'Meghnad Desai's *Marx's Revenge* is a cosmic joke with a serious purpose. Marx today would have been an enthusiastic globalizer. Globalization is good, because it brings the end of capitalism nearer. The anti-globalists don't realise that, if successful, they will simply keep capitalism going longer. Brilliant and paradoxical, Desai's book is a constant stimulus to thought.' **Robert Skidelsky**

'Meghnad Desai has produced a brilliant reconstruction of the arguments in political economy over the past 25 years in relation to the changes and events in the real world. The book also demonstrates the continuing importance of Marx's ideas for understanding globalization and its possibilities.' **Raymond Plant**

'*Marx's Revenge* is a brilliant analysis of global capitalism – a surgical operation rather than an ideological tract. Meghnad Desai is always clear and evocative; his book is not just for economists. A must read!' **Richard Sennett**

MARX'S REVENGE

The Resurgence of Capitalism and the Death of Statist Socialism

MEGHNAD DESAI

VERSO
London • New York

First published by Verso 2002

Paperback edition first published by Verso 2004

1 3 5 7 9 10 8 6 4 2

Verso
UK: 6 Meard Street, London W1F 0EG
USA: 180 Varick Street, New York, NY 10014–4606
www.versobooks.com

Verso is the imprint of New Left Books

ISBN 1–85984–429–4

British Library Cataloguing in Publication Data
Desai, Meghnad
Marx's revenge : the resurgence of capitalism and the death of statist socialism
1. Capitalism
I. Title
330.1'22

ISBN 1859844294

Library of Congress Cataloging-in-Publication Data
A catalog record for this book is available from the Library of Congress

Typeset in Cochin by SetSystems Ltd, Saffron Walden, Essex
Printed and bound in the UK
by The Cromwell Press

Contents

Preface and Acknowledgements

This book is meant to annoy and provoke, but – I hope – also to explain how we come to be where we are in what is now called this globalized world of ours. Like many others I have spent most of my life broadly on the Left, and taken part in the many agonized debates about the future of capitalism and of socialism, the betrayal of the October Revolution, and the prospects – or, indeed even the possibility – of parliamentary socialism. But during the last forty years, we have all witnessed the high tide and ebbing away of Keynesianism; the sudden rise of liberal philosophy, especially the popularity of the works of Hayek; double-digit inflation and unemployment; the changing fortunes of China and India. As an active member of the British Labour Party, I, like many others, lived through four consecutive election defeats. Then, in 1989, the Berlin Wall was brought down, and soon afterwards the Soviet Union ceased to be.

Sometime during the mid-1980s, I began to rethink a lot of the things I had taken for granted. I had read Marx since my teenage years in India, and taught Marxian economics in the heady days following the student 'troubles' of 1968. Keynesianism was my credo in academic economics, and I had written a critique of monetarism. But the electoral triumph of the Conservative Party in the midst of severe unemployment posed a real challenge. Even if one explained away their 1983 victory as due to the Falklands War (though I thought even then that this was a false consolation), the 1987 defeat of the Labour Party was pretty final. It was the end of the road for democratic socialism. The collapse of the Soviet system only confirmed the need to re-examine my ideas.

The answer came from a very unexpected quarter. I had spent some time, during a visit to Delhi in 1970–71, reading the *Collected Works* of Lenin and extracting his economic writings for a book. I had been struck by his defence of capitalism against the populist critique from the Narodniks (the late-nineteenth century equivalents of the anti-globalizers). I put it aside then, but in 1989 I agreed to edit a book based on Lenin's economic writings. Then I reread Lenin, and understood how sturdy Marxists were before the Russian Revolution in their belief in the progressive (albeit ultimately doomed) nature of capitalism.

It is this classical – that is, pre-Leninist (Leninist refers to Lenin as he came to be embalmed after his death in 1924) – reading of Marx that provides the key to understanding our contemporary world. In my books on Marxian economics, I had confined myself strictly to his critical understanding of how capitalism worked. I had only to go back to that and use those tools for understanding the resurgence of capitalism in the 1990s – but this time without the teleological expectation of its imminent demise.

Much of the twentieth century was spent waiting for the collapse of capitalism. Even now, the radical anticapitalists of Seattle and Prague and May Day demonstrations wish, expect and predict the end of globalization. But what if capitalism did not die imminently – or at least, not in our lifetimes or, say, the next hundred years? What would the world look like then? The answer to this question is not available in either classical or neoclassical economics – or what passes for radical political economy nowadays. Classical and neoclassical economists do not care to discuss the prospects of capitalism as such and the arguments of radical political economists are premised on the notion that capitalism is in terminal crisis. Hayek's concept of the Spontaneous Order is a timeless notion. Only Marx dicusses capitalism as a system that survives, but through cycles and crises, through wealth creation and destruction, through the dialectic of poverty and riches, through human actions of workers and capitalists and rentiers and landlords. And he does not need to be saddled with the stupid things written in his name: no longer, not after the collapse of the Soviet system. He does not need to be deified or hailed as an astrologer of capitalism, casting its horoscope and predicting its death at a specified date.

This book is thus an attempt to understand our contemporary world – the world of globalization, or just of capitalism. It is an account of ideas and events over the last hundred and fifty or so years. Although its central focus is Marx, I start with Adam Smith, the first person to set down the laws of what I call 'social astronomy': the laws that govern the motion of societies through history. I then go on briefly to Hegel, a risky gambit for a non-philosopher. But Hegel is essential for a corrective to the Smithian vision of the idea that the civil society (the market, as we would call it today) is self-adjusting and autonomous. Two chapters on Marx follow. Chapter 4 is a general introduction; Chapter 5 is my attempt to explain value theory, or where profits come from. Some readers may find the tables a bit offputting. If so, skip them. Nothing will be lost. They are there to reassure those who care about such things that Marx had a cogent argument at the heart of his theory. No doubt many will continue to quarrel with details of the argument.

The next fourteen chapters trace the fortunes of this notion of capitalism, especially its likely and imminent demise through the social democratic parties of Europe, but especially Germany before the 1914 War (Chapter 6). The First World War itself was a turning point in European and world history in many senses, but mostly in terms of the belief in progress and reason. I discuss the causes and the impact of the war on social-democratic parties, their splits, and so on. The Russian Revolution rates a chapter on its own, because of the crucial way in which it appropriated Marx, and set the terms of the debate on the prospects of capitalism (Chapters 7 and 8). But there were other dissident voices – fascism especially – and I trace the course of interwar history and the way in which fascism and National Socialism were responses to the breakdown of the pre-1914 liberal order (Chapters 9 and 10). It may surprise many today who are champions of market intervention, but it was fascism that based its critique of capitalism on a market-failure notion, and pushed the need for planning in a market economy. The debate about the liberal as against an interventionist model of capitalism occupied many economists in the interwar period. Thus ideas are as important as events, and I devote a chapter to theories of capitalism in Keynes, Schumpeter and Hayek (Chapter 11), and then discuss the debate on whether socialism could be based on rational economic principles which was launched by von Mises and sustained by Hayek in the 1930s (Chapter 12).

The Second World War is seen as a battle between the liberal political order and the authoritarian system within capitalism (Chapter 13). But the influence of the economic ideas of National Socialism survived in the postwar period inasmuch as planning in a market economy was widely accepted and practised. It was prewar liberal economics that lost the battle after 1914, and even through the Keynesian Golden Age (1950–75), it was the mixed economy that won the allegiance of the intellectuals (Chapter 14). I trace the long gestation of the revival of the liberal notion, relating my own first-hand experience as an economics student and then an academic from the 1960s onwards. There was also, of course, a resurgence in Marxist studies and the rise of the New Left (Chapter 15).

It was the collapse of profitability in the late 1960s/early 1970s that the orthodox economists missed and the Marxists – or, at least some, Marxists – caught. What was described as stagflation was the crisis of profitability. I trace the oil price rise and the challenge to Keynesian policies by the monetarists in Chapter 16. There is some background about the development of postwar economics to cover here, but I have avoided any technical notations or even tables. It is essential to see that the challenge to Keynes's ideas was rooted in theoretical premisses of postwar economics, and was not just some vulgar attack by 'the running dogs of capitalism' to use a favourite expression of Mao Tse-tung. Along with the crisis in advanced capitalist countries I also carry through a discussion of what was happening in the Soviet bloc and in the Third World.

The 1980s bring us to the crucial decade. In advanced capitalist countries, politicians came to power – Thatcher, Reagan, Kohl – who tackled the crisis of profitability by a deep restructuring of postwar capitalism. It was in many ways a brutal experience, but then, as Lenin said, you cannot make an omelette without breaking eggs, nor a revolution without breaking heads. It was a gamble, but it worked: these governments won democratic mandates again and again (Chapter 17). At the same time, the Soviet system could not cope with its crisis of profitability (productive efficiency), and went under. Leninist socialism had failed to deliver on its promise of greater material prosperity, let alone justice or fairness. But democratic socialism also suffered its historic defeat because the prospects of an imminent demise of capitalism were dimmed (Chapter 18).

Capitalism showed, through the new technological and institutional revolutions – IT, deregulated capital movements, the emergence of the WTO – that it still had tremendous potential. It was not about to lie down and die, nor even converge with its rivals, as its friends – like Professor Rostow – were predicting in the 1960s. This is where Marx regains his relevance. His is the only serious attempt after Adam Smith's to understand the dynamics of capitalism. None has succeeded since, though Schumpeter came near. Once the horrible legacy foisted upon him by the Bolsheviks and their cousins in Asia, Africa and elsewhere is discarded, Marx emerges as a serious but not an infallible theorist of social astronomy (Chapter 19).

This, then, is the book. It has been written for the general reader. But for the serious or pedantic, some source notes are provided. I hope readers enjoy reading it as much as I enjoyed writing it.

I have to thank Joanne Hay for her patience with me and my handwriting, since I could write a book like this only by hand, not on a machine. Her skills helped me to trace many of the references which I thought I had remembered. She has been a cheerful colleague and friend. My friend Alison Hooper gave me the idea of what I call 'Standing Marx on his head' in Chapter 5. You have to be running a business, as she is, to have that simple but sharp insight. I thank her for that, and for many other conversations. Staff in the House of Lords Library should also be thanked for finding books and references on many occasions.

Gillian Beaumont was a superb copy-editor. I thank her for her heroic efforts at improving my original manuscript, which had many unsuspected errors. If there are still errors remaining, I claim sole ownership.

Robert Skidelsky read the entire draft, and made many useful suggestions. I have not accepted all of them, but his efforts have improved the book. And yet I may not have matched his *The World After Communism,* which came out in 1995. No doubt problems and peculiarities remain which are entirely mine, so no one is responsible for any defects except me.

It is a rare pleasure to say, further, that no research council or foundation contributed a single penny towards this book. It was that increasingly rare resource which academics used to have in abundance, but no longer do – time to read and write – which made it possible for me, mainly over two summers in 1999 and 2000, to write it.

1

Two Revolutions and a Demolition

The year 1989 was a historic one for two reasons. These reasons, though separate, are intimately linked. One was the fall of the Berlin Wall, symbolizing as it did the collapse of Soviet hegemony over Eastern Europe, followed soon after by the death of the one-party state in the Soviet Union itself. The other was that it was the bicentenary of the French Revolution.

Zhou En Lai, asked what he thought about the French Revolution, is said to have replied: 'It is too soon to give a verdict.' Indeed, the bicentenary became an occasion for the airing of widely divergent interpretations of the meaning that the French Revolution had for the late twentieth century. Francois Mitterrand, as a Socialist president, wanted to claim the Revolution for socialism emphasizing the rights of man. One of his guests was rude enough to claim that human rights had been earlier and more endurably established by the Bloodless Revolution of 1688 and the Bill of Rights which followed the year after. President George Bush was too diplomatic to agree with Margaret Thatcher, who had made this claim, but then the American Revolution of 1776 had benefited from French material support as much as French, as well as English, ideas.

The Revolution of 1789 is a perennial subject of debate among historians. François Furet and Simon Schama are merely the most recent examples of historians who have espoused major revisionist interpretations, and no doubt the battle will continue.[1] But the one interpretation which has long held sway was the one that claimed 1789 as a precursor of the later revolutions – the unsuccessful one of 1848, the Paris Commune of 1871 and, of course, the Bolshevik Revolution of 1917. The Bolsheviks knew their history of 1789 intimately, and bandied about words like Thermidor and Bonapartism. And, of course, there was the Terror. Lenin as Robespierre has been a frequently used analogy. Trotsky decried Stalin as having embodied the reaction that Thermidor represented in that earlier Revolution. But throughout much of this century, if not the last two hundred years, there has been an identification of the French Revolution as a popular, democratic uprising, which brought down a feudal, aristocratic *ancien régime.* Its earlier idealism inspired the pioneers of socialism; its occurrence presaged the birth of the modern era; and its later perversion affected a host of European intellectuals and artists – Hegel and Beethoven among them.

The fact that an established and powerful regime can be overthrown suddenly, almost overnight, and replaced by those it previously ruled over, defines the word revolution. It is a simplification, of course. Bastille Day, 14 July 1789, did not change everything overnight. The Revolution was led by the middle class, and was not the friend of the masses at all times. But ever after, revolution has meant a sudden, total overthrow of one regime and its replacement by a rule of the oppressed.

It was this notion of the overthrow of the ruling – by definition oppressive – regime by its oppressed that haunted Europe throughout the nineteenth century. At the end of the long nineteenth century (1815–1914) came the fulfilment of this nightmare. During 1917, Russia witnessed two revolutions: in February and October. The October Revolution consciously claimed descent from the French Revolution of 1789. Uprisings in Germany, Hungary and Austria soon followed, with disturbances in Northern Italy. None, however, succeeded, except for the October Revolution. It was this Revolution, and its bastard offsprings in Eastern Europe, that ended in 1989.

The connecting link between the two revolutions was Karl Marx. It is his writings that are claimed to have inspired all the European revolutions from 1917 to 1923. The October Revolution, by its survival, appropriated Marx, and guarded its monopoly of his heritage with ferocious and, indeed, murderous tenacity. Marx was the prophet, they said, of their success, and the guarantee that the Socialist Revolution would conquer the world. This was not just the Russian boast. A lot of the ideological ferment during the short twentieth century (1914–89), and much of our social sciences and, indeed, our view of the relations between state and society, between economics and politics across the political spectrum, have been shaped by the way in which Marx was read by the Marxists and their friends – and, indeed, even their enemies. So did Marx and his influence also perish with the Wall?

When the Berlin Wall came down, the End of History was pronounced. Francis Fukuyama, who made this claim, was deeply influenced by Hegel's philosophy. Hegel has been portrayed as some horrendously opaque writer. Karl Popper's vulgar attack on Hegel in the second volume of his *Open Society and Its Enemies* castigated him as a father of totalitarianism, a philosophical pariah. It was a surprise to many English-speaking intellectuals and politicians when Fukuyama claimed Hegel as the one person whose prophecies had been fulfilled by the collapse of the Berlin Wall. How could it be that the philosopher castigated as a totalitarian in the 1950s could be claimed, forty years later, as prophet of the triumph of liberal democracy and capitalism?[2]

Re-evaluations of philosophers are not unknown. Indeed, revisionism is routine in the history of ideas, as of events. The Nobel laureate, Friedrich von Hayek, was forgotten and derided in his forties and fifties, only to be fêted as one of the great economist-philosophers in his seventies and eighties. Or take the fate of John Maynard Keynes. He was said to have saved capitalism from Marx and communism. But in the hour of the triumphant resurgence of capitalism, he is pronounced dead. His ideas, which were so dominant in the 1950s and 1960s, are now devalued.

What of Marx, then? Could his ideas come back? Or is he safely dead and buried, along with socialism, to which his name has been attached?

I want to argue that in the triumphant resurgence of capitalism – and, indeed, its global reach – the one thinker who is vindicated is Karl Marx. Not only that. The demise of the socialist experiment inaugurated by October 1917 would not distress but cheer Karl Marx if, as an atheist, he occupies any part of Hell, Purgatory or Heaven. Indeed, if it came to a choice between whether the market or the state should rule the economy, modern libertarians would be as shocked as modern socialists (social democrats *et al.*) to find Marx on the side of the market.

This claim is not made lightly or facetiously. Nor is it made in some desperate attempt to prove that Marx was always invariably right. For of all those who deride or even worship Marx, how many ever read him? It would surprise them to know that Marx did not advocate nationalization of industries, or the replacement of the market by central planning. He did not look to the state, even a 'Socialist' state, to alleviate the conditions of the workers. He was a champion of free trade, and no friend of tariff barriers. He did not advocate the monopoly of one-party rule, and never said that the Communist Party – the party of Marx and Engels – would lead the proletariat. He did not found a political party and, while often insufferable and undemocratic in his dealings with his fellow socialists, he never harmed a fly in his life. The use of terror, of cliquish party rule to gain power, was to him anathema: Blanquism.

Marx was no friend of capitalism, but he was its best student. He devoted more than half his sixty-five years to studying the dynamics of capitalism, but with a view to finding the forces that would finally bring about its end and its eventual replacement by communism. This was not, however, the replacement of the government of a capitalist state by a government which would bring about socialism. The idea that socialism would be brought about by the state was alien to everything he stood for.

Marx saw the incredible dynamic motion of capitalism, its revolutionary potential, as early as 1848. In the *Communist Manifesto* which he wrote with Friedrich Engels, he celebrated the global nature of capitalism. Barely thirty years old, he wrote about capitalism:

> The Bourgeoisie cannot exist without constantly revolutionizing the instruments of production, and thereby the relations of production, and with them the whole relations of society. Conservation of the old modes of production in unaltered form, was, on the contrary, the first condition of existence for all earlier industrial classes. Constant revolutionizing of production, uninterrupted disturbance of all social conditions, everlasting uncertainty and agitation distinguish the bourgeois epoch from all earlier ones. All fixed frozen relations, with their train of ancient and venerable prejudices and opinions, are swept away, all new-formed ones become antiquated before they can ossify. All that is solid melts into air, all that is holy is profaned, and man is at last compelled to face, with sober senses, his real conditions of life, and his relations with his kind.
>
> The need for a constantly expanding market for its products chases the bourgeoisie over the whole surface of the globe. It must nestle everywhere, settle everywhere, establish connections everywhere.
>
> The bourgoisie has through its exploitation of its world-market given a cosmopolitian character to production and consumption in every country. To the great chagrin of Reactionists, it has drawn from under the feet of industry the national ground on which it stood. All established national industries have been destroyed or are daily being destroyed. They are dislodged by new industries, whose introduction becomes a life and death question for all civilized nations, by industries that no longer work up indigenous raw material, but raw material drawn from the remotest zones; industries whose products are consumed, not only at home, but in every quarter of the globe. In place of old wants, satisfied by the production of the country, we find new wants, requiring for their satisfaction the products of distant lands and climes. In place of the old local and national seclusion and self-sufficiency, we have intercourse in every direction, universal interdependence of nations. And as in material, so also in intellectual production. The intellectual creations of individual nations become common property. National one-sidedness and narrow-mindedness become more and more imposs-ible, and from the numerous national and local literatures, there arises a world literature.
>
> The bourgeoisie, by the rapid improvement of all instruments of production,

> by the immensely facilitated means of communication, draws all, even the most barbarian, nations into civilization. The cheap prices of its commodities are the heavy artillery with which it batters down all Chinese walls, with which it forces the barbarians' intensely obstinate hatred of foreigners to capitulate. It compels all nations, on pain of extinction, to adopt the bourgeois mode of production; it compels them to introduce what it calls civilization into their midst, i.e., to become bourgeois themselves. In one word, it creates a world after its own image.[3]

As he sought the secret of capitalism through a study of political economy, Marx had in his mind an extension of the theory of history that he had inherited from Adam Smith and the Scottish philosophers of Enlightenment via Hegel. Smith had seen the achievement of commerce and liberty as the highest and final stage of human history. It was the prospect that the fall of the Berlin Wall would now make the universal, global achievement of capitalism (commerce) and democracy (liberty) possible which led Fukuyama to celebrate the End of History. Humankind had arrived at its final destination. Marx had the idea that there was something beyond this final stage – something that would go beyond individualist, private-property-based capitalism, as well as parliamentary democracy based on class-based parties with inherent inequality in the distribution of power. This was to be communism. It was to make human beings realize that they were free only when they recognized their mutual interdependence – that no one can be free while anyone else was not. But communism was not round the corner. There was no set timetable which one could follow.

There were some lessons to be derived from the way the world had passed through the previous stages of history. This was the original programme of the Scottish philosophers – Adam Smith, Adam Ferguson, Francis Hutcheson, John Millar. They saw human history passing from hunting-and-gathering to pastoralism to agriculture, and finally arriving at commerce – not everywhere at the same time, or in the same form, but this was the unifying thread in human affairs, much as Isaac Newton had found a unifying principle in the motion of the Heavens and the Earth. Marx, going one beyond them, saw the daisy chain as primitive communism, classical slavery, and medieval feudalism which, in its turn, was overcome by the bourgeois revolution. But if you could grasp the secret of change, then you could see that change would not stop there.

What caused these epochal stages – modes of production, as Marx called them – to persist for centuries, why did they go under, and what made a new mode superior to the old? Above all, what made capitalism triumph over feudalism, and what made it persist? What was the secret of its self-reproduction, its continued growth and survival, which made people accept wage labour when they could see that they were merely helping someone else – their employer – to get rich? Since commerce had come along with liberty, how come workers, free to do as they liked, consigned themselves to working as wage labourers?

The origins of capitalism can be placed anywhere between the fourteenth and the sixteenth century, but it was in the eighteenth century that capitalism had burst forth with immense productive powers. It had gained the ability to harness raw materials from all corners of the globe, to summon science to its aid in further revolutions in technology. It had, in short, the potential to eliminate scarcity. Why, then, was the birthplace of industrial capitalism full of misery, as Engels had so carefully observed in Manchester in 1844?[4] Could capitalism deliver on its promise of abundance, or were there inbuilt, inherent obstacles to its doing so?

To answer these questions required a deep study of the mainsprings of capitalism. The political economists – Adam Smith, David Ricardo, James Mill, the French Physiocrats – had studied this issue, but they clearly had not done so *critically*. Critical thinking was a philosophical method. It was a tool as well as a weapon. It helped you undermine an accepted dominant philosophy from within, by locating its contradictions – the weakness embedded in its strongest points. Once you understand the world, you can then know how to change it.

But change was not an easy mechanical act, like opening a door. Historical change involved vast movements of people, of events, of institutions. The changeover from feudalism to capitalism took anywhere between two and four centuries, and even then Marx claimed to have studied only the experience of Northwest Europe. Indeed, in Eastern Europe the same period saw the strengthening of the bonds of feudalism, while they were loosening west of the Elbe. Russia was yet another uncharted territory. In the final decade of his life, Marx learnt to read Russian so that he could understand the land tenure systems of Russia – the nature of Russian feudalism. Capitalism had barely penetrated there.

By then – the 1870s – Marx was, however, a very famous (as well as notorious) man. He was regarded as a dangerous subversive, possibly a regicide, by the rulers of Germany, France and England (though allowed to live in England), and his name was celebrated among the many radical parties forming in Europe. The younger revolutionaries, especially in mainland Europe – France, Germany and Russia – read him voraciously, and took his theories very seriously. They made his theories into an ideology – Marxism – causing him to make his famous remark that as far as he knew, he was not a Marxist. They wanted formulas and recipes for change. They were impatient to overthrow what he had taught them was an oppressive system prone to crises. But he would not oblige. When the German Social Democrats formed a political party claiming allegiance to his ideas, he severely criticized their political programme. When Russian revolutionaries appealed to him to say whether he predicted that Russia would have to go through the same stages as the most advanced countries of Western Europe, he demurred and told them that he had only studied Western European experience, and could not pronounce on this urgent request. He was still studying the Russian situation.

After his death in 1883, it somehow came to be said that Marx had indeed predicted the imminent demise of capitalism. The German Social Democratic Party, which had now firmly set Marxism on its banner, had a programme to achieve socialism. Indeed, the suggestion that capitalism might have mutated and changed, to increase its chances of survival, caused a big rift in the party between the followers of Bernstein (Right) and Kautsky (Left).

How this belief in the imminence of the collapse of capitalism came to take hold in the 1880s and 1890s is a complex issue which I shall pursue below. But even then, if this demise was to occur, it was to do so in the mature capitalism of England. This made some sense, because one brief hint Marx had given about the changeover from one mode of production to another was that any particular mode disappeared only after its full potential had been exhausted – when it had lost its dynamism, as it were. With mature capitalism came a mature, organized working class capable of autonomous collective action. The full chain of links was never specified, but it would be collective autonomous action by the workers which would overcome capitalism when it had exhausted its potential.

It is an easy conceit of each generation to believe that it stands at the pinnacle of progress. This was, after all, implicit in the celebration of commerce and liberty in the late eighteenth century. The European socialists of the late nineteenth century were impatient. Their contemporary capitalism looked to them mature and ripe for change. The change that came in 1917, however, sent out all the wrong signals. Old-fashioned Marxists denounced the Russian Revolution as not properly socialist. It could not be socialist, since Russia had not had any proper capitalism. But the change happened after the outbreak of the First World War, which had already bitterly divided the various socialist parties of Europe. The German SPD especially had shocked its admirers – and, indeed, itself – by supporting the German war declaration enthusiastically. So had the other socialist parties. Socialist internationalism was in tatters. Working-class parties were supporting capitalist military adventurers. This Marx had not predicted.

The Russians who led the October Revolution – Lenin, Trotsky, and others of the Bolshevik tendency of the Russian Social Democratic Labour Party (later relabelled the Communist Party) – fully expected a chain of revolutions to break out in Germany, France, and perhaps even England. When they alone survived – against all odds – they were surprised. Having opposed collaboration in Russian war efforts, unlike the German socialists, they thought their ideas, their theories, their Marxism had been vindicated.

They therefore proceeded not only to appropriate Marx, but also to reinterpret and revise Marx to harness his prestige to their cause. At this distance, it is hard to realize that in those days capitalism *did* seem beleaguered, and yet another surge of revolution seemed imminent. Even the mild Fabian socialists Sidney and Beatrice Webb wrote of *The Decay of Capitalist Civilisation* in 1922.[5] And it did not get better in the next twenty years as Mussolini, Hitler and a Great Depression visited the homelands of capitalism. It was easy to argue that socialism had indeed been established in Russia, and that capitalism had had its day. Even its best friends thought that in order to survive, capitalism would have to adopt some of the methods of socialism – control of the market, introduction of planning, social ownership.

The notion that Marx would have been shocked by the Russian situation because it was socialist, a vindication of his theories, was held by a very tiny minority, which was ceaselessly hounded by all the various Bolshevik sects: Leninists, Stalinists, Trotskyists. The delicate plant of non-Bolshevik (indeed, anti-bolshevik) Marxism withered on the vine. Even when – after 1956 and the Hungarian Revolution – the monopoly of Soviet Communist orthodoxy was challenged in the West, the New Left which appeared only encouraged the flowering of dissident sects of Bolshevism: Trotskyism, Maoism, 'original' Leninism. The rightness of the October Revolution was unquestioned. The issue was when and how the Revolution got distorted and betrayed, and by whom.

Marx's ideas were re-examined. Gaps and inadequacies were discovered. His economic theories had suffered revision and correction way back in the 1900s at the hands of Rudolf Hilferding and then Lenin. But now his lack of a theory of the state, of classes, of agency in political change, were all pointed out. His analysis of transition between modes of production was said to be too simple, too mechanistic. He had not seen the obvious weak link in capitalism and its potential as harbinger of socialism – an idea that was, fortunately, brilliantly innovated by Trotsky. He had not seen the importance of monopoly capitalism, and why it was against all that he had praised in capitalism. Monopoly capitalism was exploitative, but without dynamism, without the revolutionary potential of the capitalism of Marx's day. Monopoly capitalism lived parasitically off the colonies, the periphery, the South – by making them underdeveloped. The dialectic of progress leading to maturity and demise that Marx had adumbrated was replaced by a dialectic of development, feeding off underdevelopment in a climate of stagnation. Indeed, bad and distorted as Soviet socialism was, its technological dynamism showed that it was progressive. It had an unfortunate dictatorial tendency, but soon autonomous working-class action within the Soviet Union would replace the regime. Trotsky said so.

It was all to end in tears. After a brief and stormy seventy-five-year life, the Russian socialist venture, the attempt to speed up the pace of history, the weak link that Marx had failed to see, came to an abrupt but complete end. Capitalism was not ready to give up yet. Lenin had proclaimed that imperialism was its highest (latest) but final stage way back in 1916. As late as 1972 another prominent Marxist, Ernest Mandel, wrote a book entitled *Le Troisième Âge du capitalisme* (literally, capitalism in its old age, though the English translation was entitled *Late Capitalism*).[6] Decay and demise were thought to be imminent in the 1970s, just as they were in the 1890s. Even the friends of capitalism, such as Walt Rostow, predicted a convergence between Soviet and American industrial cultures.

But Marx had the last laugh. He was not wrong, not simplistic, not mechanical. Capitalism would not go away until after it had exhausted its potential. The information technology revolution has just begun. What more may come we do not know – biotechnology, new materials, outer space as colonizable land. The whole world is not yet fully integrated into global capitalism. Despite the pessimistic predictions of Marxist political economists such as Paul Baran, Andre Gunder Frank, Immanuel Wallerstein and Samir Amin, Asia is now the home of dynamic capitalism. There are Korean-owned factories in the UK, Japanese-owned factories in the USA, the UK, and many other countries. Latin America has, however, stagnated after its early integration into capitalism, and Sub-Saharan Africa is still to be globalized.

Many view the prospect of globalization with horror. They desperately hope that some limits will be found to global capitalism. Perhaps the environment. Perhaps the resurgence of the nation-state, or a regional superstate. Or even a global-level co-ordination among the nation-states through the UN or G-7 or G-77. Something to tame capitalism, to stop its rampant progress.

Perhaps. But then again, perhaps not. Marx would not have looked for limits to capitalism in these 'external' agents. He did not see capitalism as eternal, but nor did he see it as incapable of change and innovation and adaptation. The limits to capitalism have to be sought in the weakness of the strongest points of capitalism – that is, the dialectic method. The limits to capitalism will be reached when it is no longer capable of progress, but it will be in the daily practice of the people working the machinery of capitalism that its limits will be felt, and it will be overcome by them.

The continued dynamism of capitalism at the beginning of the twenty-first century is Marx's revenge on the Marxists – on all those who, in his name, lied and cheated and murdered, and offered false hope. The detritus of that misadventure has distorted a lot of thinking about social change. It is necessary to go back to Marx to understand the strengths of capitalism and the secrets of its dynamism. But it is also necessary to understand how the limits of capitalism will be reached. It would be an act of folly, after the searing experience of the twentieth century, to ask *when* these limits will be reached. Marx was an astronomer of history, not an astrologer.

But along with Marx, we shall need to harness others. Joseph Schumpeter, John Maynard Keynes and Friedrich von Hayek were three twentieth-century economists who also studied capitalism and sought to unravel its secrets. We shall also need to go back to Marx's precursors, Adam Smith and Hegel; they, after all, started this study of the astronomy of social motion.

I shall begin this book with Adam Smith and the original venture in understanding the laws of motion of society that was started by the Scottish philosophers. The American and French Revolutions came at the end of a century of rapid change. They have to be understood if we are to see why Hegel was much taken up by the same question that Smith raised, but tackled it in a different way. Marx went from a critique of Hegel to a critique of political economy, in a sense going back over the route Hegel had travelled. The full complexity of what Marx said – and, even more, of what he did not say – have to be appreciated if we are to understand that capitalism was the lifelong subject of Marx's studies. This subject will be discussed in the middle section of this book.

The chequered history of the ideas not only of Marx but of Smith as well, for a hundred years after his death, has to be laid out. The notion of the state regulating the economy; the convergence of socialism and capitalism; the challenge of Soviet-style Marxism and its profound influence on the social sciences; the tension between the understandings of capitalism that Schumpeter, Keynes and Hayek brought to our attention; the critique of the market in the works of Karl Polanyi, and its reversal within fifty years; the many separate attempts to search for alternatives and limits to capitalism and socialism – the Third Way; the shocked realization at the end of the twentieth century that an entire alternative philosophy – the Second Way of socialism – had disappeared from the menu of possibilities, and the desperate search for a way out – any way out – of the prospect of living under a resurgent capitalism; and the continuing relevance of Marx (and, indeed, many other nineteenth-century socialists) to that question: all these will constitute the concerns of this book.

2
Adam Smith and the Principles of Social Astronomy[1]

Isaac Newton was hailed as a great mind during his lifetime. He pioneered much of modern physics, and has a claim to be the joint inventor of calculus. He dabbled in alchemy, and was credulous about witchcraft. After a successful career as Fellow of Trinity College, Cambridge, he became Master of the Mint. The price he set for an ounce of gold, £3 17s. 9d. (£3.88¾), remained unchanged until 1933, when Franklin Roosevelt decided to take the USA off the Gold Standard – roughly two hundred years.

It was, however, for his discovery of the laws of motion of the Heavens and the Earth that Newton became a hero of the Enlightenment. He explained a great deal from a small set of principles. Once you understood gravity and motion, the rest followed. The motion of the planets and the phases of the moon all obeyed the simple principles Newton had discovered. To many people, Newton had stumbled upon God's own subtle plan. He made sense of the universe.

But if a simple underlying unity could be discovered in the physical universe, why not in human societies? If God had a secret plan which explained the harmony of the Heavens, was there not a plan similar in scope, and perhaps based on equally simple principles, for human history and human societies? Throughout the eighteenth century, in Scotland and in France, philosophers looked for this particular Holy Grail. Quite consciously, they invoked Newton's name. They were trying to find the secrets of social astronomy – the laws of motion of human societies.

The most famous of these philosophers, and the one most frequently credited with having discovered the simple principle underlying the motion of societies, was Adam Smith. But he was not alone. His teacher, Francis Hutcheson, as well as his contemporary Adam Ferguson, had some contribution to make. His elder contemporary, David Hume, and the French bureaucrat/philosopher Anne Robert Jacques Turgot were useful sources. The French savant Baron de Montesquieu is perhaps more cited in this context than is the Italian, Giovanni Battista Vico. But the possibility of discovering a design in

God's creation, a key that would unravel the secret of rearranging what seemed to be chaotic into a pattern that made sense, was the adventure in which Adam Smith was supremely successful.

There was much that was chaotic as he looked around. His own native country, Scotland, had been through multiple revolutions during the eighteenth century. A few years before his birth, the Act of Union between Scotland and England had been signed. As in all such federalizing events, there had been losers and gainers – his own father, whom he never got to know, being among the gainers. While he was still a student – though by now in Oxford – Bonnie Prince Charlie's failed attempt to claim his heritage, and the massacres of Culloden, had followed. Adam Smith was not a Scottish nationalist – nor even a Jacobite, like Sir James Steuart, who has a disputable claim to be the real father of political economy. Indeed, those who offered Smith his first lectureship in Edinburgh were keen to point out that his stay in Oxford had taught him the proper way of speaking English.

As a lowland Scotsman, Smith could not fail to be aware of the contrast in levels of development (as we would call it today) between the Highlands and the Lowlands. They were like two different worlds. But as he moved further south, to London, he could see how much more prosperous England was. When he gave up his professorship at the University of Glasgow, it was to take up a most lucrative tutorship accompanying his young aristocratic charge on a Grand Tour. Here again he could appreciate the contrast, as well as the new ferment in French thinking. France was an Absolute monarchy, which England had ceased to be in 1688. There were many small principalities in Germany. There were also one or two large kingdoms, not unlike Scotland only seventy years previously. Could the French monarchy go the way of the English? Would the small kingdoms of Germany effect a union?

Much more furious than the pace of political upheaval was the change in commerce. The landed gentry, undisputed as the ruling elite for nearly a thousand years, were now being upstaged by wealthy merchants and bankers. This had been obvious to philosophers of the seventeenth century. The fickle, erratic and quicksilver nature of this new wealth made them compare it to women. The magical allure of this money, here today and gone tomorrow, was rather like the unfathomable mystery of women's sexual power. Moralists raged against it. Politicians lamented the loss of virtue. The commoners were challenging the Lords. Money-changers had entered the temple, and taken it over.

Where had this money come from? How, after centuries of stability where the Lords dominated the social order, and even held the king to ransom, had these parvenus become important? The dying decades of the fifteenth century had seen the breakthrough in long-distance navigation. Columbus to the west and Vasco da Gama to the east are the two most prominent names among many who 'discovered' new continents. The dynamic leadership in trade and war, which had been lost to the Muslims in the seventh century, returned to Europe in the sixteenth.

The original impetus for these explorations had indeed been the Crusades and the boost they gave to finding alternative trade routes to Asia. Merchant companies were formed for overland routes as well as the seafaring ones. Trade became profitable as some of the Asian commodities became scarce. Soon kings around Europe realized that trade and the formation of merchant companies were lucrative activities which helped to finance the territorial wars they wished to fight to acquire 'real' wealth which, for them, was land. If trading wealth could be converted into larger territory, all the more reason for encouraging trade.

With navigation came trade and, of course, colonies. The Iberian exploration of the Americas and the West Coast of Africa flooded Europe with gold. Europe, which had been practically drained of precious metals at the end of the Roman Empire, was shocked by the advent of a financial revolution. A century of inflation straddled the sixteenth and seventeenth centuries. Old values were being changed as prices for some things increased faster than prices for others. Gold was suspected of possessing occult powers, as Shakespeare's characters repeatedly testify. Treasure became an object of royal policy as trade grew and colonies became profitable.

But travel had also brought knowledge of other civilizations and nations. A well-read person in the eighteenth century was well aware of China and India, and their greater prosperity and urbanization compared to Europe. They had also been made aware of tribal peoples of Pacific Islands, and of America. Their simpler techniques of obtaining subsistence, and seemingly undeveloped social practices, struck the travellers.

Just as astronomers had measured the position and motion of planets and stars, but lacked a simple unifying theory, eighteenth-century philosophers had available to them a rich array of facts about different nations, civilizations and people. They also knew their classical history well, and observed rapid contemporary change. Could there be a pattern to this bewildering jumble of facts?

From the moment he took the chair of Moral Philosophy at the University of Glasgow at the age of twenty-nine until his death at the age of sixty-seven, Adam Smith thought, taught and wrote on this subject. He lectured at Glasgow for thirteen years. His *Lectures on Jurisprudence* have survived from the final two years. He then gave up his professorship to act as a tutor to the Duke of Buccleuch. Two years of travel and tutoring bought him a pension which freed him from the need to work for a living. He had already written a book on the question of what motivated human behaviour. This book, *The Theory of Moral Sentiments,* made him famous. But in the ten years following his 'early retirement' he devoted himself to the book which gave him immortality, *The Wealth of Nations.* Its publication in 1776 was the second revolutionary event of that year.

To understand Adam Smith's answer to the question of an underlying pattern in social structures, both current and past, one has to piece together *The Wealth of Nations* and the *Lectures on Jurisprudence.* The bicentenary of the publication of *The Wealth of Nations* generated a superb series of all Adam Smith's works and gave us, for the first time, the opportunity to form a rounded impression of his life and achievements. Smith was not just the champion of free market, or the scourge of state intervention (both of which are, in any case, partial views). He was the Newton of society, the social astronomer. He did not merely found political economy or economics. He led the Scottish Enlightenment, which founded all social sciences. The systematic study of history can also be laid at its door, though this can be contested by champions of Vico and Montesquieu.

Smith started out by looking at how justice was dealt with differently in different societies. As his student John Millar observed: 'Upon this subject he followed the plan that seems to be suggested by Montesquieu; endeavouring to trace the gradual progress of Jurisprudence, both public and private, from the rudest to the most refined ages, and to point out the effects of property, in producing corresponding improvements or alterations in law and government.'[2] Millar goes on to add that Smith was unable to fulfil his intention of making his results on this public. But also at Glasgow he lectured on 'those political regulations which are founded, not upon the principle of *justice* but that of *expediency,* and which are calculated to increase the riches, the power and the prosperity of a State'. This is what he published in 1776 as *An Inquiry into the Nature and Causes of the Wealth of Nations.*

A common thread runs between the *Lectures on Jurisprudence,* now happily available to us, and *The Wealth of Nations*: that the ways in which a society obtains its subsistence and accumulates property have a 'corresponding' (to use John Millar's word) impact on its laws and governments. This, however, has to be seen in the context of progress, as well as at any one moment in time. As the arts which contribute to subsistence progress, they also improve law and government. Thus we become more civilized, more just and law-respecting as we get more materially advanced, richer as a society. This progress is gradual and, as we shall see below, not necessarily irreversible. But there is a definite optimism here – both in the prevalence of progress and in having discovered the coupling correspondence between the material side and the juridical/political side.

Virtually all social science has been an elaboration of – or a quarrel with – aspects of this fundamental proposition. Adam Smith is not even identified with these propositions, though Marx, and sometimes Hegel, are. We shall see below how far Hegel and Marx followed or departed from Smith. But the primacy of Smith is beyond doubt. The revolutionary nature of his theory can, however, still be missed.

First, it is a theory about progress – progress in justice and progress in material arts. It has a universal focus: 'from the rudest to the most refined stages'. No geographical restrictions here. The progress in justice having been traced, the theory goes on to encompass 'the effects of those arts which contribute to subsistence and to the accumulation of property' – not for their own sake, but for 'the corresponding improvements or alterations in law and government'. The study of the development of jurisprudence is thus not merely textual, or confined to the changes in forms of government. It is encompassed with (endogenized within, as we would say) a systematic study of progress in subsistence and the accumulation of property.

Progress in history occurs through various stages of modes of subsistence. Thus in his Glasgow *Lectures on Jurisprudence*, Smith starts with a discussion of how property rights, especially the right of private property, evolve and become legally secure:

> Before we consider exactly this or any of the other methods by which property is acquired, it will be proper to observe that the regulations concerning them must vary considerably according to the state or age society is in at that time. There are four distinct states which mankind passes through: firstly, the Age of Hunters; secondly, the Age of Shepherds; thirdly, the Age of Agriculture; fourthly, the Age of Commerce. (LJ[A], 14)[3]

Countries, nations – peoples, if you like – go through these stages. These are millennial, epochal stages. They are also inclusive. Thus in the Age of Agriculture, a nation will have shepherds as well as hunters-and-gatherers. There may even be some trade at the margin, but wealth will consist mainly in land and its products. In the Age of Commerce, new forms of wealth-holding will emerge. These will require complex laws guaranteeing private property rights in these new forms.

This is not a mechanical account. Thus, while 'mankind' goes through these four ages, not everyone is in the same age at once. By Smith's reckoning, the Age of Commerce had come to certain parts of Northwest Europe. It was not just that there was trade, or that merchants used credit to carry on transactions over long distances. In the Age of Commerce, the right to private property was secure against the arbitrary predations of the king or the feudal lord. Thus even France in the mid-eighteenth century had not got to the stage which Holland and Britain had attained. The Chinese had superior technology, as we now know, and perhaps a better king than Louis XVI, as Voltaire alleged. But Smith's concern is with security of private property, because it can be obtained only with the diminution of arbitrary rule and the growth of liberty. China lagged behind Britain, and even France, in that respect.

There was an interplay between progress in the mode of subsistence, and the legal and political arrangements. The higher the mode, the more complex the legal structure. Higher in what sense? In terms of the surplus affordable – opulence – from the work of farmers, labourers and merchants. Higher in the attainment of liberty defined as security from arbitrary rule and within a framework of law.

Progress is not the same as change. It implies that things are getting better rather than worse. But it is neither inevitable nor irreversible. There is no straight upward ladder of progress. There can be setbacks. In European history, the period between the fall of the Roman Empire and the Renaissance (give or take one or two hundred years on either side) – the Dark Ages – was such a period. Of course, it was not a Dark Age for other nations. Islam was the dynamic force in this period, spreading from the Atlantic to the Urals, and down to India and the archipelago of Malaysia and Indonesia. China was enjoying a robust period of technological and scientific growth. Indian merchants were trading with Africa and Europe on the Western side, and China on the Eastern side. Europe was stuck in a period of retrogression from the heights achieved in Roman times.

During the Dark Ages, for Europe, there was retrogression in technical knowledge – roadbuilding, construction of aqueducts, indoor heating – as well as a decline in the security of property and use of arbitrary rule. But change can come in many ways. Thus Smith traces the decline of serfdom and the emergence of *métayer* and later tenant farmers through a combination of the power of the clergy and the king. The clergy were interested in spreading their influence, and found in the serfs a ready group whose interests they could champion. The king was interested in curbing the power of landlords. This harmony of interests forced the landlords to concede freedom to their serfs, and once they had done so, it was in their own best interests to move to fixed money rents.

In telling this story of change from serfdom (though he calls it slavery) to free tenants, Smith makes it clear that it applies only to a particular 'corner of Europe' where the twin conditions occurred: 'The great power of the clergy thus concurring with that of the King set the slaves at liberty. But it was absolutely necessary both that the authority of the King and of the clergy should be great.' The same was not true in his view of Poland, Germany, Bohemia, Austria or Russia. But if the story is specific to Western Europe, Smith's account – his theory, so to speak – is general, based on tracing the action of the Church and of the king to self-interest. Thus of the clergy he says: 'They saw then or thought they did that it would tend greatly to aggrandize the power of [the] church, that these people over whom they had the greatest influence were set at liberty and rendered independent of their masters. They therefore promoted greatly the emancipation of the villeins and discouraged as much as lay in their power the authority of the great men over them' (LJ[A], 188).

There are two remarkable things about this whole account. It is an example of theoretical or conjectural history, which Smith regarded as his scientific method. Newton's method was empirical, and would have demanded observations or experiments. David Hume, Smith's senior contemporary, was sceptical of all accounts not based on direct sense perception. His method was scientific in Newton's sense. Smith followed Newton in seeking a single explanation. In a broad sense, it is self-interest – not selfishness, nor individual greed, as has been misunderstood by his friends and enemies. The motive of the clergy in pushing for the freedom of the serfs is based on Smith's conjecture that it must have been in the interests of the Church to do so if they did push. This is not a 'testable' hypothesis in the sense of recent scientific philosophy. But it is a powerful method in social sciences and in history where no direct observations or experiments may be possible. People individually, and collectively as institutions, do things which accord with their perceived self-interest. The Church was interested in aggrandizement, but this is not to be seen as seeking monetary wealth, or as growth in the clergy's consumption levels.

The progress from hunting to commerce is a progress in the material dimension (size of surplus), in increasing complexity of the legal structure and the corresponding nature of government. But the puzzle Smith was struggling with was his contemporary world. The Age of Commerce had suddenly burst on to the scene, upsetting old arrangements. In earlier times, land was the sole source of wealth, landlords were the ruling elite, and virtue was the cornerstone of readiness to participate in public life. Citizens bore arms as part of this virtuous tradition. Professional standing armies were anathema to this Augustinian ideal, worshipped in the seventeenth and eighteenth centuries. (There are clear echoes of this in the US Constitution: the Right to Bear Arms.) Commerce was corrupting people from this point of view, since money became a solvent of all relationships previously based on honour, status, duty. Elites everywhere wanted to put a stop to this commercialization of life. Commerce was soft; it encouraged luxuries and anonymous exchange.

Smith championed commerce. He wanted to show that the Age of Commerce was a step up from the feudal age. Property had taken more diverse forms, while at the same time legal developments made property more secure. The growing size, diversity and security of property constituted the best guarantee for liberty. By tracing progress from the Age of Hunting, he put the agricultural society, with its Augustinian idealism, in a historical context. It was a stage, but not in any sense an end-state. Far from being a noble state, feudalism tolerated – indeed, thrived on – arbitrary power of king and landlords which put unreasonable restrictions on property rights. The story of how property rights change with the mode of subsistence occupies the early part of the *Lectures on Jurisprudence*.

In early and 'rude' stages, possession alone would guarantee a property right. As a hunter, you would not only have stalked your prey and wounded it – but actually finished it off. In his lectures Smith developed the various distinctions that these steps made to rights of property. If I stalked, you wounded, but he killed, I would have no right, and you would share with him. But once you came to taming animals in a pastoral society, the laws would be more elaborate, designed to reward indirect effort as well as direct final possession. With agriculture comes settlement – a fixed abode and permanence in the possession of property, whether or not you are physically attached to it: 'The first origins of private property would probably be men taking themselves to fixt habitations and living together in cities, which would probably be the case in every improved society' (LJ[A], 22). Smith is using the word cities not in our sense, but to describe any settled community. Property in land 'is the greatest extension' of the right of private property.

Alas: '[T]he tyranny of the feudal government and the inclination men have to extort all they can from their inferiors' (LJ[A], 23) compel a further codification of laws. Thus wild game, previously free, was appropriated by those on whose land it roamed. Indeed, laws were made to the effect that only the big landlords could hunt wild game: 'there can be no reason in equity for this constitution . . .' (LJ[A] 24). Game and indeed fish should be common property going to whosoever can catch it. So indeed should these things become 'considered as common to all' which 'cannot be lessened or impaired by use, nor can anyone be injured by the use of them' (LJ[A] 24). Air, running water, the sea, navigation on rivers and seas, should be common to all. The contemporary tone of this passage is striking.

The second main method of acquiring and enhancing property is accession, that is, the right to the yield of property. Since hunters do not tame and conserve, there is no accession in the first age. But with the pastoral stage there is a some scope with 'the milk and young of animalls'. These belonged to whomsoever owned the animals. But with agriculture and private property in land, the opportunities expand – indeed, 'they multiply to a number almost infinite'. The soil and all that lies beneath it – that is, minerals and the harvest obtained by cultivating the soil – all belong to the person who owns the land. In feudal times, however, all land began to be held not in absolute allodial ownership but in service of some superior – landlord or king. Arbitrary rights, such as the right to precious metals lying under the soil, were assigned to this superior. The yield of land, or anything that had been worked on by the cultivator, was his, but anything which could be put back into its original unworked form – for example gold – belonged to the superior. 'This rule has no foundation in reason' (LJ[A] 27–30).

With progress – and, indeed, its concomitant, the accumulation of private property – comes inequality. The Age of Commerce is marked by the wealth of the few sustained by the labour of the many. In one sense, the state was needed to restrain the poor from coveting and collecting the property of the rich. The way Smith expresses this idea makes him seem more like an early-day Bolshevik than a champion of liberal capitalism. But while there is greater inequality, Smith argues that for the bulk of the population the living standard is also higher than in earlier societies:

> If we examine, I say, all those different conveniences and luxuries with which he is accommodated and consider what a variety of labours is employed about each of them, we shall be sensible that without the assistance and co-operation of many thousands the very meanest person in civilized society could not be

> provided for, even in, what we very falsely imagine the easy and simple manner in which he is commonly accommodated. Compared, indeed, with the yet more extravagant luxury of the great, his accommodation must no doubt appear extremely simple and easy; and yet, perhaps it may be true that the accommodation of a European prince does not so much exceed that of an industrious and frugal peasant, as the accommodation of this last exceeds that of the chief of a savage nation in North America'. (Early Draft of part of *The Wealth of Nations*, ED LJ p. 563)[4]

In the past, societies were more equal, but also poorer. The modern world is more unequal, but affords a higher level of consumption. It is not just that *per capita* income is higher. As Smith goes on to say further in the Early Draft of *The Wealth of Nations*, quoted above: 'In the midst of so much oppressive inequality, in what manner shall we account for the superior affluence and abundance commonly possessed even by this lowest and most despised member of civilized society, compared with what the most respected and active savage can attain to'. (ibid.)

Thus Smith poses the stark question which has lost none of its relevance even today. As globalization spreads to more and more countries, as old socialist societies collapse and the earlier certainties are destroyed, there is much unease about the increasing inequality in the contemporary world. Smith seems to argue that greater inequality coexists with – and, indeed, is causally responsible for – the fact that the living standard of the worst-off person in this unequal society is higher than was possible even for the richest in earlier societies. How had this come about?

It was the superior productivity made possible by the division of labour which, in turn, owed a lot to the fact that certainty of being able to enjoy the fruits of their labour and their property gave people incentives to work harder. Commerce made many complex and anonymous exchanges possible, since people were no longer dependent on their superiors – their landlord, their guild master. The possibility of entering into complex exchanges made a wide market accessible. This meant that if you produced ten times what was previously possible, you could still find markets for it. Thus trade helps to raise the productivity of manufacturers and agriculture as well.

The Wealth of Nations commences with an example of the pin factory, where, by breaking up pin-making into separate tasks, and specializing, productivity is raised several-fold. Division of labour is thus the key to greater productivity – but not only within the workshop, but also outside. It is by having specialists in trade and transport and finance that the market is extended, and higher productivity is rewarded by higher sales. To let the market extend as far as possible without putting restraints on the movement of goods was very important.

This was a revolutionary doctrine for those days, despite Smith's use of a laconic style devoid of flourishes. Those who disliked the Age of Commerce contrasted it with a happier past when workers had permanent masters who looked after their welfare, what was made locally was consumed locally, and exchange was not just an anonymous act but a rich social ritual with extra-economic resonance. Even today, it is not unknown for many people to criticize the growth of trade, lament the breakdown of old social bonds as monetary calculations enter social life, and, in general, pine for a quieter, happier, smaller society.

Smith argued that these earlier societies were based on dependent relationships especially for the labouring majority. They also had arbitrary laws which made property insecure. The powerful were above the law, and thus confiscated the fruits of other people's work on unnatural and unreasonable grounds. Liberty meant independence from these myriad social oppressions. With such independence, and the legal framework of secure property, came prosperity. This prosperity was characterized by a great deal of inequality, but at the same time the living standard of the worst-off was improved.

But there was more to the modern society than met the eye. In previous societies, people's dependence on other people was direct and visible, and their obligations were clear and enforceable. In a modern society of independent people with anonymous exchange, and no obligation but a contractual one, there was still a complex web of interdependence, but it was invisible. Each person acted in his or her own self-interest, to do the job they had chosen, but in consequence, they ended up providing for the myriad wants of society. The modern society needs even more and more varied interdependencies, since division of labour is so much more complex.

When Smith used the words 'Invisible Hand' in *The Wealth of Nations,* he was trying to illustrate this hidden complex interdependence of a commercial society behind the seeming array of independent anonymous exchanges. The pursuit of self-interest by the butcher, the baker, et cetera, led to the happy outcome of satisfaction of their customers' wants. But of course, behind the baker was a chain of operations – the farmer who grew corn, the miller who ground it, and the transport which delivered the grain to the miller and the flour to the baker, perhaps via a wholesaler. Nowadays there would be a bakery which would in turn deliver to the supermarket. If I fancy Italian ciabatta or French croissants, German pumpernickel bread or Greek pitta bread, all these are available as well, thanks to the invisible complex of farmers, millers, bakers, wholesalers, and the transporters who deliver them to the supermarket from which I wish to buy.

Of course, there was a time when such bread was locally made and locally consumed. Baking was a housewives' chore. Farmers grew the grain; their wives and mothers and daughters ground it and made bread. Those who did not farm, such as the local blacksmiths, exchanged an annual supply of bread for guaranteed blacksmithing services. Such local economies were rarely self-sufficient (salt and iron being two products that were not ubiquitous), but always poor. They were perhaps more equal, except for the local landlord and priest. But even they partook of limited luxuries, despite the heavy exploitation they exerted on the labourers.

There are many people today, as there were in Smith's time, who idolize this old system. Smith's answer is that with commerce, there is a greater variety of bread to be had, as well as the fact that bread becomes relatively cheap. With rising productivity, it requires less and less labour time to buy the necessities. Manufacture becomes even cheaper than products of land; you can buy a Swatch with a fraction of a week's grocery bill; a computer costs less than a summer holiday in Britain today.

Smith's challenge was thus to argue for commerce and liberty as preferable to the earlier agrarian societies, conjured up increasingly as utopias, as money and market relationships overwhelmed Northwestern European societies. Inequality was the other side of the coin of decent living standards for the worst-off. The commercial society could guarantee this because, along with security of property, it awakened the spirit of enterprise. Montesquieu had said that 'the spirit of commerce naturally attended with that of frugality, economy, moderation, labour, prudence, tranquillity, order and rule'.[5] Smith agreed, but he harnessed it to a theory of economic progress. Commerce brought luxury, and the indolent landlords surrendered their surpluses to merchants in return for a few baubles. This was all to the good, and not to be deplored. The merchant was the hero who, by investing his capital in productive labour, increased the wealth of the nation; while the landlord, the old repository of virtue, merely wasted it. The landlords lost power to the king on the one hand, and had to commute feudal rents on the other, as they became spendthrift. But the king encouraged commerce and, by granting security of property, strengthened the move towards greater freedom. Division of labour makes everyone in some sense a merchant, since exchange is part of making a living.

This progress is not wholly pure and beneficial, but Smith would argue, on balance, that it is preferable to earlier regimes. On the one hand, you have gross and oppressive inequality, but there is opulence, and even the mass of the population benefits from the abundance created by the division of labour and the spirit of commerce. There is no dependence, as in the old days, but independence. This in turn has some negative aspects too. Division of labour is mind-numbing. Workers become 'as stupid and ignorant as it is possible for a human creature to be'. Smith continues to point out the dehumanizing effects of specialized routine work in almost modern terms. This passage, with its almost Marxian overtones, concludes: 'His dexterity at his own particular trade seems, in this manner, to be acquired at the expense of his intellectual, social and martial virtues. But in every improved and civilized society this is the stage which the labouring poor, that is the great body of the people, must necessarily fall into, unless government takes some pains to prevent it'.[6]

The last half of the concluding sentence will seem startling to those who think Smith was wholly anti-government. In the context of his time, the state was mainly a warfare state; Britain was more or less continually at war on the Continent (and in America and India at times) between 1688 and 1815. The state was corrupt, and many of its officers were placemen. It was also deeply and scandalously in debt. It was likely to be influenced by 'lobbying' on behalf of merchants. Smith had warned in his *Theory of Moral Sentiments*: 'Sometimes what is called the constitution of the State, that is, the interest of the government; sometimes the interest of particular orders of men who tyrannize the government, warp the positive laws of the country from what natural justice would prescribe.'[7]

The state could not, therefore, be trusted always to follow the course of natural justice – neither the eighteenth-century British state nor any other contemporary European or, for that matter, Asian or African state. Smith had a minimal agenda for the state, of which education was an important part. But the main task of the state was to administer justice. This was commutative justice – prevention of injury to people, and of illegal encroachment on their property. Justice, for Smith, was this proper behaviour of individuals towards each other. This was especially important, because in a society of independent individuals tied together by the means of exchange, you could not rely on any feeling of brotherhood or sympathy to make people behave appropriately towards each other. He approved of prudent behaviour, but did not think it would necessarily be forthcoming. Hence the framework of laws and the administration of commutative justice. There was the natural right to physical safety, and then there was the right to property. These were justifiable.

A society run purely on self-interest would no doubt function. It was not what Smith liked, but he knew that benevolence had to be voluntary: it could not be required. A good society would come about if we were all prudent and exercised self-restraint, a stoic temperament being the best. But benevolence could not be relied upon. If it was available, however, it made a functioning society a good society.

The nub, however, remained: equal societies were likely to be poor societies. Commerce and private property led to inequality, but also to prosperity, giving adequate living standards to the masses. Commercial societies were also just, in the sense of respect for the natural rights of person and property. This was not utopia, but it was progress.

3

Hegel and the Ideal State[1]

Adam Smith thus poses the fundamental question of the modern – capitalist – economy. Liberty in the form of a guarantee of property rights brings with it inequality but, at the same time, prosperity. The prosperity that comes through the division of labour, and incentives to efficiency and innovation, translates into a decent standard of living, even for the poorest people in modern society, so that they live better than the rich of earlier days. Earlier societies were poor, though less unequal. They were arbitrary in their exercise of power and, in respect of property rights, very insecure. There was much dependence in these earlier societies, and thus no liberty.

The modern society brings many attendant problems, some of which are the unintended consequences of human actions, designed to yield good results. Division of labour leads to a numbing of the brain of the worker who has to do repetitive tasks. In this respect, the state has to ensure that education is an antidote to the lowering of sensibilities. Merchants and businessmen are forever conspiring to harm public interest by restraint of trade. Political factions driven by narrow economic interests seek to influence public policy. Free trade and competition are thus to be jealously guarded. Mere politicians are not enough; legislators – that club of more noble statesmen-like creatures – alone could ensure that *Homo civicus* was in balance with *Homo economicus.*

This was an eighteenth-century view: a precapitalist, preindustrial – indeed, as Donald Winch has put it, even a predemocratic – idea.[2] But even as Smith was writing, ideas that he and his fellow philosophers had made popular were about to destroy the Augustinian repose of the eighteenth century, and usher in the democratic age. The twin revolutions – American and French – took two contrasting stands on the Smithian dichotomy of liberty and equality. These two stands influenced much of European and, via the imperial connection, much of world history. Two hundred and ten years since Smith's death in 1790, the issue seems to many to be settled in favour of the American and against the French Revolution, but then this is to ignore the only serious critic of Smith: Karl Marx. If we are to understand him, we have to understand those two revolutions.

If early societies were unequal, they were unequal in status as well as in wealth. When we speak today of discrimination against women, or ethnic groups, or the aged, it is because we no longer tolerate an inequality of status whereby some are born superior to others. Hierarchy of status was the basis on which eighteenth-century European (and indeed, as far as we know, all other) societies were organized. The American Revolution started as a revolt against English domination over the colonies' obligation to pay the expenses incurred by the mother country. The objection was not so much to taxation as such, but to the fact that the tax proposed was not on external trade, where English right was acknowledged, but on domestic activities. In winning their battle, the colonists unfurled the flag of equality: 'We hold these truths to be self-evident, that all men are created equal' et cetera. It is easy from today's perspective to carp at the implicit omission of women and the actual omission of slaves and Indians, men as well as women. For the late eighteenth century, the establishment of a nation rather than a kingdom – and, indeed, one without a hereditary nobility – was a revolutionary step. However, the American Revolution was fought against not a foreign but a consanguine people, with only a very limited split within the colonial society. This allowed the new Republic to abolish status inequality, while leaving the wealth of the local elite untouched. Indeed, the sanctity of private property and the right to enjoy its fruits unhindered were a central part of this socially egalitarian revolution.

Not so, however, in the French Revolution. Here the enemy was home-grown: the feudal structure presided over by the king. Status inequality in France was reinforced by economic exactions which preserved wealth inequality. The egalitarian cry of the French Revolution was thus not only anti-royalist and anti-feudal, it also aspired to – and briefly, during the economic hardship of the Terror, achieved – a semblance of communist equality. And though, later on, order was restored in the form of some status inequality – first by Napoleon and then by the Restoration – the ideal of economic as well as status equality, once proclaimed, was not going to go away. The French Revolution thus required the assault on the property rights of the landlords, while championing the private property of the middle class, but this meant that the right to private property was secondary to status equality. You can hold property, but only as a citizen, not as a lord.

The mild Dr Smith was even accused posthumously of having fomented the French Revolution. His ideas were denounced as dangerously radical, and his students – especially his first biographer, Dugald Stewart – had to dress him up in conservative garb to refute these charges.[3] Liberty was a radical slogan for the eighteenth century. Private property rights had led to two nations doing away with the monarchy. The seeds sown by John Locke during the Bloodless Revolution had made rivers of blood flow.

The export of the French Revolutionary message by Napoleon's armies across Europe caused a further shake-up of these societies, especially that of the many small and large kingdoms of Germany. From Jena to Waterloo, Germany – a proto-nation at best – suffered upheaval and humiliation. The world of German gentry was turned upside down. The small, sleepy kingdoms and their residents were 'globalized' – connected with foreign lands and strange ideas. The challenge of understanding such rapid revolutionary change, but at the same time bottling it up in a rational understandable system, was taken up by Georg Wilhelm Friedrich Hegel.

There are many ways of reading and interpreting Hegel, and even more ways of misunderstanding him. In British intellectual life, Hegel's influence was decisive in the late nineteenth century, when leading political philosophers were Hegelians, but reached its nadir in the 1950s, when Karl Popper's attack on him became so fashionable that no self-respecting left-liberal person could be seen reading Hegel. At about the same time, a Hegel revival was taking place in France. Hegel continues, despite Popper, to be read and taken seriously. Indeed, Francis Fukuyama made him a name to be taken to intellectual salons in the early 1990s.

Hegel added one crucial dimension to Adam Smith's stadial theory of progress: that as progress occurred over time, humankind became more aware, more conscious, of what was happening to it. This was the march of the Idea (I caricature, but only slightly). While we were not yet in total self-conscious control of our surroundings and of events – of History – we understood them better and better as time went on. Thus, not only did our mode of subsistence change and cast its powerful spell over other institutions, as Smith had averred, but something above and beyond material progress was also happening.

Progress occurred not smoothly but fitfully, as a result of struggle, of contradiction, which gave a dynamic impulse to things and ideas. Dialectics is not something weird; it is merely a way of spotting, in any situation, the potential for change which exists, and teasing it out. At times of much smug satisfaction with achievement, and the feeling of having reached a pinnacle – as, indeed, at the fall of the Berlin Wall – the dialectical philosopher would spot the seeds for further change and, indeed, reversal. Nothing is ever finished, ever settled, until the end.

Trajectories require destination. Philosophers, no less than ordinary people, like a neat story with an end. Smith stopped at commerce and liberty, and did not see any further stage. Hegel saw the end in the future, when complete self-consciousness would become the universal property of humankind. The Idea will have won its self-realization for itself, through people's actions.

David Hume was an atheist and a sceptic, and he made no bones about it. His friend Adam Smith temporized about his own scepticism, and mouthed empty pieties about the Creator when necessary. Hegel was different. His monumental scheme for progress was in one sense futuristic and, if anything, excessively rational in a society still ruled by religion. He was thus not averse to giving Christianity a starring role in the progress story, and if people interpreted the End of History and the self-realization of the Idea as the Second Coming, so be it. He left things obscure enough – some say deliberately – to accommodate such sentiments. But it would be a mistake to think of Hegel as a cynic. The central problem which had brought him to philosophy from his schooldays in Württemberg was the loss of piety – of an active Protestant civic virtue which had hitherto, in his view, defined a moral community. This moral community was under threat of erosion. He therefore had to come to terms with the recent traumatic shock that German society had suffered at the hands of Napoleon, and the recoil into authoritarian reform to which Prussia had resorted. Indeed, bureaucratic rationality could have been invented in Prussia at the time of Hegel.

Hegel was not a sceptic, and never an atheist. His lifelong quest was to discover how public behaviour in civic society could be ethical. He viewed the events of the French Revolution and subsequent developments as a challenge to rethink how – to simplify – the old moral community could be restored in social intercourse. There was a rupture; the ideal unity between private morality and public conduct had been disrupted. Modern life had to divide individuals, in their dual capacities as men and as citizens, into private and public personae. Was this rupture an accident which could be overcome by the practice of piety, or did it have deeper causes? It was in search of answers to such questions that Hegel discovered Smith and the Scottish philosophers. He discovered political economy. Indeed, Hegel was the first philosopher in the classic mould to take economics seriously on board.

The problem facing Hegel was almost precisely the one that had faced the early-eighteenth-century English and Scottish thinkers. The age which was passing had seemed solid and enduring. Now it was going away, and they remembered how good it had been. Although it was status-ridden, in that society each person took care of the other – the lord looked after the serf if the latter was in need; the Church laid down the rules of good conduct; and relations between people were based on personal ties. Now, suddenly, money was subverting all this, introducing a new fluidity – indeed flirtatiousness – in social relationships. Things were valued in money terms; relations were based on impersonal exchange. What was solid in such a transient situation?

As we have seen, Adam Smith's answer was an almost aggressive vindication of commerce and impersonal exchange. Relations between people may appear anonymous, and motivated merely by self-interest, but they are actually intertwined in a complex but invisible way. They may appear independent and uncoordinated, but they are guided as if by an Invisible Hand. Smith was not unaware of the moral dimension – as, indeed, his first book, *The Theory of Moral Sentiments*, had shown. But he himself saw no contradiction in his theory of sympathy in individual behaviour, and his extolling of self-interest and liberty. Hegel did not dwell on any contradiction in Smith, as some late German authors did, inventing 'Das Adam Smith Problem'. The contradictions were in the real world. Without grasping the importance of the economic dimension in social life, he could not pursue his programme of rediscovering the roots of a moral community.

In a way, Hegel's project is a backward-looking, almost nostalgic one. How could we bring back the Golden Days when people were bound together by a sense of community, when private and public sphere – man and citizen – were one? The French Revolution was one indelible sign of rupture, but of course the Scottish philosophers who pioneered political economy also knew that the modern was a break with the ancient. There was no going back for Adam Smith; at best a coming to rest in a future stationary state. Hegel, however, wanted more. He wanted a better destination for the march of progress, a destination which, although out in the future, would restore the wholeness that once was enjoyed by mankind. (The male terminology is kept here, as I am trying to convey what the particular author thought, not what I would dearly have loved him to say.)

The material realm of needs about which the Scottish philosophers had been theorizing was not to be rejected in some ascetic Christian denial. Hegel came from a tradition of active Protestant but worldly citizens who once lived under a Catholic king, and whose civic life was intertwined with religion and political action. So the problem was to understand the mainsprings of material progress, but then seek the key to the forces that would transform material progress into freedom, that is, the realization of the moral community. This key lay in understanding how people became conscious of their actions and their circumstances as progress – that is, how far reason was marching alongside material growth. If History could be seen as the march of reason – and Hegel was as much a theorizer of History as a philosopher – then one could argue that the latest instalment of progress, odious though it might seem in its commercial and impersonalizing aspects, might yet be a cunning way in which Reason operates. From within the stage of History, which may seem to be going away from the true path, may come its opposite, its antithesis; and overcoming the contradictions between the two may lead to a higher synthesis. It sounds like a simple box of tricks, but Hegel was able to rewrite the stadial theory of History in these terms. Through History, he saw the growth of self-consciousness: the growth of a knowledge which, though by no means perfect, was allowing actors greater freedom.

The French Revolution was an example of this Cunning of Reason. The Enlightenment had encouraged people to think of themselves as individuals on their own, rational and autonomous, and not as a cog in a complex hierarchical machine. They had even started to question religion, and wanted a rational dogma. The autonomous individual could not accept any fetters; he wanted freedom. In Hegel's view, the French Revolution, which culminated in the Terror, was an effort to obtain absolute freedom for these individuals. Since no one could claim authority except by consent, and each person's right to rule was as good as any other's, the Revolution was caught in a frenzy. Whichever faction was in power had to pretend that it commanded universal support, and hence had to castigate every rival faction as suspect, eliminating it physically if necessary. The Terror, for Hegel, proved that absolute individual freedom was a chimera.

But as Napoleon swept through Europe and dismantled the old order, most severely in Germany, the post-Napoleonic world proved not to be such a bad thing after all. The Terror and its aftermath had wiped the slate clean, and prepared the conditions for realizing freedom for individuals within the community. Only by their social existence, fully conscious and totally voluntary – indeed, by realizing that they must internalize the need to live in a community – could individuals be truly free. The community was the Spirit as it realized itself through individuals; and as they understood fully and rationally why their freedom could not be arbitrary, but had to be lived in the community, the Spirit moved closer to its end: complete self-realization.

The community that was to realize this freedom had three facets: the family, civil society and, at the apex, the state. Adam Smith had lived in a state – the mid-eighteenth century Hanover monarchy – which was a warfare machine, very expensive and very corrupt. Fortunately, it left the private life of families, and of society in general, to itself. Parliament was on the one hand a representation of many small property interests and, in the House of Lords, of the bigger landlords. It was not an autocratic state – 1689 had seen to that – but it was not a progressive or reforming state either. Smith, therefore, wished nothing more than that the state should leave the sphere of the economy – the sphere of individual contracts and exchange – well alone. This sphere – civil society – could, Smith argued, thrive if it was left to its own devices, and did not need state regulation or interference. The contemporary state, of course, did interfere all the time, but the passionate argument that Smith put forward was the beginning of the revolution in thought whereby self-governed entities were no longer assumed to succumb inevitably to anarchy, but could thrive.

For Smith, the state had one great task as far as civil society was concerned. Since the division of labour led to prosperity, but extracted its toll on the workers by deadening their sensibilities, the state had to look after education, which was an antidote. The state had to guard individuals against alienation – as Hegel would call it – by improving the citizens.

Hegel took a very different view of the state. His state was post-Napoleonic Prussia. By the time he came to formulate his theory of the state, much had changed, even in Britain. A more rational, more tolerant state, better reflecting civil society, was struggling to emerge. The Prussian state had self-consciously embraced reform by rationalizing its bureaucracy. These reforms had shocked the Romantics, who resented the sudden novelty of the legislation which was sweeping away much that was old. They wanted organic – that is, slower – change. They wished laws were more like natural law.

Hegel was much too rational – and, indeed, much too radical – for that. Even though he did not approve of the Terror, he saw its positive contribution in hindsight. The Cunning of Reason had cleared the decks. The moment was ripe for a rational state in which all would realize freedom. This, of course, goes against an individualist and utilitarian notion of the state. An individualist utilitarian state with democratic majority voting (as Condorcet had realized) ran into contradictions. (This has come to be known in the modern theory of social choice as Arrow's Impossibility Theorem.)[4] Hegel wanted to explore the limits of autonomous individuality and blend it into a higher community in order to make it free in a different – and, indeed, he would argue, more rational – sense.

Each element in the triad of family, civil society and the state had its role in the rational order. The family was the private sphere of feeling rather than reason, sentiment rather than contract. Private property, in Hegel's view, cemented the family, especially where it was entailed by inheritance laws, so that one generation could not dispose of it as it wished. Family life represents a community in its immediate parochial form. Civil society, on the other hand, is where individuals come together as so many self-interests, exchanging and trading on a contractual basis. This was the economic sphere which had revolutionized life in the previous hundred years, in which more and more relations were based not on ties of status and hierarchy, but on contract and anonymity and juridical equality.

Hegel recognized that the activities of civil society were the key to prosperity. By extending the division of labour, and facilitating inventions and far-flung trade, the economic sphere catered to an ever-expanding system of needs. But Hegel, unlike Smith, was not sanguine about the course of the economy. On the one hand, it generated alienation by making the worker a mere cog in the division of labour. On the other hand, far from being self-regulating, it could generate extremes of wealth and poverty, thus deepening the sense of alienation. So, while much of the self-governing logic was unexceptional, for a truly rational free community, civil society had to be overseen by the state. Hegel was no *laissez-faire* political economist.

The counterweight against the bourgeoisie, the individuals in civil society, was the class of disinterested civil servants. These civil servants constituted a universal class, because their interests coincided with those of the community as a whole. They were neutral umpires settling the disputes within civil society which could not be settled by mutual agreement, guarding the law, and overseeing its implementation. Civil servants were the executive serving the single embodiment of the state: the monarch. The monarch derived his or her authority not from tradition, or Divine Right, but because only a personal embodiment of the community would be rational. An elected head was too accidental, and far too amenable to pressure from below. Only a hereditary monarch could simultaneously be impartial and personify the community. In Hegel's view, such a personification of the Spirit was essential.

Hegel's view of representation was also predemocratic. The landed estates were to be represented individually in one house of the legislature. The burghers, representing civil society, were to be indirectly represented via their guilds and corporations in another house. Individuals were not merely autonomous subjects; they were also members of a collectivity. Thus, they were a differentiated rather than a homogeneous collection. Hegel distrusted adult franchise and election of delegates, because without differentiation, an abstract homogeneous mass became a dangerous crowd. The Terror was not forgotten.

The task of the estates, as the legislature, was not to oppose the monarch but to blend private interests with public knowingly and willingly. The will could not be divided against itself. The community had to have a single, perfectly blended, consciously rational will. There had to be a voluntary internalized harmony between private interests and public good. Of course, given the division of labour, modern societies could not be like the Greek polis, with all citizens expressing the public good. Civil servants were the instruments for dedication to the public good. But the burghers and the landed interests also had to reflect the public good, even as they pursued their private benefit. This is a predemocratic, but post-1789 utopia. Neither contemporary Prussia, nor any other state, came near to realizing it. But the balance between civil society, the landed interests and the selfless executive, serving a monarch dedicated to post-Napoleonic reform, was better in Prussia in the 1820s than in England, where civil society was rampant; or in France, where, according to Hegel, Catholicism precluded full rationality.

Hegel, though dated today, was in advance of his time. His opposition to individualism and to representative democracy was based on the emptiness of abstract individual freedom. People, he thought, need to be more than free autonomous individuals. They have to have another 'identity', as we would put it today. The pursuit of hedonistic pleasure and abstract democracy would never satisfy completely. Fukuyama's Hegel is not, after all, Hegel's Hegel. There had to be a community as part of which people had to experience their freedom. Man is not an individual; he is a social being. The state, in its rational mode, could encompass both the narrow individual and the social being.

Thus Hegel contains and deals with the disruption of modern life by nascent capitalism in a different way from Smith. His two houses of the legislature – one for the landed elite, the other representing the burghers – comes very close to the British arrangements of his time. A neutral, public-interest-orientated civil service was yet to evolve. Indeed, the neo-Hegelians among late-nineteenth-century British political philosophers may even have shaped the civil service in the image of his universal class. The state had to guard civil society – the market economy – against itself in the larger interest. In this broad way of putting it, the liberal reformers and the Fabians derived from Hegel (though also from others such as John Stuart Mill) a notion of the state which was not the state of Adam Smith.

But Hegel's solution was not to be implemented as far as the legislature was concerned. The drive towards abstract freedom inaugurated by the French Revolution was to proceed until universal adult franchise and representative democracy became the most desired political arrangements. Monarchy was not accepted as the ideal Hegel posited it to be. Indeed, counterpoised to the Smithian and Hegelian solutions to the problem of economic freedom was to be Marx's vision, which theorized the French Revolution into the end-goal of History. Marx dealt with capitalism simultaneously as a tremendous step forward, but also as an eventually self-destructive system. This third solution was to shape the history of the twentieth century.

Before we come to that, some other aspects of our discussion need to be noted. First, there is the very narrow focus on Western Europe and Protestant Christianity taken as universal frameworks. Hegel's history, like Smith's, ignores the dynamic course of Islam, which flourished just at the time when Europe was going through the Dark Ages. The dialectic does not encompass those eight centuries between the decline of the Roman Empire and the Renaissance, when the most progressive civilization was the Islamic one. Nor is any progress credited to India or China, of which Hegel was not ignorant. The story of modernity is written exclusively and ignorantly, in purely European terms, where the rest of the world appears, if at all, as a victim rather than an active other.

But even discounting that, the young American Revolution which had established a republic and, at that time, one of the widest franchises – and, indeed, consciously argued the basis of its Constitution in terms of European philosophy – was all but ignored. The balance between civil society and the state was debated at Philadelphia in 1789 – that fateful year – and articulated in writings such as *The Federalist Papers*.[5] It was, perhaps, too parochial, too far away, for the Europeans, but much subsequent political theory and political struggle were to be impoverished because of a failure to look across the Atlantic. But that is an issue to be taken up later.

4
Marx I: Clearing the Decks

Between the year of Adam Smith's birth (1723) and the death of Karl Marx (1883), not only European societies but the world changed profoundly. When Adam Smith was born, there had been no breakthrough in steam-powered energy or spinning machines. When Marx was born, spinning had been revolutionized, but weaving was still a handicraft. Railways, that great manifestation of steam power, were yet to come, as were the steamships. By the time Marx died, the Suez Canal had opened, Europeans had traversed the interior of central Africa, California had been populated, and telegraphy was common knowledge. Slavery had, by and large, been abolished in Europe and North America, though at a bloody cost in the latter. Thousands of people from Central and Eastern Europe had migrated to America and some from the British Isles had been deported to the Antipodes. Huddled masses from India and China had migrated all over the world, except to Europe – to other countries of Asia, to Africa, to the Caribbean islands and, in the Chinese case, even to California. The world had been explored and mapped and settled and exploited for its minerals – gold especially – for its crops, its exotic fruits and spices. Botanical gardens in France, England and Germany became like dictionaries of global flora and fauna.

Within these 160 years spanning Smith's birth and Marx's death, the world had moved irreversibly away from its past. Even if in 1750s Glasgow it was possible to imagine that the contemporary polity ought to model itself on that of Ancient Greece, by the 1850s the world was no longer comparable to isolated city-states. Renaissance Europe had looked up to the Romans' achievements, and marvelled at the accounts they had read of the Chinese or the Mogul Empire. But by the time Marx was middle-aged, all that had been surpassed. The medieval world was in many ways at the mercy of Nature, in its day-to-day life as well as in its frequent catastrophes and crises. But the nineteenth-century European could pride himself on the fact that his life was controlled consciously by him and the powers that industrial technology had put at his disposal. There was more to come – electricity, the internal combustion engine, and air travel –

in the next thirty years. But history had escaped its cyclical fate, and become a dizzying upward spiral. Capitalism had become the established norm for organizing economic life; it was the dominant mode of production.

Marx took up the challenge of forging a new and total understanding of this rapid transformation. As in the case of Adam Smith, who lived in a period of rapid change over time and over space (as he moved from Kirkcaldy to London or Paris), Marx observed and thought about the world around him as it changed over the course of the mid-nineteenth century. He wrote throughout much of his adult life, over a period spanning forty years from 1843 to 1883. It is to him that we owe much of what we call social science today, and some powerful but technical vocabulary – mode of production, for example. He lived in Germany, Belgium, France and, indeed, was *persona non grata* in these countries even before he was thirty; he then came to London and lived there for the last thirty-four of his sixty-five years.

Marx did not, however, just study and write. Unlike Smith and Hegel, he wrote and fought and wove schemes for a total revolutionary transformation of society. He did not merely chart a different destination for History from the one that Hegel had presented; he tried actively to inch his world towards it. A philosopher's task, he said, was not only to understand the world around him; he had to change it as well. Marx was that sort of philosopher.

The world was changing quite fast anyway, without any help from the philosopher – indeed, changing so rapidly that while, in his youth, Marx thought there was not much more left to theorize about, all his life he tried to grasp the ever-changing drama of capitalism. Starting from the critique of German (Hegel's) philosophy in his youth, he ended up studying and speculating about land tenures and their potential for changing Russian society. In between, he had mapped out the anatomy of contemporary capitalism in such a way that, whatever the subsequent attacks on his theory by other social scientists, his appeal to people wanting to change their world has never died, though his death has been pronounced frequently. Currently, he is thought to be even more dead than ever before. We shall see.

Marx was born three years after the Battle of Waterloo. As part of the postwar settlement, Prussia had been given Rhineland-Westphalia, and it was in the town of Trier in that province that Marx was born. Technically, this makes him a Prussian,[1] but the dominant influence on that region had been French. Marx's father gave up Judaism, which he was convinced was a backward religion compared to Protestantism, which had the approbation of many philosophers. Thus, Marx can be labelled Prussian or not, Jew or not, as fancy takes any of his many detractors. The French Revolution and its progressive aftermath were major influences on his life, just as they were for Hegel.

Marx started at Bonn as a law student, to please his father, but after a while, before finishing his degree, he had what can only be described as a nervous breakdown. He switched to Berlin and to philosophy. He came under the influence of the Young Hegelians, especially Bruno Bauer.[2] This group was using Hegel's theory to mount a critique of established religion. In 1835, Strauss had published his *Life of Jesus,* the first 'biography' of Jesus as a human being. Bauer was writing a critique of Protestantism. By then the Prussian state had revealed its conservative side, and a purge of Hegelians was going on in the universities. Marx had to go to Jena to finish his doctorate, and was unlikely to get a teaching job given his association with the Young Hegelians. He took up journalism and engaged in frenetic writing activity. His friends were trying their hands at publishing literary reviews that were meant to be radical and subversive and, therefore, to be published from outside Prussia – the German-French Yearbook, and the like. Often only one issue was published, and the journal then had to change its title.

From today's vantage point, philosophical activity in the late 1830s and early 1840s looks as feverish as it was in the heady days of May 1968 and anti-Vietnam protests. There was a small group of bright, intellectually incestuous and immensely bitchy individuals of which Marx was, for a while, a star. On his marriage to Jenny von Westphalen, he managed to write his first major work, but like many of his other works, it was unpublished in his lifetime: a critique of Hegel's *Philosophy of Right,* the Master's last complete publication. It is a fragment, but Marx had promised his friends an earth-shattering critique of Hegel that would settle scores once and for all. And as often in his later life, he promised more than he could deliver. The introduction to this purported book did, however, appear in print, and its power and style are stunning. A star had arrived in the philosophical firmament in Germany, just as his fellow students had predicted.

Within five years of writing this fragment, however, as well as two major books – *The Holy Family* (with Engels) – a philosophical family quarrel, published in 1845; and *The German Ideology* (also with Engels) – a substantial development of his basic philosophy – Marx abandoned philosophy, and took up political economy.[3] He had already been making trouble as a journalist, and his paper had been shut down by the Prussian censors. But in 1848, on the eve of the widespread revolution on mainland Europe, he published, along with Engels, their immortal work, *The Communist Manifesto.* There had been manifestos before, and there have been many since, but only this one has managed a shelf life of a century and a half, and shows no sign of wilting yet. Apart from anything else, it ranks as a classic piece of European prose, as good in the German original as in French and English and in the hundred-odd other languages it has been translated into since.

But the 1848 revolutions failed, and Marx retired to London in serious destitution, though that proved temporary thanks to the generosity of his industrialist friend and comrade Engels, who supported him for the rest of his life. Marx spent the 1850s and much of the 1860s working on his much-promised *Capital*. Still intoxicated by the power of ideas to change reality, he and many of his friends had expected that the publication of this critique of political economy would sound the death knell of capitalism itself. Marx had given hints of his ideas in his shorter works – polemics with Proudhon and an introductory volume, *A Contribution to the Critique of Political Economy*, whose preface has been read and quoted more often than the book itself. But in 1867, when the first volume of *Capital* was published, Marx had already prepared, in draft form, the next two volumes, and enough notes on the history of economic ideas to fill three more volumes: about a thousand pages.

And then, as suddenly as he had given up philosophy and taken up political economy, he again shifted gear. The Paris Commune of 1871 was blamed on him, though he was in London and busy writing one of the most riveting 'eye-witness' accounts of it.[4] But for the next twelve years he did not go back to his drafts of the volumes of *Capital*, did not polish them for publication as he had done with Volume 1. Indeed, he did not publish any major work before he died in 1883. He spent his time supervising the publications of new editions and translations of the first volume. His fame was spreading. A Russian translation appeared even before a French one, a decade and more before an English translation came out. He read deeply and widely about land tenure systems in Russia, and about the ethnology of 'primitive' societies. He and Engels poked their noses into the fortunes of the fledgling socialist party in Germany – the first party among many to come later which swore by his theories, which he thought they had misunderstood. His readers and disciples tried to embalm his theories as Marxism – something he disclaimed: *Tout que je sait je ne suis pas marxiste.*

In terms of the ratio of posthumous publications to those published in his lifetime, Marx must hold something of a record. Smith's *Lectures on Jurisprudence* were discovered only in the twentieth century, and he had forbidden the publication of his writings, which are now available to us as *Essays on Philosophical*

Subjects. But Smith's major works – *The Theory of Moral Sentiments* and *The Wealth of Nations* – were published in his lifetime, and immortalized him. Smith died a famous man. When Marx died he was not unknown by any means; governments across Europe were aware of his notoriety, though the English did not share the German suspicions that he was a potential regicide. But it was after his death, and through the short twentieth century, that his reputation soared. All his writings were rescued and published – though, as luck would have it, the new censors, though they were his admirers, were no better than the Prussian censors of his day. We now have – bowdlerized for a while, but eventually retrieved – if not the complete collection of his writings, pretty much 98 per cent. It runs to forty-five volumes, of which perhaps a fifth, at most, were published in his lifetime.

The grave of Adam Smith in the Canongate area of Edinburgh is a modest affair. There is no statue of the sage exhorting us to divide (labour) and prosper. There are no street marches, no demonstrations with Adam Smith's face on large furling banners. There are now Adam Smith Institutes, and even T-shirts bearing his likeness. But no one went to jail or a concentration camp for quoting, misquoting or interpreting Adam Smith in a way that the rulers of the day did not approve of. All this has happened in the case of Marx. His grave in Highgate cemetery is an imposing structure, and occasionally incites vandals to attack it. Perhaps nowadays there are fewer bewildered Russian tourists getting off at Highgate Underground Station and seeking the way to the grave. But there it is. And people have gone to concentration camps, been purged from the Party, expelled, exiled, axed, murdered and liquidated for reading or misreading Marx. The fall of the Berlin Wall brought to an end that disgraceful chapter in European history, at least.

It was not always thus. For about forty years after his death, Marx's ideas were openly debated, contested, corrected, and sometimes abandoned. The German Social Democratic Party, the largest of its kind in Western Europe, took Marxism as the basis of its theory. But while Bebel, Liebknecht and Kautsky acted as official interpreters of Marxism, they had no power to punish dissidents. Left and Right factions bloomed. Marx's ideas were also debated in universities. Böhm-Bawerk, Sombart, Weber and many others discussed them. The notions that Marx's theory was inconsistent, that it was outdated, and even that it was nothing new, were all advanced.

At the core were two ideas: first, the theory of what made capitalism work, that is, how profits were generated from the exploitation of workers; and second, the immediate future of capitalism. Later on, I shall explain these ideas in some detail, because they are crucial, even to this day, to the way we think of contemporary capitalism. Here I wish to survey rather rapidly the fortunes that Marx's ideas suffered. The first volume of *Capital* had laid down the main lines of attack and, in the seventh part, detailed a theory of the cycles of profitability and unemployment in capitalism. But there was also a longer – let us call it millennial – perspective: that capitalism was just one link in the daisy chain of modes of production. Like Smith, Marx had his stadial theory of history, but as with Hegel, there was yet another higher stage or two to come, which would transcend capitalism.

The power of Marx's style in the *Communist Manifesto*, as in parts of *Capital Volume 1*, made many of his followers think that the transcendence of capitalism was imminent. Even Marx himself, during his prolonged efforts at writing what became *Capital*, feared (especially in 1857) that capitalism might disappear before he had finished his critique. This wild hope receded after 1871, and he turned his mind to the periphery of capitalism – to Russia in particular. But his German followers – along with French, Russian, and some Italian ones – were convinced that capitalism had indeed reached its limits, and its demise was not far away. But then, after Marx's death, Engels published in 1885 the second volume from Marx's notes, and it appeared that the same theory could be used to illustrate a very long and sustained period of capitalist expansion without crises. A terrifying controversy broke out. The third volume, published in 1894, talked of the tendency of the profit rate to fall, heartening the doom-mongers. How could one then see the future of capitalism? Could it sustain itself despite its exploitative nature? Could it escape punishment by subtle devices – colonies, for instance – which would rejuvenate the ailing system?[5]

Böhm-Bawerk, occupying the chair of Economics at Vienna, wrote a strong attack on the theoretical inconsistency – as he saw it – between the simple argument of *Volume 1* and the detailed account of how labour's exploitation translates itself into capitalist profits in *Volume 3*.[6] Edouard Bernstein, after spending some years in England, was convinced that capitalism had changed, and Marx's ideas were no longer applicable.[7] The left wing of the German SPD disagreed. Rosa Luxemburg, its best mind, wrote a long book trying to reconcile the three versions of the dynamics of the capitalism story, integrating the question of colonies. She, at least, remained hopeful that the workers of the advanced capitalist countries would – via a general strike, or some such device – hasten the demise of capitalism.[8] Kautsky put his money on the steady advance of workers' strength through the Party, and the parliamentary road to socialism.

The First World War, which broke out in August 1914, changed much about the way the world was and the ways in which it was perceived. Throughout the nineteenth century, politicians, philosophers, scientists and historians had greeted the growth of reason and the advance of what they defined as European civilization spreading across the world. Perhaps they had always been insulated from the grim underbelly of progress. Yet the outbreak of war was a rude reminder that the forces of irrationality, of jingoism, of mindless violence, of class and race divide, had not gone away, just because the middle classes in some parts of Europe had acquired 'manners'.

But the ruder shock was for the Marxists. The workers, instead of being internationally united, displayed the worst traits of jingoism; the German SPD enthusiastically voted for war credits. Only a handful of socialists across Europe – Ramsay MacDonald, Jean Jaurès and Lenin among them – stood out against the war and the patriotic madness. The Socialist International – a child of what Marx had started in the 1860s, which had died, only to be revived in 1889 – was split. Lenin and the revolutionary defeatists wanted out.

And then, against all expectations, Lenin and his Bolsheviks won power in Russia, in a Revolution reminiscent of Paris 1871 and, indeed, Paris 1789. Whatever else it did, for ever afterwards, Marx and his ideas became the monopoly possession of the Party that could claim to have come to power using Marxism. Revolution was not meant to occur in a backward country like Russia, according to the theory thus far received, but that became heresy, and documents were unearthed, reinterpreted and revised until the Bolshevik version became the only version of Marxism. What was an intellectual and idealistic coalition of many strands of belief was pushed into uniformity. Marx, far from being obscure, became the founder of a new religion. All non-Bolshevik readings of Marx were traduced; their proponents were denounced. Polemics, hitherto merely verbally rude, became lethal – literally so.

Within ten years of the Russian Revolution, honest open debate about Marx's ideas ceased – in the West as in the Soviet Union. No innovations or new interpretations were offered by the active political movements. Marxism retreated into a few universities. The much-hoped-for uprising in the West did not take place. Even as capitalist countries suffered a succession of problems – war damage, hyperinflation and depression – communism, the new variant of social democracy, did not triumph. Fascism, the other variant of socialism, did triumph and, for many, held out real promise. Only a long, bloody war, in which the Soviet Union first sided with Hitler and then had to fight him off at an immense sacrifice, could defeat fascism.

The Cold War followed, but not until after the Soviet Union had gained a respectable audience as an industrialized power which had somehow accomplished in twenty years what had taken a hundred in capitalist countries. Its example was studied by the newly decolonized countries of Asia and Africa. Revolutions in China and Vietnam added to the glamour of the Bolshevik version of Marx. Despite the Cold War, Marxism became a powerful force in universities, as well as in some political parties. It was almost like being back in the 1880s – but not quite, since an official orthodoxy had laid down the line. Deviations were denounced, be they from a former Bolshevik – Trotsky – or other variants of Marxism – Tito, Mao, Ho.

Then 1956 shattered it all once again. The Soviet invasion of Hungary to suppress the fledgling uprising, and the denunciation of Stalin at a secret Congress of the Communist Party of the Soviet Union, exposed that orthodoxy for the cruel sham it was. It had severed its last connection with the nineteenth-century humanist tradition in which Marx was situated. And old manuscripts written by Marx, hitherto unpublished or unpublicized, came to light. The New Left was born in the West. Western Marxism became a serious and ongoing enterprise, both inside and outside the universities. For the next thirty years, every word and line by Marx was scrutinized, debated, criticized. Marx was found to have deviated from his own theory, left huge gaps in his theory concerning class, the state, the agency for the Revolution, gender, the peasantry, the Third World, the advent of automation, the rise of Keynesianism and the welfare state, democracy, nationalism, ethnicity, race, and so on.

It was a great and moving – almost orgiastic – feast of reading and rereading, of revising and accusing others of revisionism, of great syntheses and searching critiques. In some ways it is reminiscent of the debates among the Young Hegelians that Marx and Engels mocked in *The Holy Family*. But it was a wide-ranging debate in time and across countries. Many thousands of forests were felled to print the commentaries, the theories, the prognostications. Marx was refurbished and put in his place. His crude enthusiasm for progress and technology, expressed as the march of the forces of production, was tamed in favour of an open-ended, flexible and humanistic emphasis on the other strand of his theory: relations of production. His theory of socialism was elaborated; existing socialist countries were examined and often found wanting, but not beyond redemption. Given time, it could all be fixed.

And then disaster struck. Towards the end of a century at the beginning of which many had thought that capitalism had a short shelf life, and that the alternative was socialism or barbarism – a century during which socialism, in both its Bolshevik and its fascist varieties, had indeed been barbaric – socialism in the form of the Soviet Union and all its Eastern European satellites collapsed, a collapse most vividly illustrated by the fall of the Berlin Wall. All sorts of debates about the distorted nature of socialism in the Soviet Union – the superiority, perhaps, of the Chinese or the Cuban or the Yugoslav path – became utterly irrelevant. The care with which people examined the sociology of St Petersburg in 1917, to check whether there could have been genuine working-class support for Lenin, as he claimed, or whether it was just a distorted revolution from the beginning; debates about Bukharin and Trotsky and Stalin being the correct theorizer of Marx – all became worth less than nothing.

Capitalism had survived – not only survived, but become a dynamic worldwide phenomenon yet again, for the first time since 1914. It showed a capacity for technological advance with promises of more to come. Across the world, people abandoned socialism as a cure for their problems. Warts and all, it was capitalism they wanted. Capitalism still had a lot of potential; it was not yet ready to lie down and die. Neither underconsumption and lack of markets, nor workers' organization and their rising share in total income, nor the loss of empire or the shortage of oil, or the threat of the Third World proletariat – all of these and more rehearsed as possible causes of its downfall – could stop capitalism. Now who could have predicted that?

In a short preface to the *Contribution to the Critique of Political Economy* published in 1859 (two years after he thought capitalism might end, before he had finished its critique), Marx wrote:

> No social order ever disappears before all the productive forces for which there is room in it have been developed; and new higher relations of production never appear before the material conditions of their existence have matured in the womb of the old society itself. Therefore, mankind always sets itself only such tasks as it can solve; since looking at the matter more closely, we will always find that the task itself arises only when the material conditions necessary for its solution already exist, or are at least in the process of formation.[9]

Practically all the commentary on Marx since his death, but especially since 1917, has been an attempt to deny this. This statement, denounced as a crude – indeed, naive – 'theory', was vindicated at the end of the twentieth century. Socialism was premature, since capitalism had not as yet exhausted its capacity for development. We lost sight of this simple truth only because of the contingent factors – now, fortunately, removed – that characterized the short twentieth century: 1914–89. In order to see the relevance of Marx, we must get that sorry episode out of our minds, and use Marx's theory for the purpose for which it was intended: as a way of studying the dynamics of capitalism, its strengths and its limits.

We need, therefore, to cleanse our minds of a lot of preconceptions about Marx, and harness his theory, so that we can understand the great change that we are living through at the beginning of the twenty-first century. Will capitalism go on for ever, or will it come to an end and give way to another mode of production? Will that mode be better for the poor, for the average person, for the currently rich or the poor countries? Are there any limits to the expansion of capitalism and, if so, what are they? Are these limits internal to capitalism, or external: workers' dissatisfaction or real wage explosion; ecological limits; nationalist rivalries reviving protectionism and regional blocs; religious fundamentalism, which is anticapitalist in outlook? Can any social arrangement remotely resembling socialism – in any of its variety of definitions – come about in the future, although such a future may not arrive for the next century or two?

But one or two caveats are still necessary before I can proceed. First is the fact I alluded to above: that what Marx published in his lifetime is only a small fraction of what he left in written form. The work that he prepared for publication bristles with flashes of style – there is sarcasm, irony, wit; everywhere we encounter quotations from classical and modern literature, the Bible, Shakespeare, Heine and Racine.[10] What he left behind was often notes to himself, abstracts from books he had read, summaries of other people's arguments, clarifications for himself, and some brilliant analysis. If Marx had not been deified, a lot of this would never have seen the light of day, or, if published, accorded the reverence it has been given. Indeed, in the Marx literature, there is a law of inversion. His unpublished work is accorded greater reverence than his published work, and what he wrote in his youth praised way above his mature work. This, however, has more to do with the political fortunes of his theories – especially after 1917 and then again after 1956, as I describe above – than with its intrinsic merit. But it is his published work, that small fraction of all his writings, which had effects on events. The unpublished work was retrieved systematically after the Bolshevik Revolution by Ryazanov, who was left in charge of the manuscripts handed over to the Soviets by the German SPD, which had them in its possession. These manuscripts trickled out in the 1920s and 1930s, but were again known only to a few. After the Second World War, they influenced the shape of Western Marxism as an academic discipline, but, given the weakness of Marxists in politics, did not influence events all that much. (The one major exception would be the events of 1968, in universities across Europe.) I intend, therefore, to concentrate on the writings published in Marx's lifetime, and mention the posthumous publications only where strictly necessary – such as two volumes of *Capital* edited and published by Engels after Marx's death in 1883. This will mean concentrating on the more 'economic' writings of Marx, but that is precisely my focus. When I come to discuss the future prospects for global capitalism, I shall get into what has become known in the last fifty years, because it does now have the power to influence the way we think, for example, about socialism.

The other caveat is that while Marx had, like Smith, a stadial theory of history in the background, he did not publish very much about it in his lifetime. Indeed, his speculations about universal history were wrapped up in *The German Ideology*, which he wrote with Engels, but abandoned to 'gnawing criticism of the mice' (though since these manuscripts were found, the mice must have been either very inefficient or too well fed to bother with old paper). After that, he dealt with his theory only in a devastatingly compact summary, of which more below. Throughout the 1850s he worked on the political economy of capitalism. The first book-length monograph that Marx published on his own, *A Contribution to the Critique of Political Economy*, appeared in 1859, when he was forty-one, some fifteen years after he had promised his first great book, which was going to be a critique of Hegel's *Theory of the State*.

But the 1859 book was only to whet the appetite and to keep off plagiarists. The big book he was preparing was, as usual, started in rough draft, which was then polished and polished again. This rough draft, which has became known as *Grundrisse*, has also acquired a status – in some opinions higher than that of *Capital*. *Grundrisse* contains some discussion of precapitalist formations. Some people think that these notes contradict the published summary in the *Contribution*. Since Marx prepared the *Contribution* for publication even as he had the rough drafts before him, I shall conclude that he knew what he was doing. So such brief mention as I make of Marx's theory of history will be the succinct – and, for some, crude and mechanical – version that Marx left behind. If only Marx were as easy to discuss as Smith!

We can now go back to the questions I raised above, about the nature of capitalism. Incidentally, Marx did not use the word 'capitalism' anywhere in his books. The word occurs late in his life in a letter he wrote to a Russian correspondent. For him, it was always the bourgeois mode of production.

Marx started with a critique of Hegel's most mature work, *The Philosophy of Right* – written on his six-month-long honeymoon! But it was his work as a journalist, and a significant economic event, that made him change direction.

In a way, the event was very similar to what we describe today as the impact of globalization. The revolution in the industrial technology of spinning in late-eighteenth-century England had not been followed immediately by a similar breakthrough in weaving. As the spun-yarn output rose, and its price plummeted, the demand for weavers expanded not just in England but all across Western Europe. Among these regions was Silesia, on the border between Germany and Poland. But when weaving became mechanized in the 1840s, the fifty-year-long boom in handloom weaving collapsed, and weavers' incomes shrank. This led to a revolt by weavers in Silesia. The Army had to be called out to suppress this revolt. Many people said more charitable works were needed; others that more education would do the trick; while some blamed it all on the workers' fecklessness. Demands for tariff protection were also raised. Such demands are advanced even today, in the face of globalization.

Marx began to make the link between the state and its legal framework, civil society, its search for economic gain, and the plight of the workers. He saw Germany as economically and politically backward. Pauperism was not peculiarly German; indeed, when he looked at England, which had reformed its Poor Law only a decade previously, he knew that the more advanced an economy, the more likely such problems were. But by the same token, he did not advocate tariffs, since that meant going backwards. In his first published article (apart from newspaper editorials, and so on), the Introduction to the never-published critique of Hegel, he wrote:

> [T]he relationship of industry and the world of wealth in general to the political world is one of the main problems of the modern age. In which form does this problem begin to preoccupy the Germans? In the form of *protective tariffs*, of a *system of prohibitions* of *national economy*. In Germany, therefore, we are about to begin at the point where England and France are about to conclude . . . In France and England, therefore, it is a question of abolishing monopoly, which has progressed to its final consequences; in Germany it is question of progressing to the final consequences of monopoly.[11]

Hegel had maintained that private property was the bastion of the order, with estates representing propertied people – landed and monied – with bureaucracy looking after public interest, all under the monarch. Marx challenged the assertion that the bureaucracy was above the particular estates, and hence could be trusted with public interest – that, in Hegel's terminology, it was a universal class. Marx argues against this in an a priori syllogism. This is what he was trained to do: mount an immanent critique – a critique from within, as it were

– taking as given the approach he was trying to undermine by showing its inconsistency. Since the bureaucracy was recruited from property-owning classes, it could not be above class interests. The only class that could be universal, and above particular interests, is the class not represented in the estates, that is, a class which has no property. This is the proletariat, as the Romans used to call them. In Marx's fiery words, inverting Hegel's logic, it sounds awesome:

> So where is the *positive* possibility of German emancipation? *This is our answer.* In the formation of a class with *radical chains*, a class of civil society which is not a class of civil society, a class [*Stand*] which is the dissolution of all classes, a sphere which has a universal character because of its universal suffering and which lays claim to no *particular right* because the wrong it suffers is not a *particular wrong* but *wrong in general*; a sphere of society which can no longer lay claim to a *historical* title, but merely a *human* one, which does not stand in onesided opposition to the consequences but in all sided opposition to the premises of the German political system; and finally a sphere which cannot emancipate itself without emancipating itself from – and thereby emancipating – all other spheres of society which is, in a word, the *total loss* of humanity and which can therefore redeem itself only through the *total redemption of humanity*. This dissolution of society as a particular class is the *proletariat*.[12]

Stylistically, this is a powerful piece of prose. It posits, in opposition to Hegel's destination for History, the total self-emancipation of society. It also implies a notion of freedom – against Smith – which implies that if some are not free, the rest cannot be either. Freedom is not an individual condition/state, but a joint collective state. In emancipating themselves, the propertyless emancipate their oppressors as well.

That said, this still remains a piece of philosophical legerdemain that a brash young person with style and panache could turn out. What does it mean? After all, as the sentence at the start admits, Germany has to form its proletariat. Of course, England and France have their proletariats. But then that would mean that you have to develop productive powers through private property, industrialization and pauperization to get to a proletariat before the latter is ready to emancipate us all.

Marx realized, at this juncture in 1844, that he knew very little about how the proletariat formed itself, how it grew, how it organized itself. All those questions required the study of political economy. So, for the next twenty-plus years after writing the above – now much-quoted – words, he had to put some solid theory behind that piece of rhetoric. While he wrote some polemical pamphlets and much unpublished material, it was only in 1859 that he was able to give a glimpse of his theory, and only in 1867 did the first full fruit appear. Political economy is not easy.

For the next five years, however, his perspective remained very German. It was in theorizing about Germany as an economically and politically backward society that he came to focus on the comparison with England and France, as a way of telling the Germans what was wrong with them. He broke with the Hegelians quickly and then, along with Engels, he worked out his theory of history quite rapidly. The title of this unpublished work is revealing: *The German Ideology*. The bulk of the six hundred pages of *The German Ideology* is a tedious settling of old scores, with much juvenile sarcasm about other Young Hegelians. None of these philosophers would have been remembered, had it not been for Marx's contempt of them. But at the beginning there are about a hundred pages where Marx and Engels lay down a general outline of their theory of history. Since their interest was in explaining the present and the prospect for future emancipation, they did not strictly need to explain all history. But as a Young Hegelian, Marx was nothing if not universal in his ambitions. But he soon left that aside and began, after the failure of 1848, to work on political economy.

It is the 1859 *Contribution to the Critique of Political Economy* [*CCPE*], then, which is the first major work that bears Marx's approval as worth publishing. Even then, it is only an appetizer for the big book which was to follow eight years later: *Capital Volume 1*. The *CCPE* is read today mainly for its preface, since that contains all that Marx thought readers should know about his theory of history and, indeed, a biographical account of how he arrived at that juncture.

Marx's theory of history is rather similar to Smith's stadial model. While Smith had modes of subsistence, Marx had modes of production. In both cases, a large structure of legal and political institutions was borne on the bases of the mode of production/subsistence. Marx's modes of production were just a bit more articulated. While Smith had:

- hunters/gatherers
- pastoral/nomadic
- agriculture
- commerce;

Marx has:

- primitive communism
- ancient/classical
- feudal
- bourgeois

And just to make sure that the coverage was not merely European, he throws in the Asiatic mode of production.[13] This is probably a result as much of Hegel's influence as of anything else. Hegel classified the spiral of religions – Judaic, Classical Greek/Roman, Christianity. He made remarks about Asian religions on the side, without integrating them into the upward march towards Idea. Similarly the Asiatic mode of production is a bit of an anomaly. I shall leave it aside, as did Marx. (Later, when everyone took it very seriously, Stalin sent a few hundred people to the Gulag for getting the Asiatic mode wrong. His gamble in fomenting a Chinese Revolution in 1927 had failed, and he had to find scapegoats.)

That aside, as in the case of Smith, the basic idea is to explain the present; the past is a mere backdrop. For Smith, its usefulness lay in the study of property rights and the growth of jurisprudence. For Marx, the story had to do with locating, in each earlier formation, a class which was likely to foment change. The history it is trying to explain remains – for Marx as for Smith – the history of Northwest Europe: France, Germany and England, with what we would call today the Benelux countries. Greece and Rome figure in the classical stage, but drop out later. The Iberian peninsula, Scandinavia, Eastern Europe, are not there. This is a theory of history, whatever the claims later made for it, which is designed to serve its purpose – that is, explain how Western Europe got to the modern age.

It is also totally innocent of external influences. Both Smith and Marx note that a long gap of technological retrogression occurred during the so-called Dark Ages: from the end of the Roman Empire to the age of high feudalism – four or five centuries. Northwest Europe reverted to a natural – that is, substantially non-monetary – economy. Did progress stop? If so, why should we believe in the inevitability of progress? These details were troublesome to Smith, as we can see from *The Wealth of Nations* Book V; but, as I argue, the general theory of history was not Smith and Marx's major concern: they wanted to study and change the present. Marx was the least troubled by this retrogression. But the strange thing is the total ignoring of the dynamism of Islamic society, which, between the seventh and fourteenth centuries, was both militarily and scientifically dominant over Europe. This dynamism brought Arab rule to Sicily, the

South of France, and Spain. The Crusades were a major external contact. The Central Asian steppes sent their nomadic armies to the gates of Vienna. All this is ignored. Change in Europe has to be totally endogenous. It makes sense only because by the time Smith and Marx were writing, it was almost true: Northwest Europe was master of its own destiny.

The modes are obviously millennial episodes. Smith's agricultural mode, between pastoral and commerce, covers several thousand years of European history. Marx's ancient/classical mode covers Greece and Rome, obviously, and accounts for over a thousand years. The feudal period, perhaps, stretches over another thousand years. Individual dynasties and national histories, and so on, are folded within. This is not descriptive history; it is analytical history. As such, it has to perform two tasks. It has to explain how any particular mode of subsistence/production works and lasts: what, in Marx's terms, makes it produce and reproduce itself. How do people living within these modes earn their living and, in so doing, perpetuate the conditions for their continued living? Then it has to explain the transition from one mode to another: when, why, and how do things change to make one mode concede to another? Of course, the later modes envelop the earlier ones. So, with commerce you may still have pastoral, agricultural, and even hunting modes coexisting. What is not possible in this analytical story is for commerce and pastoral modes to coexist in the pastoral phase. Time moves in one direction: forward.[14]

In Marx's case, the story as related in the Preface is stark and simple. Within a mode: 'In the social production of their existence, men inevitably enter into definite relations, which are independent of their will, namely relations of production appropriate to a given stage in the development of their material forces of production.'[15] This sentence does not deviate in any way from the Scottish notion of the mode of subsistence. The relations people enter into could be slave/master, serf/landlord, buyer/seller, tax collector/taxpayer. To carry on life from day to day, and to subsist, these relations are necessary, like it or not. 'The totality of these relations of production constitutes the economic structure of society, the real foundation, on which arises a legal and political superstructure and to which correspond definite forms of social consciousness.'[16] The first half of this sentence is merely a definition of the economic structure of society – for example, the civil society of which Hegel spoke in the context of modern times. It is the second half, with the foundation/superstructure analogy, which has caused a lot of debate. John Millar, a student of Adam Smith, was the first writer to tease out extensive conclusions from the Scottish philosophy in his *Origin and Distinction of Ranks.*[17] Marx is following in this tradition, though he influenced subsequent work more than anyone else. The problem here is: is there a one-way or a two-way link from base to superstructure, and if there is feedback between the two, does the economic structure still retain primacy? It is not my purpose to settle these questions here, as they do not impinge on what I need to get from Marx.

It is when he comes to the transition that Marx departs significantly from the Scottish model. Again to quote:

> At a certain stage of development, the material productive forces of society come into conflict with the existing relations of production or – this merely expresses the same thing in legal terms – with the property relations within the framework of which they have operated hitherto. From forms of development of the productive forces these relations turn into their fetters. Then begins an era of social revolution. The changes in the economic foundation lead sooner or later to the transformation of the whole immense superstructure.[18]

Recall Smith's development of the history of property rights. As things progressed, new property rights had to be defined. What worked under the hunting mode did not work under the pastoral mode. Settled agriculture leads to a variety of forms of property right. So there is a correspondence between productive forces/technology in a broad sense, and the framework of rights. The sting is in the idea that, after a while, the framework lags behind the forces, and becomes a fetter. It has to be changed. Since, however, this is a millennial history, the change is not merely a matter of legislation or change in customary rights. It is a bigger shift than that – hence, a social revolution. There is no immediate, or even inevitable, connection. That clause 'sooner or later' gives a lot of room for manoeuvre. But if Europe had got this far with its elaborate structure of rights and laws, and if it kept changing as necessary, there must have been a time when things changed sufficiently to mark a clean break with the past.

Of course, what the preface does not mention is the role of class. In other contexts – most famously in *The Communist Manifesto* – Marx argued that one class bears the responsibility for resisting the change in the framework as it gains from the old structure. The class that stands to gain will then challenge and overthrow the *ancien régime*. The nearest example for Marx was, of course, the French Revolution, where the feudal class was overthrown by the bourgeoisie. (This, I know, is a simplification, but it is not too inaccurate. That was certainly the way Hegel and Marx thought of it.) Of course it had not yet happened in Germany, and in England it had happened a century before the

French Revolution. So it was not a hard-and-fast rule, not an exact algebraic formula, as people later tried to make it.

The obverse side of the transition was the idea that a mode of production went under only when it had exhausted its potential. This was the quotation above (p. 44) which, I said, had been ignored by all those who got carried away by the idea of the imminent demise of capitalism. It is to capitalism that we must turn after all these preliminaries. But before I do that, one final thought about the widespread expectations about the demise of capitalism in the 1890s. Since the ancient/classical, as well as the feudal, modes lasted a thousand years each, why did anyone think that a much more productive mode would disappear in a mere century or two?

5
Marx II: Profits

The basic problem that intrigued Marx was the secret ingredient that made capitalism the powerful dynamic force that it had suddenly become. The reaction of the Silesian weavers was an example of this; the misery of the working class in Manchester so graphically described by his friend Engels was another.[1] Together, they showed that in the heartland of the bourgeois revolution, as on the periphery, the system generated a mix of growth and misery. But in the heartland the dual process was clearly visible, while on the periphery it was only the misery that was visible. Yet Marx could envision that the periphery would be like the heartland before long. But the questions were: why, how, and how soon?

As he read the classical political economists – Smith, Malthus, Ricardo, James Mill – Marx could see that they did not have the answer. Smith had seen the importance of the division of labour, and had identified it as one mainspring of the big surge in productivity. David Ricardo had taken Smith's value theory much further, and shown how the rent that landlords earned could be shown to be due entirely to growth which was shaped by forces beyond the landlords' control. Rent was a large portion of national income in the early nineteenth century, when Ricardo showed that it was unearned income; what is more, its removal would have no adverse effect on land under cultivation or, indeed, any other activity. Thomas Malthus had put up a defence of such unearned income on the grounds that it was a source of luxury spending, and such spending was necessary to avoid slumps due to shortage of demand. Ricardo was able to demolish this objection by showing that any supply produced would simultaneously generate income to meet the demand in one sector or another. He ruled out booms and slumps: any excess in one sector, he argued, would be matched by a shortfall in another sector, but eventually these imbalances would be smoothed out. The process that drove activity in different sectors was the search for profits. If profits were high in one sector and low in another, capital would flow from the low-profit to the high-profit sector. As in the tendency of water to find its own level, profitability – the rate of profit on capital – would find the same level.[2]

What Ricardo – or, indeed, any other economist – had not discussed was the source of profits. Smith had proposed that wages, rent and profits were the three broad categories of income accruing to three broad classes: workers, landlords and capitalists. Wages had been tied down to the subsistence cost of labour, give or take some moral and historical elements to determine the level of the subsistence wage. Ricardo had explained rent as arising from the original and indestructible properties of the soil. As population expanded, and more land came under cultivation, the least fertile (marginal) land earned no rent. Rent was thus the difference between the price of corn determined by the cost of production on the least fertile land, and the lower cost on more fertile land.

Thus wages were determined by the subsistence cost of labour, and rent was pure surplus. But how were profits determined? Neither Smith nor Ricardo had much to say about this. All they could say was that profit rates were equalized across sectors. But regardless of that equality, it was unclear how the level of the profit rate was determined.

Marx saw this as the major unresolved problem of political economy. Classical political economy had proposed a theory of value: the labour theory of value. This had seemed to provide a satisfactory theory of *price* determination. So if price was determined by labour values and wages by the subsistence cost of producing labourers, could not profits be consistently explained in this framework?

Marx's training in Hegelian philosophy equipped him to address this question at a level of depth and generality which was totally alien to the British way of doing political economy. He used the *method of immanent criticism*. This meant mastering the classical political economy completely, accepting its logic but then proposing a better political economy as a critique from within which to point up and resolve the internal contradictions.

Classical political economy had a labour theory of price, but not a labour theory of either wages or profits. If the labour content of a good explained its price (as all economists seemed to have agreed by then), why couldn't there be a labour theory of wages? Why should profits be thought to be residual, and not integrated within a single theory of value?

Leaving rent aside, the price of a product consists of wages, cost of material inputs, and profits. Marx began with the simple assumption, accepted by classical political economy, that the price of a good was determined by its value – that is, its labour content. He then reasoned that if price equals total labour content of the product, then one should be able to break this down into labour content of labour input, material input, and profit. But what could be the labour content of the labour input – is this not just a tautology? Surely the labour content of labour input is the number of hours worked? Wages were just the price of the hours of work. Material inputs being products of a previous stage, their contributions were matched by their labour content. But then, what is the labour content of profits?

Marx solved this conundrum by a beautiful conceptual device. Labour time was, of course, a way of measuring value quantitatively. But what the labourer did in his worktime should not be confused with this measuring rod. The worker's time was also a commodity bought and sold. Indeed, capitalism was a new phase of world history, a new mode of production where, for the first time, labour time was ubiquitously bought and sold. So the price of labour time, and the price of material input, must be explained by the same theory of value.

Marx then used a well-known device in political economy to make his breakthrough. Every commodity had two kinds of value: *value in use* (use value) and *value in exchange* (exchange value). Price was a monetary expression of exchange value; thus the labour theory of value was a theory of exchange value. Things were sold at their *exchange value*, but bought by the buyer for their *value in use*. Now, though use value was thought to be unmeasurable, it would in any case never be equal to exchange value for any commodity. A buyer would get more use value than exchange value, since otherwise he would not buy the commodity. At worst, use value would equal exchange value. For the seller, the inequality would go the other way: exchange value would exceed – or, at most, be equal to – use value. This is because while the exchange value is the same for both buyer and seller, their use values can be – and are – different.

So commodities were bought for their use value, but paid for at their exchange value, and these two values could be unequal. Labour-power as a commodity had its exchange value (wages), but it also had its use value. The use value of labour-power, bought as input into production by the capitalist, was the length of time the worker spent in the factory. Thus, while use value was not in general quantifiable, in the case of labour-power used as input, use value was precisely measurable by time spent. (Marx treated other aspects, such as intensity of effort, separately in a pioneering analysis of management of the factory process. A simple quantitative measure was minimally sufficient for this purpose.)

So, if use value was the number of hours worked, what was exchange value? Here Marx made another breakthrough, anticipating what became known in the twentieth century as input–output analysis. The wage that defined exchange value was spent on a basket of goods: food, clothing, housing, heating, transport, and so on. Now, the labour content of each of these goods on which the wage was spent could be added up to reach the measure of wage in labour time. Thus, compared to hours worked by the worker, there would be the number of hours required to produce the goods bought with the wage. Note that this does not assume that wages are at subsistence level, nor that workers, as consumers, do not have choice.

Marx had therefore cracked the basic issue of providing a single theory of prices, wages and profits. The separation of the exchange value and use value of labour-power, and their commensurate quantitative measurement, was central to his breakthrough.[3]

When the capitalist purchased labour-power from the worker, wages were paid as exchange value representing the cost of reproducing labour-power: the worker's ability to work. This was a voluntary exchange between the seller of labour-power (worker) and the buyer (capitalist). But the *use value* of labour-power for the buyer exceeded the *exchange value* of labour-power paid, as in the case of many other commodities bought. Thus the labour content of (the basket of commodities representing) the wage was typically – and, indeed, necessarily – less than the labour content of the use value of the labour-power bought.

Thus far Marx had used only the classical labour theory of value. His innovation was to treat labour-power (rather than the labourer) as a commodity, and derive quantitative expressions for its exchange value and use value. This gave him his explanation of profit. It was this explanation of profit in terms of the labour theory of value which made Marx's economics controversial for ever after.

One reason for the controversy is the language Marx used at this stage. The labour content of the wage he called *necessary* labour. The difference between use value (total hours worked) and necessary labour he called *surplus* labour or *surplus-value*. Thus:

Surplus-value (labour) = use value − exchange value
= total hours worked − necessary labour

Take a typical working week of forty hours. Let us say that the weekly wage is £200. One would need to know the typical basket of goods bought with the £200 – food, clothing, rent, entertainment. Using an input–output table, it would be possible to calculate the amount of direct and indirect labour time required to produce the basket. Thus food is produced on the farm with the farmer's labour time plus seeds, tractors, harvesters, fertilizers, pesticides, and so on. These in turn are produced by labour plus machinery and other inputs. Each of these inputs is in turn produced by labour plus machines, et cetera. All this can be measured with available data by an input–output analysis. Marx's theory predicts that when this is finally done, the labour content of the wage would turn out to be less than forty – let us say, typically, twenty hours with twenty hours of surplus-value.

From this simple calculation, Marx derived two further measures. One was the *rate of surplus-value* or the *rate of exploitation.* This use of the morally charged word 'exploitation' in what, for Marx, was a 'scientific' context was also a cause for controversy.

Rate of surplus-value = surplus value divided by necessary labour

So far, of course, the contribution of other inputs has not been discussed. After all, labour's productivity depends on machinery. Where is that contribution? This is calculated in an analysis of total value. Think of total costs as wage costs plus cost of all non-labour inputs. The contribution of machinery, raw materials, energy, and so on, can be measured in terms of labour-time equivalent using an input–output table. Thus a machine's contribution to final output will be equal to the wear and tear (depreciation, broadly speaking) which can be expressed as a proportion (percentage) of its total value. The total value of the machine as a finished good can be measured by the total labour input contained in it, as in all other cases. Thus, if a machine embodies one million labour hours of input, and the wear and tear is 2 per cent in any one year, then twenty thousand hours will be the machine's contribution to the final product.

Marx put all these various non-labour inputs together into one category, and labelled it *constant* capital. Since the capitalist also advances money (capital) to pay wages, he labelled the exchange value of labour input *variable* capital. Thus total value of output was:

Total value of output = use value of labour plus use value of constant capital
= surplus labour (surplus-value) + necessary labour
(variable capital) + constant capital

Note that for non-labour inputs, Marx assumes that use value equals exchange value. This is because in the exchange of non-labour inputs, both the buyer and the seller are capitalists; so any surplus-value will be extracted by the seller before he sells to the buyer. Even if there are discrepancies, they cancel out over the entire economy. For labour-power, use value exceeds exchange value.

This is because the capital/labour exchange is across a class divide between capitalists and workers. Thus while all inputs contribute *value* to output, only labour-power contributes *surplus-value*.

Before I examine this further, let me show Marx's analysis of the profit rate. Profit rate for Marx is the ratio of surplus-value to total capital expended. Thus

$$\text{Rate of profit} = \frac{\text{surplus-value}}{\text{total capital}} = \frac{\text{surplus-value}}{[\text{variable capital} + \text{constant capital}]}$$

Now we can connect the rate of exploitation and the rate of profit, since that clarifies the importance of non-labour inputs. A little manipulation shows that:

$$\text{Rate of profit} = \frac{\text{surplus-value}}{\text{variable capital}} \times \frac{\text{variable capital}}{\text{total capital}}$$

$$= \text{rate of exploitation} \times [\text{share of wages in total capital costs}]$$

Thus the rate of profit is a product of the rate of exploitation and the share of variable capital in total capital. Marx called the ratio of constant capital (non-labour inputs) to total capital the organic composition of capital. Thus the ratio of variable capital to total capital was one minus the organic composition. Hence the famous formula:

$$\text{Rate of profit} = \text{rate of exploitation x } [1 - \text{organic composition of capital}]$$

As far as Marx was concerned, he had thus provided an explanation of the origin of profits using the labour theory of value and violating none of its tenets. By driving a wedge between the use value and exchange value of labour-power, the capitalist reaped surplus-value. His investment in labour and machines determined the rate of profits, but the key was the contribution of labour-power.

Although it is straightforward to explain Marx's calculation today, it was very difficult for him to reach this result. Indeed, he pursued it throughout the 1850s, retiring from the field of battle to the library. Sometime during the early 1860s, he arrived at the solution almost two decades after he had written about the Silesian weavers. He had at last traced the secret of capitalism to its sophisticated way of exploiting labour, but he had done so not by a moral denunciation of capital but by using classical political economy and the labour theory of value. He had innovated the concept of labour-power and shown that the gap between its use value and exchange value was measurable. He had then linked this surplus-value to profit. It was a 'scientific' theory of exploitation.

Of course, once Marx published the first volume of *Capital* in 1867, there was a big debate among the economists in continental Europe, and this debate never abated. Even to this day, Marx's theory of profits remains controversial.

The controversy can be followed at different levels, but it centres around the proposition that only labour-power – living labour – generates surplus-value; hence profits come from living labour alone. Non-labour inputs have *value*, but do not generate *surplus-value*. But if that is true, why should anyone use machinery? Anyone who uses more machinery than his rival would lose out, since his organic composition will be high and, given a low base of variable capital, he may also have a lower rate of exploitation.

This strong objection surfaced quite early – even before 1867. Marx had worked out a rough draft of all three volumes of *Capital* by the early 1860s. He had then set about polishing up the draft of his first volume for publication. When Engels read the page proofs of the relevant parts of *Capital Volume 1*, he immediately raised this objection. Marx's reply was that he had anticipated such a critique, but in the first volume he was keeping his analysis simple, and keeping prices and values equal to each other. This was a trap, however, since if his critics say he was wrong, in the final volume he will show why he was right and they were wrong.[4]

Marx never prepared the next two volumes for publication. Indeed, he did very little work on them at all during the remaining sixteen years of his life after 1867. He occupied himself with supervising translations of *Capital Volume 1* into different languages, and making small revisions to the text. He also got diverted into studying land tenure in Russia, and making extensive notes on its ethnography. He was becoming quite famous, being (falsely) credited with having instigated the Paris Commune of 1871. He corresponded with people around the globe, complained loudly about his aches and pains (he had haemorrhoids), but he did not revise or update the two additional volumes of *Capital*.

Engels published the second volume of *Capital* in 1885, two years after Marx's death. In the preface he challenged Marx's critics to prepare the solution to the conundrum posed by Marx's calculation. If living labour alone generates surplus-value, and profits come from surplus-value alone, given the different ratios of variable to constant capital that we observe, how can profit rates be equal across different capitals? In other words, was (non-labour) capital relevant to profitability or not?

When Marx's solution was published in 1894, in the third and final volume of *Capital*, it satisfied no one – indeed, it fuelled further controversy. It became known as The (so-called) Transformation Problem. Like some other well-known puzzles – such as Fermat's Last Theorem, or Squaring the Circle – the Transformation Problem has been 'solved' several times over the hundred-plus years since 1894. Before I lay out the problem and its solution, let me dwell briefly on the reasons why this problem acquired an almost mythic status.

Marx had thought that finding the clue to profitability would yield a critical understanding of capitalism which, in turn, would help to destroy it. The hopes placed by both Marx and his family and friends in the publication of this work, which had taken almost twenty years of much misery for his family, were quite extraordinary. It was as if Marx seriously believed in the famous Eleventh Thesis on Feuerbach that he had penned in his youth: 'Philosophers have hitherto interpreted the world; the task, however, is to change it.' Having found the key to capitalism, he had accomplished the philosophical task of interpreting (understanding) capitalism in the same deep way in which Hegel had interpreted the world. Now that the root of capitalism had been traced to exploitation of the workers, the task of changing this world, of destroying capitalism, was the easier one. But if the answer Marx had found were to be defective, then so would be any programme of changing capitalism on its basis. For Marxists of a certain philosophical bent, a correct solution of the Transformation Problem became akin to a destruction of capitalism itself. This may sound exaggerated, but one attraction of Marxism was always its scientific basis. Marx, it was said, had 'proved' that capitalism was based on exploitation of labour by capital. This 'proof' made Marxists believe even more firmly in the rightness of their cause.

The enemies of Marxism took the problem no less seriously. To disprove Marx, or destroy his arguments about the origin of profits in exploitation, became almost an intellectual crusade all over Europe and North America, but especially in Germany and Austria. Eugen von Böhm-Bawerk, a professor of Economics at the University of Vienna, wrote a famous article called 'Karl Marx and the Close of His System'. He had waited until all three volumes of *Capital* were published. Now he pointed out that Marx's proposed solution, as given in Volume 3, was incoherent. Ever since, the anti-Marxists have considered the issue as settled: Marx's system is incoherent.

So what was Marx's situation? It was to posit two separate 'accounts' – one in value terms, which was not visible to the naked eye, and one in price (or money) terms, which was. (Such a procedure is not unusual in economics.

Utility that a consumer derives from consumption is non-observable and cardinally non-measurable. But from that starting point, demand curves can be derived for goods and services which are measurable.)

A1

Begin with a capitalist who is willing to advance (invest) a sum of money M. With that he buys labour-power and means of production, (Think of hiring rather than owning all machines and buildings.) With these inputs, output is produced. This is sold for a sum of

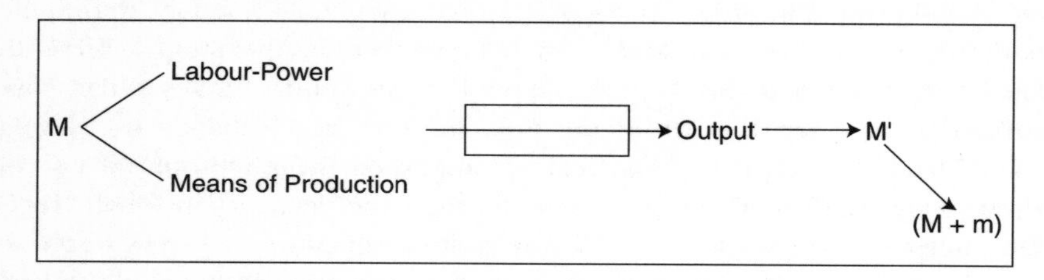

money M′ which is usually larger than M. Thus M′ equals M plus profits (m). Where does this profit come from?

Marx's answer was that while the M–M′ circuit is what you see, a value-creating process is hidden beneath this visible process. To see this, we have to peer inside the empty box in the diagram above.

A2

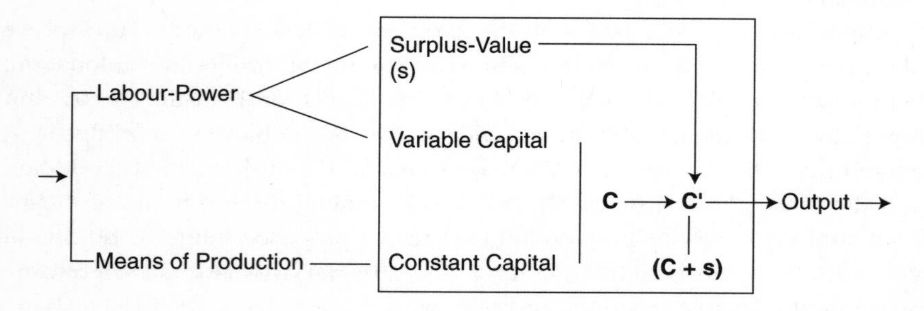

This diagram appears inside the empty box, which is between the physical input and the physical output processes. Thus we see labour-power as split up into surplus-value and variable capital, as already explained. Marx called the sum of variable capital and constant capital C; output in value terms is C′, which is C plus surplus-value (s). In physical form the output then appears at the end of the physical input–output process. The invisible surplus-value (s) is the origin of the visible money profits (m).

Marx's theory of profits thus linked the invisible value process to the visible process of money and the physical input–output process.

In the price domain, profit rates were equal, and they were measured by the rates of profits to the money value of the capital, just as in modern accounting. In the value domain, there was no compulsion for the value rates of profits to be equal, since such inequality was not visible and could not drive capital from one sector to another.

So the calculus of Volume 1, which assumed that prices matched values perfectly, had to be replaced by a more elaborate one. Values were a mental calculation by the economist, while prices and money sums were more obviously visible. Thus a bridge had to be built from the invisible to the visible. Marx posited two alternative ways to bridge this chasm. One way was to assume that the sum total of all profits (Σm)[5] in an economy was equal to the sum of surplus values produced (Σs). Thus, while an individual company's profits may not be the same as its surplus-value, over the whole economy, all profits come from surplus-value. Thus there is a bridge between profits and surplus-value. Another was to posit that the sum total of all values produced ($\Sigma C'$) is the same as the money sum of all output ($\Sigma M'$). Either way, all that these two bridges do is to create a way of translating values measured in labour time to sums of money. They are fixing the money price of a unit of labour time, whether embodied in living labour or in a machine.

Either way, Marx's solution was to say that money rates of profit are equalized by some commodities' prices being above value, while others would be below. Commodities which had a high organic composition of capital (ratio of constant capital to total capital) will have price/value ratio larger than one. For those with a low organic composition of capital, the price/value ratio is smaller than one.

Another way of putting Marx's solution is to say that while living labour generates surplus-value, there is a compensation for those companies (capitals) which use more machines to labour than the average because their price/value ratio is larger than one. Labour-intensive goods cede surplus-value to machine-intensive goods via this imbalance in the pricing process.

If the above sounds complicated, all I can say is that this is much simpler than following Marx's own treatment in Volume 3, Chapter 9. His solution was messy and incomplete. He took an example of five companies (capitals) with different organic compositions. But then, in demonstrating his solution, he multiplied the outputs by their price/value ratio, but forgot that inputs are also goods, and should also be similarly 'transformed'.

In any case, while he was wrong in the details (he had left an unrevised, unpolished draft for Engels to publish), his solution has stood the test of time. Prices deviate from values, but not by much, and also in a systematic way. We can now show that much more elegantly than Marx did, thanks to some developments, such as input–output analysis, pioneered by his own ideas. An early solution came in 1907 from the German statistician Ladislaus von Bortkiewicz.[6] Since then, solutions have multiplied, as have new objections to the way Marx formulated and solved the problem.

Logically, there are formidable problems in showing that profits come from surplus-value alone. All economic theories make simplifying, reality-denying assumptions. But even granting that, Marx's problem is complex, because the solution for any one commodity's price cannot be calculated independently of the solution for all the other commodities. The reduction of machine inputs to labour content is a nightmare bedevilled by such considerations as the longevity of the machine, and the likelihood that a machine could be made useless by new inventions, and hence valueless, despite labour time having gone into its making. (Similar problems bedevil any consideration of durable capital in neoclassical economies. For about fifteen years during the 1960s and 1970s, this led to a famous 'capital controversy' which engaged some famous economists on both sides of the Atlantic.[7])

The surprising thing is that, despite these logical problems, *empirically* the theory stands up very well. If you calculate labour values using input–output tables, and compare them to prices for a representative list of products, prices are *not* proportional to values, but the divergence between price and value is very small, and goes exactly in the direction that Marx predicted. This robust empirical result was first established by Professor Anwar Shaikh of the New School of Social Research, New York. He took input–output tables for Italy (1959 and 1967) and the USA (1947 and 1963), and examined the correlation of values and prices at one point in time and across two periods. With 25 and 83 sectors, the correlations were found to be remarkably high and stable. These results were confirmed for Yugoslav data by Petrovic in 1987.[8] So the price–value connection is close and stable across time. If values fall, so do prices, and they do so equiproportionately (i.e. with a unit elasticity). So, despite all the fuss, the empirical results support Marx.

One can accept that prices are proportional to values, but still refuse to say that all profits therefore come from the exploitation of labour. For one thing, the Marx calculus neglects the importance of innovations which raise productivity dramatically across many industries. Marx was keenly aware of the technological dynamism of capitalism, and he emphasized the constant pressure of competition which drove capitalists to cut costs and search for new ways of making old products, or even making completely new products. He used these arguments to explain *movements* in the rate of profits, yet in his view the *level* of the profit rate at any point in time was still pretty independent of the productive contribution of capital.

This book is not a last-ditch defence of Marx, so I do not go into an elaborate justification of Marx's failure to link up his qualitative analysis of the dynamics of profitability to his quantitative analysis of price/value and profitability. Yet there is one fundamental insight which can be derived from Marx's analysis which is crucial to understanding globalization as contemporary capitalism.

Standing Marx on His Head

Let us invert Marx's insight about surplus-value. Let us, so to say, stand him on his head, as he did with Hegel. The truth is that no capitalist will employ a worker who doesn't produce more value than the cost of hiring him or her. Thus, if wages rose to such an extent that this gap narrowed, a capitalist might choose to move his factory away rather than suffer a loss.

The consequences of this inversion are far-reaching. Marx saw the entire process as a conflict between capitalists and workers. He realized that in a boom, employment would rise, unemployment would shrink. This can put pressure on wages, thus raising the share of workers and lowering the share and the rate of profits. At this stage, Marx pointed out, capitalists would bring in labour-saving technology, reversing the increase in employment and wages as well as the decline in profits. This would generate a trade cycle over ten or twenty years. But Marx was also confident that the attempt to restore profits would not only generate trade cycles, but that over the long run, the rate of profit would tend to decline. Falling rate of profits was a constant theme in all classical economies. But in Marx's world, the falling tendency of profitability became entwined with the probability of the survival of capitalism itself.

I shall return to trade cycles and the long-run trend in profitability below, but one consequence of the above analysis, if we apply our inversion, is clear. If employability depends on high profitability, workers would want to *co-operate* with employers in keeping profits high. This goes directly against the doctrine of antagonism between capital and labour. If workers know the rule 'no profits, no employment', then they will struggle, not for a higher share of wages in total output, but with that share which maximizes their chance of employment. This could be the case if the alternative to high profitability is not the end of capitalism but the outward migration of capital to generate employment in other countries, and unemployment for the workers.[9]

Even as economists and policymakers denigrate Marx's theory of profit, the basic idea of surplus-value is frequently used in modern-day discussions. Thus, if we call the rate of surplus-value e, (1 + e) is the ratio of total value produced by labour to its wages. Now, what we call the competitiveness of a company, or a sector, or an economy, is often measured in terms of unit labour cost of output. The lower the unit cost, the more competitive the product/sector/economy. Another way of saying this is: the higher the rate of exploitation, the lower the unit cost and the more competitive the economy. This is because the reciprocal of (1 + e) is identical to unit labour cost of output, or the degree of competitiveness.

$$\text{Unit labour cost of output} = 1/\ (1 + e)$$

So the message is the same, regardless of the label you pin on the economic theory underlying it. Profitability is a matter of lowering the ratio of wage to output per worker, or raising the rate of exploitation. To be competitive, the economy has to raise its profitability – that is, its rate of exploitation.

Thus, the course of the long-run trend in profitability is vital to any prognosis of capitalism. If the economy stays profitable, then capitalism has a healthy future. If profitability is falling, drastic changes in the economy – and even, sometimes, in politics and society – may become necessary to restore profitability. It may even be that there is no change that will in fact restore profitability. That would be the end-game of capitalism.

Can capitalism come to an end as a result of its own internal contradictions – for example, if profitability declines? Or does it need a push from revolutionary forces which will topple it? Or, yet again, will there be a superior mode of production which will supplant capitalism, just as feudalism was supplemented in Western Europe by capitalism itself?

If we look for answers to these questions in Marx's work, it is yes to all three, depending on what text you cite. But, quite alarmingly for his followers, there is also a section of *Capital Volume 2* where Marx displays a numerical scheme of a capitalist economy which runs into no crisis, and enjoys perpetual growth. How do we evaluate these different stances on the long-run future of capitalism?

There are three strands of analysis of the dynamics of capitalism in the three volumes of *Capital*. Since all three volumes were written in draft at the same time, in the early 1860s, one has to presume that these are not just mistakes in revisions but consistent aspects of the same model. There is also – as we shall see later – an apocalyptic vision, practically repeated from the *Communist Manifesto*, which sits uneasily with the rest of *Capital*.

Thus Marx has three responses, not altogether contradictory, to the question of the dynamics of capitalism.

Cyclical growth

There is a cyclical pattern to a capitalist economy which is due to the way in which the rate of profit fluctuates. Capitalists employ workers to make profits, but as they employ more workers, unemployment goes down. This puts pressure on real wages. As real wages, as well as employment, go up, the share of profit goes down, and there is a squeeze on the rate of profits. At this boom stage of the cycle, capitalists retaliate by investing in labour-saving technology, thus slowing down the growth of – even reducing – employment. As unemployment increases, the pressure on real wages eases, and they may even go down. This is the slump. Profitability improves; this encourages capitalists to expand their business now, with the new technology, and the cycle continues its upward course.

This is succinctly described in Chapter 23 of Volume 1 of *Capital*, 'The General Law of Capitalist Accumulation'. The final third of the chapter lays out the theory summarized above; there then follows detailed empirical information for the British economy, urban as well as rural, between 1846 and 1866.

Marx was the first classical economist to develop a theory of the cycle. Ricardo would not admit to the possibility of a general glut, and John Stuart Mill could only begin to admit doubts about this Ricardian doctrine that his father, James Mill, and David Ricardo himself, had shoved down his childhood throat (Mill got his first lessons in economics when, as a youth of twelve, he went on walks with Ricardo). But a glut is not the same thing as a cycle. In his *General Theory*, in a later century, Keynes showed the high likelihood of a glut – underemployment equilibrium – in a market economy, but did not himself develop a theory of the cycle. (Many Keynesians did – about which more below in the appropriate place.) Marx had a theory of the cycle in which the economy never quite rested in equilibrium at full employment, or at less than full employment. There is an inherent tendency to disequilibrium in tracing out a cyclical pattern in a capitalist economy driven by profitability, but one where profits arise from employing workers.

The cycle of which Marx speaks was about ten years in length, and by the time he was writing, in the 1860s, one could trace about four cycles of ten years starting in the mid-1820s. A French statistician, Clément Juglar, published a treatise on trade cycles in the early 1860s, though Marx does not cite him.[10] Marx's basic idea of the mechanism of the cycle has endured remarkably well. In the 1950s, the LSE economist A. W. H. (Bill) Phillips published a seminal article about the relationship between money wage rates and unemployment which gave birth to the Phillips Curve.[11] Phillips looked at British data for 1861–1913 and, in that fifty-two year period, found six-and-a-half eight-year cycles. The cycle traced out fluctuations in money wage rates and in unemployment – much in the way Marx describes, though Phillips made no mention of Marx. Of course, what attracted much more attention was not the cycles, but a curve Phillips had fitted to his data which appeared to show a stable long-run (pan-cyclical) relationship between the rate of change in the money wage (wage inflation) and unemployment. For about twenty years following the publication of Phillips's article in 1958, economists thought they had found the Holy Grail for combating inflation by choosing an appropriate combination of inflation and unemployment read off the Phillips Curve. It was all to end in tears, but again that is for later chapters (see Chapter 14).

The essence of Marx's theory is that cycles arise from a basic antagonism between labour and capital, while at the same time, they are mutually interdependent – workers need jobs, which only capitalists can provide; capitalists need workers to produce, so that they can make profits. Exactly a century after the publication of *Capital Volume 1*, a Cambridge economist, Richard Goodwin, devised an elegant mathematical formulation of Marx's model.[12] Using the predator–prey model well known in biology, he formulated the Marx cycle in terms of a pair of differential equations. It encapsulated Marx's insights in the context of a growing economy, with cycles in two basic variables – the share of wages in national income (or share of profits, as the two added up to one) and the proportion of the labour force employed (or the proportion unemployed, as these two also added up to one). The economy described by these two equations had two building blocks:

- rate of growth of real wages (and therefore of the share of wages in national income) goes up as employment rises beyond a certain threshold;
- rate of growth of employment goes down as the share of wages in national income goes up.

This stylized economy has interesting 'equilibrium' properties – a constant growth rate sufficient to absorb additions to the labour force, a constant profit rate to sustain that growth rate and employment. But the economy is never *at* equilibrium. It constantly revolves around this equilibrium, either above or below it. Goodwin made several simplifying assumptions to get his model down to two equations: a constant rate of population growth and of productivity growth; a constant capital–output ratio in that capitalists invested all profits and workers did not save. He has no taxation, no foreign trade, no public sector, no welfare state.

These simplifying assumptions can be relaxed, but that takes away the simplicity and elegance of Goodwin's story. Basically, he has shown that Marx's cycle can be formulated mathematically, without necessarily taking on Marx's paraphernalia of surplus-value, et cetera. Wages and profits are two shares in the national income; labour and capital are two claimants fighting over it. But their fight also has to acknowledge their mutual interdependence. The mathematical formulation that Goodwin proposes generates cycles of constant length and constant amplitude. Thus the 'crises' do not get bigger or more frequent in this scenario, as a lot of Marxist rhetoric asserts. The profit rate stays constant *over the cycle,* though it fluctuates up and down during the cycle. The rate of unemployment over the cycle is also another constant, though it fluctuates up and down from one year to the next. Thus one answer to the dynamics of capitalism is that it will perpetually revolve around some steady average values of profitability and unemployment. But if that is the case, will capitalism never end?

Balanced growth

Marx's followers, as well as his detractors, did not read this message of the longevity of capitalism as central to *Capital Volume 1.* Other chapters in the same volume (especially the penultimate one, Chapter 32, of which more later) and his other writing had sounded the death-knell of capitalism. But the saga of crises of increasing severity was promised for later volumes, which were eagerly awaited.

In 1885, Engels published the second volume of *Capital*. Tucked away in the very last chapter of this volume was Marx's second answer to the question of the dynamics of capitalism. It was formulated in a series of tables of figures, or 'schemes', as Marx called them.[13] These schemes were designed to illustrate the relations between output, income and expenditure in a growing economy. Marx was pioneering much that has now become routine in national income accounting, but was quite difficult to conceptualize in those early days.

Take an economy that has no growth. Obviously this is an abstract example as far as a capitalist economy is concerned. But we simplify in order to clarify some concepts. As in the example above, think of the economy as producing machines and wage goods, both non-durable. To simplify matters further, we translate machines and wage goods into their labour values, so that we need not worry about adding up disparate items.

We have the following simple scheme:

	Constant capital	Variable capital	Surplus-value	Total value
I (Machines)	4,000	1,000	1,000	6,000
II (Wage goods)	2,000	500	500	3,000
Total value	6,000	1,500	1,500	9,000

Department I (as Marx called it) produces machines worth 6,000 units. In doing so, it uses up 4,000 units of machine inputs and units of labour inputs whose wages appear as variable capital worth 1,000. Labour, in turn, generates surplus-value of 100 per cent. Similarly, Department II uses up 2,000 units of machine inputs and 500 units of variable capital as wages for labour. Again, there is 100 per cent surplus-value.

At the end of production, as much new-machines value is produced (6,000) as is consumed by the two departments. Variable capital of the two departments (1,500) plus the surplus-value generated (1,500) can be spent on the wage goods. Then the economy can start all over again. There is no growth, no change; just constant repetition. The point, of course, is that looking across the first row and down the first column, you see how outputs come from inputs and, in turn, become inputs again for the next period's output. In this way, the interconnections of the economy are brought out.

In modern national income analysis, the 6,000 units of machine inputs consumed during production do not count as income. What counts is 'value added'. This is not just the surplus-value (1,500) but the variable capital as well. Thus in modern parlance, we have:

Wages: 1,500 (variable capital)
Profits: 1,500 (surplus-value)

But in terms of expenditure, net output is just the 3,000 units of wage goods. There is no net investment in this economy. Only consumption and consumption equals income.

Consumption: 3,000
Net investment: 0

Gross investment in this economy is 6,000, but all of that is for replacing capital used up in production. Gross national income will be 9,000. In a modern economy with durable capital, replacement is a very small part of total output, so we use Gross National Product rather than Net National Product as a quick measure of income.

Now take a growing economy, one in which the output of machines exceeds their use as replacement inputs. If the example above is simple reproduction, this is now expanded reproduction. In the table below, similar numbers are used, but you have to think of this as a different economy, not the previous economy in a different time period.

Input–Output

	Constant capital	Variable capital	Surplus-value	Total value
Department I	4,000	1,000	1,000	6,000
Department II	1,500	750	750	3,000
	5,500	1,750	1,750	9,000

In this economy, 6,000 units of machines are produced, but only 5,500 are required to reproduce the same level of output. Thus 500 machine units are surplus, and they cannot be consumed. On the other hand, the 3,000 units of wage goods produced are confronted by 3,500 units of variable capital and surplus-value. There is an imbalance here.

Marx proceeded to resolve this imbalance by a simple rule. Let Department I capitalists invest one half of their surplus-value, keeping the ratio of constant to variable capital unchanged. Department II capitalists can then 'mop up' the excess supply of machines. This is a mechanical rule, and it sounds puzzling. Marx, of course, was not trying to model an economy so much as to think through how the national income accounts of a growing economy might look. But his simple rule was to have a profound effect on debates among Marxists for nearly fifty years after the publication of *Capital Volume 2,* because the consequence of this simple rule was to show that such an economy could grow for ever and ever, and never suffer a crisis.

Let us just follow through the consequences for a couple of periods, and see how this happens. We begin with Department I capitalists investing 500 (half of 1,000) surplus-value in their industry, with ⅘ going to extra machinery and ⅕ to extra labour. And so on.

Income-expenditure

4,000 + 400	1,000 + 100	500	6,000
1,500 + 100	750 + 50	600	3,000
6,000	1,900	1,100	9,000

Income expenditure accounts above show that in this economy, there are 3,500 units of income, of which 3,000 (1,900 + 1,100) are spent on wage goods and 500 are net investment in machine goods. But in the next period we have higher inputs and higher output.

Input–Output

4,400	1,100	1,100	6,600
1,600	800	800	3,200
6,000	1,900	1,900	9,800

We are back again with more machines than are required for replacement – in fact, 600 surplus compared to 500 in the previous period. But the same rule works again:

Income expenditure

4,400 + 440	1,100 + 110	550	6,600
1,600 + 160	800 + 80	560	3,200
6,600	2,090	1,110	9,800

It is pointless to go further, because at this stage something almost miraculous has happened. From this period on, Department I capitalists invest ½ of their surplus-value and Department II capitalists invest 3/10 of their surplus-value. They never have to change these proportions. They never have to change the ratio of constant to variable capital. The economy will grow at 10 per cent each year. There are no cycles, no crises, no problems. Capitalism lives for ever, without any cycles but in steady-state growth.

As we can imagine, this was a rude shock to the first generation of Marxists, who were taking the message very seriously. How could there be trouble-free perpetual growth in capitalism? Were there no limits to the growth potential of the system, no barriers to its upward march? Will capitalism live for ever?

Today, we see this scheme as a planning model of an economy divided into two sectors. Indeed, this scheme became the germ of the Soviet Union's first planning model, which was constructed by a Russian economist, Grigorii-Alexandrovic Feldman. In this world, the planner can direct Department I to accumulate at 50 per cent, and Department II at 30 per cent. No consideration of prices, or of profitability, is relevant in a planning model.

But all that, of course, was in the future. In the 1880s, neither Marxists nor, indeed, anyone else had any other economy-wide models to compare Marx's model with. Marx succeeded not only in explaining the national income accounts to himself and (thanks to Engels) to his readers, but he managed in addition to hit upon what is nowadays called a balanced growth trajectory of a two-sector model.[14] Not until the 1960s did the economists get back to studying two-sector models using an identical machines/wages goods classification. Of all such models, Marx just happened to construct not only the first but also the only one which hits a balanced growth path in the second time period after starting. It was not a typical model of a capitalist economy; it was pretty well unique.

I will come to the agonizing debate among the Marxists in Chapter 6, but suffice it to say that the luminaries of the Marxist pantheon – Lenin, Rosa Luxemburg, Bukharin, and many others – took part in this debate. The debate has resonance today, as people ask whether there are limits to globalization or whether it can go on for ever.

For our purposes, note that the model of cyclical growth of *Capital Volume 1* could be seen as cycles around a constant growth rate, though obviously actual economies do not follow models precisely. When we come to *Volume 2*, Marx extends the constant growth to both (all) sectors of the economy, and eliminates cycles altogether. What happens to the pressure on profitability? Are there infinite supplies of surplus labour, so that wages never rise and profits never fall? Or are we describing the very long-run trajectory which will be one of perpetual – if not constant – growth, and cycles would be just wrinkles around this growth path? After all, there has been perpetual – albeit fluctuating – growth in capitalism for the last two hundred years (at least, but income data go back only that far), and in the long run, cycles have not affected the system enough to make it break down. Could we stand Marx (yet again!) on his head and get an optimistic message about the future of capitalism from his writings? Not quite – not yet, anyway.

Falling rate of profit

Marx had always planned *Capital* as a three-volume work. The first volume set out the basic concepts at an extremely high level of abstraction. Simplifying assumptions were made – for example, in the first volume, that values and prices were proportional; that the economy could be analysed in macroeconomic terms, as if it were producing a single good; and that capital was non-durable. In the second volume, Marx outlined the circuits of money capital, physical capital and commodity capital as they interacted. He explored the problems of the durability of capital and then, in the last part, looked at national income accounts in terms of a two-sector breakdown, as we saw above.

It was all going to come together in a more complex fashion in the last volume. Here Marx explored (somewhat messily, as we saw) the price–value transformation problem; he also explored the different kinds of capital as they emerged historically: merchant capital, industrial capital, financial capital. He offered his own theory of rent in a challenge to Ricardo's celebrated theory. He also, most significantly, stated the *Law of the falling rate of profit.* This was the third piece of speculation about the dynamics of capitalism.

Every classical economist, from Adam Smith onwards, had a theory of the falling rate of profit. The idea that the rate of profit would fall as the economy progressed was central to classical political economy, though the reasons why this happened varied with different authors. The economy could run out of profitable opportunities (Smith), or run into the barrier of inflexible supply of land, so that rent would eat up profits (Ricardo), and so on. It was also a matter of taste whether the eventual state reached in such a case – the stationary state – was a happy one or a dire one.

Marx's method of immanent criticism meant that he had to fight the classical economists on their own ground. If they had a theory of the falling rate of profit, so would he. Of course, given his prognosis of the eventual breakdown of capitalism, his theory of falling rate was bound to lead not to a stationary state but to another mode of production. Marx, of course, avoided any speculation about the nature of socialism in his life's greatest work. But the falling rate of profit was a standard piece of political economy.

The falling rate of profit story in *Capital Volume 3* catches up with the cyclical analysis of *Captial Volume 1.* As capitalists struggle to restore profitability after each episode of overfull employment/labour shortage/real wage growth, they have to adopt a technology that replaces labour by machinery or, in Marx's theory, the organic composition of capital rises. But if the rise in the organic composition of capital does not raise the rate of surplus-value sufficiently, then the rate of profit will fall. That is the simple, first-step reason. Since I have explained these concepts above, a simple formulation should suffice:

$$\text{(Value) rate of profit} = \frac{\text{Surplus-value}}{\text{constant capital} + \text{variable capital}} = \frac{s}{c + v}$$

Rewrite this as:

$$= \frac{s}{v}\left[1 - \frac{c}{c + v}\right]$$

$$\varrho = r\,[1 - g]$$

Here, ϱ is the rate of profit as measured in value terms rather than money terms, r is the rate of surplus-value and g is the organic composition of capital.

Now, if g goes up, then ϱ goes down unless r goes up to compensate. But the organic composition of capital may increase the rate of surplus-value as it increases. Not only does it have to increase r, but it has to increase it by enough to cancel out the depressing effects of a rise in g on ϱ. In simple terms, the technology must raise labour productivity sufficiently to cut the unit cost of labour. Otherwise, the rate of profit will fall. This is pretty much what the financial pages of newspapers and beleaguered finance ministers always say. Wages must not rise faster than growth in productivity.

But of course, one can add many complications to this simple formulation. Thus we could have durable fixed capital of which only a portion is used up in any one period, and so we need a 'stock' measure of constant capital, not just the current flow. We are dealing with values rather than money amounts, and we have to look at the (money) rate of profit rather than the (value) rate of profit. And while Marx and all the classical (and neoclassical) economists assume that profit rates equalize across all sectors, we may wish to look at sectoral rates of profit.

The central problem is that Marx is said to have predicted that the rate of profit would fall. After 1870 and the birth of marginalist, neoclassical economics, any discussion of the rate of profit went out of fashion, except to deny that it had any tendency to fall. Neoclassical microeconomics shows that in a competitive economy, profits would be zero in equilibrium in a firm and an industry. Another part of the theory says that profit rates would be equalized across all firms and industries in equilibrium. Indeed, Friedrich von Hayek has said that the very mention of the rate of profit disappeared for a while, because Marx had made the notion so unpalatable, associating it with exploitation.[15] Economists spoke of the natural rate of interest instead – a rose by any other name, et cetera.

It is not my purpose here to attack or defend neoclassical economics. It is very useful for training minds, but only moderately useful for studying actual economies. But what of Marx's predication that the rate of profit had a tendency to fall? Has it fallen? If so, why do we still have capitalism? If not, was Marx not wrong?

When Marx develops the theme of the falling rate of profits in Volume 3, part 3, he calls it The Law of the Tendency of the Rate of Profit to Fall. A tendency, not a certainty. Once the simple mechanics are expressed, as we saw above, then qualifications follow. Wages could fall below subsistence level. Methods of production may develop which not only increase labour productivity generally, but raise it faster in machine-making and other sectors which generate the commodities that make up constant capital (raw materials, energy) so that the *value* of constant capital rises less rapidly than its physical amount. In such a case one may see a lot of machinery and raw materials being used by the workers, but in terms of value, the organic composition of capital may not be rising. Modern computer technology is a ready example of this, since the price of computing has fallen precipitously over the last thirty years. Yet we see people using more and more computers, and the ratio of computers per worker has risen in physical terms, but not so much in value terms.

A major qualifying factor is foreign trade – the possibility of exporting capital as well as that of cheap imports of raw materials and wage goods. This has as much relevance today, with globalization, as it had in nineteenth-century England. If the rate of profit is low in a developed country but high in a less developed country, where the organic composition is low, then exporting capital and repatriating profits is an obvious answer to the problem of a falling rate of profit.

Such countereffects 'hamper, retard and partly paralyse this fall (in the rate of profit)'. Yet Marx was not conceding defeat. These countereffects 'do not do away with the law, but impair its effect'. This is because, being a shrewd observer of economic data, he must have noticed that the rate of profit was not falling rapidly in mid-nineteenth-century England, so he concluded this paragraph from which I have been quoting by saying: 'otherwise it would not be the fall of the general rate of profit, but rather its relative slowness which would be incomprehensible. Thus *the Law acts only as a tendency.* And it is only under certain circumstances and after long periods that its effects become strikingly pronounced' (*Captial Volume 3*, p. 239).

We shall see below what the long-run trend of the rate of profit has been. But in the course of combating a fall in the rate of profits, Marx briefly mentions two mechanisms. One is new inventions, which would make commodities cheaper, or find new demands and raise profitability. The other is the process of mergers and takeovers, which increase the concentration of capital. This process eliminates smaller capitalists and creates larger units. But of course, it happens in the course of the cycle as a way of combining units in which individual profitability may be falling, but this could be averted by the merger.

Along the way, as the rate of profit tends to fall, there are cycles, of course. After all, the course of the rate of profit is the reverse side of the coin of the investment cycle – or the accumulation process, as Marx calls it. Thus the cycle discussed in Volume 1 is augmented at this stage by looking at overproduction of capital, that is, overinvestment and overproduction of commodities. This is part of the greed process that drives accumulation. Yet the crisis, when it comes, causes a massive fall in prices; capital is devalorized and quickly depreciated; unemployment increases. Thus the seeds of recovery are within the crisis itself. The value of capital falls; hence a given amount of profit is now a higher *rate* of profit.

Marx concludes this discussion of the falling rate of profits with three observations. These observations appear to be unconnected to the previous discussion, and could have been put in this place quite arbitrarily by Engels, who had the formidable task of finding order in the manuscripts Marx had left. Yet these observations are very pertinent to our purpose.

> Three Cardinal facts of Capitalist Production;
> (1) Concentration of the means of production in (a) few hands, whereby they cease to appear as the property of immediate labourers and turn into social production capacities. Even if they are initially the private property of capitalists. These are the trustees of the bourgeois society, but they pocket all the proceeds of this trusteeship.
> (2) Organization of labour itself into social labour, through co-operation, division of labour, and the uniting of labour with the natural sciences. In these two senses, the capitalist mode of production abolishes private property and private labour, even though in contradictory forms.
> (3) Creation of the world market.
> The stupendous productivity of developing under the capitalist mode of production relative to population, and the increase, if not in the same proportion, of Capital values (not just of their material substance) which grow more rapidly than the population, contradict the basis, which constantly narrows in relation to the expanding wealth, and for which all this immense productiveness works. They also contradict the conditions under which this swelling capital augments its value. Hence the crises. (*Capital Volume 3*, p. 226)

The puzzling thing about these three observations is that while they are perspicacious, they fail to mention either the collapse of the rate of profit as a possible conclusion to this section on the Falling Rate of Profit, or the eventual breakdown of the capitalist system. Not only here, but nowhere else in *Volume 3*, is the apocalyptic vision of the *Communist Manifesto* or Chapter 32 of *Capital Volume 1* revisited. Capitalism grows, and does so in a contradictory way, via crises and cycles. The rate of profit has a tendency to fall, but there are countertendencies which break this fall. What are we to make of this?

The *Communist Manifesto* is the work of hot-headed youth. It survives to this day as a rousing, inspirational, visionary piece of prose. Even after a hundred and fifty years, it can generate debate and command attention. The popular version of Marxism derives from the Manifesto. Lenin got it wrong: It was not *Capital* that was the Bible of the working classes in Europe, but the Manifesto.

Capital is a very different kind of work. It is neither visionary nor millenarian. It does not cover the grand compass of history that the Manifesto or the few chapters of *The German Ideology* cover. It is a critical study of the working of capitalism as a mode of production. It is an immensely demanding and difficult piece of work – not only because of the inherent difficulty of the subject, and Marx's uncompromising way of presenting his material (nothing reader-friendly here), but also because the last two volumes had to be reconstructed by Engels from an unpublished and unfinished manuscript. But it is the work that occupied Marx for most of his life after 1851 – intensely until 1867, and intermittently in the last sixteen years of his life.

Yet *Capital* fails to come up with a single story about the dynamics of capitalism that in any way predicts – even with various conditions attached – its eventual downfall. It is not that Marx ever says it will never reach its limits, but these limits are logical rather than time-specific. There are cycles. There are crises. But these are underlaid by steady growth and a rate of profit that has only a partial tendency to fall.

There is one paragraph in the penultimate chapter, Chapter 32, of *Capital Volume 1*, 'Historical Tendency of Capitalist Accumulation', a much-quoted paragraph, that does rekindle the spirit of the *Communist Manifesto.* The last part, part 8, of *Capital Volume 1* is a historical account of the emergence of capitalism from its feudal origins, using England as an example. The whole part is entitled 'The So-Called Primitive Accumulation'. It was designed to trace the history of the transition from feudalism to capitalism and to account for the emergence of the two classes, bourgeoisie and proletariat, whose existence, with asymmetric ownership of means of production and the necessity to sell labour-power, was at the heart of the wage/exploitation relationship.

Chapter 32 comes after six previous chapters recounting the horrific story of the Enclosures, of the dispossession of the English peasantry and its removal from arable land between the fifteenth and eighteenth centuries, the emergence of the English capitalist farmer and of the industrial capitalist. Then follows Chapter 32, which is mostly concerned with the destruction of small, independent producers and the rise of capitalist production. Thus 'petty commodity production' (a model of economic production still used in modern neoclassical economics textbooks) is destroyed, and capitalist production emerges. This is more or less as already described in the Manifesto.

The last three paragraphs then describe a long-run vision of the development of capitalism that has been much more the 'popular' message of Marx (quoted frequently even nowadays in many left-wing weeklies) than the analytical material I have been discussing. This may be because it was the only chapter of *Capital* included in a two-volume selected works of Marx and Engels published during the 1930s period of the Popular Front.[16] This was probably the first widely available collection of Marx's writing. It was what the Third International wanted people to read of Marx and Engels:

> As soon as this process of transformation has sufficiently decomposed the old society from top to bottom, as soon as the labourers are turned into proletarians, their means of labour into capital, as soon as the capitalist mode of production stands on its own feet, then the further socialization of labour and further transformation of the land and other means of production into socially exploited and, therefore, common means of production, as well as the further expropriation of private properties, takes a new form. That which is now to be expropriated is no longer the labourer working for himself, but the capitalist exploiting many labourers. Thus expropriation is accomplished by the action of the immanent laws of capitalist production itself, by the centralization of capital. One capitalist always kills many. Hand in hand with this centralization, or this expropriation of many capitalists by few, develop, on an ever extending scale, the co-operative form of the labour-process, the conscious technical application of science, the methodical cultivation of the soil, the transformation of the instruments of labour into instruments of labour only usable in common, the economizing of all means of production by their use as the means of production of combined, socialized labour, the entanglement of all peoples in the net of the world market, and with this the international character of the capitalistic regime. Along with the constantly diminishing number of the magnates of capital, who usurp and monopolize all advantages of this process of transformation grows the mass of misery, oppression, slavery, degradation, exploitation; but with this too grows the revolt of the working-class, a class always increasing in numbers and disciplined, united, organized by the very mechanism of the process of capitalist production itself. The monopoly of capital becomes a fetter upon the mode of production, which has sprung up and flourished along with and under it. Centralization of the means of production and socialization of labour at last reach a point where they become incompatible with their capitalist integument. This integument is burst asunder. The knell of capitalist private property sounds. The expropriators are expropriated.
>
> The Capitalist mode of appropriation, the result of the capitalist mode of production, produces capitalist private property. This is the first negation of individual private property, as founded on the labour of the proprietor. But capitalist production begets, with the inexorability of a law of Nature, its own negation. It is the negation of negation. This does not re-establish private

> property for the producer, but gives him individual property based on the acquisitions of the capitalist era: i.e., on co-operation and the possession in common of the land and of the means of production.
>
> The transformation of scattered private property, arising from individual labour, into capitalist private property is, naturally, a process incomparably more protracted, violent and difficult than the transformation of capitalistic private property, already practically resting on socialized production, into socialized property. In the former case, we had the expropriation of the mass of the people by a few usurpers, in the latter, we have the expropriation of a few usurpers by the mass of the people.[17] [At the end of the last paragraph, a footnote is attached quoting a passage from the *Communist Manifesto* which expresses the same idea.]

The first paragraph is obviously one of the most quoted of Marx's writings. This is the millenarian vision that gives him his prophetic image. It sees capitalism as a global phenomenon: 'the entanglement of all peoples in the net of the world market'. But there is also a fall in the number of capitalists who devour each other in the relentless march of concentration of capital. The workers' misery grows, and there is the 'revolt of the working class, a class always increasing in numbers and disciplined, united, organized by the very mechanism of the process of capitalist production itself'. This, then, is the dialectical intertwining of capital and labour. We then get the connection between this process of increasing concentration and the prediction in the preface to *CCPE*: 'The monopoly of capital becomes a fetter upon the mode of production . . .' It is this incompatibility between the forces of production constantly developing and the relations of production – monopoly of the capitalist – which is bound to undermine capitalism. Then comes the *Sturm und Drang*. 'The knell of capitalist private property sounds. The expropriators are expropriated.'

This, though justly famous as a piece of rhetoric, sits uncomfortably with the analytical parts of *Capital* I have outlined. How does concentration increase, and does its increase suspend the growth-cycle mechanism or the surplus-value/profit relation? If, in Volume 3, we know that the decline in the rate of profit cannot be suspended, but only retarded by the growth of concentration, is it a falling rate of profit which eventually brings about the collapse of capitalism, or the revolt of the working classes, or both?

Yet this revolutionary vision was what gave Marxist parties their constant optimism. The scientific parts do not, in my view, quite fit in with this apocalyptic vision, since the analysis does not lead to this conclusion. After all, Marx could have written this paragraph in 1848, before he discovered the secret of surplus-value. What was the point of all that study and three volumes, if he could just repeat the *Communist Manifesto*?

These thoughts are not incidental to our discussion. They are central to it, because Marxism got hooked on the revolutionary message while giving as its scientific basis the much more complex and, in my view, innovative and unique analysis of capitalism, which does not lead to such revolutionary conclusions. So a tension remains. But the tension is in Marx's own work, not merely in the minds of his followers.

There are two simple ways of seeing this. This chapter should have been the end of *Capital Volume 1,* then it would have been a high note to end on. But Marx follows it with a perfectly straightforward discussion of 'The Modern Theory of Colonization'. Having charted, as it were, the full history of capitalism from its origin to its future destruction in Chapter 32, why is there a discussion of what is an important issue, but one which should have preceded the prophecy of the end? This is a minor point, although since Marx prepared Volume 1 for publication, and oversaw several translations and editions without changing this order, one wonders why he put his apocalyptic vision in the penultimate chapter. But there is another reason for noting the tension. Chapter 32 goes on for two more paragraphs beyond the expropriators being expropriated. First we have the fundamental point that capitalist private property relies not on the labour of the proprietor, as petty commodity production does, but on the socialized labour of the workers. This is the negation of its own negation of the individual proprietor.

The last paragraph of the chapter then says that the transition from scattered private property arising from individual labour – a sort of John Locke world – into capitalist private property is a protracted, violent and difficult process. This is, after all, the process Marx had been tracing in the previous six chapters, a process occupying four to six centuries. Yet he feels confident that the next stage – 'the transformation of capitalistic private property, already practically resting on socialized production, into socialized property' – will take less time. It is difficult to say whether by this Marx meant that the change was imminent, or just inevitable. The left/right divisions among Marxist parties were to hinge on this ambiguity. The fiery prose makes the change seem imminent; the other – less flamboyant but more analytical – parts can at best support inevitability, if that.

A hundred years-plus on, it is the analytical parts which are of help in understanding the dynamics of capitalism. Inevitability has no calendar time attached to it. It is like the Second Coming. For everyday political and economic conduct, it is the sober analysis of the course of the cycle and the projections of growth, the interplay of inequality and poverty, which are most relevant. This sort of 'mild' reading of *Capital* will no doubt surprise and shock many readers. Few have ever read *Capital* through all its three volumes. Much more has been written about Marx's theory of history, about historical materialism, than about *Capital* and its critique of political economy. Even in writing about *Capital*, the value–price problem has inspired a greater debate over the last hundred years than the dynamics of capitalism. Engels asserted that Marx had discovered the laws of motion of capitalism, and this has been accepted uncritically. No one has asked what these laws said about the future of capitalism. It has been taken for granted, even by some high authorities, that in *Capital* Marx provided an analytical argument for the breakdown of capitalism.

Yet what we discover is that on reading *Capital*, one could conclude that capitalism will live through cycles, and a slow as well as cyclical tendency of the rate of profit to decline. As capitalism grows, it spreads globally, and its crises become worldwide. But could it be that Marx provides a better argument for the long-term survival of capitalism than his detractors or followers have given him credit for?

6

The Future of Capitalism I: How Soon the End?

Introduction

When Marx died, in 1883, capitalism was in one of its long downswings. There was a long-run downward trend in prices. This was due to more rapid transport facilities – steamships, the Suez Canal – and new breakthroughs in communications – telegraph, transatlantic cable. Territories previously unknown to Europeans, or only marginally on their horizons, were pillaged to provide food and raw materials. Australia and New Zealand, India, North and South America all became sources of raw-material supplies. Railways had spanned countries in Europe, and were spreading across North America. India had its first railroad in 1853. Cotton textile mills – spinning and weaving – had also taken root in India, as well as all over Western Europe and North America.

England had preached the doctrine of free trade and liberalized its food import policy. This was the essence of the Corn Law debate, which preoccupied the nation in the 1840s. Not all the 'newly industrializing' countries followed the free-trade rule. The USA and Germany held out, and France was always a reluctant free trader. Free trade was to Britain's advantage as the first industrialized country, which needed markets for its manufacturers and investment opportunities for its savings. The City of London became the versatile instrument for dispersing the savings of the wealthy to the profitable outlets in the rest of the world. Savings from Western Europe began to flow into the Americas, and Central and Eastern Europe. Western Europe was to reach the farthest corners of Asia and, within the next twenty-five years, colonize Africa as well.

For any country which wanted to aspire to the club of industrialized countries, there was the Gold Standard.[1] Russia joined up in 1897, as did Japan. The 'cross of gold' was cursed by American farmers who had incurred large debts in the inflationary years of the Civil War, and were now paying them back as prices of their products fell in terms of gold.[2] But gold became the universally preferred currency, with silver as a junior partner. India had a silver rupee, and silver coinage was widespread from the American West to the steppes of Europe.

There was also a massive movement of people from the heartlands of Europe to the Americas and the Antipodes. Indians migrated to Southeast Asia, to Africa and to the West Indies – mostly as indentured labourers, but also as traders and moneylenders. Gandhi was invited to South Africa in 1891 as a barrister to fight their case. Chinese workers went to the west coast of the USA, and to Australia and Southeast Asia. The movement of labour was not completely free, though. The surplus white populations of Europe moved to the Americas and the Antipodes. The brown and yellow peoples of Asia moved to the periphery – Africa, Asia, the fringes of America. This pattern was not to break until a hundred years later.

Yet this was a globalized world. The scramble for Africa was to reach its climax soon after Marx's death. But in a sense, capital moved freely – though never evenly – across the globe, as did labour. Technological advances were shrinking distance as well as time. Sir Charles Napier was able to telegraph the capture of Sind in 1843 to his masters in Whitehall in a single-word message – Peccavi (I have sinned [Sind]). The globe was pretty well fully mapped; no new discoveries of any significance remained.

Economic growth accelerated in the period 1870–1913, the first episode of modern globalization. Data on income for this early period are always scarce and somewhat unreliable. Even the notion of national income was new and, as we saw above, Marx struggled to come to terms with nation income accounts. But now we have some good results, thanks to the pioneering efforts of Angus Maddison.[3] The data focus on the more 'advanced' capitalist countries of Europe (Austria, Belgium, Denmark, Finland, France, Germany, Italy, the Netherlands, Norway, Sweden, Switzerland and the UK) plus Canada and the USA, Japan and Australia. The populations of these sixteen countries reached about 150 million in 1820, 295 million in 1870, and nearly 495 million in 1913. Along with the trebling of population over the ninety-three years, income had also grown. In the first fifty years (1820–70), it grew at an average of 0.9 per cent *per capita* per year in real terms. In the next period (1870–1913), this average went up to 1.4 per cent. Should anyone think this slow, income doubles in eighty years at 0.9 per cent, while at 1.4 per cent it does so in fifty years.[4]

So *per capita* income roughly trebled, and population likewise. Thus total income – GDP for these sixteen countries – increased ninefold over the century. This, of course, was unprecedented. Within this overall total, some countries – Canada, the USA, Germany and Sweden – grew more rapidly, while the pioneer industrialized country – the UK – was slower. There were cycles, of course. Long swings (called Kondratieff cycles after the Russian economist who first wrote about them in the 1920s) spanning fifty years were dated as downswings from 1810–17 to 1844–51, and upswings from 1844–51 to 1870–75; downswings again 1870–75 to 1890–96, then an upswing 1890–96 to 1914–20. These dates are rough and ready, and Kondratieff claimed a greater regularity to his 'waves' than modern research concedes.[5] But for our purposes, it gives a picture of cyclical growth, which is endemic to capitalism, as Marx was the first economist to point out. Of course, the growth was not even – either within a country, or across the globe or over time. Income and wealth inequalities were very acute in the feudal ages. With capitalism, these inequalities did not increase but, thanks to urbanization and the availability of new luxuries, became highly visible.[6] The growing urban population, with crowded housing and teeming streets, brought the fear of 'the mob' to the rich classes. Concerned middle-class intellectuals and radical reformers began to question the nature of this industrialization and economic progress which caused so much visible misery. In England, Thomas Carlyle and John Ruskin were in the forefront of a critique of this new order, while Robert Owen from Lanarkshire had proposed a radical solution as early as 1813. For the first time in human history, it became possible to argue that poverty could be eliminated. Studies by Charles Booth in London and Seebohm Rowntree in York highlighted the low living standards of the poor.[7] Inequality of income and wealth had risen with the spread of capitalism, as Adam Smith had predicted; but were the poorest strata of society enjoying a better standard of living than even the well-off of previous centuries?

Such thoughts were rarely in the forefront of many people's minds. If the middle classes and the ruling elites of Europe worried about anything, it was the agitation of workers. Trade unions were forming, as well as political parties claiming to speak for workers. There was a movement everywhere for the extension of the franchise. The aristocracy which ruled over much of Europe (France and the Netherlands excepted) had enough difficulty accommodating the parvenu bourgeoisie's demand for political power, let alone the mass of workers. In a variety of ways in this period (1870–1913), there were reforms which meant that the spectrum of the ruling elite began to move steadily downwards and outwards from the aristocracy to the bourgeoisie; or the bourgeoisie conceded power to the working class. As capitalism entrenched itself more and more, so did the workers' movement for political power and economic betterment.

The German Social Democratic Party[8]

A working-class party with mass support emerged in Germany in 1875. This in itself was a paradox, since Germany was not at that time the most advanced country in terms of either capitalist production or political participation. The party was a merger of a faction claiming allegiance to Marx, and another which followed Ferdinand Lassalle. Lassalle was a popular Romantic figure who believed in an Iron Law of Wages which, he said, could be abolished only by abolishing capitalism. Marx thought Lassalle confused and dishonest, but Lassalle's early death facilitated the merger of the two factions. At a congress in Gotha, the SAPD (the Socialist Workers' Party of Germany) was established. This could have been the first 'Marxist' party (its name was later changed to the Social Democratic Party of Germany: SPD), but its programme did not please Marx: he thought it was too Lassallean. Indeed, he let it be known via a letter to Wilhelm Bracke, one of the leaders of the new party, that he and Engels would be 'dissociating ourselves from the said Programme of Principles and stating that we had nothing to do with it'.[9] He did not want anyone to think that he and Engels controlled the party from a distance, but he thought that the programme was 'thoroughly reprehensible and demoralizing'.[10] He pointed out several flaws in it which purported to reflect his theories, but were really Lassalle's. The very first words – 'Labour is the source of all wealth and culture . . .' – were wrong. Labour was *not* the source of all wealth: 'Nature is just as much the source of use values (and surely these are what make up material wealth!) as labour'.[11] He also pointed out that it was fallacious to say, as the first sentence did: 'all members of society have an equal right to the undiminished proceeds of society'.[12] In his critique, Marx took this proposition as a possible blueprint for distribution in a communist society, and subjected it to his incisive criticism:

> 'The instruments of labour must be elevated to common property'! This is probably meant to mean 'converted into common property'. But this just incidentally.
>
> What are the 'proceeds of labour'? Are they the product of labour or its value? And in the latter case, is it the total value of the product or only that part of its value which labour has created over and above the value of the means of production consumed?
>
> 'Proceeds of labour' is a loose notion, used by Lassalle in place of definite economic concepts.
>
> What is 'just' distribution?

Does not the bourgeoisie claim that the present system of distribution is 'just'? And given the present mode of production is it not, in fact, the only 'just' system of distribution? Are economic relations regulated by legal concepts of right or is the opposite not the case, that legal relations spring from economic ones? Do not the socialist sectarians themselves have the most varied notions of 'just' distribution?

To discover what we are meant to understand by the phrase 'just distribution' as used here we must take the opening paragraph and this one together. The latter presupposes a society in which 'the instruments of labour are common property and the whole of labour is regulated on a cooperative basis' and from the opening paragraph we learn that 'all members of society have an equal right to the undiminished proceeds of labour'.

'All members of society'? Including people who do not work? Then what remains of the 'undiminished proceeds of labour'? Only the working members of society? Then what remains of the 'equal right' of all members of society?

'All members of society' and 'equal right', however, are obviously mere phrases. The heart of the matter is that in this communist society every worker is supposed to receive the 'undiminished' Lassallean 'proceeds of labour'.

If we start by taking 'proceeds of labour' to mean the product of labour, then the cooperative proceeds of labour are the *total social product.*

From this the folowing must now be deducted:

Firstly: cover to replace the means of production used up.

Secondly: an additional portion for the expansion of production.

Thirdly: a reserve or insurance fund in case of accidents, disruption caused by natural calamities, etc.

These deductions from the 'undiminished proceeds of labour' are an economic necessity and their magnitude will be determined by the means and forces available. They can partly be calculated by reference to probability, but on no account by reference to justice.[13]

Marx's letter had little immediate effect. The Lassalle faction had a majority in the SPD, and their views, however confused they may have seemed to Marx, prevailed. But then Bismarck saw the danger of a large working class combining with the various middle-class reformist parties and advancing the interests of workers and of democracy. Germany had a larger adult male franchise at this time than other advanced countries – 33 per cent as against an average of 17.8 per cent for the twelve European countries, with the UK at only 14.9 per cent in 1869–73. Only France (43 per cent) and Switzerland (38.7 per cent) had a larger franchise. Bismarck therefore made the SPD illegal in 1878; most of its leaders were exiled, and only in 1890 was the ban on its activities lifted. During those years, the SPD continued to contest elections, and its performance improved from 312,000 votes in 1881 to 1,427,000 in 1890.

But the ban on the party and its exile also radicalized the SPD: it became more overtly Marxist. Its intellectual leader, Karl Kautsky, collaborated closely with Engels, who was still around as the authoritative voice of Marx.[14] The 'Critique of the Gotha Programme' was published in 1891 – albeit with a few deletions, to save the faces of some leaders who were then still alive. But by now, the SPD had become the largest and most respected of all the fledgling socialist parties in Europe. Its doctrine fused socialism and democracy, reform and revolution. It was the leader of the parties that met in Paris on the centenary of the French Revolution, 14 July 1889, to found the International Workingmen's Congress. Marx and Engels had founded the first such Congress in 1864, but it had been dissolved in 1874. This, then, was a revival and a refoundation of that Congress, with many more countries represented and with much larger parties. They were committed to democratic methods for the achievement of power, and their goal was a socialist one.

The Socialist (or Second) International, as the Congress became known, declared on 14 July 1889: 'Our aim is the emancipation of the workers, the abolition of wage-labour and the creation of a society in which all women and men irrespective of sex or nationality will enjoy the wealth produced by all the workers.'[15] The repetition of sentiments similar to those Marx criticized in the Gotha Programme, 'the wealth produced by all the workers', is telling. But as a recent historian of socialism has pointed out, while *the long-term goal* of the movement was 'the destruction of capitalism and the establishment of a society where production would be subjected to the associated control of the producers', much of their immediate and short-term perspective was reformist – 'to make working-class life under capitalism endurable and dignified'. There was, however, a problem which Marx could have warned them about – and did, in his various analytical statements about the course of capitalism: '[T]he more successful the socialists became, the more dependent they found themselves on the prosperity of capitalism.'[16]

This paradox was felt acutely by the SPD. Its establishment and growth coincided with a period of rapid growth for German capitalism. *Per capita* income was growing at 1.6 per cent *per annum* (doubling over the period 1870–1913), and the German population grew by 70 per cent. In 1891, when it launched its new – specifically Marxist – Erfurt Programme, it relied on a long-term revolutionary perspective, but immediately stuck to reformist demands:

universal adult franchise, secret ballot, direct election of officials, graduated income tax, an eight-hour working day, prohibition of child labour under the age of fourteen, et cetera.

Yet the tension between the revolutionary and the reformist demands would not go away. Was the SPD confronting a system that was expected to continue despite crisis and inceasing concentration of capital, and hence fighting for immediate short-term gains? Or was it a revolutionary party fighting to hasten the inevitable end of capitalism? The tension stems – as we saw in Chapter 5 – from an ambiguity in Marx's own formulations. The revolutionary vision of the *Communist Manifesto* is reiterated in a chapter in *Capital Volume 1*, but the complex analytical understanding of the way capitalism works leads Marx to a much more nuanced understanding. Which was it to be?

Political parties – once they reach a certain size, and have mass membership as well as an electoral agenda – cannot be built on ideological clarity. Instead of choosing one strand or the other of Marx's thought, the SPD chose Marx. His word was authoritative, but when it contradicted itself, another authoritative figure – Karl Kautsky for the most part – had to interpret and reconcile differences. This practice of elevating one person's thought to such an uncritical position was to bring nothing but trouble later on. But the SPD became wedded to Marx's writings in a serious way. It was an ideological political party. Its battles thereafter were not merely with the German ruling classes, but within its own ranks – between the trade unionists and the theorists and, among the theorists, between the Left, which was for the revolutionary path, and the right, which was for the reformist path. The quarrel was, of course, about the dynamics of capitalism.

The trade unionists who formed the right wing of the SPD were interested in achieving higher wages and buoyant employment for their members. These demands could be more easily satisfied under a boom than under a slump. Their use of the strike weapon was instrumental rather than political. But the 'politicos' – the intellectuals on the Left, and even some on the Right – were interested in the breakdown and disabling of the capitalist order. Lassalle had argued that trade unions could not challenge the Iron Law of wages. What was needed was a complete overthrow of capitalism by democratic means. If the successive crises of capitalism could become more and more serious, then the Left was vindicated in its strategy of fighting to destroy the system. Yet, while capitalism lasted, crises caused misery to the workers, not to their bosses.

But even on the Left, there was a strand that could argue for the rapid growth of capitalism. In Marx's formulation, workers could become a disciplined army by working in large-scale industrial establishments – the larger the better. Capitalism had to grow, if workers' revolutionary organizations were to become stronger. To oppose the growth of capitalism while it was still in its early stages – that is, while the bourgeoisie was still fighting the forces of reactionary feudalism – was 'objectively' to undermine the struggle. Nor was there any mileage in dreaming of a quick transition to socialism. Such dreams were being entertained among Russian Marxists, and as we shall see later, it was Lenin who defeated them by using Marx's theory which had 'proved' that socialism could come only after the full development of capitalism. That, of course, was nearly twenty-five years before Lenin came to power.

Debating Capitalism: The German Debates

The debate about the course of capitalism that broke out among the European Marxists was sparked first by Edouard Bernstein. During the SPD leaders' exile, Bernstein went first to Switzerland, but in 1888 he was exiled from there as well, and went to England; although the SPD was legalized in 1890, he stayed there until 1901. It was during this period that he constructed his revisionist theory, which challenged the prognosis of a revolutionary end to capitalism. As a leading Marxist in the SPD, a close associate of Engels and an editor of the party's theoretical review, *Sozial-Democrat* Bernstein had toed the received line of Marxism. He had – as he later wrote to the veteran SPD leader August Bebel – 'tried, by stretching Marx's teachings, to bring them in accord with practical realities'. These realities were the continued survival of capitalism and the relatively mild nature of the business cycles.

Capitalism, Bernstein realized by looking at its British variant, had a capacity for adjusting to the challenges thrown at it by new social developments, as well as new technology. So he wanted not just a little local criticism of this or that aspect of Marx's theory, but a fundamental revision. In a series of articles between 1896 and 1898 in SPD's *Neue Zeit*, entitled *Probleme des Socialismus*, he threw doubt on the thesis of ever-growing crises and increasing misery for the working classes. He thought there might be an evolutionary, reformist road to socialism as an alternative.

Bernstein was the first apostate of the new Church of Marxism that the SPD had established after Marx's death. It is a moot point whether Marx himself would have been that insistent on the literal truth of all his writings. He was often dictatorial in his dealings with his associates in the First International – as the Russian anarchist Bakunin, complained. But in his correspondence with the

Russian Marxist Vera Zasulich, he was much more modest about the scope of his theory of history than his disciples were claiming. Marx's personality is not at issue here. He was human, all too human, and hence liable to gross errors. But by the end of the 1890s, adherence to what the leaders of the SPD – Karl Kautsky, August Bebel, Wilhelm Liebknecht – had decided was his doctrine was the Truth. This doctrine was based more on that single paragraph in Chapter 32 of *Capital Volume 1* than on the rest of *Capital* put together. Thus one tenet of the Erfurt Programme adopted in 1891 said:

> For the proletariat and the disappearing middle class, the small businessmen and farmers, [monopoly capitalism] means increasing uncertainty of subsistence; it means misery, oppression, servitude, degradation and exploitation.
>
> Forever greater grows the number of proletarians, more gigantic the reserve army of labour, and sharper the opposition between exploiters and exploited . . .
>
> The abyss between propertied and propertyless is further widened by industrial crises. These have their causes in the capitalist system and, as the system develops, become ever more extensive and devastating.[17]

This is popular Marxism, Marx as he has been served up to millions of socialists the world over. This picture of capitalism is not sustained by Marx's theory of crises as outlined in *Capital Volume 1*, part 7, or in the theory of falling rate of profits in *Capital Volume 3*, as I have already argued. Certainly an ever-increasing reserve army is not a necessary part of the theory; at best, one may sustain a prediction of a rising army from one downturn to the next, but even that is empirically hard to sustain for many periods in the late nineteenth century. Bernstein's answer was: 'I set myself against the viewpoint that we have to expect a collapse of the bourgeois economy in the near future, and that Social Democracy should be induced by the prospect of such an imminent catastrophe to adapt its tactics to that assumption.'[18]

Kautsky – as the keeper of the flame, as the Pope of Marxism – was furious:

> your Marxism has collapsed. You have not further developed it to a higher form but have capitulated before its critics. . . . You have decided to be an Englishman – take the consequences and become an Englishman. . . . The development which you have undergone . . . heads away from German Social Democracy, although not from Socialism. Try to achieve a place in the English movement and become a representative of English Socialism.[19]

Here, Kautsky was inadvertently hinting at a problem which was to become much more serious for socialists of all hues. Capitalism had been developing on a global scale. It had developed unevenly in various countries, and this unevenness was part and parcel of the process of capitalism. But socialist movements were national, since their focus was on the capture of political power, either peacefully or by revolutionary means. Socialist movements were gripped by the French Revolution model of seizing power. But if capitalism was a global phenomenon, how could it be successfully challenged by socialists in a single country?

Marxist debate continued uneasily, taking Marx's theory as one of global capitalism but applying it to particular countries where particular parties flourished. Yet the revolutionary Left was internationalist – German, Polish, Russian, French, Dutch. The most perspicacious among them was Rosa Luxemburg, a Polish economist who spent her active life in the SPD and died in 1919 at the hands of some disgruntled German soldiers. Rosa Luxemburg posed the question of the dynamics of capitalism at a much deeper intellectual level than Bernstein or anyone else.

One of the problems, of course, was dating the expected final crisis of capitalism. How imminent was the collapse of capitalism? SPD rhetoric was ambivalent on this point, but it retained the idea that the crises were getting ever worse. As I said in Chapter 5, not even the apocalyptic Chapter 32 can be read as predicting an imminent collapse of capitalism. All it says, in a rather roundabout way, is that the transition from capitalism to socialism will take less time than the transition from feudalism to capitalism. But that could mean anywhere between four and six hundred years. No political party could live on that sort of promise to its followers. So the SPD had to shorten the timetable.

But there was the matter of Marx's Schemes of Reproduction at the back of *Capital Volume 2*. Were these schemes of the actual or possible progress of capitalism – crisis-free and stable growth in perpetuity – or were they a demonstration of the impossibility of such an outcome, given that it assumed co-ordinated investment behaviour among capitalists? In any case, how could Marxists believe that the ever-expanding production of commodities – of use values – would find a market? Workers were supposed to be getting poorer as the economy expanded, so they should fail to provide a market for consumption goods. Surely this failure on the part of workers to provide a market should undermine the system. After all, the only purpose of investment was to produce things which could be sold at a profit. And if things cannot be sold, why should capitalists keep investing?

The obverse of this question was to ask why capitalism had not self-destructed, as many thought Marx had prophesied. Bernstein had argued that the emergence of large units – of concentration of capital – had improved the capitalists' capacity to control output and avoid overproduction. But if so, concentration had the opposite effect to what Marx had predicted, eliminating rivals and intensifying the class struggle. So the continued survival of capitalism beyond the nineteenth century became a subject of heated debate among European Marxists. During this debate they raised many issues which became part of mainstream economics once Keynes had hit upon the problem of effective demand in his 1936 book *The General Theory of Employment, Interest and Money.* But when they were writing, the mainstream economics of their day was not concerned with the problem of underconsumption or overinvestment, certainly not in the works of the major economists such as Menger, Jevons or Marshall.

The best of this rather vast and untidy literature is *The Accumulation of Capital* by Rosa Luxemburg. She was on the left of the SPD and a trenchant critique of Kautsky, who was combining a revolutionary theoretical stance (against Bernstein) with a reformist practice (against the Left). The merit of Luxemburg's contribution is that she mounted an immanent critique of Marx's Schemes of Reproduction, thus being the only Marxist in all these years to use Marx's method against himself. In the Scheme – as will be recalled – the two Departments (sectors) producing machine goods and wage goods expanded in parallel without a shortage of workers, a shortage of demand or a lack of credit. Indeed, Marx had not even posed the problem of money in this context. Where did the capitalists of Department I find the money to invest *before* they were sure they had sold all their output – that is, realized the value and the surplus-value? (Recall Chapter 5 and the diagram $M \rightarrow C \rightarrow C' \rightarrow M'$.) How could Marx ignore the problem of selling output, of finding workers, or the need to have money to buy material inputs and labour-power?

In her book, Luxemburg made two major contributions to Marxian economics. First, she connected the problem of demand in an advanced capitalist economy with its imperial periphery. Marxist parties had sprung up, of course, in advanced capitalist countries, and their perspective was Eurocentric (they, of course, called it internationalist). Germany had no empire to speak of at this time (that being one of its quarrels with Great Britain and France). Luxemburg said that empires were markets for the developed countries' products, especially their machine goods (railroads were one example). This gave a rationale for the continued expansion of Department I. At the same time, colonized territories provided cheaper raw materials and foodstuffs. These supplies kept the labour content of the wage-goods basket from going up. So workers' real wage in terms of their wage goods could go up, without their money wages going up and reducing profits. Thus there would be a wedge between real wage in terms of wage goods and real wage in terms of the product produced by the worker. This wedge was significant for Great Britain.

Whatever the technical details of the argument (and there was a fierce debate about Luxemburg's immanent critique of Marx), Luxemburg restored a global perspective to a Marxian theory of capitalism. The national perspective in which the SPD had been caught up was expanded. Economic historians ever since have denied that empires were profitable to the ruling countries, but the idea of imperialism extending the life of capitalism beyond its imminent demise became part of Left economics. As sinks for their surplus outputs and sources for their raw materials, colonies became tied up in a logic of symbiotic dependency on the core countries. Of course, what Rosa Luxemburg did not foresee then was that these peripheries could become locations for surplus capital, which could then employ cheap local labour. Then the migration of capital abroad hurts the workers at home. This was yet to come.

The other theme Luxemburg introduced was the addition of a 'third Department' to Marx's scheme. This Department's role was to absorb surplus output, and produce output for which the demand came not from workers, or from any other consumers, but from governments. This was the armaments industry. Thus the armaments industry could absorb surplus machinery from Department I and make armaments which governments buy.

So the perspective here is that capitalism needs a 'sink' sector which can absorb surplus output of machines. (Recall that Marx had to solve the problem of surplus output of machines in his scheme.) Of course, the armaments sector, like every other sector, had to earn an average rate of profit. It generates some employment, of course, because otherwise surplus-value would not exist in the sector. When, later on, this insight was expanded into the notion of a waste sector, Department III could be publicly owned, and need not even make a profit (more about that below). The question still remained: how was the government to pay for such purchases? One way would be to tax profits or wages. Marxists assumed that workers' consumption would be taxed to finance arms purchases. This made sense in Germany, where indirect taxes were the main source of government revenue, and for financing arms expenditure. In Great Britain there was income tax, even death duties.

Since Luxemburg criticized and improved upon Marx, she was much criticized herself.[20] Orthodox defence of Marx was advanced by many writers. But again, the details do not concern us here. Marxists firmly accepted the idea that the continued survival of capitalism was a puzzle to be solved. Luxemburg explained it by linking the core countries with a periphery. Imperialism here did not mean political domination: it was an exchange relationship in which the core sold machine goods and bought raw materials. Such a process, of course, was not permanent: sooner or later, the periphery would be saturated and the market would dry up. That might yet be a limit to capitalism's ability to reproduce itself, according to Luxemburg.

Other answers to the question of capitalism's survival took a more revisionist path. Instead of mounting an immanent critique of Marx – conceding his assumptions and then subverting his conclusions – they mounted an external, empirical critique. Marx had assumed a competitive economy, much as the classical economists had done. In his day, most industrial establishments were roughly equal in size, and there were many of them. Capital was free to move from one sector to another, and there were no monopolies – in theory, at least. But now, at the turn of the century, it was argued that steel, chemical and electrical firms were gigantic. In any industry there were a few large units and many small ones. In these sectors, the USA and Germany were the leading countries. Great Britain was left behind. There was a pronounced tendency for cartels to be formed in these newly industrializing countries. Some Marxists said that these cartels presaged a new world of non-competitive behaviour.

To this tendency for large industrial units to form cartels in order to control the market was added a peculiar German institution. When the Industrial Revolution occurred in Great Britain, the industrial enterprises were financed by country banks and private borrowing. By the end of the nineteenth century, country banks had been swallowed up into a few large clearing banks, and had withdrawn from industrial financing. Instead, an active stock market had developed, and British industry was substantially equity-financed. In Germany, however, the banks took a very active role in financing companies. Banks owned shares in industrial companies, and bank directors sat on the boards. Banks were the dominant partners in German capitalism.

This combination of large units forming cartels, financed in turn by large banks, led Rudolf Hilferding to advance the idea of finance capitalism [*Finanzkapital*].[21] This was a new phase of capitalism – unlike, it was said, what Marx had theorized about. So the so-called laws of Marxism were suspended. The fall in the rate of profit could be postponed, and the paramount importance of banks was a new factor. There was control over markets, and a large credit supply to finance stockpiling of surplus products to be sold when conditions became more favourable.

Hilferding did not offer any new value theory, nor even any demonstration of how the existence of large units financed by banks modified or nullified Marx's calculations in the three volumes of *Capital*. If some units made incredible profits, did this mean a departure from the notion that all sectors made the same rate of profit? If so, how were unequal rates of profit sustained? These questions are not simply academic. Luxemburg tackled the difficulties she encountered within Marx's theoretical structure. Hilferding introduced a corrective to Marx's descriptions, but he did not improve upon the theoretical structure.

One Capitalism or Many?

Finance capitalism was an idea specific to German capitalism – or perhaps at most to continental Western Europe. Great Britain's experience did not fit into this pattern (though just around the turn of the nineteenth century, some British commentators began to look with envy at the dynamism of the German economy). The USA shared the cartel phenomenon with Germany, and feeble attempts were made at trust-busting by the US Congress around this time. But when it came to the role of banks in industrial financing, the Anglo-Saxon pattern was in contrast to the German one. Stock markets remained important in the USA and the UK. It was beginning to look as if there was not a single model of capitalism, but several.

Marxism was also weak in its appeal to American and British socialists. There were followers of Marx in these countries, but Marxism was never a philosophy for a political party of any substantial size. Indeed, Anglo-Saxon socialists deliberately turned away from Marxism. The rise of the anticlassical marginalist theory of economics caught on very quickly. The Fabian socialists debated Marx's theory of surplus-value, but were soon convinced that the theories of marginal utility and marginal productivity afforded a better explanation of value and of distribution.[22] Goods had value not because of their labour content but because they were scarce in relation to the demand for them. Consumers equate marginal utility (a measure of use value) with price. Producers bought different quantities of factor input – labour, machinery, and so on – and each factor received its marginal product. That maximized profits for the producer. But then, in the process of competition among producers, these profits were reduced to a bare minimum: normal profits. Abnormal profits were zero. Profits and profitability disappeared as a subject of inquiry from the new – neoclassical – economics.

But British socialists – and, indeed, the radical wing of the Whigs – were alive to John Ruskin's and Thomas Carlyle's critiques about the effects of capitalism on the quality of life, and what we would call today the alienation of workers. Their bent was reformist. The Fabians had a strong belief in the power of a neutral and technocratic civil service to effect changes in the market economy. It was at this time – in the 1890s and 1900s – that British neo-Hegelians were most influential in their view of the state. Recall that Hegel did not believe in *laissez-faire.* Civil society had to be regulated against its own excesses by the state, guided by the bureaucracy. While the neo-Hegelian political philosophers were mainly at Oxford, economists at Cambridge – chiefly Alfred Marshall and his successor as Professor of Political Economy, Arthur Cecil Pigou[23] – developed the economic theory for market intervention via taxes and subsidies. Economic welfare could be enhanced by limited but suitable acts of state intervention into the working of the market – smoking factories, noise and air pollution had to be taxed, and workers' education had to be subsidized. The objective was a mitigation of capitalism.

Marx had nothing to say about market intervention. In this respect, he was very much a classical economist in the mould of Adam Smith and David Ricardo. The system had its own logic, and it developed along those lines due to the profit-seeking behaviour of capitalists. Such reforms as could be won, such as shorter working hours, were the result of the class struggle, though this could take different forms in different countries. Thus a shorter working week was legislated for in France across all industries, Marx observed, while in England it had to be negotiated industry by industry between the employers and the workers.

Marx's early work on alienation was not to come to light until the mid-twentieth century, and Marxists regarded all such criticisms of capitalism as Romantic. Nor would Marxists be able to accommodate the Christian, Nonconformist roots of British socialism. Marxists were atheists. They also held firmly to the view that whatever its future, and however much misery it might cause, capitalism was a progressive mode of production, to be preferred to all that had gone before. The Romantics, they argued, were merely nostalgic about a past that never was – or, if it was, should not be any longer.

Russian Debates

The same debate surfaced in Russia in another guise.[24] Russia had abolished serfdom only as recently as 1861, and throughout Marx's life, he regarded the Tsardom as the bulwark of reaction in Europe, never forgetting the role it played in defeating the 1848 Revolution in Germany. Yet Russia had one of the earliest Marxist groups. *Capital* was translated into Russian five years after its publication in German, in 1872, even before it appeared in French. The translator, Nikolai Frantsevich Danielson, translated all three volumes, and corresponded with Marx and Engels. Danielson, who wrote under the pseudonym Nikolaion, was the leader of the Narodniks, the People's Party. The Narodniks went among the Russian peasants to study their living conditions, and proposed radical reforms. One major plank of Narodism was the notion that since Russia had within its countryside institutional arrangements for common ownership of land, with periodic redistribution within the village, it should avoid breaking this up and introducing private landownership. Indeed, Russia could skip the horrible miserable stage of capitalism, and go straight to socialism, which would require common ownership. They cited Marx in their support, as proving that capitalism was an undesirable stage to go through. There would be a unique Russian path.

Another more determinedly Marxist group was led by Plekhanov, and the Marxists challenged the Narodniks for leadership among the politically conscious Russian youth. Of course, both these groups were banned, and their publications had to be clandestine. Their leaders were frequently in exile or in Tsarist jails. It was from one such Russian Marxist exile, Vera Zasulich, that Marx received a letter in 1881.[25] The letter asked him to adjudicate on the dispute between the Marxists, who believed that Marx's laws of historical materialism predicted that every country must go through the same stages of successive modes of production – ancient, feudal, bourgeois and socialist – and the Narodniks, who believed that Russia could skip capitalism and go straight from feudalism to socialism. Please, Sir, could you settle our argument?

Marx wrote a succinct reply to Vera Zasulich. He made four rough drafts of the letter. These rough drafts have been pored over since they were published by Ryazanov in the 1920s. As usual, more truth has been sought in the drafts than in the final version. But in my view, all the drafts reveal is how good an editor of his drafts Marx was. Out of these prolix drafts he fashioned a terse reply. First, he modestly denied any claim to have found General Laws of History. His theory applied only to Western Europe. He had been studying Russian conditions carefully, but he did not think he knew enough to be able to pronounce on them. The Russian *mir*, the institution that allowed collective ownership of property, was indeed a strong one, but it was difficult to say how it would survive. He could not rule out Russia defying the trend, but somehow he could not predict it either. Russia could go either way. As he had said in response to a Russian review of *Capital Volume 1*: 'if Russia attempts to become a capitalist nation . . . and in recent years it has made great efforts in this direction, it will not succeed without having first transformed a good part of its peasants into proletarians and afterwards, once it has crossed the threshold of the capitalist system, it will have to submit to the implacable laws of such a system.'[26]

This was indeed a very flexible 'late' Marx: there are no inevitable Laws of History as such. But if you get into capitalism – as Russia was indeed trying to do in those days, as official policy – then the system had its 'implacable laws'. Engels had little time for such 'possibilist' views. A Russian Revolution had to be in tandem with a revolution in advanced Western countries. Thus in the preface to a new Russian edition of *The Communist Manifesto*, published in 1882, signed by both Marx and Engels, it is the latter's views which seem to have prevailed:

> But in Russia we find, face to face, the rapidly flowering capitalist swindle and bourgeois property, just beginning to develop. More than half the land is owned in common by the peasants. Now the question is: can the Russian *obstchina*, though greatly undermined, yet a form of the primeval common ownership of land, pass directly to the higher form of communist ownership? Or on the contrary, must it first pass through the same process of dissolution such as constitutes the historical evolution of the West?
>
> The only answer to that possible today is this: if the Russian Revolution becomes the signal for a proletarian revolution in the West, so that both complement each other, the present common ownership of land may serve as the starting point for a communist development.[27]

This Russian translation was by Vera Zasulich, but Marx's reply to her letter of the previous year was not widely known at this time. This formulation gives a lot of importance to a proletarian revolution in the West. A Russian Revolution, obviously not proletarian at such an early stage of capitalist development, had to be complementary to the proletarian revolution. Only then could Russia skip capitalism and move straight on to communism – not otherwise, though Engels did not spell it out, since he thought there was no possibility of a Russian revolution at that stage.

But Russia was marching headlong into capitalist development. The Tsar had decided that modernization from above was the best bet. Foreign capital – largely French – was to be attracted. Railways had to be built, ports developed. Russia was to become a major exporter of grain to the industrialized countries of Northwest Europe. As usual, cotton mills began springing up with the same attendant squalor as in Manchester fifty years previously, as so well described in Gorky's novel *Mother*. The Narodniks disliked the far-reaching changes in Russia intensely. Their argument was that capitalism was a hothouse plant imported from abroad, and unsuitable to Russian conditions. It had no future in Russia, because the poor Russian peasantry could never constitute a large enough market for the much greater volume of output that factory production would generate. Capitalism would soon become unprofitable but, in the meantime, cause a lot of misery. The Narodniks were thus in favour of resisting capitalism by all possible means.

The Marxists were against such behaviour, and considered the Narodniks' analysis flawed. The rising star of Russian Marxism, Vladimir Ilyich Ulyanov, later to be known as Lenin, wrote a series of pamphlets and books during the 1890s refuting the Narodniks' critique of the prospects of capitalist development in Russia.[28] One of the books, Lenin's first in print, was called *A Characterization of Economic Romanticism*. The Narodniks were economic Romantics. Their leader, Danielson, had tried to demonstrate his thesis by using Marx's Scheme of Expanded Reproduction from *Capital Volume 2*. But in a long article, 'On the So-Called Question of the Home Market', Lenin showed that Danielson was misreading Marx. Marx had indeed shown why there were no such home-market (i.e. effective demand) limits to capitalism. In this article, Lenin extends Marx's Scheme by going back to a situation where there is a natural economy – non-market subsistence production, with such surplus as there is traded by barter. Then he shows how, as this natural economy is broken up by the introduction of market exchange, a parallel home market emerges. Peasants become prosperous. There is migration to the city for employment in factories. (Economists today know this as the Lewis Model of Development, after the Nobel laureate W. Arthur Lewis's classic article in 1954.)[29] Thus the 'peasantry' is no longer homogeneous; it is differentiated.

Since many who oppose globalization nowadays say, as the Narodniks did, that the switch to cash crops from subsistence crops ruins the Third World peasantry, it may be worth quoting Lenin's conclusion. Lenin begins by quoting from Danielson: 'Being in need of money, the peasant enlarges his crop area excessively and is ruined.' Then comes his answer:

> But only the prosperous peasant can enlarge his crop area, the one who has seed for sowing, and a sufficient quantity of livestock and implements. *Such* peasants (and they, as we know, are the minority) do, indeed, extend their crop areas and

> expand their farming to such an extent that they cannot cope with it without the aid of hired labourers. The majority of peasants, however, are quite unable to meet their need for money by expanding their farming, for they have no stocks, or sufficient means of production. *Such* a peasant, in order to obtain money, seeks 'outside employment', i.e., takes his labour-power and not his product to the market. Naturally, work away from home entails a further decline in farming, and in the end the peasant leases his allotment to a rich fellow community member who rounds off his farm and of course does not himself consume the product of the rented allotment, but *sends* it to the market. We get the 'impoverishment of the people', the growth of capitalism and the expansion of the market. But that is not all. Our rich peasant, fully occupied by his extended farming, can no longer produce as hitherto for all his needs, let us say footwear; it is more advantageous for him to buy it. As to the impoverished peasant, he too, has to buy footwear; he cannot produce on his farm for the simple reason that he no longer has one. There arises a demand for footwear and a supply of grain, produced in abundance by the enterprising peasant . . .

Lenin then goes on similarly to analyse the decline of handicrafts and growth of markets. Then:

> Again, we get the impoverishment of people, the growth of capitalism and the expansion of the market; a new impetus is given to the further development and intensification of the social division of labour. Where will that movement end? Nobody can say, just as nobody can say where it began, and after all that is not important. The important thing is that we have before us a single, living organic process, the process of development of commodity economy and the growth of capitalism. 'Depeasantizing' in the countryside shows us the beginning of this process, in genesis, its early stages; large-scale capitalism in the town shows us the end of the process, its tendency. Try to tear these phenomena apart, try to examine them separately and independently of each other, and you will not get your argument to hang together; you will be unable to explain either one phenomenon or the other, either the impoverishment of the people or the growth of capitalism.[30]

So there were no limits of effective demand on capitalism's growth. Later on, the proletariat may grow in size along with capitalism, and dig capitalism's grave. But for Lenin in the 1890s, capitalism was the *progressive* option, although he was fully aware of its impoverishing effects. Marx's views on free trade may also be interesting. In *Economic Romanticism*, Lenin cites a speech Marx made on free trade in Brussels in January 1848.

> The whole line of argument amounts to this: *Free Trade increases productive forces.* If industry keeps growing, if wealth, if the productive power, if, in a word, productive capital increases the demand for labour, the price of labour and consequently the rate of wages rise also. *The most favourable condition of the worker is the growth of capital. This must be admitted.* If capital remains stationary, industry will not merely remain stationary, but will decline, and in this case, the worker will be the first victim. He goes to the wall before the capitalist. And in the case where capital keeps growing, in the circumstances which we have said are the best for the worker, what will be his lot? He will go to the wall just the same.[31]

Yet despite the last sentence, Marx supported free trade – as did Lenin in this pamphlet – because it led to a development of the productive forces. This is because:

> instead of comparing capitalism with some abstract society as it should be (i.e., fundamentally with a utopia), Marx compared it with the *preceding stages* of the social economy, compared the different stages of capitalism as they successfully replaced one another and established the fact that the productive forces of society develop thanks to the development of capitalism.[32]

This is what I call classical Marxism, a nineteenth-century perspective forged in an era of globalization, when capitalism was spreading to new territories and old countries, when the state never sought to regulate the economy, and when capital and labour were globally mobile. While Marxists debated the future of capitalism, even in the face of what was in fact one of its most vigorous expansions, they did not seek the reversal of its development, or even its slowing-down. The hope for Marxists was in the acceleration of capitalist development, the sooner for it to reach its end. Thus there is no Romanticism either in *The Communist Manifesto* or, fifty years later, in Lenin's writing about the 'deserted village': handicrafts abandoned, the peasants migrating to become factory workers. History was moving forward, and Marxists were riding along with it.

And then suddenly, the Cunning of Reason – as Hegel would put it – struck again. As it had done before during the Dark Ages for Europe, History decided not to go forward. The First World War started in August 1914, and the wheels of History did the unexpected. For the next seventy-five years (1914–89), the short twentieth century, neither capitalism nor Marxism was the same.

7
War and Revolution

The First World War broke out on 4 August 1914. It altered, in a fundamental way, virtually everything that had been taken for granted on all sides in European life during the previous hundred years. It shocked a generation of intellectuals who had put their faith in reason and gradual progress – people such as Bertrand Russell and Bernard Shaw, for whom 1914 became the entry into a world of unreason.[1] But it also stopped and reversed the course of globalization. Capitalism had enjoyed unrestricted access across the world – with capital and labour mobility, with free trade spreading its reach, and the Gold Standard to maintain monetary discipline. This was the liberal order. Some people were arguing right up to the eve of war that free trade would render wars impossible.

The war was to disillusion liberal utopians like Norman Angel. Capitalism was to go into a different phase for the next seventy-five years, but few could foresee that. No one had actually thought that a war would break out. After all, the two Moroccan crises – 1905 and 1911 – had been contained by diplomacy, and German ambitions in North Africa had been checked. There had been a build-up of naval power and of armaments. We now know that the German army had planned the war, right down to the last detail of railway timetables. Yet the war was not foreseen.

The Marxists had the best reason for not being surprised. There had been a debate about imperialism and war, and how socialist parties should deal with it, for many years. At the Stuttgart Conference of the Socialist International in 1907, there was an antiwar resolution more radical than the SPD would have liked, but more to the taste of the new socialist wave coming from the East – Rosa Luxemburg representing Poland, and Lenin fresh from the 1905 Russian Revolution. The French socialists argued that a future war should be converted into a workers' insurrection. The SPD had just lost several seats in the 1907 election, because the German public was in one of its jingoistic moods. The revisionist wing of the SPD wanted no truck with French insurrection, denouncing it as Sorrelian anarchism. Yet when the debate ended, the resolution was fairly radical:

> If the outbreak of War threatens, it is the duty of the workers and their parliamentary representatives in the countries involved, with the aid of the International Bureau, to exert all their efforts to prevent the War by means of concerted action. They shall use the means which appear the most appropriate to them, and which will necessarily vary according to the sharpness of the class struggle and the general political situation. If War should nevertheless break out, they have the duty to work for its speedy termination, and to exploit with all their might the economic and political crisis created by the War to arouse the population and to hasten the overthrow of Capitalist rule.[2]

This was the Internationalist line, yet it allowed for particular national differences. Rosa Luxemburg wanted the weapon of mass strike to be explicitly mentioned, as did the French, but the Germans kept it to 'the means which appear the most appropriate'. Yet there was to be no co-operation with the war effort. Workers had no fatherland. They would use a war to hasten the collapse of capitalism.

But once hostilities commenced, this internationalism evaporated. The biggest shock to the International was the behaviour of the SPD parliamentary delegation. It was well known that the revisionists and the trade-union elements were pragmatic and willing to work with the system, and they formed the majority in the SPD parliamentary delegation. By then in the 1912 election it was the largest single group, with 110 out of 445 seats obtained with four million votes. The SPD slogan was always 'For this System, not a penny, not a man'. Its Erfurt Programme was dedicated to opposing the government at every step, but especially rejecting every military budget. But all along the way, especially after its setback in 1907, the SPD had to face the dilemma of any parliamentary socialist party. If the electorate wanted a jingoistic response, could a party which wanted to win seats continue resisting? Could a party which aimed to capture votes afford to appear antinational?

The SPD had on its left the very radical elements represented by Karl Liebknecht, Rosa Luxemburg, Franz Mehring and Klara Zetkin. At the centre left was Kautsky, still hoping for an evolutionary parliamentary path to socialism.[3] But the rest were willing to work for immediate gains – the trade unionists – or did not even want the system to destroy itself – the revisionists. This uneasy coalition had been glued together by the two-speed Erfurt Programme: reform immediately, but ultimately revolution. The SPD played out all the scenarios that parliamentary socialist parties have experienced since; it was simply the first. There was the usual battle between the active party and the bureaucracy, between the headquarters and the local branches, between leadership and the Conference, with each side accusing the other of sectarianism and preaching unity.

But while the peace lasted, elections were fought, and the size of the SPD's parliamentary delegation rose steadily. It had 81 seats by 1903, went down to 43 in 1907 and up again to 110 in 1912. Yet the SPD remained a pariah in German society. The conservatives and the agrarian centre party, the national liberals and the progressives – all were ultimately for the system, and only the SPD was against. As the conservative Herr von Oldenburg auf Januschan said in the Reichstag to ringing applause: 'The King of Prussia and the German Emperor must always be in a position to say to any lieutenant, "Take ten men and shoot the Reichstag".'[4] He meant, of course, the socialists in the Reichstag.

It is difficult to say whether the parliamentary tactics of the SPD, despite all the contradictions and compromises, would have succeeded in getting them into power. As the first and the largest parliamentary socialist party sworn to Marxism, the SPD raises fascinating counterfactual questions at this juncture.

The war confronted the party with all its dilemmas in one go. When it came to the crunch, the SPD voted unanimously for military credits, the first time it had ever done so, on 4 August 1914. By previous agreements, the SPD always voted as a bloc after intraparty discussions. There was a majority for approval, but a strong vocal minority argued that a yes vote violated the Erfurt Programme as well as the Stuttgart Conference Resolution against a war. The shock of the SPD's vote was felt among all the socialist parties across Europe. The vanguard Marxist party had gone chauvinist. European socialism would never be the same again. Marxist parties were split for evermore.

There has been an endless debate about why they did it, but since then we have learnt that proletarian internationalism is never practical politics, and that being a parliamentary political party is a synonym for compromise. At that time, the sense of shock and betrayal was palpable. During the course of the war, the SPD broke up, and in January 1917 the Left – radical and centre – started their own Independent Social Democratic Party (USPD). Kautsky joined, with Luxemburg and Liebknecht. When the war ended in German defeat, and a republic was declared, the first president was Friedrich Ebert, formerly a General Secretary of the SPD and a pillar of its right wing. In the uprising which ensued, his former comrades, Luxemburg and Liebknecht, were bludgeoned to death by military officers. By then the Russian Revolution had happened, and German Communist Party had been formed.

Before I come to that other major effect of the First World War – the Russian Revolution – let me quote what Carl Schorske says in his classic work on the SPD about why the delegation voted as it did:

> The decision of the Social Democratic Reichstag delegation to vote the War credits was taken in an atmosphere somewhat reminiscent of that of another August 4 – that of 1789, when the nobility of France, seized by a paroxysm of fear, voted away its privileges and, in effect, publicly renounced its own principles of social organization. As in 1789, the hard facts of political life – above all the threat of force against the nobility – operated to strengthen the left wing of the second estate, so in 1914, the cold facts favoured the right wing of the German Social Democratic Party.[5]

The disarray of the Second International was total. In France, Jean Jaurès, a pacifist socialist, was assassinated for holding on to his antiwar principles. In the UK, the fledgling Labour Party, neither Marxist nor pacifist, joined in the cheering, with only Ramsay MacDonald among its leaders holding out. The contradictions between global capitalism and the various individual national economies could not be resolved. Capitalism regressed into a cluster of separate national economies at war for the present but failing, when peace came, to revert to a global system. This was the phase of 'capitalism in one country' which was to be the twentieth-century pattern. It was deglobalization with a vengeance.

Isolation was forced upon the German economy, almost from the first day. Germany was very dependent on raw-material imports, and did not have an imperial network on which it could rely. Walter Rathenau, a dynamic young businessman, proposed to the German military authorities on the second day of the war that they should allocate the scarce raw materials in a properly co-ordinated way. He was immediately absorbed into the German war machine, and became its first central planner. The idea of planning was not unknown to economists; the Italian economist Vilfredo Pareto had written about a fully planned economy, and another Italian economist, Enrico Barone, had taken Pareto's speculations much further. It is a story to which I shall revert later. Rathenau's efforts inaugurated a practical experience in planned allocation of resources.

The idea that an economy could be controlled like a machine was foreign to much of nineteenth-century thought. Marx never discussed it with any seriousness, since for him, the economy was a self-organizing process. Some day, 'society' would run the economy in a conscious way, but that was in the future.

Classical and neoclassical political economy treated the economy as a self-regulating organism. Socialists had written about establishing isolated self-governing communities. Charles Fourier had plans for a series of publicly owned factories (phalansteries), but it was not clear how resource allocation would take place. Marx had heaped ridicule on Proudhon's anarchist plan for a labour-value-based economy. The market was a very sophisticated allocation system, inequitable though its results might be.

The Germans called their experience of a planned war economy 'war socialism'.[6] Here was the first example of an advanced economy run consciously from the centre: what socialists had spoken of in vague terms was alive and concrete. German experience of war socialism attracted great attention in Russia, especially when Russian socialists became enamoured of the German achievement. Lenin read about the German war economy in some articles by Yuri Larin while he was in exile in Zurich during the war. His admiration for the German experience was to shape his thinking later, when he came to power in Russia after November 1917. More of that below.

But the other belligerent powers also began to think about some central co-ordination of production plans and allocation of scarce materials. Trade unions were welcomed through the portals of power for the first time. There was continuous full employment. The Gold Standard was suspended. Economies had to be run by committees of bureaucrats, army staff and businessmen. International trade was severely disrupted, and capital movements dried up.

A new logic of economy was suddenly born. There had been wars before and armies had always been like planned economies. But this was total mass war: nothing could escape the war effort. Although business stayed in private hands, the market was no longer the logic of the economy. This was new territory. This was a new phase of capitalism.

In the middle of the war, two major events took place which changed the Western European focus of capitalism. The first event was America's entry into the war on the Allied side. Thus was born the Anglo-Saxon alliance which prevailed throughout the twentieth century. American personnel, resources and values began to assert their importance in the Old World. America never had feudalism, and its only imperial experience was the Spanish–American War. Its capitalism could not be regarded as mature and ripe for revolution. Indeed, European Marxists knew little about the USA, and did not factor it into their speculations. America's entry into European politics was to have a long-term influence on the dynamics of capitalism. The other totally unexpected event was the February Revolution in Russia, which then became the October (November) Revolution, when the Bolsheviks seized power from the Kerensky government. The Russian Revolution was reminiscent of the 1789 French one. It was a sudden coup. The powerful and aristocratic Tsardom was toppled, but instead of a liberal democracy or an oligarchy, Russia got a Marxist party in power. This was as much a surprise to the Bolsheviks as it was to their enemies.

But there was no prospect that the Bolsheviks would hold on to power. They themselves had thought that it would take a revolution in Germany, and perhaps France as well, to sustain a Russian revolution. But the war was not yet over. Germany imposed a humiliating settlement on Bolshevik Russia, and famine stalked the land. Yet the Bolsheviks were convinced of their premiss that Germany must rise in revolt. And so it did, after German defeat in 1918.[7] There was a naval mutiny in Kiel, and the dissident Spartacist faction within the Independent Social Democratic Party, led by Luxemburg and Liebknecht, joined the revolutionary German forces. The Bolsheviks were willing to send wagonloads of scarce food grains to Germany to sustain the Revolution. It did not stop there. There were uprisings in Austria and in Hungary, where socialist parties of a Marxist bent came to power. There was unrest in Northern Italy. For a while in late 1918–early 1919, it looked as if it was 1848 again, and Europe was fulfilling Marxist prophecies.

Everywhere there were workers' councils, sometimes workers' and soldiers' councils – soviets, as they were called during the 1905 Russian Revolution, and again in 1917. And then it all ended as suddenly as it had started. The German, the Austrian and the Hungarian revolutions died out. By late 1919, only the Bolsheviks were still in power. What was more, they survived a blockade imposed by Western powers and a civil war in the midst of famine.

The survival of the Russian Revolution, with its Bolshevik leadership, profoundly altered the shape of the twentieth century.[8] For one thing, authority in Marxist matters passed from the SPD to the Bolsheviks. The High Church of Marxism established by Kautsky now became the much more intolerant Calvinist one of Lenin and, later, Stalin. Marx's word became infallible even as it was distorted. From being a giant yet imperfect intellectual, Marx became deified. Criticism of Marx, which had been widespread in the thirty years before the First World War, was outlawed in Marxist parties. All Marxist parties had to belong to the Third International founded by the Bolsheviks, and all had to sign up to certain basic tenets. From being parliamentary parties with a long-term revolutionary perspective, Marxist parties became antidemocratic, conspiratorial and centralized. That was Lenin's model of a revolutionary party, and that was what had worked in Russia, so it had to work everywhere else.

But the question for Marxists of that generation was: how could Russia have a socialist revolution, given the backward state of its capitalism? How could a revolution so contrary to the predictions of Marxist theory be labelled Marxist? How could there be a proletarian revolution in a country with only a fledgling proletariat? Was Lenin's revolution not a refutation of Marx rather than its fulfilment? If there was to be a Marxist revolution in a backward capitalism, were the advanced countries off the hook, as it were? Or was the Russian Revolution an aberration, an accident of history?

It is easy from today's perspective, after the collapse of the Soviet Union, to dismiss these questions as of no importance whatsoever. Some may argue that if Marx's theory did not fail in 1917, it definitely did so in 1989. But the importance of suspending this hindsight is that much of our way of thinking about capitalism and socialism, about Marx and the market, has been profoundly influenced by the peculiarities of the Russian Revolution. Its occurrence, its survival, its enormities under Stalin and its later senescence under Brezhnev, have to be understood. So let me debate the nature of the Russian Revolution in what follows as if we did not know that the Soviet Union had collapsed. Shift your focus to, say, 1980. How can we comprehend the Russian Revolution?

The Russian Revolution: A Historic Miscarriage?

> [that] a Russian revolution, even if temporarily successful, would be an historical miscarriage, needs no further proof . . .
>
> (Trotsky, *The War and the International*, pp. 20–21, [cited in Cliff, *Lenin*, vol. 2, p. 21])

There is perhaps a never-ending debate on the nature of the Russian Revolution. 'The Revolution Betrayed' is the constant cry, but there is a great deal of disagreement on when, and by whom. Various explanations containing contingent, structural and historical reasons tracing the roots of the betrayal back several decades, if not centuries, have been advanced.

Those who wish that Russia were a parliamentary liberal (bourgeois, if you like) democracy locate the betrayal between February and October 1917, (old-style calendar). The weakness of the Tsar's previous commitment to the Duma, the fragility of the middle class, the slow growth of local government, the contingent failure of Kerensky or any number of ministers, the split in the Socialist Revolutionaries (SR: a peasants' party) and so on, can be advanced for this view. There is a large body of White Russian debate along these lines.

Another variant is to shift the date to December 1917, with the blame to be laid on the Bolsheviks' rejection of the Constituent Assembly's decision. Here, those who aspired to a parliamentary social democracy, the Mensheviks and the left SR, would join the debate. The Bolsheviks gained a slim majority in the Congress of Soviets, late in October 1917, but did not retain this in December. They should have resigned then. This may be so, but as we shall see below, anyone who knew the Bolsheviks should not have been surprised by the tenacity with which they stuck to power. However, it is only in the *ex post* context that this seems a crucial event. Neither the German nor the Hungarian socialist revolution lasted very long. There was no reason why the Bolsheviks should have had any greater luck. Indeed, this seems to have been the attitude of the other parties in the period immediately after October. They did not expect the Bolsheviks to last. The question remains: why did they survive? The key here is Lenin.

Six months previously, in April 1917, Lenin had entered Russia, and three months later he had to go into hiding. But the Bolshevik majority in the Congress of Soviets coincided with the collapse of the other arm of the dual government – the Cabinet resigned. The Winter Palace did not even need to be stormed (*pace* Eisenstein) – the Cabinet just shuffled off. *Ex ante,* that is, a month to a year, or even twenty years, previously – no one would have given the Bolsheviks much chance of success. The crucial difference the Bolsheviks made in this situation was that *once they won power, they knew how to hold on to it.* Lenin's writings in the period 1902–05 (*What Is To Be Done; Two Tactics of Social Democracy*) have been read mainly as the argument that a socialist party should be small and disciplined and conspiratorial, and that it should eschew the parliamentary path. Many people believe that this thesis is vindicated by Lenin's success in October 1917. But I should like to argue that winning the majority in the Petrograd Soviet had little to do with the Leninist model of the Party. The Bolsheviks had been recruiting to become a mass party in the changed circumstances post-February, thus repudiating the Leninist model, and gained increasing success until October. The membership of the Party, 24,000 in February 1917, increased tenfold by August 1917 to 240,000. Sverdlov, Party Chairman at that time, claimed 400,000 by 16 October, but there are doubts about this claim. In 1918, at the 7th Party Congress, he claimed 300,000.[9] The Party had lacked a centralized structure and discipline even as recently as July 1917, when it had got into an adventurist uprising in which it lost much prestige. In the general mêlée caused by the split in the provisional government, Kornilov's march on the capital and the pathetic response of the Cabinet, the Bolsheviks won majority support increasingly after July, and eventually in the Second Congress of Soviets.

No, the Bolsheviks did not win power by virtue of the Leninist party structure. The Leninist centralized apparatus helped them to *retain* power once they had won it. The tight discipline, the elite leadership concept, the constant requirement of total commitment to the party cause – all these helped the Bolsheviks to weather every storm from October 1917 to the end of the civil war (1921). They even survived the Kronstadt revolt[10] and the Left opposition. This was where Lenin's tightly knit party structure helped. Lenin kept control of Russia once he got a majority, just as he had done with the Russian Social Democratic Labour Party (RSDLP), when a single majority vote in a contest for the editorial boards of the Party journal *Iskra* was enshrined for ever by sheer ruthless attack on the other sides until they quit. The Mensheviks were, after all, the majority faction in the RSDLP membership in 1902, as later, but the Bolsheviks claimed to be the majority after winning that single vote.

For Leninists, the events of December 1917 do not matter. They are convinced that the October Revolution was a proletarian revolution, and that the first workers' state (dictatorship of the proletariat) came into being then. They see it as Marx's vision of 1848 vindicated, thanks to Lenin's genius for political organization. Teleology becomes difficult to avoid. The split in an obscure Russian party in 1902 acquires worldwide significance; seeds of the later defeat for the Mensheviks are sown there; Lenin's correctness in every aspect – economics, politics, philosophy – begins then, and lasts for ever.

It is this Leninist 'tendency' (interpretation?) that will concern us more in the context of our overall theme. This interpretation then has a further dimension. The more influential one – in the West, at least, since de-Stalinization – is the Trotsky interpretation. This says that the Revolution was betrayed by Stalin in the late 1920s: by the doctrine of Socialism in One Country; by the substitution of Party bureaucracy for worker activists (substitutism); by the break-up of the coalition between workers and peasants (though this last is underplayed); by Stalin's collectivization policy. This view was a minority one during the years up to 1956: the 'Trotskyites' were said to have been traitors to the Revolution. The majoritarian view was that, despite everything, Stalin was still leader of the socialist camp; the Soviet Union was still *the* socialist country; the

Russian example was the strategy (the Leninist strategy) to be followed by other socialist parties. The purges unnerved a few; a few more went with the Molotov–Ribbentrop Pact; but for each person who left, the Popular Front and the 1941–45 phase of the Second World War brought more into the Communist Party. It was this strength that brought the PCF into sharing power in France, and even made the American Communist Party respectable in the USA during the war. While the Cold War restored the prewar status quo of Communist Parties in the Anglo–US axis, the Party retained its respect on the Continent. It was not the Cold War, nor the McCarthyite witch-hunts, but Khrushchev's speech to the 20th Party Congress that broke the majority view. By and large, the Communist Party as a serious political force was finished on the Left. Raphael Samuel has brilliantly recalled what it meant to be a Communist in the days before 1956.[11] Today, it would be impossible to re-create that. The Leninist torch in Western Europe passed to the Trotskyist groups after 1956. They now attracted those who would claim to be the true inheritors of Marx and Lenin. Leninism, the Third International and the years since 1917 have created a peculiar situation for European socialism: there is no non-Bolshevik Marxist movement left. If you're not a Leninist, you're not a Marxist.

The Trotskyist Story

The Troskyists had to perform a neat trick in order to win the allegiance of radical youth, and to hegemonize the New Left – to be able to inherit the virtue of the Russian Revolution and Lenin's mantle without incurring the blame for the horrors which Khrushchev admitted, which were known to the West anyway. This was done by taking up Trotsky's cry of 'The Revolution Betrayed'. But how could the Revolution be betrayed by an individual, however powerful? Surely historical materialism as a method demanded that a class analysis of the betrayal of the Revolution be carried out. How did bureaucratism gain strength? How could a workers' revolution degenerate into a Bonapartist disaster? Countless books, articles, pamphlets and polemics on this have been offered. Factions have split; people have been expelled from mini-versions of the Stalinist Party. Endless apologia still fill the pages of journals and books.

If you grant that what happened in 1917 was a workers' revolution, you have to explain how the working class lost its strength and its revolutionary tradition sufficiently, and rapidly enough, for the Revolution to have been betrayed ten (give or take a few) years later. One version which was crucial in capturing the New Left for Trotskyism was in Issac Deutscher's biography of

Trotsky.[12] Apart from creating Trotsky as a great Romantic figure of the Russian Revolution ('the prophet', exploiting Trotsky's Jewishness to advantage in the post-Holocaust years), Deutscher offered his own explanation of the degeneration of the Revolution: that while the original working class which made the Revolution was solidly socialist/Marxist, the civil war took its toll. Members of the working class – urbanized for a generation or more, educated into socialist politics by the Bolsheviks, fully conversant with the theoretical debates and tough in their revolutionary practice – occupied key positions in the new government, but the civil war caused irreversible damage: through hunger, through death in combat, through sheer fatigue. This exhausted, decimated working class was ripe for defeat by the bureaucratic forces of Stalin. The new working class had been recruited from among the peasantry, and had no immersion in working-class culture, no experience of trade-union struggles, no knowledge of theory and no stomach for revolutionary practice. Thus they could be made passive in the face of Stalin's corruption of the original Leninist revolution. Thus, by winning physical permanence as a workers' state in defeating the White counter-revolution, the Russian Revolution lost its soul.

This is an attractive thesis, because it blames the degeneration on an external factor, agreed on all wings of the Left to be evil – the White Russians. It also has a Romantic air. The brave, hardy workers died defending the Revolution and, in so doing, lost the cause they died for. It avoids the issue of anything internal to the Revolution. Lenin and Trotsky appear as above criticism, since it is the civil war that is the culprit. The rise of the secret police, the militarization of trade unions, the manipulation – if not the closure – of debate in the Party after the opposition had been silenced, the very practice of centralizing power in the Politburo that made way for Stalin, the many tergiversations of Trotsky in the period between Lenin's death and his exile – all these are left unanalysed by this version of events. The critiques by the Left opposition and the Left anarchist groups of the shift of policy towards greater centralization in factories as much as in the political party are ignored in this analysis. It is too neat, too convenient.

This interpretation of Deutscher can be supplemented by others, but there has always been another interpretation. Just as the frailty of the liberal-democratic impulse is blamed on the absence of the middle class, the frailty of the social-democratic impulse is traced to the absence or the small size of the working class. How could Russia move on to socialism from such a weak capitalist base? The working class was numerically small and concentrated. How could one hope that in the absence of a mature capitalism, which Marx took to be the necessary precondition for socialism, Russia could have socialism? Only the socialist pretensions and protestations of the petty-bourgeois Bolshevik leadership, it is said, persuaded people into thinking that Russia was a workers' state. This was, by and large, the Menshevik line, and to some extent it was also reflected in the critique of the October Revolution by the moderate faction of the German USPD (Karl Kautsky) as well as the Far-Left faction (Rosa Luxemburg).[13]

This is the classical (that is, pre-Lenin) Marxian model of the transition to socialism. Capitalism goes away in the fullness of time, when its relations of production – wage labour, privately owned means of production, production for profit and accumulation to increase profit and lower values – no longer contribute to advancing the forces of production – that is, productivity growth. Any premature seizure of power by the proletariat in conditions of scarcity, in conditions where the law of value is still binding, results not in socialism but in distorted development. This classical view was certainly held by Lenin in his controversies with the Narodniks in the 1890s. In this view, the transition to socialism is a long process, expected to take 'decades, if not generations'. In the meantime, until it exhausted its potential, capitalism, despite its antagonistic contradictions, remained a progressive mode as far as the Marxist was concerned. This is why the Russian Marxists were against the Narodnik theory of jumping over the intermediate phase of capitalism and constructing socialism on the basis of collective landownership in Russia's countryside.

But the problem with this argument is that it does not explain what happened in October 1917 and, even more so, why the Bolsheviks, however fragile their claim to power then, were able to hold on to it through civil war, famine, and economic breakdown. Why was there no serious opposition to the Bolsheviks in Petrograd until the Kronstadt revolt in 1921?

The explanation for the Bolsheviks' success lies precisely in the small size of the working class. It was not only small but also highly concentrated in a few urban centres, not mature in its experience of open debate and legally free association (as the German working class was), which made the Bolshevik political strategy of a centralized party feasible. It was not, however, this small working class that gave the depth of support to the Bolsheviks. That would hardly have been enough. It was the peasantry, both in the countryside and in the cities in soldiers' uniform, which supported the Bolsheviks. The October Revolution was a peasant revolution led by a Marxist party which could see revolutionary potential only in the working class. When the revolution which brought the Party to power happened, it could understand this only as a workers' revolution.

It is necessary to go over some familiar ground if we are to understand that the coming to power of the Bolsheviks (i.e. their gaining a majority in the Second All-Russian Congress of Soviets and the putsch which sent the Cabinet packing on the eve of the opening of the Second Congress) was a contingent event, but their ability to hold on to power and retain support was a result of the nature of the working class, the character of the Russian peasantry, and the structure of the Leninist Party.

What happened in February 1917 was a bourgeois revolution, with worker and peasant support. But the bourgeois parties could not retain support, since they would not meet the peasants' demand for land. Nor could they keep control of the workers as they asserted their rights in the newly created free environment. In theory, with Menshevik and SR support, the bourgeois parties could have formed a stable coalition, but they had to contend with the urgent demands made by the wartime conditions and the Tsarist opposition as exemplified by Kornilov in July. To retain power, they needed soldiers' support, and these soldiers – mostly peasants – wanted peace as well as land.

After July 1917, the Bolsheviks moved into a majority position among workers, and by promising land and peace they won support in the soldiers' and peasants' soviets. Their policy of land, bread and peace, with elements of the SR programme, did the trick. The depth of working-class support for the Bolsheviks – crucial between July and October in St Petersburg – did not persist. Even in Moscow, the Bolsheviks found that it took four days in late October to gain control. As the hardships of the civil war began to bite, the Mensheviks and the left anarchists gained considerable support, with the Bolsheviks losing among the workers steadily after mid-1918, as industries declined and unemployment rose. Disenchanted workers left the Bolshevik Party. It was the Bolsheviks' ability to seize the moment in October 1917, and capitalize on it ever after, that was crucial.

The argument that the peasantry was crucial to the continuance of Bolshevik power has been made before. One way to look at the nature of the Revolution would be to see who gained from it, whose 'entitlements' changed most dramatically as a result. If we do this, it is striking how uneven the gain is as between peasants and workers. The peasants immediately gained land; the number of landless declined (one of the reasons for the failure of the poor peasant committees [*kombedy*] set up by the Bolsheviks to improve the mobilization of food in the countryside in 1918) and the number of smallholders and middle peasants increased. The peasantry had no reason to doubt that the White armies would take away their newly won land. Now that they had their land (which fundamentally improved wealth distribution in the countryside), the peasantry's struggle with the government was about the amount of food they could sell and the price at which they could sell it. During the years 1918 to 1920, the government tried to force delivery of food grains to the army and the cities. The army was provided for, but as far as the cities were concerned, the public distribution system did not provide the bulk of even the reduced ration. It was the open market in the cities, and the workers' private attempts at foraging in the countryside near the cities, which provisioned the towns. The peasants successfully held out by reducing their plantings, by stockpiling food, and so on, until the end of the civil war, when the policy of compulsory delivery was abandoned. By 1921 the peasantry had successfully translated their support for the Bolsheviks into real economic gains: private landownership on a wide scale, and a free market in food grains.

This was in stark contrast to the workers' position. Despite the claim that it was the workers' state, the workers did not gain in either economic or political terms. The decree to establish workers' control in factories was passed soon after the Revolution. Yet after the Treaty of Brest-Litovsk in February 1918, the workers began to lose their special position. One-man management was favoured over workers' control, and factory committees were disbanded by the end of 1918. The workers' right to manage industries – either at factory level, or through trade unions at a central level – was never again conceded. A last attempt on behalf of trade unions was made by the Workers' Opposition in March 1921, but this was defeated. As Lenin argued, it is:

> the party as the vanguard of the proletariat which leads the non-Party worker masses . . . to enable them eventually to concentrate in their hands the administration of the whole national economy. Why have a party, if industrial management is to be appointed . . . by the trade unions nine-tenths of whose members are non-Party workers?[14]

The workers also suffered a considerable reduction in their trade-union privileges. In the celebrated debate on trade unions in 1921, Lenin's compromise won against the syndicalist view of workers' opposition and Trotsky's proposal to militarize the unions. Yet early in the new year of 1922, unions were statized, as Trotsky had proposed. The working class was nationalized by the Bolsheviks.

In terms of income, the workers suffered inasmuch as by 1922–23 their real wage was only 50 per cent of its 1913 level. There was growing unemployment and closure of factories in the 1918–23 period. While workers who were Party members identified strongly with the state, and even manned the second-rank offices, there was a decline in workers' membership of the Bolshevik Party. The workers' many grievances came to a head in early 1921, and culminated in the revolt of the sailors in the Kronstadt. But while peasant resistance led to concessions to the peasantry, the workers' resistance led to further control of urban areas by the Party. After the debate on unions at the 10th Party Congress in March 1921, dissidence was outlawed and the Workers' Opposition was banned. The small size of the proletariat made it easy for the Bolsheviks to crush any resistance. The peasants won because there were more of them.

Thus an examination of who gained and who lost from the Revolution would show that the peasants definitely gained what they wanted, and they increased their gains subsequently until by 1921 they had everything they wanted – land and a free market for food grains. They still lacked any industrial goods they could spend their money on; nevertheless, their gains were solid. The growth of the bureaucracy in the government and the Party obviously benefited the urban middle class, which had not necessarily supported the Bolsheviks, but knew from long experience how to turn almost any situation to their advantage. The workers were the one group which lost massively all the time, while they were being told that it was a dictatorship of the proletariat. Their loss was not only temporary, not only confined to the civil war. They did not make up their gains under the NEP (New Economic Policy), either. They did not gain because they had no numerical strength. Their concentration in a few urban areas did not help – partly because of the rapid drop in employment after June 1918, and partly because it was precisely this concentration which made it easier for the Bolsheviks to control them through their soviets, their trade unions and their Party branches.

There is no reason to attribute cynicism to the Bolsheviks. They were convinced that they represented the working class, which was in the vanguard of the Revolution. They had always operated on behalf of the workers, with little machinery for continuous consultation. Before coming to power, they knew from their support in strikes, lockouts, and so on, how strong their support was. After the Revolution, the Bolsheviks' first priority was to retain power in the Party at all costs. Their majority on 26 October 1917 gave them their mandate for ever. They sincerely thought that they represented the workers until, in the course of the civil war, the working class was decimated by war and economic decline. In 1921 the Bolsheviks found that they were leading a workers' movement with no workers, but they were used to working without continuous feedback, without elections and all their paraphernalia. So they carried on after 1921. The Party became a party of apparatchiks who formed the bulk of the membership. No subsequent event could alter this basic transformation.

It is therefore possible to argue that the February Revolution was a bourgeois one which was under pressure from peasants, soldiers and workers. The Bolsheviks had the cohesion and the determination to capitalize on the moment when the majority in the Congress of Soviets was in their favour. Once in power, they genuinely believed (a) that it was vital for them to hold on to power; and (b) that their Party represented the working class. In order to hold on to power, they had to placate the peasantry – this they did by providing them with substantial economic gains. They never abandoned their presumption to represent the working class even when, on their own analysis, the Party was losing working-class support. In presuming that, as a Marxist party, it was the vanguard of the working class, and that the working class, as a (the only) revolutionary class, must have made the Revolution, the Bolsheviks reflected deeply held Marxist beliefs. Thus, even as the working class disintegrated before their very eyes, they never wavered in their belief that they led a workers' state.

The material reality was otherwise. The peasantry – together with the soldiers, who belonged to the same class – provided the bulk of the muscle for the Revolution and the civil war, though the workers were more articulate and visible in the capital. The peasantry, having got what they wanted, consolidated their gains, and were challenged only after 1929. The continuously active element in the political struggle to strengthen the state was provided by the Party, which had an increasingly middle-class careerist membership even by 1921.

The importance of characterizing the October Revolution as a peasant revolution with the ostensible leadership of a Marxist party is that one need not agonize about the workers' state being corrupted or becoming degenerate. From the beginning, it was not a workers' state in any material sense. Except for the ideology of the party in power, nothing made the regime in 1917–23 or thereafter a *workers'* state. Nobody betrayed it. One can only speculate as to why the belief that it was a workers' state persisted despite self-acknowledged contradiction in fact. But there is a sound economic basis for the preponderance of the peasantry. The civil war put more power in the hands of the peasantry than they would have had in normal times. When there is war and famine (partly caused, as is often the case, by war), food becomes pivotal, and the producer/seller of food has a lot of economic clout. When the producers of food form the bulk of the population, and provide the manpower for the army, their political power as a class can be formidable. As a country, Russia was able to survive throughout the civil war on a volume of industrial production only one-sixth of the prewar level; it could not enjoy the same luxury with food. The industrial proletariat was materially less important as well as numerically smaller than the peasantry. The workers may have been important as a political group to be mobilized in the capital during February–October 1917, but in economic terms, Russia could fight a civil war without their economic contribution – and, moreover, did so. (This is not to detract from the role workers played as soldiers when they were recruited into the army, nor to deny that a few groups – railway workers, for example – made a crucial contribution.) As time went on, the working class could be increasingly ignored.

The fact that the industrial sector in Russia was small even at its full production level (as of, say, 1914) is not only undeniable, but formed an important part of Lenin's analysis that the underdevelopment of Russian capitalism was a major factor in applying Marx's theory to Russia. His debates with the Narodniks in the 1890s made this clear. After 1917, he returned to this analysis with the need to industrialize Russia rapidly – albeit by the state capitalist route. In this respect, Lenin adhered to the classical Marxian view that the extension of the capitalist mode was a progressive phenomenon. Of course, after the establishment of what was, in his view, a workers' state, the continuation of capitalist social relation – hierarchy of decision-making (one-man management); importance of economic (profit) calculation; Taylorism and other techniques (piecework) for maintaining a high rate of surplus-value; wage labour – had to be justified somewhat differently. This realization of the need to advance on the capitalist front economically, while the political context had shifted, did not occur until after Brest-Litovsk. For the first six months after October 1917, the Bolsheviks did try running the economy on the Paris Commune model – decentralized power in the factory committees, workers' control, maximum mass initiative and participation, and so on. But from March 1918 onwards, economic reality impinged, and Lenin reverted to the centralized management model.

His choice was dictated not only by the small size of the industrial sector but by its decimation as a result of war and revolution. Indeed, despite all the debates about management style, et cetera, industrial production did not revive until after the civil war. As it happened, it was the decision to go for planned industrialization on a massive scale in the second half of the 1920s that caused the first structural change in the Russian economy. By this time it was clear that it was the peasantry which held the surplus. If the industrial working class was to expand, some way had to be found to wrest this surplus from the hands of the peasants. Preobrazhensky's *New Economics* was explicit on this.[15] Even then, the First Five Year Plan was financed not from the surplus extracted from the peasantry, but by cutting the industrial real wage.

Collectivization of the peasantry was one way in which the ruling elite – the Party and the bureaucracy – could smash the political power of the peasantry. But the peasantry retaliated immediately with massive destruction of capital stock (livestock especially) and permanently low productivity. Thus, even if a higher *share* of the agricultural surplus could be extracted, the *size* of that surplus was permanently low. This meant that Soviet industrialization was permanently hampered by the problem of accumulation. It could be sustained only by forcing the industrial working class to accept a low real wage. To do this, it was essential that workers had no access to political power after displacing the peasantry from its powerful position.

Under the NEP, a Bukharinist alternative of development via an enriched peasantry and light consumer industries was proposed. After sixty more years of experience of economic development, it is obvious that only foreign loans/aid can underwrite such a course. In some ways, China under Deng Hsiao Ping shifted to a Bukharinist road after 1978, but it had a better agricultural performance under the communes to go on. But just at the time when it looked as if the blockade might be lifted, and Britain might establish economic relations (via a TUC visit to Russia in 1927), Stalin encouraged the Chinese Communist Party to attempt a seizure of power. The attempt failed, sending the Chinese Communists into the wilderness for twenty-odd years. It also stopped the thaw in Western relations with Russia. So foreign investment was out.

The pattern of Russian economic and political development was therefore determined by three interrelated factors: a weak industrial working class, a small Marxist party determined and able to retain power, and a large and powerful peasantry. With the peasantry's support and the workers' forbearance, the Party defeated the forces of the feudal and capitalist classes. It subjugated the workers successfully through the years of the civil war, so that by 1922 they had no political clout. The bureaucracy then subjugated the peasantry in the early 1930s via collectivization, but had to pay for it continually in terms of low real wages. As the industrial working class grew numerically, increasing repression was necessary to deny it any access to political power. But in such a case, how do we characterize the Russian economy and state in Marxian terms?

If we think of Marx's preface to the *Contribution* as outlining a general, universally valid historical scheme, there are several problems in interpreting the Russian developments. If we set up feudalism–capitalism–socialism as a simple chain, the question arises: what mode prevailed in Russia after 1917? It cannot have been capitalism, given the nationalization of the means of production and the ruling party's characterization of the state as a workers' state. It cannot have been socialism in any sense of the term, given the low economic and political position of the working class. There is no reason why we should fall into this trap. Capitalism in Russia was by no means fully developed. Indeed, it had hardly begun to transform the economy. By 1917 industrial capitalism had about 150 years of history, and even in such a brief period, a variety of ways of combining state action with private ownership had already been seen in the experiences of England, France, Germany, Scandinavia, the USA and Russia. The experience of German war mobilization during the First World War, which immensely impressed Lenin as a possible model for state capitalism, was another demonstration that capitalism and centralized state control were compatible – albeit for a short time, and under a bourgeois state.

But not only was the transition to capitalism variegated in form; there is no need to assume that movement in history is always forward – to 'higher' modes of production. There could be long periods of backward lapses in the progress of history. So, if capitalism is abolished, what follows need not be any form of socialism, whether or not the state degenerates. Those who assert that Russia became a workers' state in 1917 need to find a way of characterizing the non-capitalist Russian economy as some sort of post-capitalism mode. The Trotskyist view distinguishes between state capitalism as defined and defended by Lenin and state capitalism as established by Stalin – the former a transitional compromise; the latter a degeneracy. The difference between the two phases is hardly great enough to distinguish them. One has to assert that the state had altered its character in the meantime – degenerated in some sense – but this is begging the question. The social relations of production in Russian industry did not alter after March 1918. Since we have already argued that the political formation was not a workers' state to begin with, there is no need to distinguish between varieties of state capitalism.

Collectivization by reducing the agricultural surplus required greater sacrifice on the part of the working class, but even throughout the civil war, the sacrifices were made mainly by this class. There was a marginal improvement in the consumption levels of urban workers during NEP, but this was soon lost. It is quite possible to argue that the political compulsions of the battle against the peasantry by a bureaucratic ruling class led Russia to become trapped in an inefficient and backward form of state capitalism, with more repression and absolute exploitation of workers than the needs of accumulation require.

These speculations on the nature of state capitalism in Russia are germane to our discussion only as a way of drawing out the consequences of abandoning the labelling of post-revolutionary Russia as a workers' state. Once that notion is dropped, the controversy about the betrayal of the Revolution, the degeneration of the workers' state into a bureaucracy, and the changed form of state capitalism disappears. But – even more – the international context of developments in Europe after 1917 also becomes easier to understand. The Bolsheviks genuinely believed that theirs was only the first of many workers' revolutions in Europe, especially in Germany.

Indeed, Soviet foreign policy – as well as the strategy of the Third International in 1918–23 – was predicated on this happening. The collapse of the German Revolution has been blamed on – among many other factors – Comintern advice as well as the leadership of the KPD (Kommunist Partei der Deutschland). But inasmuch as the Russian Revolution was not a workers' but a peasant revolution (i.e. a revolution with majority support) in which a workers' vanguard party was put fortuitously at the head, why should we expect workers in more mature capitalist countries to foster a revolution? What material and ideological conditions were required for the European working class to rebel, and were they present in 1918? If the European working class failed to be revolutionary in 1914, why should it be so in 1918? This is the question we take up next.

The Failure of the European Proletariat

The European proletariat, according to Lenin's analysis, failed twice. First in 1914, by chauvinistically backing its masters in fighting the war, and the working-class leadership in voting war credits in various parliaments. Secondly, in 1918–23 it failed to take advantage of the collapse of the old regimes by establishing a workers' state – that is, following the Russian example. Let us analyse these two phases in their proper order.

If we read the history of the SPD from its Lassallean origins through the unification at Gotha and subsequently, it must come as a surprise that anyone, least of all an astute politician like Lenin, expected the SPD to oppose the German war effort.

The SPD had always had the vision of the transition to socialism as a very long process. Its parliamentary activities could be seen as having contributed to bringing about a peaceful bourgeois democratic revolution in Germany. Germany had not attained the bourgeois democratic stage by 1914. In this, it lagged far behind the USA, Britain and France. The aristocracy was very powerful as a ruling group in Germany, and the capitalist–industrialist was definitely a subordinate partner. Marx identified the date of the bourgeois revolution in France as 1830 and Britain as 1832 (preface to *Capital Volume 1*, second edition). But this is historically inaccurate. In terms of eliminating the political (much less the economic) presence of the aristocracy, France could be said to have achieved it only after four revolutions between 1789 and 1871. It was only the Third Republic which permanently brought about civilian political rule in France to the exclusion of aristocratic influence. Indeed, one could say that the Paris Commune, even as it was defeated, strengthened the hands of the bourgeoisie *vis-à-vis* the aristocracy. It is obvious now that this did not happen in Britain at any time during the nineteenth century. Although the franchise was extended in 1832, 1867 and 1884, it was only after 1911 and the reform of the House of Lords that one could claim containment (though not abolition) of the aristocratic influence in British politics. (The USA is an exception, since it starts as an agrarian/patrician republic and takes on a more popular form in the 1820s with the Jackson presidency.)

In Germany, on the other hand, the 1848 Revolution had failed to establish a bourgeois democracy. The rights of industrial workers were so limited that Lassalle even saw the Prussian monarch as the best bet for workers' advancement (this was less fanciful than may be thought today, given the moves Bismarck made not much later in inaugurating a paternalist welfare state, with workers' insurance, etc.). In the various separate Länder, voting rights were circumscribed. The Reich, once established, had a more progressive franchise than some regions. The SPD was in the forefront of the move to democratize the German Reich.

The universal hostility with which workers and their leaders were regarded by Bismarck and the ruling parties threw the SPD on to its own resources. It is hard to remember now that in the 1870s and 1880s there was a sort of apartheid between the working class and the rest of society. The workers were denied access to social and sports facilities, to banks, and so forth. This was not exclusive to Germany, merely more extreme there. It was this separation that made the SPD not just a party but a movement. It organized workers' clubs, their sports activities, their holidays; it printed their newspapers. Denied ordinary police protection for their meetings, the party had to organize its own volunteer guards.

The SPD's progress in the Reichstag, spectacular though it was, continued to be devalued by the aristocratic monopoly of power in Germany. The SPD constantly pushed for admission to the citadels of power on a basis of equality. It eschewed exclusionary politics as far as possible. Beyond retaining its unique hold on the working-class vote, it tried tentatively to get into a coalition with the Liberals, only to be thwarted by coalition politics played by the Right. The SPD – at least its majority – was never pacifist or antimilitaristic. Indeed, its policy on the defence budget was not for its reduction but for its financing by progressive taxation. It wanted army recruitment to be open to all, including workers. It wanted workers to be part of the Reich.

In Russia the situation was different. Parliamentary politics was even more of a sham, having begun only in 1905. The Bolsheviks had no hope of ever coming to power via the parliamentary route. They were way behind the Mensheviks and the SR in terms of popular support. They could take a defeatist, antimilitaristic stance, since nothing was affected by it. Even then, Lenin had to struggle hard to get his defeatist policies adopted as late as April 1917 by the St Petersburg Bolsheviks. The German situation was qualitatively different. The SPD was not the counterpart of the RSDLP (Bolshevik) but of the Mensheviks plus Bolsheviks plus various Legal Marxist elements, if we use the Russian analogy. It was always bigger, and had more popular support than all those factions put together in Russia.

Lenin and the few like-minded groups were in a minority even in the Zimmerwald meeting of the dissidents of the Second International in 1916 – that is to say, they were an extreme sect even among the dissidents. The split in the SPD had a similar structure. The majority SPD stayed together, helping the war effort just as the labour/social-democratic leadership of every other belligerent country did. The minority which split in 1917 and formed the USPD contained the Left Centrist factions of Kautsky and Bernstein, as well as the Liebknecht and Luxemburg group, which became the Spartacist League.

The war transformed the corporate status of labour leaders and, in consequence, of workers in all the belligerent countries. In Britain, tripartite arrangements between government, capitalists and workers became institutionalized. In Germany, the trade-union wing of the SPD actively collaborated in the war effort, and won admission to corporate status. The war, and the SPD's conduct in it, although anathema to the Bolsheviks, improved workers' corporate status in Germany. Once the Kaiser regime lost its credibility, because of the defeat, Germany witnessed, in November 1918, the completion of its bourgeois democratic revolution. But this bourgeois democratic revolution was effected by the

SPD, which was the only force capable of forming a government. This was Germany's equivalent of the February Revolution but, unlike in Russia, there was a strong bourgeoisie with a parliamentary tradition. At this juncture the SPD commanded overwhelming majority support, and achieved what it had been fighting for since 1891.

The November Revolution in Germany was precipitated by the workers. Many workers' and soldiers' councils were formed in the big cities. There was even a close parallel with the Russian situation inasmuch as the Berlin Federation of Workers' and Soldiers' Councils approved the arrangement (and the names of the Cabinet members) under which the SPD and USPD united to take power. At this juncture and later, the popular cry was 'unity', not the overthrow of capitalism. By the long-held doctrine of the SPD and the tenets of classical Marxism, the moment for a transition to socialism had not arrived. This could come only after a further maturing of capitalism, and only when the Socialist Party could carry the majority of the population voluntarily with it. This majoritarian democratic urge was as strong for Rosa Luxemburg and the Spartacist League as it was for the SPD/USPD. The disagreement was over whether this was the opportune moment. In Luxemburg's view, capitalism had destroyed itself, and had no further creative life left in it. If socialism were not launched, the alternative would be barbarism. But even socialism had to come with majority support in the workers' and soldiers' councils.

But while, in Russia, the bread, land and peace programme led to a coalition between workers and peasants/soldiers, this was not the case in Germany. Land for the peasantry – an SR plank in Russia, never a RSDLP one – was never on the SPD agenda. They saw that as the guarantee of a counter-revolutionary restoration, as in France after the French Revolution, not as a progressive step. Luxemburg criticized the Bolsheviks' precipitate moves in that direction precisely because she saw the dangers of an independent smallholding peasantry for a socialist government. All wings of the old SPD were agreed on this.

Even within the workers' councils, however, the SPD had a majority. The minority was the USPD, with the Spartacist faction commanding little support. The Spartacist League never emulated the rapid pace with which the Bolsheviks moved into a majority position in the All Russian Congress of Soviets between its first and second congress. The first All German Congress of Workers' Councils supported the SPD/USPD government overwhelmingly as late as early December 1918. Thus in late December, when the government mobilized the army to provoke a confrontation with the Spartacists, it had overwhelming support. The Spartacists were seen as a putschist sect. In the heady days following 9 January 1919, Liebknecht even thought briefly that they could take power. This was against Spartacist policy, and took people like Luxemburg and Leo Jogiches by surprise. But there was no chance, even in Berlin, that the Spartacists could take power. There was not even a Winter Palace to storm. The only building workers occupied for any length of time was the *Vorwärts* (SPD newspaper) building.

The defeat of the Spartacist uprising was bloody and swift. Luxemburg and Liebknecht were mercilessly killed. Many who defended *Vorwärts* were also killed. Within days the elections to the National Assembly were held, and the SPD/USPD won a majority. Although its popular following was much exaggerated later by the Third International, at the time of the uprising Karl Radek clearly thought the Spartacist League should have limited itself to certain demands far short of taking power. The martyrdom of Luxemburg and Liebknecht became useful for the Third International but they did not follow a Leninist strategy, nor did even the Bolsheviks think that a Russian-style uprising was on the cards. Indeed, the Bolsheviks pointed out to the Spartacists how, in July 1917, they had to discourage their hot-headed workers from rising up. Then Lenin had to go into hiding. His German counterparts were less fortunate.

Although January 1919 was an inopportune moment, the Third International still had a German revolution on the cards. The newly born KPD tried twice in the next four years, once in March 1921 and then in September 1923 – it failed both times. By the same token, when the Kapp putsch – much like the Kornilov affair – was threatened, the SPD and the trade unions were able to mobilize the workers in a general strike against the *coup d'état*. The Kapp putsch collapsed.

The Bolsheviks sincerely – and almost palpably – expected the German working class to start a revolution. Lenin's analysis, from the day of the outbreak of the war, of the conduct of the Second International demanded such an uprising. Even before the end of the war, during debate in the Bolshevik Central Committee on the Brest-Litovsk terms, some people, such as Bukharin and Radek were willing to follow a policy of no surrender on the grounds that to do anything else would be to harm the German Revolution. Lenin had to remind them that there was a distinction between an almost certain expectation that the revolution would come, and acting as if it had already happened.

In its first crucial test, this Leninist prediction failed. It is quite clear from the course of German history between November 1918 and September 1923 that the German working class was quite willing to defend the legitimacy of the state against Bonapartist coups by coming out overwhelmingly on strike. It is also clear that, unlike in Russia, workers and soldiers could not be said to be in alliance; their interests diverged. But it is also true that an attempt to overthrow the state by a left-wing putsch, as in Russia, had no chance of success. One question that arises from such an analysis is maybe to ask: why did the working class defend state legitimacy even in a post-defeat environment? Did it believe it had something worse to fear from the Kapp putsch, just as the Russian peasantry had something worse to fear from the White army? Was this consciousness of a stake in legitimacy a false consciousness, a manipulation by centralist leadership of the SPD, or was it something which was acquired over the years of maturing?

The Leninist analysis of the nature of the revolutionary potential in Europe and the tasks of the Marxist party was extremely narrow. In four words: follow the Russian road. Although many exhortations of flexibility, and so on, may be cited, the twenty-three conditions for adherence to the Third International laid it down that success would come only to parties modelled on Leninist lines: a highly centralized, elitist party, avoiding the compromises of parliamentary socialism. Indeed, the Russian road was thought to be so universally applicable, and in such detail, that Lenin expected the Hungarian Revolution to be born ready with workers' and peasants' soviets – with almost a restaging of the Second Congress of Soviets in Hungary, as in Russia. Germany was also expected to bristle with soviets, acquiring a Congress of Soviets along Russian lines. The qualitatively different structure and alliances of classes in other countries – or, rather, the fortuitous coming together of peasants, soldiers and workers – was totally unappreciated.

The Third International was thus saddled at the outset with an impatience about the imminence of workers' revolutions, and with a rigid certainty that the Russian Party was the only correct model. It is easy to blame the bureaucracy of the Third International (as Cliff does in *Lenin*, Volume 4) for mistakes, but the theory of revolution laid down – the Leninist theory – was itself at fault. It did not appreciate that it is only in a country with a small working class, untrained in democratic and open trade-union practices, and concentrated in a few urban centres, that the Leninist party can establish itself. Where the working class is large, and has experienced the give-and-take of struggle and compromise in trade unions and legal political participation, a workers' party can maintain predominance – if not a monopoly of workers' loyalty – only by being open, by being seen to deliver partial gains, by playing the political game. The German SPD was such a party. Given the history of working-class politics in Germany, a Leninist party could not be suddenly conjured up to take power. As already argued above, even in the Russian context, the Leninist party did not win power as a result of its organizational peculiarities. It came to power by accident, but retained it by design. For the KPD, the problem was one of gaining power, and a minority putsch was not a feasible way of doing so in a country where the state was seen as legitimate.

8
War and Imperialism (in theory and in practice)

The suddenness of the outbreak of the First World War affected everyone, not just the Marxists. It was a big shock for the liberals, whose faith in free trade as an antidote to war was rocked. As I mentioned above, in the case of intellectuals like Bertrand Russell and Bernard Shaw, the surge of unreason shocked them. It may have been only a thin veneer in middle-class Victorian behaviour, but there was a general belief in reason and the inevitability of gradual progress. In this sense, Marx was a part of this tradition inaugurated by the Enlightenment. The incorporation of intellectual ingenuity and scientific knowledge into technological innovations had led to the Industrial Revolution. The innovations just kept coming, science kept on advancing, and industrial growth continued – albeit interrupted – for the longest time the world had experienced. From about 1780 to 1914, capitalism had grown and spread. How could reason not be triumphant; how could progress be reversed?

If the nineteenth century believed in reason, the twentieth century opened the floodgates to the discovery of unreason. The roots lay in the past – indeed, in the nineteenth century itself. Nietzsche had already been putting his case to anyone who would pay attention. In Vienna, Sigmund Freud was exploring the subconscious. The roots of nationalism had been traced back to the myths of Antiquity in Germany as long ago as the early nineteenth century. The 'mob' had emerged as a new reality, thanks to the trebling of the population during the period of capitalist expansion in Europe. There was a fad for things oriental and ancient. Theosophists were fashionable, and Wagner evoked the old myths in his music.

Powerful forces had been unleashed by the French Revolution and the Napoleonic Wars that followed. The French Revolution gave birth to a civic nationalism which very soon took an imperialist form. But the French Revolution was also dedicated to reason, and socialism, which considers itself part of the march of reason and progress, was also born here. Reason and unreason became a dialectical duo from then on. The difference compared to earlier phases of history was that the revolution in technology – of transport, of industrial production, of warfare – equipped the forces of unreason with the tools of rational technology. In a way, the First World War was the first war of globalization, of advanced industrial capitalism. It was global in its reach; hence a world war rather than merely a European war. The mass mobilization of the people and the harnessing of the economy for a total war were also unusual. But so also was the destruction of cities and the slaughter of the youth of Europe, of Asia and of America.

This was a war of empires, and colonies were involved in the motherland's fight. But were the empires a cause of the war? Among the many reasons that were to be cited for the war, the Left latched on to imperial rivalry as the major one. We have already seen the preparation the Second International had made for the eventuality of a war. In the event, the nationalism of the people – even of the working class, in whom much hope had been placed – was to prove overwhelming. In the name of the nation and the empire, Europeans were ready and willing to inflict incredible violence on each other. Was it nationalism, imperialism, or an atavistic aristocratic feudalism which was causing such mayhem? How could Europe, the seat of reason, at the end of a glorious century of liberal progress, indulge in such uninhibited cruelty? How could Europeans be so beastly to each other?

Of course, cruel and unjust behaviour towards fellow human beings was nothing new to history. It was only that briefly during the nineteenth century, in the small Northwestern corner of Europe, it seemed – at least to the well-off – that such beastliness had ceased. The European abroad, in his civilizing mission, had been anything but kind or human or civilized. Starting with the Iberian peninsula's outward expansion in the sixteenth century, the encounter between the European and the inhabitants of the rest of the world had never been very peaceful. Asia, with its ancient settled urban civilizations in India and China, escaped lightly relative to the native tribes of North and South America, the settled kingdoms of Mexico and Central America, the natives of the Antipodes and of Africa. Attitudes changed as divisions among the European Christians after the Reformation brought doubt and scepticism to the fore. By the eighteenth century, the Enlightenment had encouraged a healthy curiosity about other cultures, and Europeans began to learn and codify languages around the world, to record the habits and institutions of other people. Voltaire admired China as an example of good governance for France; Rousseau celebrated the Noble Savage. Europe was indeed becoming civilized.[1]

The advent of industrialization changed the context of European expansion abroad. A new wave of empires in Asia and Africa took shape during the era of industrial capitalism. The search was no longer for gold, spices or fine textiles, but for markets and raw materials. Territorial possession still mattered, but control over trade was more important. Thus India was substantially put under British rule, but China suffered only from control over sea ports. Much of Latin America stayed independent after its freedom from Spain, yet became part of the mercantile network spreading out from London and Paris.

Imperialism, in the sense both of territorial possession and of economic penetration, was a strange combination of reason and unreason. For the English radical liberal J. A. Hobson, imperial entanglements were a sign of precapitalist aristocratic hunger for land when land was no longer a major source of wealth. He wished England were not involved in a futile war in South Africa at the turn of the century, fighting in the bush, where there was not much to be gained. The buoyant markets for British industry were in Northwest Europe, because that is where the purchasing power was, not in Asia or Africa. Hobson therefore regarded imperialism as an atavistic throwback which would soon pass away as reason and economic calculation prevailed.[2]

Joseph Schumpeter, an Austrian economist who taught for many years at Harvard, wrote a short pamphlet on imperialism in 1919.[3] He was not a Marxist, but he had read Marx in great depth and admired his work. Indeed, he had quite consciously proposed an alternative theory of profits in his book *The Theory of Economic Development*, to which I shall come later. But capitalism, for him, was the realm of rationality, of efficiency in resource use and pursuit of profit. Mere territory as such need not represent wealth, except for the sentimental attachments landlords of a certain age had for land:

> Imperialism is thus atavistic in character. It falls into that large group of surviving features from earlier ages that play such an important part in every concrete social situation. In other words it is an element that stems from the living conditions, not of the present, but of the past – or, put in terms of the economic interpretation of history, from past rather than present relations of production.[4]

Thus Schumpeter attributes imperialism to older modes of production. His theory may have sounded strange, especially to Marxists, in 1919, but he did boldly predict: 'If our theory is correct, cases of Imperialism should decline in intensity the later they occur in the history of a people and of a culture.'[5]

By the late twentieth century, the imperialist episode of world history had passed. No one was able to predict that accurately, but the First World War was the last war between European imperial monarchies. Yet this reliance on irrationality as an explanation of imperialism and war did not fit in with the rational spirit of the age. While the radical wing of the British Liberal Party had some anti-imperialists, empires, by and large, were thought to be good and profitable. Kautsky took a similar position to Hobson. He, too, thought that with the progress of time, advanced capitalist countries would realize that it was in their interests to collude rather than fight. It was the logic of cartelization. Germany and Great Britain would collude, inviting any other country – France, for example – to join a super-capitalist club to exploit the rest of the world jointly. When it finally happened, it was France and Germany who started a super-capitalist club with the Treaty of Rome in 1960.

Marx – though he was a creature of the Enlightenment and a firm believer in reason – had seen capitalism as a mode of production in which the rational pursuit of profits and accumulation by capitalists could lead to irrational outcomes such as crises. Thus, while for Adam Smith individual rationality led to a benevolent collective outcome, for Marx the opposite was the case. Searching for the causes of the First World War, Lenin picked up on this insight. For him, the war was the irrational yet logical consequence of capitalists' competition. In 1916, while in exile in Switzerland, he wrote his most widely read pamphlet, *Imperialism: The Highest Stage of Capitalism.* It was not published until 1919. In a sense, this pamphlet did not influence the Marxist debate during the war, nor did it play any part in the schism in the Second International. But it decisively formed the view of capitalism that Marxists – as well as many other socialists, and many conservatives – took during the next seventy years.

Imperialism combines Hilferding's insight about cartels and banks (finance capital) with Hobson's concept of imperialism. But Lenin's views were diametrically opposed to those of Hobson. Hobson thought imperialism irrational and unprofitable, but by 'imperialism' he also meant territorial possession – a vertical relation between centre and periphery. Lenin argued that imperialism was a result of desperate competition between rival cartels of different nations fed by bankers' credit and armaments manufacturers' greed. It smashes the economies in the periphery. He did think, though, that this expansionary process was self-destructive: partly because of the violent military confrontation such as the world was witnessing, but also because the periphery will also become proletarianized, and eventually rise up against capitalism.

Despite its high reputation, *Imperialism* is not by any means Lenin's most cogent work. He starts here the muddled thinking of many on the Left for whom size means something bad. Thus large corporations and trusts, and a high degree of concentration, are taken to be, *ipso facto*, evil. The fact that the technological imperative makes it uneconomic to have small-scale steel mills (as Mao was to find out in the late 1950s) implies that steel mills will be large and few – unlike, say, cotton textile mills. But I fail to see why this should in any way change the logic of profitability and surplus-value as laid down by Marx. While Rosa Luxemburg had tried to include imperialism in a classical Marxist schema, Lenin – like Hilferding before him – let the empirical descriptive data cloud his judgement. Although it is powerfully written, *Imperialism* detracts from Marxian economic rigour. Indeed, Lenin's debates with the Narodniks show a much greater level of rigour than his *Imperialism*.

There is another ironic aspect to *Imperialism*. Lenin had argued against the Narodniks that capitalism was inevitable for Russia and, indeed, that Russia's problem was the underdevelopment of its capitalism rather than too much of it. (This is similar to Marx's criticism of Prussian policy in the Silesian weavers' case: that the Germans sought protection, while England and France had already gone beyond protection.) After the Revolution, as I said above, once the initial euphoria died down after Brest-Litovsk, Lenin extolled the merits of state capitalism – the system that he had read about as war socialism in Germany. This was not socialism, but it was better than private capitalism. The aim was to speed up accumulation in Russia, and the way to do this was through good accounting, hierarchical management, and workers' discipline. Trade unions had to be subordinated to the need for accumulation. Thus, Lenin comes back to a classical Marxist perspective that capitalism has to develop before the possibilities of socialism can be realized. This became even more important after 1919, as any hope of a German revolution faded.

Lenin made this argument explicitly in many of his pamphlets after coming to power. The main one was *The Chief Task of Our Day: 'Left Wing' Childishness and the Petty-Bourgeois Mentality*, published in December 1918. This was repeated in greater detail three years later in May 1921, in *The Tax in Kind*, which inaugurated the New Economic Policy. This is typical of Lenin's exhortation in this period:

> Keep regular and honest accounts of money, manage economically, do not be lazy, do not steal, observe the strictest labour discipline – it is these slogans justly scorned by the revolutionary proletariat when the bourgeoisie used them to conceal its role as an exploiting class that are now, since the overthrow of the bourgeoisie, becoming the immediate and principal slogans of the moment.[6]

Lenin characterized state capitalism as a transition stage between private capitalism and socialism. For him, Russia was in the phase of state capitalism. In December 1918, he described Germany as the epitome of state capitalism:

> Here we have the 'last word' in modern large-scale Capitalist engineering and planned organization, subordinated to *Junker-bourgeois Imperialism.* Cross out the word in italics and, and in place of militarist, Junker, bourgeois, imperialist State put also a State, that is a proletarian State, and you will have the sum total of the conditions necessary for Socialism.
>
> Socialism is inconceivable without large-scale Capitalist engineering based on the latest discoveries of modern science. It is inconceivable without planned State organization which keeps tens of millions of workers to the strictest observance of a unified standard in production and distribution.[7]

State capitalism was later to become a pejorative label with which Trotskyism characterized Stalinist social formation in the Soviet Union (see Chapter 7). I want to emphasize that Lenin saw workers' control of the state combining with large-scale capitalist organization and planning. The attitude to capitalism is not negative here, and in 1921 Lenin went on to repeat this passage from his 1918 pamphlet with approval. In the intervening period, Russia had fought and won the civil war, but at great cost. By May 1921, Russia needed to coax grain out of the newly emboldened peasantry. Lenin extolled the benefits of free trade – that is, exchange between town and country rather than compulsory procurement – as a way of obtaining the surplus food grains. He wanted Russia to retreat from war communism, a short utopian experiment in creating an economy without money or trade. This could only be an emergency measure during the civil war and the terrible famine that accompanied it. Now, in May 1921, Lenin was back with his preferred model of state capitalism: 'The whole problem – in theoretical and practical terms – is to find the correct methods of directing the development of Capitalism (which is to some extent and for some time inevitable) into the channels of State Capitalism, and to determine how we are to hedge it about with conditions to ensure its transformation into Socialism in the near future.[8]

This justified paying foreign experts extra-high salaries – to give 'concessions' (that is, admit foreign or domestic private capital into expanding large-scale enterprises). The key was to get out of the 'small-proprietor (both small-patriarchal and petty-bourgeois)' state of the economy, and move onwards to large-scale capitalism. The argument here is completely in the spirit of classical Marxism. Capitalism is better than feudalism; large-scale organized capitalism is better than petty commodity production; and then, of course, socialism is better than capitalism. In the absence of a German revolution, Lenin reinforced the necessity of state capitalism for Russia. This was, of course, in one sense an innovation in Marxism, since the German war economy had been an innovation – a large-scale developed capitalist economy subjected to wartime planning. Russia had innovated by undertaking a seizure of power by peasants and workers, before the economy had matured into capitalism. So Lenin grafted the statist version of German capitalism on to the Russian situation, and celebrated the virtues of state capitalism.

Later, I shall address the vital issue of whether you can have capitalism, even state capitalism, without capitalists. For the present, I want to contrast the very positive way in which Lenin treats capitalism – both before the war, in his debates with the Narodniks, and in his days as a practical policymaker after the Revolution – with his very negative and dark views of capitalism in *Imperialism.*

It is the dark, negative view which has been seen as Lenin's legacy. Indeed, it is seen as Marxism for the twentieth century. The Third International, as the new orthodoxy of Marxism, put forward a very different version of Marx's views on capitalism from the one that was prevalent between 1883 and 1913. It said that capitalism was in its terminal crisis. It had no future, although various traitors of the working class – chief among them socialists of the Second International – might try to deny this. In its death throes, capitalism would take off the mask of liberalism and reveal its true predatory nature, resorting to militarism. But communist parties everywhere were to give revolutionary leadership to the working class, fighting off the collaborators of social democracy. Socialism was imminent, as the Bolsheviks' success in Russia had shown. A world revolution was imminent.

Capitalism, in this view, had no progressive features and no future either. The timetable for its imminent collapse – already foreshortened by the German Marxists in their debates during the 1890s and 1900s – was now thrown away, since it was a matter of a very short time. This idea that capitalism was in terminal decline influenced many non-Marxist intellectuals – Schumpeter for one. Even Walt Rostow, in his *Non-Communist Manifesto* (1960), could only visualize convergence between the Soviet and the American models in the future.[9] The radical American journalist Lincoln Steffens, summed up the sentiments of many when he said on his return from Russia in the early 1920s: 'I have seen the future and it works.'

The future belonged to communism – the Bolshevik version of socialism and capitalism had had its day. In the hour of the break-up of the largest democratic

Marxist party and the defeat of the German Revolution which was to have been the vanguard of the World Revolution, the Bolsheviks convinced themselves – and many others, as the next few decades unfolded – that the future was socialist, and capitalism was finished. What was to be the verdict of history?

Away from the Marxist debates on imperialism, actual empires were also shaken by the First World War. At the end of the war, the old imperial powers – Great Britain, France, Belgium and the Netherlands – retained their empires, but the war had unleashed a nationalist awakening. There was an interesting contrast in their reactions. The maritime, commercially driven empires and the land-based, agrarian/feudal ones had different outcomes, confirming – at least partially – the Hobson/Schumpeter insight that older sources of wealth were obsolete. The empires that survived were maritime ones with far-flung possessions. On the mainland of Europe and West Asia, however, the two great empires – the Austro-Hungarian Empire and the Ottoman Empire – dissolved. Their colonies in Southeast Europe and the Middle East were to be theatres of conflict (just think of Kosovo or Palestine). Once again, Northwest Europe had won against its Central and East European rivals. Tsardom was also destroyed, though the Russian Empire was to reconstitute itself as the Union of Soviet Socialist Republics.

But in the surviving empires themselves, there was an upsurge of nationalist sentiment. Most colonial peoples fought for the Mother Empire, but in the process their consciousness was transformed. Their masters, who had seemed invincible, were not really so. Their economies were harnessed to industrial production so that they could support the war effort. Great Britain began to think of the industrialization of India at this time, and conceded constitutional reform towards a slow march to self-government. The sacrifices of Australian soldiers at Gallipoli still rankle in that country as an injustice perpetrated by the mother country.

Everywhere in Europe, war speeded up democratization. Adult franchise was extended either during the war or soon afterwards – women especially won their franchise (in Britain after a violent militant suffragette movement) across Western Europe. Liberalism had been checked by the war, but it survived in the older industrialized countries. But in going from a restricted franchise of propertyholders to universal franchise, its contradictions were brought out. In Hegel's scheme, the propertyless had no representation. In Marx's critique of Hegel, he made a virtue of the fact that the proletariat – the propertyless – were outside the representative institutions of the Hegelian state. But now, this had been put right. There was to be franchise for men and women, regardless of property qualification. (It took some decades before women were granted the same franchise as men, but a beginning had been made during the 1914–20 period.)

The victory of the Northwest European powers over the Central European ones was, paradoxically, aided by an ex-colony. It was America's entry into the war in 1916 which tipped the balance in the favour of the Allies. The United States of America had fought for its independence from the mother country. The American Revolution of 1776 was the child of John Locke and the Bloodless Revolution of 1688. It associated freedom with private property. Freedom was won after a battle against a mighty military power. The British had misjudged America's resentment at illegal impositions. They also miscalculated – not for the last time – the character of the rebellion. Earl Gower, for example, told the House of Lords during the American War of Independence that the rebels were vastly outnumbered by loyalists who, 'having tasted the difference between British liberty and American tyranny, would gladly return to their allegiance'.[10]

But of course, US independence was just another version of British liberty, without a feudal aristocracy. There was the blind spot about Negro slaves, but then in 1776, even the Christian Churches defended slavery as legitimate private property. The failure to deal with slavery was to cost America a civil war of its own, and even then, it would take another century for Black Americans to become a full part of civil society. Yet apart from that no doubt massive fault, America was a socially egalitarian society. It had economic differences, but not status-based ones: no lords, dukes or kings. As the poor of Europe poured in, they were integrated; if not immediately, by the second generation. The immigrants lived in poor urban conditions when they arrived, as did the workers of Manchester whom Engels had observed. But their children did not linger in the same place or in the same jobs. There was land to move into, and a thriving economy. Once the North had won the civil war, America took off as an industrial nation. The decimation of Native Americans was to come late in the nineteenth century.

The American Civil War started in the same year as the abolition of serfdom in Russia: 1861. Here were two countries of continental size, relative underpopulation and tremendous potential. But over the next fifty years, these two countries followed remarkably different trajectories. America became an industrial power by the end of the nineteenth century, and proved its strength in the First World War. It came to rescue, as it were, the revolutions of 1688 and 1776 – the John Locke revolutions. It came – perhaps somewhat naively in the person of Woodrow Wilson – with a liberal-democratic programme for a postwar settlement. For cynical European diplomats, brought up on the power-grabbing settlements of the Congress of Vienna and every other postwar settlement before it, this was a radical departure. The Yankees were an unknown quantity, but they had resources to spare even after a war. The prospects for capitalism and for liberal democracy were to be profoundly affected by American intervention in a European civil war.

First, although the war spelt the end of globalization in the economic sphere – a retreat from the free movement of labour and capital that had prevailed between 1870 and 1913 – it inaugurated a globalization of politics. From now on, wars were seen to be the concern of the world's (not just Europe's) Great Powers. But the Americans were also naively committed to the democratic principle in international affairs – hence the League of Nations rather than just a Concert of Europe, a desire to induct not only the Great Powers but every nation into the task of global governance. It was premature, and it failed. Secondly, America gave support to the liberal order in Europe's domestic affairs. Its commitment to democracy was absolute. When, during the next twenty-five years, Europe was to experiment with a variety of non-democratic forms, and liberalism was at bay, it was the American adherence to the Revolution of 1688 which – along with the mother country, Great Britain – carried the day. Despite the visceral anti-Americanism among Europe's intellectuals, this is not a truth that can be denied, even with hindsight.

Thirdly, America was capitalist, and unashamedly so. The French Revolution and its egalitarian economic message never penetrated far into America. The thirty years preceding the First World War were perhaps the high point of continental European socialist influence in American political life. Marx's death was an occasion for a giant meeting in Cooper Union Square in New York, where tributes were paid to him in many languages. The IWW (Industrial Workers of the World) was a European-style revolutionary workers' union. The immigrant Europeans had brought much of their ideological baggage with them, and in the urban centres of the East Coast and Chicago, their numbers mattered. But eventually, America stayed liberal and capitalist. Its politics continued to be an ideology-free zone, as they do to this day. This is not to say that there are no differences among parties, but political theory – Marxist, socialist, fascist – has not had any lasting impact. Its citizens (except the Black citizens in the South) did not have to struggle for suffrage, as the Europeans did. They believe they have rights inherent in their citizen status, and these rights are not granted by but defined against the government. Compared to contemporary Europe, America in 1916 was a liberal-democratic utopia. And it was wealthy.

Was there a reason for American exceptionalism? Marx had one. He was familiar with American developments all through his life, though America did not as yet did not loom very large in European minds. He wrote occasional articles for the *New York Tribune*, and in the 1870s he even thought about migrating to the States. But it is his systematic views on American capitalism that are of interest here. In the very last chapter of *Capital Volume 1* – the chapter following the apocalyptic Chapter 32 – Marx outlines 'The Modern Theory of Colonization'. Why this chapter comes last is a question I speculate about later. But during his description of colonies and their peculiar features, Marx contrasts the capitalism of the Old World and that of the New World in the following (somewhat lengthy) passage:

> The great beauty of Capitalist production consists in this – that it not only constantly reproduces the wage worker as wage worker, but produces always, in proportion to the accumulation of capital, a relative surplus population of wage workers. Thus the law of supply and demand of labour is kept in the right rut, the oscillation of wages is perceived within limits satisfactory to Capitalist exploitation, and lastly, the social dependence of the labourer on the Capitalist, that indispensable requisite, is secure; an unmistakable relation of dependence, which the smug political economist, at home, in the mother country, can transmogrify into one of free contract between buyer and seller, between equally independent owners of commodities, the owner of commodity capital and the owner of commodity labour.

This, then, is capitalism in the Old World, in the mother country. Marx continues:

> but in the colonies, this pretty fancy is torn asunder. The absolute population here increases much more quickly than in the mother country because many labourers enter this world as ready made adults, and yet the labour market is understocked. The law of the supply and demand of labour falls to pieces. On the one hand, the old world constantly throws in capital, thirsting after exploitation and 'abstinence'; on the other, the regular reproduction of the wage labourer as wage labourer comes into collision with the most impertinent and in part invincible impediments. What becomes of the production of wage labourers, supernumerary in proportion to the accumulation of capital? The wage-worker of today is tomorrow an independent peasant, or artisan working for himself. He

> vanishes from the labour market, but not into the workhouse. This constant transformation of the wage labourers into independent producers, who work for themselves instead of for capital, and enrich themselves instead of the Capitalist gentry, reacts in its turn very perversely in the conditions of the labour market. *Not only does the degree of exploitation of wage labourer remain indecently low.* The wage labourer loses into the bargain, along with the relation of dependence, also the sentiment of dependence on the abstemious capital.[11]

I have emphasized the sentence where Marx calls the degree of exploitation in America 'indecently low'. Of course, the question to ask is: if the degree (rate) of exploitation is low, how did American business make profits which, in turn, attracted foreign capital to its shores? The answer, of course, is in the contrast Marx made between absolute and relative degrees of exploitation earlier in *Capital Volume 1*, as between part 3 (The Production of Absolute Surplus-Value) and part 4 (Production of Relative Surplus-Value). In the first case, workers' productivity is low, and it is by extending working hours that the capitalist extracts enough surplus-value. In the latter case, one can combine high wages with even higher productivity. High wages require a lot of capital to be used. But in terms of labour values, the variable capital in the New World is a higher ratio to constant capital than in the Old World, and this again may be despite the fact that American industry uses more capital than European industry.

In more modern parlance, high wages but still higher productivity would imply a lower share of wages in total output in America than in Europe. If the rate of exploitation is low, the inverse of one plus the rate of exploitation will be high. And that, readers may recall, is the same as the share of wages in total income. American industry was more capital-intensive, but its productivity was higher because of American ingenuity – the innovativeness which had so impressed the British visitors to the Great Exhibition of 1851 at Crystal Palace.

The available data bring this out. Of course, Marx did not have such data to hand, but it is still worth checking how sound his instincts were. In 1870, American productivity – GDP per man hour – was 100 relative to an average in fourteen other advanced countries of 62 (Germany 50, France 56, UK 104). In 1913, it had moved even farther ahead. Again taking the USA as 100, the fifteen-country average was 54 (Germany 50, France 48, UK 78). (Indeed, the average did not move back above the 1870 average until 1973.)

The American economy had grown at 4.5 per cent between 1820 and 1870 and 3.9 per cent in 1870–1913, when the average of all fifteen countries (i.e. including the USA) was 2.4 per cent and 2.5 per cent respectively. Thus, in the first fifty years, American GDP would have grown eightfold (doubling every sixteen years), and in the next forty-three years it would have more than quadrupled (doubling every eighteen years). But America also started with an advantage of a favourable natural resource/population balance. Thus in 1820 (at 1985 US prices) American income *per capita* was $1,048, while UK's was $1,405, Germany's $937 and France's $1,052. By 1913, despite a massive growth in population, the relevant figures became USA $4,854, UK $4,024, Germany $2,606 and France $2,734. Thus America – a fairly high-income country, though not the richest, in 1820 – outstrips the richest industrial country, the UK, by 1913, and leaves Germany and France relatively further behind.

By 1913, the USA was not only the richest capitalist economy, it was also the most populous, with a population of 97 million compared to the UK's 45.6 million, Germany's 67 million and France's 40 million. In terms of total GDP, the USA's was about $460 billion compared to $175 billion for Germany, $108 billion for France and $180 billion for the UK (all roughly rounded up). America was as large in economic terms as the three top European economies put together. Size counts – at least in international relations when it comes to war.

Marx did not go into all this. Perhaps he should have done, since American profitability foretold the new phase of capitalism, in which high wage/high profitability became a reality. This combination of high wage/high productivity → low share of wages as well as high capital productivity was not accidental. A lack of feudal aristocracy meant that as westward expansion took place, land was not monopolized and parcelled into latifundia in the USA, as it was in South America. This made the labour market tight. But there were also higher levels of literacy in the USA compared to Europe. To become a citizen, an immigrant had to demonstrate the ability to read, and some knowledge of the American Constitution. The higher literacy in America is thus a part of the concept of citizenship as a right, not as a gift.

The next two decades were to be a contest between liberal and authoritarian political forms. But capitalism also faced its biggest challenge – at home, and also from rival modes of economic organization. Thus, as Marxism lost its hold on democratic politics, it emerged to challenge capitalism and democracy in its authoritarian state capitalist version. But there were also challenges from right-wing authoritarian forms – from fascism in particular. This is our next story.

9

The Interwar Years: Return to Normality, 1919–29

Introduction

The First World War gave great impetus to the removal of the aristocracy from its ruling position everywhere in Europe. The Hohenzollern monarchy was replaced by a republic whose president was an SPD apparatchik: Friedrich Ebert.[1] The revolutionary Left of the German SPD now formed the Spartacist League, and burnt itself out in a Romantic and adventurist uprising towards the end of 1918/beginning of 1919. The old right-wing and revisionist trade-unionist leadership retained its hold and retrieved the situation. Rosa Luxemburg, that most brilliant of theorists and agitators, perished violently at the hands of the Freikorps, a mercenary group of German officers.[2] For ever afterwards, the Bolsheviks were able to claim her as a martyr and the old SPD as traitor to the revolutionary tradition.

But the fact that the SPD had come from a pariah status to that of a ruling party – that an old European monarchy had crumbled, to be replaced by a republic – was a revolutionary enough event. The Habsburg Empire collapsed, to be replaced by the Austrian Republic and independent nations in Hungary, Czechoslovakia and elsewhere in Southeast Europe. The aristocracy also retreated from power in the UK; no twentieth-century Prime Minister has sat in the House of Lords since the Marquess of Salisbury, who retired in 1902. The powers of the House of Lords were curtailed in 1911 – even before the war.[3]

The aristocracy also lost reputation as a result of its bungling and sometimes callous leadership in the armed forces. Everywhere a democratic equalizing spirit prevailed. In future, merit was to count for more in the leadership stakes than birth. With the spread of the franchise, accountable governments were going to be properly elected. Trade unions had shown remarkable patience over wages throughout the war; now they were going on the march. Across Europe, labour unrest became a formidable force. Even the British Prime Minister, Lloyd George, was intimidated by the combined forces of the railwaymen, dock workers and coalminers. Hobson and Schumpeter were more right than anyone else: the war may have been the last atavistic blow of the feudal aristocracy which clung on to power until 1914. Now they were sacked.[4]

Socialism: One or Many?

The war transformed the position of socialist parties. Of course, the split in the Second International and the establishment of the Third International created a schism, but it also clarified matters.[5] The reformist, parliamentary socialist parties stayed in the Second International, willing to work within the political and economic system. The political situation had been dramatically transformed in an antimonarchical, more democratic direction. The economic system stayed the same. Capitalism survived, but – as we shall see – it, too, had been transformed. This transformation of capitalism did not, however, help the socialist parties. The problem was not with them; it was with capitalism.

The twenty years after the end of the First World War were the worst in the history of capitalism, and they left a deep impression of crisis and breakdown in the minds of anyone who was alive during those years. For the Third International predicting the imminent demise of capitalism, these years were like an early Christmas. The reformists, it seemed, were to be proved wrong, and the revolutionaries right. As the reformists persisted in their moderate policies, and got squeezed by the adverse effects of a failing capitalism, the communists blamed them for obstructing its final collapse. The apocalyptic vision of Chapter 32 seemed to be more relevant than the more nuanced conclusions elsewhere. Marx the crude anticapitalist, the astrologer of the end of capitalism, took hold in the propaganda war in place of the man who had understood the dynamics of capitalism better than anyone before or since.

Two visions of socialism thus emerged, contesting the political terrain. On the one hand was the vision of the Second International, which I will call Socialism *within* Capitalism (SwC). Here the aim was to humanize capitalism, moderate its adverse effects, improve the conditions of workers and the poorer strata, create better public services – health and education, transport, protection for the elderly and the unemployed – by building a welfare state. But all this was to be done without fundamentally challenging the profit system. The most radical step envisioned was that of taking some industries – often the faltering ones – into state ownership. The increasing extension of state ownership and control became, for the most radical elements of the Second International, a way of conquering capitalism by stealth. The British Labour Party enshrined a commitment to take over the means of production into public ownership in its constitution in 1917, as the famous Clause Four (section four). The problem for SwC was that its success was predicated upon a prosperous, well-functioning capitalism. As we saw in the case of the SPD before 1914, the trade unions and SPD members thrived in times of high employment and a booming economy. But at such times, the pro-capitalist parties – liberal, conservative, Christian Democrat – did well in elections. Socialist parties usually come to power – particularly during this period, 1919 to 1939 – only when the system is in trouble: strikes, high unemployment, hyperinflation, and so on; and that was precisely the time when the cause of SwC could not advance. The task became one of preserving capitalism and making it work better. This may be called betrayal by the Bolsheviks, but it made a lot of sense. Workers were the first to suffer when capitalism was malfunctioning. It was a Romantic fallacy to think that every crisis was full of revolutionary opportunities.

The Bolsheviks of the Third International wanted Socialism *outside* Capitalism (SoC). Having established a workers' government led by a Marxist party (at least, so they thought), they had gone in a direction not predicted by classical Marxism. Russian capitalism was underdeveloped, as Lenin had argued consistently since 1890, but here they had workers' power with the task of accelerating capitalist development. This was not socialism as envisaged in *The Communist Manifesto*, or even in the 'Critique of the Gotha Progamme'. This was state capitalism, but even that – compared to what the Bolsheviks had thought was its apogee in Germany – was a sickly creature in Russia. As the prospect of European revolution receded – by 1921 at the latest – the Bolsheviks were stuck with the unusual prospect of building up an alternative to capitalism which would achieve the development of the Russian economy. Never daunted, they defined theirs as true socialism – not so much coming after the maturity of capitalism, but running a race to the top alongside it. Since the Germans had used planning during their war years, the Russians were to use planning on an economy-wide basis. For primitive accumulation, they were to use the countryside: via exchange, as Lenin thought; or confiscation on the lines of the Enclosure movement, as Stalin practised. Since the early decades of capitalist development had been violent and pauperizing, who could blame state capitalism for being the same? The building of a developed economy at an accelerated pace, using techniques similar to those used in the history of capitalism, but without capitalists – that was Socialism outside Capitalism.

There was, of course, a third vision which never got a chance – or, at least, has not as yet: the classical Marxian vision of Socialism *beyond* Capitalism (SbC). As in Hegel's trajectory, it was a self-conscious society, aware now that capitalism as a system of *private* property profiting from the *social* division of labour could not offer any further betterment, that would proceed to take control over the economy – society, mind you, not state. In Marx's writings, not much is said about this, but there is no doubt that it is society that takes self-conscious control, not the state. Marx did not work out how, and through what modalities, because he did not think this was an urgent problem: in due time, society would find its own solution. There was to be a transitional stage while the proletariat took power and abolished class distinctions. There is a strong anarchist strand in Marx's vision of socialism. Once people have consciously grasped their interdependence – once Adam Smith's Invisible Hand becomes visible to everyone – then they will proceed to arrange economic affairs in such a way that everyone's needs will come first. People will continue to work – not selling their labour-power, but being part of a generalized social exchange. There was an element among the Austrian Marxists (Otto Neurath in particular) which thought that money would be abolished under socialism. Indeed, by then – thanks to the developed powers of production of a mature capitalism, which would just have been overtaken by socialism – there might even be no scarcity. Each person would work for himself or herself as they worked for society. Each person would take part in conscious decision-making as to how the economy was to be run.

This is a utopian vision in a double sense: that it has not been worked out in detail; also, it has never had to face the harsh reality of day-to-day living. How conscious control can be exercised by 'society', how people's needs and wants can be communicated, how such a society would decide about saving and investment, are all questions left unexplored. There has not been even a hypothetical blueprint – a simulation or scenario construction of this vision. It is evoked briefly and occasionally in the polemics of Trotskyist factions with orthodox (Stalinist) Communist parties, but neither side has gone beyond slogans. There was one unresolved issue with all three visions. If capitalism was to be a global system, yet unevenly developed in different countries, should socialism not be realized on an international – if not global – level? But if, according to classical Marxism, one has to wait for the full maturity of capitalism (until, as it were, it runs out of its progressive steam), will this mean that capitalism has to be developed, in the last developing country, the latest one to develop, before it can be overcome? The debates between 1883 and 1913 had a very narrow Western European perspective. Even the USA had not been factored into the socialists' visions of the future. It seemed that the most developed country – Great Britain – or the fastest-developing one – Germany –

would fall to socialism first. Presumably (and this was not clarified anywhere), the less-developed areas of capitalism would then switch over to socialism. This issue was left in a muddle, since the rhetoric was internationalist, but the unevenness of capitalist development, even in Western Europe, meant substantial qualitative differences in the prospects for socialism, as and when it was to come.

The Second International, given its reformist perspective in the medium term, and only a long-term revolutionary aim, had little trouble with this. While the many conferences (such as the one at Stuttgart in 1907) tried to approve a unified resolution, it was always recognized that different countries would go their own way. None of the parties was in power, and thus had no power to coerce the others. It had to be live and let live. It was to be like that for the next eighty years.

The Third International was altogether different. For one thing, it was led by a national party which had come to power and had not only the prestige of the first successful revolutionary party, but the resources to enforce its will. The Bolsheviks were, in any case, not a democratic consensual party but a hierarchical, top–down, leadership-dominated party. The International would thus also be led hierarchically by the Russian party. But the Russian Bolsheviks were also heavily committed to the doctrine of internationalism – the idea that socialism, when it comes, will come simultaneously in many countries, led by the advanced ones. The reality was shown to be otherwise by 1921, and this had to be reconciled with the theory by an elaborate rhetoric of betrayal by the social democrats. Yet Russia's precipitate revolution had to be justified. In a sense, revolutions did take place simultaneously in Germany, Austria, Hungary, Northern Italy and Russia, but only the least developed economy held on to the revolution, for reasons explained in Chapter 7. Trotsky, along with Parvus (Alexander Helphand), had advanced the notion that the weakest link in the chain of capitalist countries might be the first to break, and then the revolution would spread. He held on to this view even after 1923, though there was little hope of any insurrection anywhere else, and the final desperate attempt at revolution had failed in Germany. In fact, though it would not admit it in theory, the Third International, like the Second International, also had to live with different speeds of revolution in different countries. 'Socialism in one country' was a matter not of choice, but of fact. As it happened, Stalin implemented it rather than Trotsky or Bukharin, but that is a contingent, not a systematic or structural, outcome. It could easily have been one of the other two.

Rupture, Restoration and Rupture

There was 'socialism in one country' but also different socialisms in different countries at that time, because capitalism itself deglobalized in the interwar period. Trade between countries slowed down. The Gold Standard had been suspended during the war, and the belligerent European countries had to make painful attempts to restore it. America emerged as the most powerful and prosperous nation, with the largest stock of gold. Great Britain – thus far the leader of the global capitalist order – had to sell its foreign assets to finance the war, and was to take six years to get back on to the Gold Standard, only to abandon it seven years later. Its ability to invest abroad was weakened. The British government, like that of every other belligerent country, had amassed a huge public debt after nearly sixty years of sound public finance. France had been physically ravaged, and insisted at Versailles on a crippling reparations settlement with Germany. Woodrow Wilson's idealism was twice defeated: once by his own Congress, which rejected America's adherence to the League of Nations, in a way confirming the vigour of American democracy. But also, the Versailles settlement, in effect, was more like the older European treaty, with its land-grabbing, than Wilson's old-fashioned idealism. For France, this had not been a world war, merely another round in the Franco–German struggle.

The twenty years 1919 to 1939 can be (somewhat arbitrarily) divided into three phases. The first phase (1919–25) was the return to normality, though it was not the normality of the prewar liberal globalized order. The next phase (1926–30) was normality for this new world of deglobalized capitalism. The third phase (1931–39) was the disastrous period of the Great Depression and an ineffectual recovery until the outbreak of another world war changed the context. Capitalism nearly went under. It faced challenges from the Left and also from the Right, which experimented with an illiberal authoritarian variant of 'capitalism in one country'. The outbreak of the Second World War, provoked by Germany under Hitler, enabled capitalism to fight back and, under US–British leadership, re-establish the liberal free-trade version of 'capitalism in one country' as the dominant model. It was to take another fifty years after 1939 for globalization to resume its nineteenth-century course. By then, the authoritarian version of socialism in one country had also collapsed.

The return to normality (1919–25)

But I am running ahead of the story. During the twenty years between the wars, it took some time before politicians and policymakers realized that the pre-1914 world was not going to be restored. The immediate postwar years were inflationary across much of Europe. In the UK, wages rose by 20 per cent on average in 1919 and 1920. The war years had been years of full employment, and unions had become strong. It was the same story in France. Germany was saddled with reparations payments, exhaustion from defeat, and militancy on the labour front. In the UK, the Cuncliffe Committee on Currency and Foreign Exchange reported that a return to the Gold Standard as soon as possible was vital to the City of London's fortunes. This would require taking control of inflation, and in 1921 there was a severe deflationary cut in the government budget; wages fell by 20 per cent, and unemployment rose sharply. A more severe dose of deflation was administered in 1925 when Winston Churchill, as Chancellor of the Exchequer, reluctantly endorsed his Treasury experts' advice to restore the prewar parity between sterling and the US dollar at $4.86 to the pound. John Maynard Keynes was appalled, because he would have preferred restoration at a lower parity. The UK economy was saddled with an overvalued pound for the remainder of the decade. Throughout the rest of the 1920s, unemployment in the UK was to remain at 10 per cent.[6]

But the years 1919 to 1925 were also years of political turmoil in the UK. Ireland's independence was accompanied by Partition and the retention of Ulster as part of the UK after a civil war. In India, the Jalianwala Bagh massacre of peaceful demonstrators by General Dyer in April 1919 flared up into a massive non-cooperation movement led by Mahatma Gandhi. There were demands for a measure of political autonomy – dominion status – by countries of the white commonwealth. The Balfour Declaration on Palestine was to open a can of worms whose effects are still being felt. The Lloyd George coalition was broken up by the Conservatives, but they could not hold on to power, and in 1924 a Labour government came in. The circumstances were not auspicious for its success, and in less than a year the Conservatives were back in power. Three governments in three years was not the norm for British politics.

Germany suffered much greater trauma. The Weimar Republic was the proud creation of the SPD. It was potentially the first modern welfare state, building on Bismarckian foundations but becoming much more universal. But inflation remained a problem; the economy had suffered a huge destruction of its capital, and government revenues remained low.[7] Foreign investments had not resumed. When Germany failed to pay reparations, France occupied the Ruhr, and forcibly exported coal and steel in lieu of reparations. The German government was outraged at such an affront, and decided to sabotage its currency. All German officials in the Ruhr continued to be paid and, with an even lower output than an already impoverished Germany had, inflation became astronomical. The value of the mark plunged until billions of marks were required to buy one dollar. Germany faced left-wing rebellions throughout these years, and in Munich in 1924 the Nazi Party's new leader, Adolf Hitler, tried a putsch to make Bavaria independent. All such attempts were defeated by the Republic, but the level of political violence rose sharply. An international intervention led by the Americans rescheduled the reparations debts, and American credits were promised to help Germany recover. By 1925, all seemed well. A new currency had been introduced which would promise stability, but the hyperinflation of 1923–24 ruined many middle-class families who had hoped to live on their savings.

America was the only economy which had a prosperous decade in the 1920s. There was no long period of return to normality or change of gear in 1925. Prohibition did not help, except to corrupt politics, but though farmers did not share fully in prosperity, manufacturing and finance flourished. The stock market became the subject of many more people's active interest than ever before, and Wall Street enjoyed a boom. America became a banker to the European economies. Great Britain and France had to repay what they had borrowed during the war, and in the meantime America was recycling credits to Europe, especially Germany. Instead of London, New York was emerging as the pivotal centre of international finance. Yet American central bankers did not have the global perspective that the Bank of England had when it 'managed' the Gold Standard in the nineteenth century by small and subtle changes in the short-term interest rate. American policy focus was national rather than international. It was to be a generation before America was ready to take up economic leadership. During the interwar years, neither the UK nor the USA could exercise such leadership.

Away from Western and Central Europe and North America, there were new stirrings. Japan had emerged on the world scene early in the twentieth century by defeating Russia in 1905. It had reached a sufficiently high level of economic development to join the Gold Standard. It acquired an empire for itself by conquering Korea, and it was quite clear that Japanese leaders intended Japan to behave like any other member of the imperialist club. Asia had now entered global political society after an absence of a century and a half. China had become a republic in 1911, and the Nationalist Party Guo Min Dang had assumed the leadership of China's modernization. There was still a lot of resentment in China against the domination of foreign powers in the Treaty Ports, but China – like the other populous Asian country, India – was hesitantly embarking on the path of capitalist development. Shanghai was a modern city, just as Calcutta was becoming one, with modern modes of transportation: tramways, buses, trains.[8]

Republicanism – though not democracy – had come to the former Spanish colonies of Latin America. They were as yet predominantly agricultural, with a very fragile industrial sector. Argentina was the leading economy, developing its agricultural resources and emerging as a major exporter of meat and grains. Very much as in the Antipodes, agriculture was to be the basis of its capitalist modernization – this was unlike the Western European model. Only Russia held out. Its civil war had taken a heavy toll, but the peasantry – recently revolutionized, and in possession of land for the first time in decades – stuck by the Bolsheviks. They held the whip hand, and in 1921 the government had to acknowledge their clout. Any revival of the Russian industrial economy was presaged upon the peasantry's willingness to part with their surplus food grains. The industrial sector had little to sell in exchange, and the terms of trade were bound to be in favour of the peasants. Lenin, in inaugurating the New Economic Policy, had offered a compromise whereby some food surplus was yielded as a 'tax in kind', and the remainder would be by exchange. There was to be no forced requisition of food surpluses, as had been tried in the period of war communism (1917–20), which caused one of the worst famines Russia had experienced.[9]

By 1925, an uneasy truce between the industrial and the agricultural economy had been established in Russia. The terms of trade kept seesawing, but by then the government had eliminated all opposition from the workers' side. All parties except the Bolsheviks had been banned, their leaders jailed or exiled. Trade unions had been 'militarized' (to use Trotsky's favourite expression) and harnessed to the government's aims, not those of their members. Nationalization was halted, and some private enterprise was allowed to flourish. Lenin had died in 1924, but for the time being, the leadership was collective – Stalin, Trotsky and Bukharin being at the top. Visitors from the West – Bernard Shaw, Bertrand Russell and H. G. Wells – were impressed by what they saw, and reported back. Russia was going to be a normal member of the international community.

Normality (1925–29)

The five-year period spanning the second half of the 1920s was as close to normality as the interwar years got. Politicians and intellectuals began to understand that there was no going back to pre-1914 days. That world of capitalism – a globalized world with a relatively small role played by the state in the economy; with rules of international monetary discipline, and prudent fiscal policy at home – had gone for ever. Countries were still interconnected by trade and credit relations, but what was emerging was an interstate or international economy rather than a global one. The state (often mislabelled the nation-state) emerged as a major player in the economy. The war had made the state take on responsibilities for its citizens' welfare. The 'social state'[10] that now emerged separated its citizens from foreigners. Passports were introduced across Europe, impeding free mobility. The state was expected to deliver welfare only to its own citizens. The rest were foreigners, immigrants, refugees. Everywhere the demand was for 'a land fit for heroes' – our heroes, not everyone else's.

The Weimar Republic, having come through its traumas, was the best equipped to deliver this dream. Its welfare legislation, its extension of trade-union rights, its sober conduct in international relations, made it a standard-bearer. It was to disappear in the next storm, but the SPD was delivering on the reformist part of the Erfurt Programme (now, of course, disowned). There was no doubt that despite the many economic problems it had faced, the SPD, in power, was delivering on its promises.

The British economy had been led into a second phase of deflation by the return to the Gold Standard at $4.86. The loss of export earnings put a squeeze on the coal industry, and the miners went on strike. For the first and only time in its history, the TUC declared a general strike. It was perhaps the bitterest moment in terms of open class warfare. The Labour Party was weak; the Liberals were divided. The Conservative government stood firm, and the strike did not change much; its romantic glow brightened as it receded further into the past. Unemployment remained high, and there was a squeeze on real wages. Yet the Baldwin government lasted its full term – the only one to do so in the 1920s.

France managed its re-entry into the Gold Standard better than the UK. The gold price of the French franc was fixed to allow depreciation, which helped French exports. The Third Republic had survived the war intact, and was able to hold on to people's allegiance, thanks to the victory over the old enemy. Paris became the international centre of art and literature, even English literature, with Irish, British and American writers crowding the pavement cafés.

The French socialists had also split between a Second International and a Third International wing. But in any case, the French Socialist Party had not been as strong as the SPD and had to wait a while before it was summoned to power.

Russia, too, enjoyed a normal five years, though there was growing disagreement about economic strategy. Trotsky wanted to move from the gradualist NEP, which had ceded much power to the peasantry, towards an accelerated industrialization programme, to be financed by a more favourable (to the industrial sector) transfer of agricultural surplus. Bukharin was for a continuation and consolidation of the NEP, with balanced growth for agriculture and industry. For a while, it even seemed likely that Russia might get foreign assistance. A TUC delegation from the UK visited Russia in 1927, and there was serious talk about a resumption of trade and credits. But then the Third International flexed its muscles, and encouraged the fledgling Chinese Communist Party to launch a revolution in the urban centres of Shanghai, Canton and Hangchow. It was ruthlessly suppressed by the Nationalist government under its leader, Chiang Kai-shek, who had received training in Moscow. This was a repetition of the adventurism of the German Communist Party between 1919 and 1923, though it had better reasons than the Chinese Party. The British delegation's favourable report was ignored by the government. Russia was seen as a rogue state, not as a normal, responsible member of the international community.

Had Germany survived the war better, it would have been Russia's natural economic partner, but Germany was in no position to export capital. The French had invested heavily in Tsarist Russia, and their debts had been repudiated. The British withdrew hastily: Russia would have to tackle its accumulation problem in isolation. This was not by choice. Lenin had welcomed foreign experts and concessions. The Bolsheviks could be flexible if Russian economic development was at stake, though they were dogmatic about foreign parties. In the face of isolation, the path of forced industrialization beckoned. Stalin outmanoeuvred Trotsky by siding with Bukharin, and Trotsky went into exile. Now Stalin took over Trotsky's policy of rapid industrialization, and eliminated Bukharin from the leadership. Two more Romantic martyrs were consigned to the revolutionary Marxist pantheon.

In devising a planned economy for the industrialization of a backward economy, Stalin was on untrodden ground. Marx's schemes for expanded reproduction became the toolbox for the First Five Year Plan of the Soviet Union.[11] The two-Department division – machine goods and wage goods – was used as a base. Machine-goods production – basic industries – was given priority.

Consumption was to be controlled with an iron-law tenacity; all the surplus was to be invested to expand the machine-goods sector. Department I was in the driving seat. Newly recruited untrained workers, many migrating to towns from rural areas, were brought in on low wages. Throughout the First Five Year Plan, real wages were to fall. But indeed, much worse was yet to come. By 1929, Stalin had consolidated his power, launched Russia on the path of rapid industrialization, and become acknowledged as the successor to Lenin in the Orthodox Communist Church of Marxism. From now on, the critical tradition in Marxism was exiled from Communist parties around the world. Every reading of Marx, everything written about Marx, Lenin or Russia, had to be strictly in line with Stalin's views. If even Marx's writings deviated from Stalin's view of Marxism, such writings were to be ignored, suppressed or excised. It was no longer necessary to read *Capital*; Lenin's *Imperialism* was to be the received text, next to the *Communist Manifesto*. All debates about price–value transformation, or the Schemes of Reproduction, or the checking of the facts about the rate of profit against the prediction of its fall, were ruled out as uninteresting scholasticism. The answers were known. Marxism became a bundle of catechisms.

But in one respect, the Third International did better than the Second International. The leaders of the latter, if they came to power, were ruling in imperialist countries. They compromised on their anticolonialism and served their domestic interests. The Third International took a bold and uncompromising stance against imperialism and colonialism. So as far as the countries of Asia and Africa were concerned, the Third International, dogmatic as it could be, was on their side. Thus at an Anti-Imperialist Congress in Brussels under Third International auspices, the young Jawaharlal Nehru was initiated into the beauties of simplified Marxism. This was in 1927, and even after he became Prime Minister of India, twenty years later, the impression that Marxism made on him – in its somewhat crude, catechistic form – was not forgotten. Many of what are now called Third World countries produced leaders who were recruited into anticolonial struggles via the Marxism of the Third International. They were told that imperialism was the latest form of capitalism. To be anti-imperialist was to be anticapitalist. Capitalism, they were told – in a travesty of much of Marx's writing on colonies – was an agent of retarded or distorted development. Marx had welcomed the British East India Company's role in destroying the old precapitalist institutions in India; his only complaint was that they had not finished the job properly in 1857, when the company was replaced by the British government. He and Engels had approved of France's takeover of Algeria. In Marx's view, capitalism was a progressive force which had to destroy older modes even if this destruction was effected by a colonial power. Marx was not a nationalist. This embarrassing legacy was suppressed or explained away. Marx became cast as a firm anti-imperialist writer as well as an anticapitalist one. The Narodniks' delusions about skipping the capitalist stage altogether and jumping on to socialism were now given Marxist garb. Russia had implemented the Narodnik programme and skipped – so the faithful were told – the intermediate stage of exploitative private capitalism. Now everyone could do that.[12]

Whatever the merits of their economic message, the communists were unflinching in their support for all anticolonial movements. The popularity of the Soviet Union and catechistic Marxism in Third World countries was a small payment back for such support when few in the European heartland were willing to help. The record of the British Labour Party or the French, Dutch or Belgian socialist parties is pitiable in this respect.

India was going through one of its quiet phases during 1925–29. Gandhi had retreated to his ashram, and the Congress Party had begun to take part in legislatures created as part of the 1919 Reform. China had consolidated the rule of nationalist leadership by suppressing the communist uprising. The prospects looked good for agricultural exports, and for a small degree of industrialization in some of these countries. The penchant for free trade having abated, tariff protection was used everywhere to promote industrialization or to enrich farmers. The liberal order was much compromised.

The real – and much bigger – threat to the liberal order was yet to come, but its portents could be seen in Italy if one looked carefully. Like every other European country, Italy had troubled postwar years. The socialists were numerous but they, too, split, and the communists had been active in the spontaneous strikes in the industrial north. But Italy also had its share of right-wing authoritarian and monarchist parties. In the Versailles Treaty, Italy did get Trieste from Austria, but its demand for Fiume was not accepted. An Italian poet, Gabriele D'Annunzio, had led a motley crew of adventurers, and captured Fiume for Italy. He fancied himself as a leader, and his ritual consisted of insignia of death and black shirts for his followers. He set the fashion for authoritarian leaders. The liberal coalition in power was weak, and could not cope with the problems. Then Benito Mussolini, a former left-wing leader in the Italian Socialist Party, formed a coalition of left and right groups. The philosophy of the party was a mixture of left-wing socialist sentiment and right-wing nationalism, but the main message was that parliamentary democracy was *passé*, and a strong leader was needed to tackle Italy's problems. Mussolini had succeeded in getting a sizeable number of his followers elected, and he had been invited into a coalition Cabinet. By 1925 he had become head of the government, thanks to an atmosphere of crisis created by his followers' march on Rome. The Fascist Party was an all-class coalition with workers, peasants, the middle class and the wealthy. But the main demand was for simple slogans and drastic solutions. Mussolini soon established himself in total control of the government. Indeed, it was an intellectual in his government, Giovanni Gentile, who invented the expression 'totalist' – or, as we say, 'totalitarian' – for his government. But Mussolini was not the real thing; he was only a harbinger of much worse to come.[13]

American prosperity continued to astonish the world. Europeans had a tough time overcoming their arrogance and ignorance about America, but Hollywood films had begun to disseminate details of American life and culture around the world. Cinema was the first industrialized cultural medium, even before radio and television, which had the capacity for universal appeal.[14] The silent films from Hollywood could be seen anywhere. Charlie Chaplin became a world-famous clown, perhaps the first of his kind. Cinema had started in Europe in the 1890s, but by the 1920s the USA had eclipsed European film industries. Hollywood saw cinema as an industry, and applied the logic of capitalistic profit-making to films – their production, distribution and exhibition. The diverse European film industries – British, French, German, Swedish – saw cinema as a craft or an art form, like opera. They produced the occasional classic, but constantly lost the battle for markets to Hollywood, which became a magnet for European actors, directors, cameramen and writers. Although it was American-owned, Hollywood created the first global cultural factory via its films. American culture began to bid for the crown of global culture. For Europe, culture was an elite concept; it was something the lower classes did not have, or could not enjoy. Anything popular was likely to be labelled philistine. The Americans had no aristocracy, and while there were rich and poor, the middle class constituted a larger proportion of the population in the USA than in Europe. In any case, even the workers had high incomes and could spare money for the cinema, for eating out and for sport. It was this culture, the culture of mass consumption, that Hollywood exported. It had immediate success around the world. Europe could fight back only with subtle tactics of cultural protectionism, by sneering at American philistinism, or by futile attempts to compete with America on its own terrain. The pattern was set: Hollywood had a film industry; Europe had art films. India, China and Japan followed Hollywood's example, and developed large and profitable film industries. Latin America followed Europe.

The years of normality were super-normal – indeed, snug – for America. The Republican Party won all the three presidential elections: 1920, 1924 and 1928. Warren Harding was replaced by Calvin Coolidge, who in turn was succeeded by Herbert Hoover. An engineer turned successful businessman, internationally known for his successful relief efforts in post-revolutionary Russia during the famine and the civil war, Hoover was a new politician – a meritocratic, technocratic exception to the usual run of corrupt party-machine politicians. He would have been marvellous at the management of a smoothly functioning capitalism, or even at tinkering with small marginal repairs. But what he was to face was a total breakdown of capitalism. No meritocrat or technocrat ever again became President of the USA.

The first flush of mass consumerism came to the USA in this period. Radios, electric cookers, even washing machines, were now widely available. Household gadgets proliferated as did office equipment – typewriters, calculating machines, cash registers. Car prices suited middle-class pockets, thanks to Henry Ford and the new assembly-line technology. The black Model T became a ubiquitous presence all over America. Here again, the European car industry stuck to the elite, hand-crafted, luxury product. It was to take many more years until this new Industrial Revolution would be mastered by Europe. For a while, America retained its lead as the front-ranking capitalist economy. American buildings became taller, its corporations became larger, and the stock market soared to previously undreamt-of heights. It was the Indian summer of interwar capitalism.

Then, in 1929, disaster struck.

10

The Interwar Years: Crisis and Catastrophe

In modern mathematics of dynamic systems, there are new speculations which go by the name of catastrophe or chaos theory. Chaos theory is a way of studying systematically, in mathematical terms, the way the behaviour of a dynamic system can alter its character. A system can be described by as few as two equations and two variables; three equations exhaust almost all the interesting results which can be obtained. The example I gave above in Chapter 5, of Richard Goodwin's two-equation characterization of Marx's model, is a dynamic system. Such systems are characterized by variables (two or three) and their coefficients – the strength of the influence of one variable on another. A system can be static – that is, with no movement from one period to the next: Marx's Scheme of Simple Reproduction is an example of this. Or the system can exhibit steady-state growth – at a constant rate per period. Marx's Scheme of Expanded Reproduction starts from an arbitrary point, but converges to such a steady-state growth. For a small change in coefficients, such a system can display regular cycles alongside growth, as Goodwin's system does. Tweak the coefficients a little more, and the system can plunge into catastrophe and display chaotic behaviour. All these possibilities are contained within a simple two- or three-equation non-linear dynamic system.[1]

In 1929, the capitalist system flipped from its normal cyclical growth pattern to a catastrophic depression. There was to be no full recovery from this catastrophe for the rest of the interwar period. Output and employment fell lower in this period, relative to normal capacity, than ever before. The crisis hit the most powerful capitalist economy, the USA, the hardest.[2] Unemployment went up to 25–30 per cent of the total labour force. Farmers went bankrupt by the millions. The stock market collapse – the Great Crash – ruined many recently enriched people. Every attempt to revive the economy – tariffs against foreign imports – depressed it further. In the few cases – such as that of the UK – where tariffs helped, the cost was borne by other countries which could no longer export as much as before.

The Great Crash of 1929[3] was followed by the Great Depression. By 1931, all the developed capitalist economies hit rock bottom simultaneously. Those economies which had already deflated in the 1920s – the UK being a leading example – had less far to fall than those – like the USA or France – which had enjoyed a boom. Germany had recovered by 1925, with unemployment much lower than the UK, so its fall was quite steep. There were spectacular bank failures, the Kredit Anstalt in Vienna being the most notorious. Wages fell precipitously, but even more so the prices of agricultural products. Asian and Latin American – India, Argentina, China – countries which had enjoyed an export boom in the 1920s lost tremendous amounts of export revenues.

The causes of the Great Depression have been debated endlessly. There is a separate debate in each major capitalist country – the USA, the UK, France and Germany – which seeks the causes in local history. Thus in the USA there is a debate about the role played by the Federal Reserve System (Fed), and whether the Fed's failure to pump up money supply could have caused the Depression.[4] The other strand of explanation, especially in the UK, is a Keynesian one which lays the blame on Treasury orthodoxy about public spending, and failure to tackle unemployment for fear of running a deficit. There is also the question of the Gold Standard and the ways in which an overvalued pound prevented recovery. Bank failures and the weakness of Weimar governments compounded the problems in Germany, and so on.

But in the main, it was the demise of the global economy, with its vigorous mobility of capital and labour, free trade in commodities and the non-interference of governments, which had shifted the interwar economy on to a lower level of activity. The system, however, remained international, and the connections – weaker relative to the prewar period of credits and trade – were still important. The stock market crash dried up bank credit in the USA; this led to the recall of outstanding debts from Europe, spreading the liquidity shortage there. Tariff wars worsened; the USA was the worst offender with its Hawley–Smoot Act, which raised tariffs. In the UK, the Conservative Party was protectionist, while Labour and Liberal were free-trade parties. But even the Liberals, with their leading economist John Maynard Keynes, went protectionist in the 1930s. There were talks about an Empire Free Trade Area (somewhat like a Common Market) to boost intra-imperial trade, keeping the other countries out. France devalued to grab more exports. A beggar-my-neighbour game was played by the leading capitalist countries. The weak connections of the international capitalist system were severed further. Economic isolationism replaced economic internationalism.

Some historians have laid the blame on the breakdown in economic governance. The pre-1914 global economy had British hegemony, and the Bank of

England, it is argued, saw to it that liquidity was adequately provided. It did this by small and subtle manipulation of interest rates. In the interwar period, there was no hegemon.[5] New York was powerful, but did not think the global economy was its concern. Its focus was domestic. Thus restricting bank credit in wake of the crash was a purely domestic response to a domestic problem. (It was a perverse response, but then that was the conventional wisdom of the day.) The international repercussions were ignored by the Fed even when they were pointed out by the Bank of England (among others).

Hindsight is a convenient tool for historians and social scientists. We know now that a depression could have been avoided by following Keynesian policies – by expanding demand through either higher public spending or monetary laxity. But at the time – 1929–32 – there was no clear answer. Even Keynes had not figured his way out of the impasse, though in general he had moved against the doctrines of fiscal orthodoxy with balanced budgets and fear of deficits. The problem was (and I say this with the double hindsight of writing in a context of reglobalized capitalism) that few could grasp the fact that the change from a global capitalism to one where capitalism in one country was the norm required rethinking the logic of capitalism. In a global economy, with free trade and expanding markets, a shortage of effective demand can never be a problem for any country. If it is not competitive – either because unit labour costs are too high, or because the exchange rate is overvalued – it would have a supply-side problem. The global economy, in the fifty years before 1914, had expanding markets and free trade. The last phase of that period, 1896 to 1914, had been a long upswing of the Kondratieff long wave. Markets could be found for the larger and larger volumes of industrial output. The growing urban populations of the European economies provided markets for agricultural exporters. America and the Antipodes had room enough for surplus European labour. The discoveries of gold in California and Australia had kept world liquidity in good shape. An open economy with competitive prices does not face demand shortages if there is free trade.

This was also the way Rosa Luxemburg grasped the logic of Marx's schemes of expanded reproduction. She was asking: where does demand come from for all this extra output? In her view it was necessary to rule out the possibility of an expanding domestic market – workers had to be poor and exploited. But there was a market abroad: she labelled it imperialism. If one thought of all the industrialized countries as a single economy, there was only the periphery to exchange with. So as long as foreign markets were buoyant, capitalism could expand without limits. That was the secret behind Marx's scheme.

But now, the global markets were impeded by tariffs, depressed by debts, and faced exchange rate fluctuations which had been absent under the Gold Standard. Economies had been export-orientated, but now exports were depressed as tariffs were imposed by country after country. In order to be profitable, capitalists had to find new markets. These turned out to be domestic markets. An economy's dependence on domestic markets was reinforced in the 1930s. The UK was – surprisingly – first off the mark. After spending the 1920s in a high-unemployment (10 per cent on average) phase, it recovered first: the key was to sever international (at least, outside the Empire) links even further. It abandoned the Gold Standard, and cut interest rates drastically. Tariffs were raised. Public spending did not expand, but a devaluation, plus a loose monetary policy, sparked off a recovery. It was housebuilding for the middle class that led this recovery, plus the market for consumer durables – cookers, sewing machines, washing machines and, in a few cases, even cars. It was not an export-led recovery; it was a home-demand-led one.

In the popular imagination, bankers deserved the most blame. American farmers who had their mortgages foreclosed, small businesses which had to file for bankruptcy, even rich punters whose credit with their stockbrokers was curtailed – they all knew it was the banks who had denied them money. In the American political imagination, the farther west you go, the more people are suspicious of banks. Populists in the Texan Panhandle or in the prairies had little time for fancy cheques; it was the silver dollar they trusted. But in fact they had incurred debts in good times, when prices were high. For America, the boom did not end in 1914; it had continued until 1929 – now they had to pay back, with prices 50 per cent lower.

Bankers in Europe were perennially identified with the Jews. This was one of the strands of Europe's thousand-year-old anti-Semitism. England had begun the painful task of learning tolerance early in the nineteenth century. Catholics were the first to gain official tolerance and then, after a few more decades, Jews. It was not that prejudice ever went away, but at least it did not wear an official cloak. This was not the case in France, Germany or Austria. Left-wing movements had proliferated in the postwar years, and so had right-wing ones. They often shared a diffuse hatred of big businessmen, profiteers and bankers. Racism and anti-Semitism were very much at home in these movements. The more serious Marxists tried to focus on class rather than race or religion, but at the popular level the slogans often blurred the distinction.

It was in such a context that the National Socialist German Workers' Party (NSDAP – a title identical to that of the party founded at Gotha in 1875, except for the word National) rose to prominence. After an adventurist attempt at a putsch in Bavaria, which collapsed, the National Socialists revived only after 1929. The tightness of budgets and the collapse of international credits finally undermined the SPD's beloved Weimar Republic. Various liberal and conservative parties tried to form governing coalitions. A strong leadership overriding the Constitution was much in vogue. The National Socialists emerged as the largest single party in July 1932, with the Communists and the SPD not far behind. But the Communists were under Stalin's orders to fight the SPD, not the National Socialists. Despite a setback in another election in November 1932, Adolf Hitler, leader [*Führer*] of the National Socialists, was invited to be Chancellor by President Hindenburg in January 1933.

There is an uncanny parallel between the October 1917 Revolution in Russia and the National Socialist takeover in Germany in 1933. In both cases, the winning party came to power by chance, and few thought it would survive. But in both cases, observers reckoned without the leader and the nature of the party. The Bolsheviks were led by Lenin, and – as I argued in Chapter 7 – it was Lenin and his tenacity in holding on to power which was unique. The Bolsheviks had become a mass party by October 1917, yet it was Lenin's model of a tightly knit, strongly led party which was crucial to holding on to power. Hitler's case was similar. His immense capacity for evil, which emerged later, should not detract from his ability to consolidate his power once he had been invited to be Chancellor. He, too, had built up a party which relied on strong leadership, a mass party which was hierarchical in its structure. He, too, could deploy militant party members in fights against the police or against other parties, mainly the SPD. Upon coming to power in January 1933, he used constitutional powers to bar the Communist Party (KPD) and held new elections in which the National Socialists swept the board. Then he could rewrite the Constitution. By June 1933, Germany had become a totalitarian state. What took Mussolini several years, Hitler did in six months. Lenin consolidated his position by dismissing the elections of the Constituent Assembly as irrelevant. Hitler did it by banning the KPD and holding new elections which allowed him to do as he liked.

Lenin and Hitler are not, of course, the same. Lenin, despite his penchant for violent prose and use of the NKVD-OGPU, never caused the carnage that Hitler did. Lenin genuinely thought Russia was just a junior partner in a worldwide revolution that would be led by Germany. There is no racism or anti-Semitism in Lenin's rhetoric against capitalists or bankers. I make comparisons between them because the speed with which each consolidated power was unexpected for both their friends and their enemies. By their achievements in this respect, regardless of what one may think of communism or fascism, they illustrated a peculiarity which has marked the twentieth century: the retrospective light their success has cast on obscure political events – in Lenin's case, the 1903 split in the Russian Social Democratic Labour Party between Mensheviks and Bolsheviks; in Hitler's case, the Beer Hall putsch of 1924. The twenty-five-point 'manifesto' of the German workers' party (as the National Socialists were known in 1920) would have been consigned to 'the dustbin of history' (to use Trotsky's memorable phrase) had Hitler not come to power. The small split in the editorial board of a Russian left-wing magazine with a very small circulation – *Iskra* – would not even have merited the dullest academic study had it not been for the events of 1917. There were to be similar surprises of small beginnings rapidly acquiring worldwide significance in the case of the Chinese and Vietnamese Communists, or in the horrific doings of the Khmer Rouge in Cambodia. Nothing is so obscure, so bizarre, or so far-fetched that it can be safely ignored as unlikely to succeed after those experiences.

Leadership was the vital ingredient in each case, whether for good or for evil. But there was also the changed political context in the twentieth century. Population had trebled in Europe over the course of the nineteenth century and, despite the toll taken by the war, kept on growing. The masses changed politics as the democratic impulse became strengthened with the collapse of monarchies and aristocracies. This tendency was fuelled by the new media – newspapers, radio and films. Propaganda was a twentieth-century invention. The technological innovations were made by individual genius inventors who could also exploit their business possibilities – Edison and Marconi, and the Lumière Brothers. The newspaper barons – William Randolph Hearst, Lords Northcliffe and Beaverbrook – had counterparts in other countries. Print was cheap, and newspapers were affordable for those on the the lowest income. The tabloid came into its own at this time, giving a respectable and wide circulation to yellow journalism. The propagandist politician was well aware of the power of radio and the cinema, as Lenin's writings and Hitler's actions testify. Even a dictator had to be popular – unlike a king, who expected and received loyalty.

The National Socialists had a muddled mixture of left- and right-wing views. They hated profiteers, but not capitalism. They disliked bankers, but were not averse to money, like some utopian socialists. They hated the Jews with passion, but that was the only certainty in their programme. Hitler took care to project an image of fiscal orthodoxy and monetary discipline. His Finance Minister, Count Schwerin von Kosigk, was from outside his party, and remained Finance Minister until 1945. His choice for central bank governor was Hjalmar Schacht who had a reputation for sound money. German business was afraid of the nationalization agenda which the National Socialists had put forward in their various election manifestos. Some in the party – like Feder – even took it seriously. But Hitler never believed in any economic theory. He needed funds for his party, and he was friendly to big business, which was betting on any outcome which would protect them. But the National Socialists also needed the co-operation of business to win the primary battle they faced – against unemployment.

The National Socialists claimed that they halved unemployment between 1933 and 1935. German unemployment had trebled from an average of 1.9 million in 1929 to 5.5 million in 1932; the monthly figures showed an even wider range: 1.25 million in July 1929 to 6.1 million in 1932. Employment fell from 20 million in 1929 to 11.4 million in early 1933. Measures to reduce unemployment had been started – mainly work creation schemes – even before Hitler came to power. The economy had also reached the bottom of the cycle in 1932, and started recovering for normal cyclical reasons. But these facts are clearer in retrospect than they were at the time. Unemployment was the spectre haunting capitalism; free-market economics and fiscal/monetary orthodoxy, favoured by the liberal order, were failing to get rid of it. Indeed, in 1933, Harvard University's Economics Department was warning the newly elected President, Franklin Roosevelt, of the dangers of inflation if he did not balance the budget.

The National Socialists brought unemployment down to 2.8 million by 1934 and only 2.1 million by 1935. Like everything else about Hitler's regime, their achievement has led to a lot of debate among historians of Germany. But there is no doubt that statistical fiddling (redefinition of unemployment, etc.) played only a marginal part in this – less, perhaps, than comparable efforts in the UK during the 1980s. There was also no massive public works scheme financed by large deficits. At this juncture, in 1935, tax cuts plus some monetary easing seem to have worked, with a large multiplier. Trade unions had been smashed early in the course of the Hitler regime, and businessmen were shrewd enough to see that their profit lay in co-operating with the new regime. Workers were happy that they had jobs – with or without unions.

This moderate reflation was not the main aim of Hitler's economic strategy.[6] After 1935, German rearmament began in earnest, and there was total mobilization of the economy to this end. Hitler saw the economy as a resource for his political aims; these required rearmament for a future war for territorial expansion – for *Lebensraum*. He launched a Four Year Plan for this purpose.

Details apart, there are great similarities between the Soviet Five Year plan of 1929–33 and the German Four Year Plan. This similarity is brought out if we refer back to Rosa Luxemburg's critique of Marx's Scheme of Expanded Reproduction. As I said in Chapter 9, Stalin used the scheme (as developed by a Russian economist called Feldman) to prioritize Department I: machine building. But recall that Luxemburg had said that a Department III – armaments – could absorb surplus as well. For the Soviet Union, as for Germany, the problem was one not of absorbing surplus but of allocating scarce resources. Stalin chose Department I because his was a much more underdeveloped economy; he did not have a large Deptartment I to start with. Despite the depredations of war, the German economy retained a much larger capacity for machine goods – steel, electricity, transport vehicles, engineering – than the Russian. Thus Hitler's choice was between expanding either the wage-good sector or armaments. His entire political philosophy was geared to the rearmament of Germany.

Hitler's challenge to the liberal order that the Allied Powers represented at this stage (i.e. long before *Kristallnacht*) was to harness capitalism while rejecting free markets. He abandoned the liberal tenets of free trade, free mobility of capital and labour, and *laissez-faire*, but without challenging capitalism and profit-making. Planning replaced the free market. Tariffs and import substitution replaced free trade. Labour was denied free mobility; private capital was told to co-operate if it wanted to remain free and profitable. The subsequent history of the war and the Holocaust has so totally destroyed the National Socialists' reputation that few today would admit that much of the planning in developing countries after 1945 – in India, for example – drew on ideas from this experiment. The Soviet Union was claimed as a model more often, but wherever capitalism and planning have coexisted, the original model has been the German one.

But Hitler not only challenged the liberal economic order, he also challenged its political tenets. The nineteenth-century liberal order in Europe had been pushed reluctantly by various social forces into extending the franchise. It had thus become steadily more democratic. This was so, of course, in Western Europe. In the USA, the liberal order had been much more democratic for much longer than in Europe (again excepting Black and Native Americans). Women did not have suffrage on either side of the Atlantic during the nineteenth century, but government had to be accountable to an elected legislature, and there had to be the possibility of different parties coming to power. France, the USA, the UK, were all in this mould. Germany before the

First World War had not quite got there; the SPD would never have been allowed to come to power, and the Kaiser was not accountable to the Reichstag. After 1919, the Weimar Republic had joined the liberal club. Hitler challenged this by establishing a one-party state within capitalism. The Soviet Union had rejected liberal democracy.

The rejection of liberal economics as well as liberal democracy was to stay in fashion after the Second World War, but it wore more pseudo-Marxist clothes and was called – inaccurately – socialism. The fundamental difference between Stalin and Hitler hinged on their attitude towards capitalism. Stalin's challenge to the liberal order was that economic development and industrialization to a very high level could be achieved without resort to private property and profit-making. It was to declare the profit motive redundant to accumulation and economic growth. Hitler's challenge was to declare the free market wasteful and unnecessary for economic growth under capitalism. Germany had already experimented with planning during the First World War. There had been a long tradition of rejecting free trade as an English doctrine, and Friedrich List was very much a German economist who also captured the American imagination. Marx had nothing but contempt for List, and vigorously supported free trade. List believed in free movement of labour and capital within a customs union [*Zollverein*], but tariffs against foreign goods. The European Community, with its single internal market and tariff barriers against imports, represents a Listian model rather than an Adam Smith one. But Hitler rejected the domestic *laissez-faire* aspects of List. It was this double rejection that made the National Socialists (stripped of their virulent anti-Semitism) the precursors of post-1945 socialism in many developing countries.

The reaffirmation of the liberal political order was accomplished by Franklin Roosevelt in his New Deal.[7] He, too, rejected pure *laissez-faire*, though the New Deal eventually made few inroads into the liberal economic order. Social insurance and trade-union rights were entrenched; farmers won special privileges in terms of protected prices; and for every potential house-buyer there was easier mortgage financing. Agriculture was thus insulated from the free market to aid recovery. Banking was reformed to restrict its freedom of diversification into other regions or other financial services (the Glass–Steagal Act). But Roosevelt's interference with free markets was minimal, though it was novel enough to arouse great opposition. Nor – contrary to later impressions – did he deviate much from fiscal orthodoxy. He demonstrated American power by taking over the task of fixing the price of gold in his US Treasury. Roosevelt's goals were to save democracy and capitalism by minimal tinkering. He reaffirmed the strength of the liberal order even as he mildly challenged it.

Yet the liberal order did face its biggest challenge during these ten years. Capitalism, during this time, seemed to be fulfilling every dire prediction made in the vulgar catechisms of the Marxism preached by the Third International. The reserve army of unemployed workers had greatly expanded, and the wages of the employed were precarious. (Prices of foodstuffs fell more than money wages, and statistics show a rise in real wages for those who were employed in this period.) The lower middle classes – the self-employed and small-scale industrialists, shopkeepers and farmers and professionals – were all being thrown on the scrapheap to join the reserve army. Output had halved, if not worse. There was no quick cyclical recovery and, unlike in the 1870s, the masses were larger and more articulate.

During the immediate postwar period (1919–23), there had been left-wing revolutionary uprisings in Germany, Hungary, Austria, Northern Italy and, of course, Russia. As I said above, all except the Russian Revolution collapsed. Workers chose to reject the communist alternative, and stuck to reformist socialism. But even at that time, the UK and France did not see any serious revolts. There were problems in Ireland and India for the UK, but nothing serious at home. Here, during the Great Depression, was yet more fertile ground for a communist revolution, but in no advanced capitalist country did that happen. Right-wing authoritarian regimes in Germany and Italy set the pattern for Hungary and, later, for Spain and Portugal. Socialist parties were banned in the fascist countries. In the UK, the Labour Party came to power in 1929, the worst time for a socialist party. Within two years, it was overwhelmed.[8] It failed in the task of stabilizing capitalism, much less reforming it. But the UK did not lurch into fascism, despite the ambitions of Oswald Mosley. It was a parliamentary right-wing party, the Conservative Party, which formed the backbone of the National Government with Ramsay MacDonald.[9] It was this coalition which was able to abandon the Gold Standard – something the previous Labour government was told could not be done. The Liberal Party was decimated in the 1931 election, and Labour Party seats fell to a very low level. But neither a left nor a right revolution occurred.

The situation in France was similar. Here there was a greater proliferation of right-wing movements – *Action Française* in particular. The Third Republic was used to coalition governments as well as short-lived ones. The socialists came to power in 1936 and Léon Blum's government – albeit much beleaguered –

managed one long-term reform in working conditions: paid holidays. It fell because of the Spanish Civil War, and its failure to support the Republicans openly and boldly while the fascist powers supported Franco. Yet France did not go fascist – not until 1940.

A novel experiment in socialism was carried out in Sweden.[10] The Swedish Social Democratic Workers' Party [Socialdemokratiska Arbetare Partiet – SAP] had adopted a revisionist stance very much in accordance with Edouard Bernstein's philosophy. It was interested not in the final downfall of capitalism but in the immediate improvement of working conditions. It secured a third of the popular vote throughout the 1920s, and came to power in 1932. It had made a long-term pact with the Farmers' Party. This coalition of workers and farmers stayed in power for the next forty-four years, allowing it the strength to come as near to the best Socialism within Capitalism that one could get. The SAP was able to overcome unemployment by pursuing progressive taxation and high public spending, while never abandoning a policy of stable prices. Jobs were created by a housebuilding programme and work-creation programmes, and workers were given maternity benefits and paid holidays. Sweden was the pioneer in establishing a tripartite wage-bargaining structure at national level: trade unions and employers, with government as referee. It was also blessed with some of the most imaginative and unorthodox economists – Myrdal, Lindahl, Lundberg and Ohlin, all of whom, in one way or another, were inspired by Knut Wicksell, the best-known Swedish economist. The Swedish economists claimed – quite rightly – to have anticipated Keynes's theories.

The rejection of the communist alternative by advanced capitalist democracies twice during the interwar years is not accidental but systematic. It was a preference by the bulk of the working class – now fully eligible to vote – to stay with the possibility of a reformable capitalism: a system which, despite inequality and exploitation, afforded trade-union rights. Economism, which Lenin and Luxemburg had denounced as the limited vision of trade unionists, proved strong enough to reassure the workers that better days could come. Democratic governments, even right-wing ones, attempted to alleviate their hardships. They faced (perhaps self-imposed) fiscal and monetary constraints. There was much agitation and violence. But the callousness with which nineteenth-century statesmen could treat the unemployed was no longer possible. The First World War had democratized the liberal order.

There was also the contingent fact of the stupidity of the communist parties ruled by the Third International under Stalin's command. They fought socialist parties, and divided workers everywhere. In Germany, they were even willing to collaborate with Hitler in order to eliminate their SPD rivals. Stalin had labelled the parties of the Second International 'social fascist'. The communists isolated themselves, and lost. For at least once in his life, Trotsky was brilliant in his clear-sighted analysis of Stalin's mistaken policy in Germany. But he was in exile, and could not accomplish anything.[11]

Stalin, of course, had just committed the biggest and most unnecessary blunder of his political life. Impatient with the slow rate at which agricultural surplus was being mobilized for industrialization, and unwilling to pay the price at which Russian peasants wanted to sell their surplus foods, he launched the collectivization campaign in 1931.[12] Never had a government launched a war upon its own people so ruthlessly. The expression 'class warfare' was meant analogically, not literally, by Marx and Engels.

There had been insidious examples of a war against the countryside during the period of war communism (1919–21). The Bolsheviks had lost that war, but not the civil war – thanks to the peasantry's support. Now Stalin launched a programme against the countryside on the dubious grounds that it was not the ordinary peasants but the rich *kulaks* who were the class enemy. In fact there never were many rich kulaks – not after the peasants' land-grab of 1917–18. There were a lot of small landowning peasants who had just obtained the possibility of making some income by selling surplus produce. It was this peasantry which had stayed faithful, while the sailors had revolted in the famous Kronstadt rebellion of 1921, and the left opposition, with proletarian support, had backed them. Lenin and Trotsky were able to crush Kronstadt and decimate the left opposition because the countryside was bought off with the NEP. Now, in this brutal campaign, Stalin won physically, but Russian agriculture was put back by decades. The peasants destroyed their cattle, and such meagre stores as they had. The productivity of Russian agriculture plummeted, and was not to recover for forty years. Instead of mobilizing surplus more efficiently – which could have been done through market exchange, as Lenin had realized in 1921 – Stalin reduced the surplus drastically for the foreseeable future. The Soviet Union was to suffer from low availability of wage goods for the next forty years.

Collectivization was an unnecessary panic measure. Stalin faced no challenge within the Party, nor did Russia face an external threat. Nothing, absolutely nothing – in Marxian economics or any other economics, for that matter – recommends such foolishness. It was a throwback to Russia before Peter the Great, which increased the misery of industrialization a hundredfold. No country had succeeded in making collectivization of agriculture work; few have tried it. If there had to be an advertisement for private property, it came not from the rich industrial capitalists but from the almost precapitalist smallholder in the Russian countryside.

But Stalin managed to keep all this misery well hidden, just as he also kept the world in the dark about his concentration camps. In the 1930s, foolish enthusiasm for the 'New Civilization' that the Soviet Union represented was displayed by Sidney and Beatrice Webb.[13] It was a poignant moment for those pioneers of reformist socialism. They did love bureaucracy, which for them – as for Hegel – represented the selfless universal omniscient class, so they loved the epitome of bureaucracy: the USSR. But not to value the freedoms which had been so hard won by ordinary people in their back yard, and had been lost in the Soviet Union, was bankruptcy of the intellect. They did not even have the excuse of having joined the Communist Party. Many others, communists and fellow-travellers, were to repeat such acts of intellectual bankruptcy throughout the period of Stalinism, which ended only in 1956.

By 1935, Stalin realized the seriousness of the German threat. Germany had historically coveted lands on its eastern frontier, and – like France on its western front – Russia was Germany's arch-enemy on that front. The Weimar government had collaborated quietly with the Soviet Union even in the area of military co-operation, but Hitler was different. He was now in power, and Stalin's German gamble had failed, just like his Chinese gamble. Stalin changed his tactics and launched the idea of a popular front. Communists were to co-operate with socialists and 'all progressive forces'. This period led to an efflorescence of Marxian studies in the West. Of course, the communists acted as the keepers of orthodoxy. The Marxism projected was a rather crude version of the windmill–feudalism, steam engine–capitalism type. But there was a big growth in Marxist historiography, sociology and philosophy. Translations and publications of hitherto-unpublished manuscripts – the *Grundrisse,* for example – were encouraged. Of course, there had been a powerful German tradition in Marxist philosophy, thanks to Georg Lukačs and the Frankfurt School.[14] But by 1936 the Frankfurt School had migrated westwards, ending up in the USA. Lukačs had been silenced – or, at least, made into an intellectual helot of the Third International.

There was very little innovation, however, in Marxian economics.[15] The Soviet Union had, of course, abandoned any serious inquiry into Marxian economics, or even its use, except to exorcize ghosts and dissidents. But by this time (1936–39), Keynes had become the topic of interest, thanks to his *General Theory.* Attempts were made to draw similarities between Keynes and Marx, to give Keynes a left-wing interpretation. Marxian economics as we know it today is a post-1936 Western enterprise. In some ways, the debate about Marx – interrupted in 1913, and finally killed off in 1929 – resumed in 1936. But this time, it had no political party of any significance behind it. Marxian economics came back as an academic discipline rather than a political weapon – except, of course, for the Communist parties in the West. But they did not matter, for it was clear to Stalin and the Third International that whatever the rhetoric about capitalism being in its terminal crisis, the chance of a Communist revolution in the West had been missed. Revolution was to be the rhetoric, not the reality, of Western Marxism.

It was also clear by 1936 that a Second World War was not far away. Japan had already invaded Manchuria in 1931, and moved on to China by 1937. The Spanish Civil War was a test run for new military hardware. Only the Anglo-Saxon powers – the USA and the UK – stayed firm in their delusions of peace. The League of Nations, idealistically launched after the Treaty of Versailles, had failed to police the world, and the Allied Powers were unprepared for war. In the UK, only Winston Churchill saw the danger of German rearmament clearly, but he had burnt his boats by his old imperialist stance on India. Italy had invaded Abyssinia (Ethiopia) and got away with it, as had Japan in China. There was no rule of law in international relations. Hitler took advantage of this, reoccupied the demilitarized Rhineland, forced Austria into an Anschluss, and staked a claim for parts of Czechoslovakia, which were readily conceded by the British Prime Minister, Neville Chamberlain.

An imperialist mentality still lingered in Europe. The French and the British conceded that Germany had 'legitimate aspirations' to an empire. But while the British and French empires were overseas, Germany wanted territory in Europe. Since 1648 and the Treaty of Westphalia, sovereignty of a kingdom or a state had been recognized in European diplomacy. This did not prevent war, as the history of Anglo–French relations throughout the eighteenth century shows. Nevertheless, territorial aggrandizement on the European continent was frowned upon, even fought against. Napoleon had tried most spectacularly to acquire a European empire, and had finally been rebuffed at Waterloo by a coalition of European powers led by Great Britain. Hitler was reopening the possibility of a land-based empire for Germany in the East. The response of the Western Allies – Britain and France – was to concede Czechoslovakia, but to balk when it came to Poland. Stalin conceded Hitler's demands by signing the Molotov–Ribbentrop Pact. This won both sets of enemies of Hitler some time to rearm, but the unfinished agenda of European imperialism was to lead to a Second World War.

It became a world war because Japan had designs on the Asian possessions of the European imperial powers. Japanese imperialism shared Hitler's *Lebensraum* logic, if only to find the markets and raw materials for Japan's growing economy. The Second World War became the final war of European imperialism, but now fought without monarchs playing an active executive role. Germany involved the USSR by invading it in June 1941. Japan made it a full world war by attacking Pearl Harbor in December 1941. For the second time in a century, the USA was involved in a European war but this time its own back yard was under attack from Japan.

11

Curing Capitalism: Keynes, Schumpeter and Hayek

Economics has a very high – albeit somewhat controversial – reputation today. Economists are frequently quoted in newspapers, often consulted by governments and international agencies. In a number of countries, an economist has served as Finance Minister – a technopol[1] – to carry out deep reforms or structural adjustments: Balcerowicz in Poland, Aspe in Mexico, Manmohan Singh in India. The economist has been ubiquitous as soothsayer, sage and saviour.

But it was not always so. During the interwar years, when the economic world was in a serious crisis, economics was neither prescient in predicting the crisis nor quick in offering solutions when trouble did come. Orthodox liberal economists – the overwhelming bulk of the profession – believed that the economy, left to the free play of markets with minimal government interference, would be self-correcting. They had failed to see the fundamental structural breach in global capitalism caused by the First World War. This was partly because they kept on advocating policies to get back to prewar normality, but partly also because economic theory as built up between 1870 and 1920 – the marginal revolution – was a theory in which neither space nor time played a crucial role. The Theory of General Equilibrium associated with the name of the French economist Léon Walras was a monumental logical construction of great elegance which showed how myriads of separate but interconnected markets for commodities and services, for labour, land and capital, could come into a simultaneous – hence general – equilibrium. The economy was seen as a stationary, unchanging, phenomenon or, at best, as growing smoothly (naturally), with no abrupt structural breaks. The British School under Alfred Marshall had spent much energy trying to understand the workings of the economy industry by industry, and began to admit that the market might need corrections at the margin, where private and social benefits might not be identical. The Austrian economists, led by Carl Menger, were ferociously jealous of the liberal economic order. They saw no need for any interference. An elaborate theory was constructed by Eugen von Böhm-Bawerk to justify the return to capital as coming not from the exploitation of labour but from adopting more elaborate and time-consuming technology. Time brought no uncertainty, and was represented as past (embodied in machinery) rather than future. All the schools of economics were fiercely anti-inflationary, and preached budget discipline. But they agreed on one proposition: left to itself, the economy would produce full employment of resources.

It is useful here to examine an example of liberal thinking. Ludwig von Mises was a leading member of the Austrian School, a student of Böhm-Bawerk and a very influential thinker during the twentieth century. His pioneering book *Socialism* (1922)[2] was a thorough examination of the question of whether a socialist economy with collective ownership of means of production, and suspension of free markets, was feasible. I shall discuss him below (Chapter 12). But this is how he described the working of a liberal economy, repeating his statement without amendment in 1932:

> where production is perfectly balanced there is no unemployment. Unemployment is a consequence of economic change, and where production is unhindered by the interferences of authorities and trade unions, it is always only a phenomenon of transition, which the alteration of wage rates tends to remove. By means of appropriate institutions, by the extension, for example, of labour exchanges, which would evolve out of the economic mechanism in the unimpeded market – i.e. where the individual is free to choose and to change his profession and the place where he works – the duration of separate cases of unemployment could be so much shortened that it would no longer be considered a serious evil.[3]

Thus unemployment was transitional or frictional, as economists would say today. If it persisted, the fault lay with 'the interferences of authorities and trade unions'. At the time of the Great Depression, leading economists repeated more or less the same message. The economy was only temporarily out of equilibrium; interfere as little as possible, and everything will be all right.

As I have said, the fifty years preceding the First World War were years of steady growth for economies, stable or falling prices, and rising standards of living in the advanced capitalist countries. But there were also cycles over that period. Marx was the first economist to make cycles a central part of his theory, but he saw them as an integral part of growth in capitalism. Cycles were not integrated into the theory of general equilibrium; indeed, even today, integrating cycles into general equilibrium remains a fruitful area of research. There were many statistical accounts of cycles, and many 'cranks' had theories of why they happened. The famous British economist William Stanley Jevons tried to build an explanation of cycles based on the frequency of sunspots, which in turn affected agricultural output and prices. Some people thought that cycles were caused by the surplus or lack of bank credit, and blamed the Jews for that. The Theory of General Equilibrium kept clear of money or credit; it modelled the real economy as a set of barter transactions in which money played no role.

There was one major exception, and that was the Swedish economist Knut Wicksell.[4] Wicksell had come somewhat late to economics from journalism because he was agitated by 'the population question' – the cause of poverty among the working classes. He thought overpopulation was the major cause of poverty, and advocated birth control. He wrote a pamphlet called 'A Few Words on the Most Important Causes of Social Misery and its Remedy, with Special Reference to Drunkenness' when he was only twenty-nine. He was a pacifist who believed Sweden ought to capitulate if Russia invaded, and he was irreverent about Christianity. He steeped himself in Walras's theory, and mastered the Austrian School's capital theory. He was well versed in classical economics, and familiar with Marx's work. Unlike many others in his profession, Wicksell had socialist leanings.

Wicksell focused on the interest rate – the cost of borrowing that an investor faced and the rate of return he could obtain from that investment. Marx called the latter the rate of profit, but – as Hayek explained later in the 1930s[5] – that made profit a dirty word for economists. Wicksell called the rate of return the natural rate. Some people saved their money and put it in banks, or bought finance assets – bonds, shares. But in the main, savers were passive, and happy with a stable rate of return. Banks could then fix their interest rate for borrowers also to be quite stable, and not change it frequently. But the natural rate may suddenly go up, because of a new invention or a new market. If the natural rate were to go above the rate of interest, entrepreneurs would have an incentive to borrow. This would lead to new factories, shops or railroads, and increased employment. Such extra activity would have its own positive effects on demand, and other people would find that they could borrow and make money. This is a boom which becomes a cumulative dynamic process. A depression is exactly the reverse, with bank credit being too expensive for entrepreneurs, since they cannot hope to make a return on capital high enough to cover the cost of borrowing. Businesses do not get started, or if they do start, they soon shut down. Bankruptcies rise and they, in turn, damp down further activity. So the cycle is an interplay between the investors/entrepreneurs and their expectation of the rate of return, and the conservative bankers who fix their interest rates with stability in mind.

Wicksell's theory was much more realistic than anything that had gone before it in orthodox economics. In Walras's theory, entrepreneurs worked for zero incomes – for charity! But Wicksell had no explanation of how booms turned into depressions – how, that is, the cycle had a turning point.

Joseph Schumpeter was a maverick member of the Austrian School. He was also very sure of himself, declaring that he wanted to be the best rider of horses, or the best economist, or the best lover, in Europe. He confessed towards the end that he had achieved two of his three ambitions, but did not elaborate on which two. Before he was thirty, he wrote his most influential book, *The Theory of Economic Development.*[6] It was not translated into English until 1934, but his argument was well known. Schumpeter had mastered liberal economics, but he had also read Marx very closely. His book was a careful and detailed answer to Marx's question about the origin of profits. Schumpeter had an alternative answer to that of Marx: profits came not from exploitation of labour but from *innovations,* and it was the entrepreneur who launched innovations.

By innovations, Schumpeter meant much more than just a better mousetrap. His notion of innovation spanned new leaps in industrial technology: the steam technology of the 1780s; the railroads of the 1830s; steamships and, later, electricity, steel and chemicals in the late nineteenth century; automobiles and aeroplanes in the early twentieth. Today we would add the microchip revolution and the Internet. He also included new transport routes such as the Suez Canal and the Panama Canal, the discovery of new territories, new financial services – cheques and clearing banks. Many of these innovations had been anticipated by scientific or technological *inventions,* but the commercial opportunity for the exploitation of these inventions was perceived only by a person of vision and large ambitions – the entrepreneur. Ferdinand de Lesseps, who thought of and raised money for the Suez Canal, would be one such. In the 1990s, it would be Bill Gates with Windows.

Innovations often clustered together and made for an Industrial Revolution. But they came only periodically and discontinuously, in waves. One wave of innovations would break the mould of the old stationary economy. The pioneers would borrow money and launch their innovations. They would enjoy a temporary monopoly, and make immense profits (if, that is, they were successful, since there are also failures in this life). These innovations would launch the economy on a growth path with an upswing that might last twenty to twenty-five years. But imitators would soon come in and erode the entrepreneurs' excess profits. Output would multiply, but prices would start falling and profits would go down. A downswing would set in until another wave of innovations hit the economy. All in all, Schumpeter thought a cycle set off by a wave of innovations lasted fifty years, rather like a Kondratieff wave.

But innovations were also destructive. Steam-powered cotton-spinning made cottage spinning redundant; the same applied to weaving, as we saw in the case of the Silesian weavers. The cotton textile industry of Britain so cheapened these products that older handicraft methods in India were wiped out, as they were in European countries. Railroads made canals and horse carriages redundant. This was 'the gale of creative destruction'. Prices of products and services fell precipitously, output expanded, but many older businesses were ruined.

Thus capitalism grew by innovations, from wave upon wave of creative destruction. Profits rose sharply and then, as competition increased, fell to normal low levels until another wave came along. Along the way, labour productivity increased by leaps and bounds, raw materials could be brought from great distances at low prices, goods came within the reach of ordinary people. Progress occurred, but at the expense of destroying old technology and businesses.

So Schumpeter's view of capitalism is a dialectical one – the good and the bad are inextricably intertwined. You cannot have innovations and growth if you protect old technologies and restrict enterprise for fear of losses. It also allows for growth and cycles, for the ups and downs of the profit rate. It is much as Marx and Engels had described the achievements of capitalism in the *Communist Manifesto*: 'All that is solid melts into air'.

Nineteenth-century liberal economic theory concentrated too much on demonstrating that the markets would equilibrate – so much so that they ruled out booms and busts. In underpinning Adam Smith's vision of the Invisible Hand with their new and sophisticated value theory, they missed out on his vision of growth, and the notion of unintended consequences. While they proved with great elegance (and the proofs have been made even more mathematically rigorous since) that the market 'works' to establish a stationary equilibrium, the liberal school of thought forgot that the market and capitalism were not the same thing. Markets are ubiquitous in capitalism, but they work in the context of a dynamic ever-changing disequilibrium. The purpose of the economists' 'market' is to allocate resources efficiently. The purpose of every capitalist is to make profits and expand the business – to accumulate. For the economist, a market works when profits are eliminated. For capitalism, this would be catastrophic. Whether the market works or not, the system has to be profitable, that is, generate sufficient profits to keep enough companies in business so that they can provide employment and generate output.

Schumpeter combines these two views by looking at the market and zero profits as a condition of a stationary economy, and positive but fluctuating profits as a condition of a growing economy in disequilibrium. Eventually, every growth wave peters out and reaches a stationary state until the next wave comes along. In between the fifty-year-long Kondratieff waves, there were ten-year cycles such as Marx discussed (called Juglar cycles) as well as very short three-to-four-year ones (called Kitchin cycles). The Great Depression of 1931 was a confluence of a downswing of all three types of cycle. That was Schumpeter's answer, but he had no policy proposal for how an economy could come out of these. There, he remained an orthodox liberal economist.[7]

There were economists who argued that the Great Depression, far from being a problem that had to be urgently solved, was a cure for the unhealthy features of the economy. Thus it had to be allowed to run its course, no matter how long it might take and however much misery it might cause. Cycles were signs of excesses and imbalances. Booms were based on false optimism on the part of investors, fed by the banks' failure to match the cost of credit to the rate of return. Friedrich von Hayek, a thirty-year-old Austrian economist, captured the imagination of many young economists with his book *Prices and Production*,[8] based on lectures given at the London School of Economics. Developing the insights of Wicksell and Mises, he said that booms were the creation of bankers' credit expansion at low rates of interest. This then led to investors embarking on projects with long gestation periods, so that resources were diverted away from consumer-goods production to investment-goods production. This caused inflation, and an unexpected fall in real wages, leading to demands for higher wages and more credit by producers still embarked on their investment projects. If the projects were allowed to finish, then productivity was raised and a larger volume of consumer goods became available, and prices could fall again. But typically, banks panic and curtail credit before the investment projects come to fruition. Then the depression follows. Projects are abandoned incomplete, and all that capital is 'malinvested'. The answer was not to give extra credit in order to let the projects finish – to reflate – but to let the economy work out the bad effects of excess credit until the rate of interest is once again equal to the natural rate – that is, the profit rate that can be earned.

Hayek's theory caused a lot of excitement, because he combined a theory of bank credit with a theory of a 'real' cycle. He introduced a whole generation of British and American students to the intricacies of Austrian capital theory. In his lectures he used some interesting diagrams, and his style was highly abstract and austere.

The young Paul Sweezy – later America's most famous Marxist economist – came from Harvard to the LSE because he was told, he said, that 'Hayek had the key to capitalism'.[9] But Hayek was an old-fashioned liberal economist. In his world, an economy could develop calmly and steadily, without any cycles, as long as the market was allowed to work naturally, and prices were not 'distorted'. It is bankers charging too low an interest rate that sparks off a boom which has to be paid for by a long depression.

Hayek's theory failed to provide a cure; indeed, he himself was against any quick fix. Money supply and bank credit needed to be controlled so that they would cause neither inflation nor boom. But even then, Hayek's whole philosophy was against any solutions which did not come naturally from a free play of market forces. The Great Depression of 1931 was too severe for people or policymakers to heed his austere advice. Hayek was also soon displaced by Keynes in the public imagination, and was not to vindicate himself until the 1970s.

It was Keynes who completely transformed economics by his book *The General Theory of Employment, Interest and Money*.[10] When it came out, in 1936, Keynes did not just revolutionize economics; he saved its reputation and, indeed, made economics the one social science which acquired a prestige equal to that of natural sciences. If economists are in worldwide demand today (even as people tell jokes about them), it is thanks to Keynes. Above all, Keynes gave people hope; things could be made better by using human reason and ingenuity. The market did not know best, and whatever the outcome of the market's workings might be, it was possible to do better.

In the preface to *The General Theory*, Keynes says that his book is addressed to his fellow economists. It is not a popular, easy read; it is a difficult, unevenly written, demanding book. Its message has been disputed ever since it came out, and even today, books and monographs contesting the Keynesian terrain are being written. But much of that can be left to academic economists. For my present purpose, it is enough to note how Keynes created macroeconomics. He gave us a theory of the single economy disconnected from the world economy. Keynes was much concerned with British problems; he had also bombarded Roosevelt with his solutions for the American economy. But he chose to theorize about an economy which is more or less closed: neither international trade nor capital movements mattered. For this 'capitalism in one country', Keynes fashioned the tools for regulation and control. He found a solution that was neither the German war socialism/Soviet state capitalism nor the liberal free market of Mises and Hayek. His cure did not require a totalitarian control over the economy, as the National Socialists had imposed on Germany. Keynes was a godsend for the liberal political order. He fashioned an economic recipe for countries which could avoid economic catastrophe. But, as a price, he asked for the abandonment of liberal economic theory.

The most controversial (to this day) of Keynes's propositions was that a free market economy, left to itself, was most likely to end up in underemployment equilibrium. This implied that full employment was not automatically guaranteed by a free market economy left to its own devices. The economy could get to a level of employment below full employment, but it would stay at that level. There would be people involuntarily unemployed. This proposition went against all classical and neoclassical theories, whether based on a labour theory of value or a marginalist value theory. To this day, this proposition – that a free market economy could be trapped in an underemployment equilibrium, implying the possibility of involuntary unemployment – is challenged. Modern macroeconomics, as I shall show below, has modified these propositions so much as to restore the liberal economic theory Keynes challenged (as if to validate my claim that Keynes is still debated, the day after I first wrote this, Samuel Brittan returned to the issue of 'the polemics for and against the legacy of Keynes[11]').

But for fifty years, Keynes ruled the roost – he not only had a theory, he also had a cure. The cure was government spending, which would provide initial employment and disburse income. After this initial injection of spending, there was a multiplier process which increased income and employment severalfold. The initial government spending could be recouped in additional tax revenue paid from the extra income. The multiplier process depended on what Keynes called his psychological law that consumption as a ratio of income was less than one. The higher the income, the lower the ratio. Thus savings went up as people got richer. But consumption was a stable function of income, on which governments could rely. It was private investment which was likely to be volatile, sensitive to changes in expectations about the future profitability of any investment undertaken. If investors were optimistic, if their 'animal spirits' were buoyant, then the economy could even reach a state of overfull employment. But if they were pessimistic, then they would postpone investment. Even if banks cut interest rates, investors would not respond. Hence the role of public investment, which is not motivated by profitability. Public investment takes up the slack between savings and private investment.

Keynes showed that the standard answers of orthodox economic theory are not valid. If there was unemployment, wage reduction was neither possible nor likely to be efficacious. Workers bargained over money wages, and could not unilaterally cut their real wages. (After all, real wages had gone up during the Depression, because while money wages fell, prices fell more.) But cutting real wages, even if it were possible, would only lead to reduction in demand, because lower wage incomes would make business unprofitable. Interest rates could not be cut to revive investment. Businessmen were more concerned with future profitability, and interest costs were of minor importance. But there was a limit to how low interest rates could fall, because in times of trouble people hoarded cash, and would not give up their command over liquidity unless the interest rate was high enough. Thus the free market was blocked at each stage, for theoretically cogent reasons.

Keynes's theory used the newly available measures of national income, consumption and investment. He provided a simple way of balancing the books of a national economy and, in so doing, he also found ways of enhancing income and employment. It was a theory not of business cycles but of the determinants of the level of income attained by an economy. It was to lead to a vast new army of specialist economists who were able to advise governments how to achieve high employment and income. Keynes gave the world a new language, and a grammar to go along with it. The vocabulary of economics was changed, as was its reputation for doing good.

Keynes's timing was perfect. He had been making policy recommendations throughout the Depression, and warning people that he had a new theory to propose. To Bernard Shaw he said that he felt his new theory would be like Einstein's theory of relativity – totally revolutionary. But the publication of *The General Theory* in 1936 led to a bitter debate, with the older generation doubting the validity of his claims and the young swallowing it whole. He fought a hard battle to answer his critics. Some of these included Swedish economists who had already practised what he preached, and even advanced not dissimilar theories. But the cyclical recovery from the low point of 1931 faltered in 1937. This proved Keynes's point that although unemployment was still 10 per cent in the USA and the UK, the economy was unable to move up to full employment by itself, and was in fact moving down. Orthodox balanced budgets had to be abandoned. Even Roosevelt was ready to follow this radical course in 1937. Keynes actively encouraged the UK government to borrow to finance rearmament, pointing out that the revival in the economy would pay for itself. He had given governments a perfect reason to do what they loved to do but were afraid of doing: borrow for public spending. While he always held to the view that a budget should be balanced over the cycle – deficits in slump, surpluses in boom – he was quite happy for governments to borrow as long as interest rates, the cost of borrowing, could be kept down. This required control over capital movements. Given such control, savers could not export their savings for higher returns abroad, and investors could not borrow abroad either. Keynes made a virtue of the deglobalized world economy. He preferred economies to be insulated from capital movements, since this made the government's task of managing the economy easier.[12]

The nation-state that emerged after the 1914–18 war is better defined as a 'territorial social state'.[13] For the twenty years after 1918, it could not deliver on its promises to look after the economic well-being of its citizens. Its political agenda fell foul of liberal economics. The downturn in capitalism squeezed the state even harder. Some countries, like Germany, sought a solution in a totalitarian government, albeit with a planned, regulated version of capitalism. Keynes gave the state new tools so that it could manage capitalism without planning or physical controls which, as a liberal, he abhorred. By manipulating taxes and spending, keeping interest rates low, and shutting the economy off against capital movements, the democratic state could have its cake and eat it too. It was a miracle solution, and it worked like a dream for the next forty years.

It was thought that Keynes had provided an answer to Marx. Unlike Schumpeter, Keynes had little respect for Marx, and found his economics turgid. But in one sense Keynes was advancing a fundamental anti-Marxian proposition: that a reserve army of unemployed was not only not necessary for capitalist accumulation, but positively harmful. A high level of employment and high profits were reconcilable as long as the government was ready to step in and top up if there was a lack of effective demand. Marxists had a problem with Keynes.[14] When *The General Theory* came out, the tactic of the Popular Front, on the part of the Third International, required that communists should be positive and co-operative. They were to cultivate the 'progressive forces'. And Keynes was loved by these progressive forces as answering the challenge of unemployment. So the communists dithered between praising Keynes – for substantiating Marx's insights about capitalism's tendency to be crisis-prone – and criticizing him for deluding the people that jobs could be created by inflationary finance. This dual model of embrace and denial lasted as long as Keynesianism ruled the roost.

Of course, had there still been a critical tradition of Marxism alive in the 1930s, there could have been a more nuanced approach. Keynes was pointing to the significance of what Marx had called 'the realization problem': that goods not only have to be produced by labour – thus transferring surplus-value, et cetera – but have to be sold, and the surplus-value has to be 'realized' as profit. If goods are not sold, the surplus-value is just notional, unrealized. Labour has then been exploited in vain. In terms of Chapter 5, C′ has to become M′. But Marx, like all the classical economists he was criticizing, did not have a role for public spending in his model. His capitalism was entirely private-sector. Keynes had not been the first to advocate public works as a cure for unemployment. He was, however, the first to construct an economic theory of the aggregate level of output in which the level could be high or low thanks to government spending.

Rosa Luxemburg was not in Stalin's good books at that time, so no one related Keynes's theory to Luxemburg's Department III. Remember that Luxemburg thought an armaments sector paid for by government taxation would solve the realization problem of Marx's Scheme for Expanded Production. Keynes's advocacy of government spending in theory, and his encouragement of the British government's rearmament in 1937–38, were perfect fits to Luxemburg's model. Of course, Department III need not be armaments; it could be anything which did not compete with the excess supply of Department I goods. A Polish economist, Michal Kalecki, who was familiar with the work of Marx and Luxemburg, arrived independently at a model similar to Keynes's. His equations were reflective of Marx–Luxemburg schemes.

But in one respect Keynes had gone beyond all this. In all classical and neoclassical economics, you either spent or saved. If you spent, you bought consumption goods (Department II). If you saved, you were automatically assumed to have invested – bought Department I goods. Keynes saw that in a monetary economy, you had a third choice. You could hold on to your savings in liquid form, as a bank deposit, or not spend it. Banks, in turn, could hand out money only if there was demand for credit from entrepreneurs. If animal spirits were mouselike rather than tigerish, then there would be no demand for credit. Lower interest rates would not help – indeed, they could not be lowered if people wanted to hold interest-bearing deposits.

If we search through the three volumes of *Capital*, we find that Marx has similar insights about why a monetary economy – one where money is required to settle debts, and claims and barter are not enough – may lead to such a gap between selling and buying. Having sold something, in a monetary economy, you can hang on to your money. In a barter economy, every sale is a purchase. As I explained above, the elegant theory of general equilibrium built up between 1870 and 1920 was a theory of barter in which money played no role. Not only Marx, but John Stuart Mill too, had similar reservations. It is, after all, common sense – though it may be impossible for economic theory to take it on board.

Economists however, do not respect common sense. A thing has to work in theory for them before they will accept that it could work in practice, not the other way round. Keynes's claim was that his theory provided a complete argument using habits of thought, as well as some concepts with which orthodox theorists were familiar. His theory of liquidity preference was a linchpin – one of the three pillars, along with the psychological law of consumption/income relation, and the influence of expectations of future profitability on investors. People preferred to hold on to cash; preferred liquidity unless they were offered a reward – the interest rate – to part with it. Thus interest rates did not balance savings and investment, as in the old theory. Interest rates were rewards for parting with liquidity. So a monetary economy followed different rules from an economy based on barter.

Keynes's monetary theory remains an embattled part of his *General Theory*. Many people felt that the link between government spending and full employment was the most important, most practical part. The theoretical frills about liquidity preference did not matter. Keynes was driven by the fear that there would be a glut of savings, but liquidity preference would prevent interest rates from falling to low levels, even to zero. This fear proved unfounded in the postwar years. No one seemed to mind. There was enough there to regulate employment in the economy. But Keynes also downgraded the importance of money supply. For general equilibrium, a money-free exchange of goods – supply and demand – determined the *relative* prices of all commodities; the total money supply, via the quantity theory of money, fixed the *absolute* level of prices. Thus the ratio of, say, twenty sheep to one cow would be determined in the general equilibrium model, but sheep at £10 and cow at £200 would be determined by the total money supply. If the money supply doubled the ratio of 20:1, sheep/cows would not be affected. That was the 'real' economy. But the absolute prices would double: sheep would cost £20 and cows £400. If you increase the money supply, prices rise. Inflation – the rise in prices – was therefore, in orthodox theory, a purely monetary phenomenon. And liberal economists were against inflation much more strongly than they were against unemployment, which they considered transitory.

By 1936, there had been no inflation in the UK for nearly fifteen years. Across advanced capitalism, the period 1924–36 had been one of stable or falling prices. The inflation shock of the aftermath of the First World War (1919–23) everywhere (and 1919–24 in Germany) was not forgotten by the orthodox economists. Remember the warning sent by Harvard economists to Franklin Roosevelt in January 1933, mentioned in Chapter 10 above. Keynes did not seem to be unduly worried about inflation. *The General Theory* does have a chapter on Price Level (Chapter 21), but in converting his theory to a recipe book, Keynesians neglected inflation, just as they ignored money supply. Keynes had downgraded monetary policy because he thought it did not act quickly enough to cure unemployment – if it had any effect at all.

Keynes was not an inflationist, as he was later portrayed. Early in the Second World War he published a pamphlet, *How to Pay for the War,*[15] in which he used *The General Theory*'s logic to show how inflation could be avoided during war years. But a neglect of inflation, and of the money supply, became a feature of post-1945 Keynesianism. There was a similar nonchalance about the size of public debt. Public debt, it was said, was owed by the majority of the people to a small section of debt-holders – rentiers. There was thus no consequence except a distribution of income from taxpayers to rentiers. As long as interest rates could be kept low, and money supply was plentiful, debt was a non-problem for the Keynesians – or so they thought.

These problems were to come back to haunt Keynesians in the 1960s and later, but the key proposition which triggered the attack on Keynesianism was one that was also its highest achievement – the effect of full employment on wage demands. It was difficult in the 1930s to worry about sustained full employment. During the Second World War, William Beveridge – as well as Michal Kalecki – saw the danger. Keynes had, of course, dealt with it in *How to Pay for the War,* but not in *The General Theory*. If employment went up, sooner or later real wages would be hiked up. There would come a time in the upswing when the rise in wages would cut into profitability. The share of wages would rise high enough to erode the share as well as the rate of profits. The volume of profits – the mass of profits, as Marxists called it – might be higher, because total income would be higher at full employment. But as Marx had argued in *Capital Volume 1,* part 7, capitalists will have to do something to restore profitability – the rate of profits. This was what happened after twenty years of full employment in the postwar period. Capitalists did do something: they fled abroad in search of higher profits.

But again, I am moving ahead of my story. Keynes had provided the cure for capitalism, constructed a 'new economics'.[16] There was a 'Keynesian revolution' – to use the title of Nobel laureate (and my teacher) Lawrence Klein's book.[17] Capitalism had survived its worst years. For a while, it was rescued by rearmament and war. But Keynes had given it the recipe for peaceful development in a non-totalitarian context. Never again would capitalism face a similar collapse. Never again could capitalism be said to be in terminal crisis. Lenin had lost his battle with capitalism – though few were to see it in such a light, thanks to Hitler's invasion of Russia in 1941.

12
Can Socialism Work?

Austria, for its relative size, had an enormous impact on the intellectual life of the twentieth century. The Habsburg Empire was mocked by Robert Musil as Kakania in his novel *The Man Without Qualities*. But if some saw the Austro-Hungarian Empire as decadent, others could see an efflorescence of artistic and philosophical activity there. Sigmund Freud, Ludwig Wittgenstein, Bronislaw Malinowski and Friedrich von Hayek have made their imprints on modern times. Inasmuch as ideas matter, Vienna has been the centre from which emanated forces which still shape our lives.

It is no surprise, then, that the most important and far-reaching debate on the nature of socialism took place in Austria. This was due as much to real-life events – material circumstances, one could say – there as to the lively intellectual life of Vienna. Of the many European revolutions sparked by the First World War, the Austrian was the only case of a democratic socialist one. The Austrian SDP was a sister party of the German one, but it had its own Marxist tradition – Austro-Marxism was much less dogmatic than its German counterpart. Its leading exponent, Otto Bauer, used to argue his case in the magisterial seminar held by Eugen von Böhm-Bawerk, the scourge of Marxism. This was a seminar where the marginalist theory of Carl Menger was discussed and developed. At various times, Rosa Luxemburg and Nikolai Bukharin attended.

Marginalist theory had sprung up independently in three centres. In England William Stanley Jevons, in France Léon Walras, and in Austria Carl Menger had, around 1870, proposed an alternative to the classical labour theory of value. There had been some precedents for this in earlier decades, Walras *père* being one of those pioneers. But the marginalist revolution made economic theory more analytical and more firmly grounded in individual behaviour. Its key insight was that exchange value was explained by use value, but in a subtle way. Individuals in their daily activity so managed their resources that they balanced the marginal utility – the utility (use value) derived from an extra unit of a commodity they consumed – with the price (exchange value) they paid for it. The more one had of a good, the lower the utility from the extra unit consumed.

Thus each consumer – taking the price as given – consumed until the marginal utility was in balance with the price. Different consumers would, of course, consume different amounts, since their tastes differed, as did their incomes.

The same story could be told on the production side. Producers would maximize profits by equating the marginal revenue – the extra revenue gained from selling one more unit – to its marginal cost – the extra cost of producing that unit. Every consumer and every producer took the price as given, as beyond their manipulation. Yet these prices were determined as a result of the interaction between their various purchases and sales. What is more, Walras showed that all the markets would clear simultaneously. There would be a general equilibrium.

The half-century before 1914 was the battleground between the classical and Marxian labour theory of value, and the marginalist (later labelled neoclassical by the British economist Alfred Marshall) theory. They both, however, shared the vision of a self-organizing, self-equilibrating market. Marx was perhaps the exception inasmuch as he predicted that such self-organization could be bedevilled by cycles and crises as the system reproduced itself. But in essence, this was an analytical retelling of the Adam Smith story of the Invisible Hand. The underlying structural interdependence of our economic activities is not visible to us, but it is there none the less. We do not consciously calculate marginal utilities, any more than businesses are conscious of marginal costs. But the entire system functions as if we did. The result is a self-propelled system which produces high levels of well-being without – or, indeed, because of the lack of – any interference on the part of the state, or any monopolies of labour or capital.

Economics has always puzzled and baffled those who come into contact with it. On the one hand, economists speak of daily life activities – buying, selling, working, saving. Yet they do so in a reality-denying framework of assumptions and inferences. No empirical evidence has been advanced for the existence of anything called utility, marginal or otherwise. Economists have felt no need to identify it, measure it, or even inquire of psychologists whether such calculating behaviour makes any sense to them. They are happy that utility and its mathematical treatment give them what they want: a theory of price formation. Their approach is aprioristic rather than empirical: anecdotal rather than experimental. Yet it is immensely effective in making sense of the seemingly complex and chaotic nature of economic life.

Millions of consumers, facing equally rich arrays of commodities and services, make decisions to buy goods or take up jobs, to change careers – even, some would say, to cheat and commit crime. All this can be explained by a single simple framework, with no need to know anything about who they are, what their class or caste or culture is, what the things they buy and sell are. To infuriate the reader, the economist proceeds to do all this in a diagram or using calculus. What could be the point of it all?

Marginalism did lead to an extensive mathematization of economics. Economists fought off historians and other social scientists by extolling their abstract individualistic approach. Yet their elaborate theories had one very simple foundation: given a choice between alternatives, and a resource constraint that precludes having it all, people economize. They choose sensibly and rationally to get the maximum out of what they have. As prices change, or as their tastes change, they adapt and substitute one thing for another. Leave them to it, and best results follow – for the individual as much as for society.

This a priori structure of economic reasoning is not only devoid of any historical, sociological or political detail, but it is also relatively ideologically neutral. Walras, one of its pioneers, was a socialist who had a lifelong interest in co-operatives. The English branch – as it developed under the Cambridge School of Alfred Marshall and Arthur Cecil Pigou – was in favour of mild intervention in selected cases. It was the Austrian version of Carl Menger that championed the liberal ideology most passionately. This was not just a technical mathematical exercise; for the Vienna School of economists, it was a comprehensive social philosophy.

This philosophy was that a capitalism unencumbered by monopolies and cartels, by trade unions and meddling bureaucrats, and presided over by sane politicians who kept taxes low and budgets balanced, and adhered to the Gold Standard, was the best guarantee of peace and well-being for all the people – rich and poor alike. Any attempt to do better than the market – to alleviate poverty, increase employment, provide social security via taxation, or curb private property rights in any way – would not only fail, but would have the opposite effect of that which was intended. The poor would stay poor or get poorer, jobs would shrink rather than expand, provision of social security would make people feckless and unable to look after themselves. Let good be done by the market, which had no primary objective of doing good, but only of maximum profits and maximum utility.

Extended to international relations, this philosophy advocated universal free trade and the extension of the liberal order across the world. Everyone was capable of benefiting from the market, regardless of race, religion, gender, class or status. No one should be presumed to be incapable of rational behaviour. Persistent irrational behaviour could arise only from extraneous non-economic constraints, mainly imposed by the political authorities. This was a universalist creed to which all could subscribe.

The challenge to this set of ideas came from Otto Neurath.[1] Neurath had done his doctoral thesis in Germany under the German Historical School, rivals to Menger and the marginalists. He studied the economic history of Antiquity as well as ancient economic thought on trade, commerce and agriculture. He wrote two dissertations rather than one – typical of his entire life – in which he worked on economics as well as philosophy, was an activist in the Austrian Revolution and a bureaucrat, edited a German literary classic with a 500-page introduction of his own, and so on. Neurath was a socialist, and his key idea was that a socialist economy should be run on different principles from a capitalist economy. Money led to misallocation of resources and inequality, because expressing prices in money terms distorted their use values. The wartime planning that Germany had undertaken struck him (as indeed it had Lenin) as a bold experiment in direct, non-price-based allocation of resources. War gave primacy to productivity (use values) rather than profitability (exchange value). Thus monetary exchange could be replaced by barter.

Neurath developed this idea further during the Austrian Revolution which, alone among the revolutions inspired by the First World War, brought a social-democratic (Marxist) party to power. Marxists had refused to speculate about the details of how a socialist economy would be run, since Marx had discouraged such utopian speculation. Neurath was not one to follow this advice. He began to devise a plan for an economy which would be geared to the maximization not of profits but of happiness: 'Maximum profit is the purpose of the individual business in the capitalist economy . . . a maximum of happiness, of the enjoyment of life in a community and of utility is the purpose of a socialist economy.'[2]

But of course, happiness cannot be measured any more than utility. Neurath then pioneered a measure of living standard. He took variables that are now familiar to economists, such as nutrition, health, life expectancy, housing, clothing, incidence of crime. He was also concerned to build these up in a single measure, and its level, as well as its distribution, were to be the concern of the socialist planner. Neurath described his plan in great detail. There had to be a Central Economic Administration, helped by the Centre for Calculation in Kind. This Centre would compute the standard of living as 'a universal statistic', and model the economic interrelationships as they produced outputs measured in aggregate by such a statistic. (Nowadays we have Gross National Product [GNP], and most countries have statistical offices for its calculation. The Human Development Index in the United Nations Development Programme [UNDP]'s Human Development Reports is an internationally comparable measure combining life expectancy, education and income. Neurath was decades ahead of his time.)

There would be other organizations for rationalizing production to increase 'economic effectiveness, workers' performance and their health and well-being', for banking, for co-ordinating regional economic activity. Once money was abolished, banks were to become distribution centres for productive equipment. Production decisions were to be taken by factory councils on which workers would sit as well as housewives (as consumer representatives). There would then be local, regional and federal tiers of the councils where these decisions would be co-ordinated. There would be scientific experts employed at all levels – nutritionalists, educationists, psychologists, and so on.

The core of the socialist economy was its moneyless nature. As Neurath wrote in an essay in 1923: 'The theory of the Socialist economy acknowledges only one manager or producer – the society – who organizes production and shapes the standard of living on the basis of an economic plan, without calculation of losses or profits and without taking the circulation of money as a basis, be it in the form of coins or labour.'[3] Thus there was to be no market, no purchase and sale, only direct allocation of all goods based on scientifically calculated perceived need. Production decisions were subject to democratic control, and money or profits were to play no role in a socialist economy. In the brief lives of the Bavarian and then the Austrian revolutions, Neurath had a go at implementing some of his ideas, but eventually they remained a mere blueprint.

Despite their non-implementation, Neurath's ideas were taken very seriously by his contemporary anti-socialist liberal Viennese economists. Ludwig von Mises devoted a substantial part of his 1923 book *Die Gemeinwirtschaft: Untersuchungen über den Sozialismus* (*Socialism: An Economic and Sociological Analysis*).[4] Mises took up the question of 'natural calculation' – moneyless exchange based on direct allocation. He argued that such moneyless exchange would lead to inefficiency and irrationality. This, he said, could be proved with the aid of economics as it had been developed: 'Only through the rationalization inherent in economic calculation based on the use of money could the human mind come to understand and trace the laws of action.'[5]

Mises's attack is a very thorough one. The essence of his argument is that it is neither possible nor rational to calculate use value directly. Exchange values, as reflected in money prices determined by the free play of market forces, is the best measure of use value there can be. There are infinite variations in consumer tastes, in workers' skills, in the versatility of different inputs, and it is beyond human ability to arrive at all the appropriate barter prices centrally. And even if you could make barter calculations for consumer goods ready for final consumption, it is impossible to do so for capital goods in the absence of markets: 'In societies based on the division of labour, the distribution of property rights effects a kind of mental division of labour, without which neither economy nor systematic production would be possible.'[6]

Thus, when it came to choosing between two different production processes – for example, replacing mainframe computers by personal computers – it would be impossible to do natural/barter calculations for the rate at which they should be exchanged. A socialist economy might stick to old methods rather than try new ones, since no risk-taking may be permitted. In a capitalist economy, such things happen by entrepreneurs risking capital in new processes and, in many cases, going bankrupt. One could think of an unchanging stationary economy in which all barter ratios could eventually be arrived at, but this was a fiction. No real economy can be immunized against change.

Mises inaugurated rather than settled a debate that went on through the interwar period. Hayek took up the baton from Mises and, after he arrived at the LSE in 1931, arranged for an English translation of Mises's book. He also edited and contributed to a collection of articles on this question of economic calculation in a socialist economy. *Collective Economic Planning* is subtitled 'Critical Studies on the Possibilities of Socialism'.[7] Four articles, by a Dutch, (Pierson), a German (Halm), an Austrian (Mises) and an Italian (Barone) economist are brought together, with an introduction and conclusion by Hayek. This was a time of intense debate about alternatives to a capitalism which had obviously failed, since the world was still suffering the after-effects of the Great Depression of 1931. The Bolshevik experiment in planning was taking place in the Soviet Union, apparently with amazing success. The National Socialists had committed themselves to controlling the market system to generate jobs. Roosevelt had already embarked on the New Deal. Governments everywhere were abandoning orthodoxies of free trade and the Gold Standard. The world seemed ripe for socialism.

The socialist calculation debate launched by the Austrian liberal economists turned out to be different from what they had intended. The problem was that the major weapon used by the liberals proved to be double-edged. The problem of price calculation in a socialist – or, indeed, any – economy could be set out mathematically, thanks to the work of Walras. Enrico Barone had indeed preceded Mises (though Mises did not know this) and set out the problem in his 1908 article 'The Ministry of Production in the Collectivist State'.[8] Here the economy is set out as a series of equations of demand and production for consumer goods, existing capital and new capital. We know (thanks to Walras) that the market can solve these equations. But how likely would it be that the central planner would be able to mimic the independent actions of millions of consumers, workers and producers?

In this way of presenting the problem, there was a subtle but – for the liberals – disastrous shift of emphasis away from Mises's concern with property rights and risk-taking in a dynamic economy. The issue became not one of running an actual economy but one of solving a computational problem. There was a delicious irony here – *pace* Mises. All Walras's equations of demand and supply abstracted from money. Indeed, the only role money played in Walras's system of equations was as a unit of account – that is, to denote the exchange value of saying ten pairs of shoes equals one refrigerator, you could say shoes cost thirty dollars a pair and the refrigerator costs three hundred dollars. But what the Walrasian general equilibrium actually mimicked was a gigantic calculation of barter – moneyless – exchange. All the institutional and historical specificities of capitalism were brushed out in the process of mathematizing the system.

So then the question was: could the Planning Ministry solve myriads of equations actually, as the market did virtually? Walrasian economics had removed human agency, since consumers could be represented by their equations, and so could producers. The economy which these equations modelled was in any case a stationary economy, since dynamics was not introduced at this stage of general equilibrium theory. The equations were meant to mirror the daily, or even hourly, calculation of prices by the hidden hand of the market. The larger issues of freedom, property rights, risk-bearing, entrepreneurship, had been left out as unnecessary complication for the solution – if not as irrelevant.

The answer to the socialist calculation came from the USA. A distinguished senior economist – F. M. Taylor, who was by no means a socialist – took up this question in his Presidential Address to the American Economic Association. His was the 'value-free' approach of an economist-as-a-scientist. His suggestions were elaborated in an elegant mathematical *coup de grâce* by the Polish-born Chicago economist Oscar Lange. The Lange–Taylor solution to the socialist calculation problem became the answer to the liberal attack.[9] In his 1929 article 'The Guidance of Production in a Socialist State', Taylor put forward the observation I made in the paragraph above. If you can write down all the information in a system of equations – that is, if you can assume complete knowledge on the part of the planner of all the consumer preferences, technical input/output combinations, supplies of natural resources, and so on – the planner's task is one of solving equations. Summing up the debate, Hayek commented:

> Now it must be admitted that this is not an impossibility in the sense that it is logically contradictory. But to argue that a determination of prices by such a procedure being logically conceivable in any way invalidates the contention that it is not a possible solution, only proves that the real nature of the problem has not been perceived. It is only necessary to attempt to visualize what the application of this method would imply in practice in order to rule it out as humanly impracticable and impossible. . . . [W]hat is practically relevant here is not the formal structure of this system, but the nature and amount of concrete information required if a numerical solution is to be attempted and the magnitude of the task which this numerical solution must involve in any modern community.[10]

This emphasis on the impracticality of myriad numerical calculations turned out to be a tactical error on Hayek's part. Although he said several other things which were cogent, the issue of computability became the main one. In the 1930s Oscar Lange was one of the best economic theorists, and something of an authority on Walrasian general equilibrium. He was also a socialist (after the Second World War he went back to Poland and served in various high capacities in the Polish government). Lange broke the logjam of practicality with a very simple device.

All the debate about socialist calculation had presumed that a developed market economy would become socialist. This would involve collective ownership of means of production, but substantial freedom of consumer choice as well as occupational choice. So one could leave labour markets and consumer goods markets intact – it was the market for capital goods which was eliminated. So this was not the problem that the Bolsheviks faced in Russia – of development and primitive accumulation in a backward economy. Nor was it the same as the problem posed by Neurath, since some prices could be allowed to exist. This was not war socialism; this was market socialism.

Lange solved the computation problem by proposing that the new socialist regime could adopt the existing prices to begin with. These were clearly equilibrium prices in some sense. All the planner had to do from then on was to tweak the prices up or down as new information became available. Thus there was no need to gather all that information, because the existing prices summarized it. This was a sturdy tenet of Walrasian theory, and remains a core assumption of the theory of efficient markets. So the theory of market equilibrium was used to subvert or overcome the capitalist order!

Lange said further that the central planner did not have to make all the production decisions either. All one had to do was to instruct the managers of individual production units to mimic the profit-maximizing rules – equate the price given to marginal cost. Profits would go to society, but production would be efficient in the sense of the market. Socialism was not only not irrational or impracticable; it was perfectly compatible with the logic of Walrasian general equilibrium. Indeed, some economists went further and argued that since income distribution would be more equal, some of the defects of the market under capitalism would be eliminated by socialism. You needed socialism to see how Walras really worked. Thus, starting from Otto Neurath's total rejection of market prices, the socialists had succeeded in moving the debate so that market prices became the virtue of socialism, rather than things to be avoided. Market calculation was not only possible but desirable in a planned economy.

Not all socialists liked market socialism, but what the Lange–Taylor solution did was to take the absurdity out of the notion of a socialist economy. It did not do this by making a realistic, administrative blueprint of the daily functioning of the economy, as Neurath had tried to do. Nor did the solution fundamentally challenge the role of money or prices or markets. Since Walras and his followers had reduced a real-life economy with a myriad problems to a set of equations, assuming away all difficulties, realism was never a ground on which the socialists needed to fight. In his review of the Lange–Taylor book (as well as a book by the British economist H. D. Dickinson[11]) in 1940, Hayek tried to point out patiently that this 'solution' solved none of the real-life difficulties. For example, goods made in anticipation and bought 'off the shelf' could be considered to have demand and supply curves. But big, bulky products – ships, large machines – were made to order, and had no demand or supply curves. Or again, he pointed out that saying that factory managers should treat prices as given does not clarify for how long they were to stay given. But then, the Walrasian system did not delve into such nitty-gritty issues. It was the lack of realism in mathematical economics, hailed as a pinnacle of achievement of the marginalist school, which proved the undoing of the liberal critique of socialism.

The problem was that the Walrasian model bore no relation to any actual capitalist economy, where change and uncertainty are endemic, where there are risk-takers and bankruptcies, where new products and new processes are tried out all the time. This dynamic disequilibrium process was not theorized by Walras, but the Austrian School had not supplied an alternative. Menger had genuine philosophical differences with Walras, but these were brushed aside in celebrating the defeat of the labour theory of value by the new theory. Marx had fallen into a similar trap when he took up Ricardo's theory of competitive equilibrium (dressed up in different terminology). Thus his disequilibrium dynamic insights hung loosely around his equilibrium calculus of prices and values. Ideas, especially unrealistic ones, can have powerful real consequences in the world of economics.

It is difficult to exaggerate Lange's impact on the socialist calculation debate. His article came out in 1938 in a book which also reprinted Taylor's essay.[12] The issue was immediately considered settled. By this time, Keynes's *General Theory* had come out and put Hayek, as well as many other champions of the liberal order, on the defensive. The world was drifting towards another war. Academic as it was, the socialist calculation debate was seen as having been won by the socialists. After 1945, when socialism was again a possibility, its impracticability or irrationality could not be raised as an objection. For all those who adhered to Socialism within Capitalism, Lange–Taylor market socialism was the answer. For the young bloods of the British Labour Party – Hugh Gaitskell, Evan Durbin, Douglas Jay and James Meade – market socialism was to be their ideal solution if ever they could implement it. The same message was picked up across Western European socialist parties.

The debate illustrated, in a poignant way, the unintended consequences of human action, a favourite workhorse of liberal philosophers. But with sixty years' hindsight and on the other side of the collapse of statist socialism (see Chapters 17 and 18), it is worth looking at the argument to see where the inefficiencies of socialism lay. It was Hayek who saw immediately, even before Lange's response was published, that the economic problem of a socialist planner was wrongly posed, because the economic problem of a capitalist economy was wrongly posed. Once this is appreciated, the symmetry between market capitalism and market socialism, with the implication of the irrelevance of capitalists and property rights, is seen to be a flaw in theory rather than a possibility in practice. Yet Hayek's insights in the late 1930s were to be ignored for another fifty years.

Hayek's lecture to the London Economic Club in November 1936 was published under the title 'Economics and Knowledge' in February 1937 in LSE's journal, *Economica*.[13] It is no exaggeration to say that this is one of the most innovative articles in economics written in the twentieth century. Indeed, it was so innovative that it remained unappreciated until the 1970s. Even today, its insights have not been fully taken on board by economists. Hayek argued that while economists had understood the importance of the division of labour ever since Adam Smith, they had not realized that the division of knowledge was much more crucial to economic life. The Walrasian theory routinely assumed that consumers had perfect knowledge of prices of all the goods they could choose from. Producers knew the full set of alternative technologies, as well as factor prices and goods prices, before maximizing profits. The cost of gathering this knowledge was not taken into account; indeed, the entire point of the market was that it economized on such information.

Knowledge about technologies, tastes, and skills was dispersed across individuals. Each individual knew and, indeed, needed to know about his own environment and the local 'neighbourhood'. No one could know everything. Information kept changing, and these changes were perceived by individuals at local levels. There was a weak connectedness between these bits of dispersed knowledge – some slight overlap in local 'neighbourhoods' of knowledge.

People did not need to know much else, because all this information was signalled by prices. People acted separately and individually in an uncoordinated fashion. The co-ordination task was performed by the market, and prices had telecommunication properties. People could search for better bargains within the neighbourhood of their current knowledge, learn from looking at prices, and adapt. There was a lot of search, a lot of groping around, before the optimum was reached. But then new information would come in again. There was no equilibrium – no resting place, as in the model of a stationary economy. Contrast this picture of a constantly restless search for a better price or a better product by far more customers to the way in which a perfect market is modelled in Walrasian economics. Hayek speaks of:

> [A] perfect market where every event becomes known instantaneously to every member. It is necessary to remember here that the perfect market which is required to satisfy the assumptions of equilibrium analysis must not be confined to the particular markets of all the individual commodities; the whole economic system must be assumed to be one perfect market in which everybody knows everything. The assumption of a perfect market, then, means nothing less than that all members of the community, even if they are not supposed to be strictly omniscient, are at least supposed to know automatically all that is relevant for their decisions. It seems that that skeleton in our cupboard, the 'economic man' whom we have exorcized with prayer and fasting, has returned through the back door in the form of a quasi-omniscient individual.[14]

Thus a lot of equilibrium theorizing is a tautology, making excessive claims about the availability and ease of acquisition of knowledge. All theorizing makes reality-denying assumptions, but these seem to be extreme even in that category.

A more plausible story is that individuals do the best they can (i.e. optimize) relative to the knowledge they have. As they learn from experience that what they knew does not correspond to objective facts – from changes in their own tastes or other relevant events – they change their behaviour. Each position is a small edging towards an equilibrium relative to knowledge. Yet this keeps changing. The economy is never at equilibrium, because it is never at rest.

This may all seem like common sense to non-economists. After all, when you go shopping, you have a list of what you want to buy; you go to a supermarket and do your shopping in one fell swoop. You may never care to know that if you had gone around all the shops, you would have found that some prices are lower in some shops than in others. Not knowing will save you time. Your purchases are what you want, given what you know. For more expensive items bought infrequently – say a house – you will search a bit more, but you will not worry about the price of all the houses in all locations, not only today but as expected to prevail in the future.

But again and again we find, in the course of this attempt to understand our world, that ideas, abstract unrealistic ideas, are taken very seriously. It is the clash of rival sets of abstract ideas which has consequences exceeding anything common sense can make happen. Hayek was undermining the entire basis of equilibrium theorizing as it was – and still is – taught in economics, yet his ideas were ignored at the time. An entire generation came to believe that capitalism and socialism were symmetrical; markets and planning were the same thing. The consequences of ignoring risk-taking, property rights, bankruptcies, and innovations were that the achievements of Soviet-type economies were exaggerated as much by their enemies as by their champions. The defenders of capitalism thought the race was in terms of material output, and the models of economics were the best guide in assessing relative success. The idea that an economy is a self-organizing process in which there is a constant search for betterment on the part of millions of individuals, all acting on the basis of local knowledge – an idea that Marx shared with Hayek – was forgotten. The point was not that a socialist planner could not compute all those equations. The point was that even making the most extreme assumptions, it is impossible to centralize knowledge. What is more, it is inefficient – grossly inefficient. Half of Europe had to learn that lesson in the coming half-century, after the end of the debate on socialist calculation.

13

Foundations of the Global Order

The Second World War broke out in Western Europe in September 1939. Japan's invasion of Manchuria in 1931, and of China in 1937, continued on to other parts of East and Southeast Asia. So in that sense, September 1939 is an arbitrary date. Even in Europe, the Spanish Civil War had been raging in 1936–38, and by then Hitler had started his incursion into Austria. The brief period between France's withdrawal from the Ruhr and its reoccupation by the Germans – say 1924–36 – was the only 'peaceful' episode in Europe.

But from another viewpoint, the war on the Eurasian landmass became a world war only in 1941. Hitler's attack on Russia should have surprised no one; it took the pressure off Britain, which was the only nation at war with Germany in Europe at the time. Various resistance groups from the countries either defeated by Hitler (Poland, for instance) or collaborating (like France) were also operating from the UK. But it was Japan's bombing of Pearl Harbor which triggered the USA's entry, and made it a world war beyond the Eurasian landmass. Although the USA had to fight on two fronts, the outcome was never in doubt after 1941. A combination of the USA and the USSR was more than Hitler could stand up to. The Japanese proved tougher opponents for the Americans. The battle across the Pacific, with no other Allied forces to speak of, meant that the Americans fought their Asian battle singlehanded (the Chinese under Chiang Kai-shek deserve a mention, but no more). In Southeast Asia, British and Indian troops stopped the Japanese short of the Indian border.

The Second World War settled one of the two battles the liberal order had to face. The authoritarian model of capitalism – fascism – was defeated. It proved to be unimaginably evil in its genocidal tendencies, but its intolerance went beyond the Jews and covered homosexuals, gypsies, and many conquered nationalities. The fact that Buchenwald was the site of one of Goethe's last visits showed the full tragedy of European civilization. All the humanistic aspects of the Enlightenment were eliminated from fascism. Anti-Semitism was by no means a Nazi invention, nor was it exclusive to Germany. It had been part and parcel of European Christianity. But Nazism took anti-Semitism to its limits, and showed its horrible possibilities when pursued with the most modern technology of death.

But of course, Stalin was no slacker when it came to the science of brutality. From the mid-1930s onwards, the Russian concentration camps had been full – at first mainly of dissident Mensheviks, Social Revolutionaries, Left oppositionists and ex-friends of Stalin, but soon other Bolsheviks, peasants thought to be kulaks, and finally just about anyone who offended anybody from the lowest to the highest in the Stalinist bureaucracy. Here was another delinking from the humanist aspect of the Enlightenment. The pity is that Marx, one of the finest figures in Enlightenment philosophy, was prayed to in support of such barbarism. Rosa Luxemburg, in her final years, had raised the cry 'Socialism or barbarism'. Here was socialism *as* barbarism.

Yet the Soviet Union was an ally, and had borne the brunt of the Nazi attack. It was also pivotal to the defeat of Hitler. The Western front no doubt helped, as did the battle in North Africa. But the prestige of the Soviet Union was immensely enhanced as a result of the war, and with it the prestige of Soviet economic planning. The Russo–German War became a battle of two planning models. From 1936 onwards the National Socialist planning model had concentrated almost exclusively on preparations for war. It was very much in tune with what the German High Command had been planning almost from the day after its defeat in 1918. The total mobilization of resources, with privately owned industries harnessed to the war economy, was the first full implementation of planning in a capitalist economy.

Stalin's industrialization was an alternative path to a war economy. He was starting from a weaker base than Hitler, and he started earlier. But twelve years of 'state capitalism' – 1929 to 1941 – had given the Soviet Union a solid base in Department I goods, with a high capacity for quick diversions into armaments: Department III goods. In the cases of both Germany and the USSR, the consumer/wage-earner was the loser in terms of real wages, though there was full employment.

At an immense cost in human lives – 25 million dead – and in material destruction, Stalin won the battle. Soviet planning, originally inspired by the German war socialism of 1914–18, proved a better way of building a war economy than Germany's own model, also inspired by the same experience but relying on a combination of private capital and public ownership. The liberal detractors of socialist planning – Mises, Hayek, and others – were out of favour for the time being. Socialist planning was not impossible; it was efficacious for the one purpose that mattered in 1941–45.

But the unplanned capitalist economy of the USA also showed its production potential. During the New Deal, some interventions in the 'free market' had already been made. The UK probably used a more *dirigiste* approach to organizing production for the war than the USA did. The immense size of the American economy – which I noted above in the context of the First World War – meant that the Americans fought a war on two fronts without much privation on the consumers' part. Anti-British Americans threw eggs at Lord Halifax when he was British Ambassador to the States during the war. He remarked that the Americans were lucky to have eggs to throw at him. Eggs, guns and butter were available in the USA. US GNP was more than twice that of the UK and France, plus Germany.

The war did make the case for a 'mixed economy' – private enterprise with government oversight. The British model went farther by going on after 1945 to state ownership of 'the commanding heights'. The Americans dismantled their control apparatus, but the idea persisted that the state had to – and could – run the economy. The adoption of a full employment target and the general philosophy of Keynesian economics reinforced this idea. The economy could not be left to the market.

So the war settled the argument in favour of a liberal political order – constitutional representative government with universal adult franchise – but the argument for a liberal economic order was not advanced. If anything, it was relegated to a museum of outdated economic philosophies. Economics gained in prestige, but not as a moral philosophy; it was now based on an operational approach. Economists built quantitative mathematical models and forecast economic outcomes. Their techniques were used to route transport ships in the war, to predict demand for rationed foods, to calculate the production potential and its required rate of growth.

The private sector did not complain about these developments: the large industrial corporations thrived on war contracts. A state/corporate symbiosis developed in which the corporations could rely on the state to keep the order books bulging. But in return, the New Deal state demanded recognition of trade-union rights. American unionism was immensely strengthened by the war and, of course, the continued dominance of the Democratic Party from 1933 to 1952. The symbiosis was, of course, between large corporations, organized labour and the federal government. Small businessmen operating at State or local level remained unhappy about these bureaucratic inroads. They drifted towards the Republican Party.

But they were in a minority. In 1944, when Friedrich von Hayek published

The Road to Serfdom, there was an embarrassed silence even from private industry.[1] Hayek was taking the liberal economists' purist line that any interference with the free market – from a local shopping mall regulation to state ownership of the means of production – was a sign of loss of liberty, with the looming prospect of totalitarianism. It is a cogent, well-written book, to which I come below, but the lack of any discerning scale between one kind of intervention and another lessened its immediate impact. *The Road to Serfdom* became notorious for a while when Winston Churchill used it to accuse the Labour Party of being likely to adopt Gestapo methods if it ever came to power. Little did the Conservative Party know that Hayek included them among the enemy. He had chosen a very lonely road.

The reasons for the retreat of free-market liberalism go back, of course, to the First World War and the deglobalization which began in 1914. But the USA had stayed a free-market country; it believed in competition and legislated against cartels. There was a popular – indeed, a populist – dislike of big business and banks. Geographically, this was a Midwest and Southwest phenomenon. The Depression gave it a much sharper edge, and wider popularity. When Roosevelt came to power, he faced persistent demands to break up the cartels and restore competition. Louis Brandeis, a Supreme Court judge, was known as the radical champion of the trust-busting movement. The balance in the industrial sector seemed to be against market interference and for the enforcement of competition.

What saved the situation for Roosevelt was Keynes and his theory.[2] By looking at the urgent issue of unemployment with a macroeconomic focus, Keynes defused the burning issues of cartels versus small businesses. Everyone, Keynes promised, could be better off at a higher level of employment – both large and small businesses. And then, soon, the logic of a war economy reinforced the case for preserving large corporations which could be relied on to deliver the war contracts. Planners prefer to negotiate with few large firms; it is administratively more efficient.

Technological innovations were also making life better for larger corporations. The Second World War, even more than the First, was fought in laboratories and universities. Natural scientists were recruited, as were mathematicians and economists. The turning of scientific invention into feasible production was better done by large firms. They soon started recruiting scientists directly, and set up their Research and Development (R&D) divisions. The happy marriage of science and industry, of university and government, during the war laid the foundations of what Kansas farm boy, later President, Dwight

David Eisenhower was to call the military–industrial complex. Keynesian macroeconomic policy was the framework that held together these separate corporate elements: large industrial companies, universities, trade unions and government procurement agencies.

The liberal idealist was thus harking back to a bygone age – if it ever existed in real life, not just in economics treatises. Competition had never been a part of European capitalist culture. Even Great Britain had *laissez-faire* tolerance of restrictive practices rather than a positive policy on competition. Thus noncompetitive practices – barriers to entry enforced by the old school tie, for example – flourished. The City of London was one place where informal cartels and selective class-biased hiring were routine until the 'Big Bang' in the 1980s. Austria and Germany, where the champions of liberal order flourished, were hardly vibrant examples of competitive behaviour. Only during the middle of the nineteenth century – and only in Great Britain during a period spanning 1835–85 at the most – could we say that a semblance of the competitive order obtained, but even that was bolstered by the country's monopoly position in international trade in manufactures as the pioneer industrializing country. And of course, the Empire afforded *de facto* protection even then. You had only to educate the natives that British was Best.

There was also the changed perception of communists. Even as some suspicion persisted, Uncle Joe was a popular figure. In his train followed a new awareness of the thoughts of Marx and Engels and Lenin. It was a reductionist Marxism, but texts hitherto unpublished began to flow out. Writing and debating about Marx became a more widespread practice. Neoclassical and Keynesian economists began to confront Marx. Schumpeter paid him a handsome tribute in his 1942 book *Capitalism, Socialism and Democracy.* Joan Robinson's *Essay on Marxian Economics* and Paul Sweezy's *Theory of Capitalist Development* were both products of the 1940s. Sweezy also brought the price–value transformation problem to the attention of the English-speaking world by publishing Böhm-Bawerk's 'Karl Marx and the Close of his System' with Bortkiewicz's solution (discussed in Chapter 5).[3] Historians and sociologists were informed by the publications of the Frankfurt School *émigrés* who were now in the USA.

This influence was even greater in Western Europe. The French Communist Party gained in reputation by being identified with the Resistance. In the UK, the Communists' popularity had begun in 1936 and continued, despite the Molotov–Ribbentrop Pact, right through to 1945 and beyond. The Labour Party had never been Marxist, but now had many younger members who were. Its Chairman, Harold Laski, Professor at the London School of Economics, though he was not a Marxist, was very sympathetic towards Marxism. In 1948, on the occasion of the centenary of *The Communist Manifesto*, the Labour Party issued a reprint with an official – albeit anonymous – foreword, and a hundred-page introduction by Harold Laski. It was a rare moment in the Labour Party's history, never to be repeated.[4]

The war also boosted anti-imperialist forces. The two leading Allies, the USA and the USSR, both had strong anti-imperialist, anticolonialist elites. This caused a problem for the UK, especially since Winston Churchill was a convinced imperialist. When it came to the problem of India, Churchill was under great pressure to accommodate the Indian National Congress's demands to be given a large official role in the war effort. India was crucial as a supplier of men and material for the war, and Churchill would take no risks. But the course of negotiations during the war made it clear that the UK was on its way out of its largest colony.

For the nationalists of India and Indonesia, and elsewhere in Asia and Africa, political independence had to be the key to economic independence. By that they meant freedom from foreign – usually imperialist country – ownership of agricultural, mineral, industrial, commercial and financial firms. It meant a right to block free trade and use tariffs. The liberal homilies on free trade had not gone down well in the periphery. It was Friedrich List rather than David Ricardo who was the hero. With the rejection of free trade came parallel scepticism about the free market. The economics of Keynes and the example of the USSR, as well as Japan, had convinced the Asian nationalists that rapid economic growth fostered by the state was a top priority. The Indian National Congress had set up a National Planning Committee in 1938 to draw up plans for industrial development. Industrialization was the magic recipe for economic independence. Marx, Lenin, and the Soviet Union loomed large in any such perspective.

By 1943, it was clear that the Allies were on a winning trajectory. Stalingrad had not fallen, and a German retreat from Russia was beginning. The Japanese had been halted on the borders of India and Burma on their southern flank, and in the Battle of Midway in the Pacific. The planning for the postwar settlement was to be a judicious mixture of Metternich and Woodrow Wilson. The Great Powers were to be in charge of postwar peace, but there would be a United Nations. The Great Powers would hold the ring as Permanent Members of the Security Council, but a General Assembly would allow for representation from all independent countries. There was much idealism in the air about the potential of the UN. Experience was later to erode much of that idealism.

But it was the postwar economic settlement that was to prove more effective in laying the foundations of the Keynesian Golden Age, because Keynes was a major player in its creation.[5] By this time Keynes had a towering reputation and an official perch in the British Treasury. As he designed the postwar foreign exchange arrangements, he was acutely aware that the UK could be impoverished due to financing the war effort. He wanted control on capital movements as well as restriction on free trade. But the Americans had allowed land lease even before they became a party to the war. This abandonment of American neutrality (there was a strong pro-German lobby in Washington, DC) was not costless. Cordell Hull, Roosevelt's Secretary of Commerce, was a staunch defender of free trade. He wanted the British to dismantle the Empire Free Trade Area, which he considered imperialist and protectionist. If the British wanted American products to fight the war, they had to promise not to divert American exports away from their markets. Thus a liberal trade arrangement was essential to any postwar settlement.

Keynes knew, however, that British reserves of gold and foreign exchange would be low, and a convertible pound would be unsustainable, so there had to be some capital controls. Britain had long enjoyed the benefits of Empire countries keeping their sterling balances in London. During the war, these countries had provided men and material, and accepted payments which were in effect sterling debts of His Majesty's Government. These debts were going to hang over the UK; thus free reserves were even smaller than they appeared to be. Keynes also knew that his economic theory was about a relatively closed economy. Trade was a 'leakage' in the Keynesian model. Free capital movements would disrupt the control a government would have on savings and investment or interest rates. Thus Keynes wanted capital controls for any country aiming for full employment, and for the UK because of its special responsibilities.

The Americans, represented by Harry White, wanted free trade and free capital movements.[6] America had no shortage of reserves, and a vast capacity for exports. They wanted restoration of the Gold Standard, and for America to capture world markets. There was nothing sinister about this – it was precisely the way the world economy had been in the nineteenth century, except that it was the British who were the dominating economic power while the Americans, among many others, were on the receiving end. Trade is, after all, a consensual act, open to competition. So if the Americans sold to the world, it was because their goods were cheaper and better. But the likelihood that Europe would slip back into its protectionist habits, and that Congress would then retaliate, and the Great Depression would recur, was a constant nightmare for Roosevelt, Hull and Morgenthau, the Treasury Secretary.

The compromise reached at Bretton Woods was that the Americans would base their dollar on gold at a fixed price of $35 per ounce. Thus gold and the dollar were equivalent. The world did not need gold to settle trade deficits; dollars would do instead. To save the face of the British, sterling was also designated a 'key currency', and its price was fixed in terms of the dollar. The other European countries were still occupied; it was presumed that they would join this arrangement as and when an International Monetary Fund was set up whose purpose was to monitor the system of fixed exchange rates. It would also have resources available to help any country that was in temporary balance-of-trade deficit. This would avoid the currency depreciation which had bedevilled the 1930s. The Fund would be built up by initial contributions from its members. Given the economic circumstances, the Americans made the largest contribution, and thus got the largest share of votes in the Fund's governing body. As members joined, the contributions of the advanced capitalist countries were obviously larger than those of developing countries, so they had the bulk of the votes. Contributions also determined the amount a country could borrow. In the first twenty years of the Fund's existence, it was very much a body for developed countries run by developed countries whose currencies were fixed in relation to the dollar. These countries' deficits were meant to be temporary and cyclical rather than sustained and structural. Only the American deficit did not matter. It was indeed necessary for other countries to acquire these dollars so that they could trade with each other. America had to be the world's provider of liquidity.

The twin institution of the International Monetary Fund (IMF) was the International Bank for Reconstruction and Development (IBRD). At its foundation, its purpose was much more reconstruction of the war-affected economies of Europe than development. In 1943–44, development was not yet the big idea it was to become soon after. A pioneering article by Paul Rosenstein-Rodan, then of University College London and later at MIT, focused on reconstruction in Southeast Europe.[7] The IBRD later became known as the World Bank and increasingly, through the 1950s and 1960s, it became involved around the world, giving long-term loans as well as providing expertise for development of the decolonized countries. There had, of course, been 'colonial development' promoted by each of the imperial governments, a response to the mounting pressure of anticolonial movements in the Dutch, French and British empires (the Portuguese and Belgian empires were exceptions to this). The World Bank recruited many of the colonial development bureaucrats in its first intake. A new theory of development was not invented until a few years later (see Chapter 15).

The two Bretton Woods institutions were to take care of short- and long-term capital needs. They were there to insure against competitive devaluations or a lurch into a fascist autarchy for purposes of development. But trade was still an outstanding issue. The third institution, the International Trade Organization (ITO), was proposed as a result of the Havana Charter. But this institution was not acceptable to the US Congress, as it feared for America's economic sovereignty. Luckily for the postwar economic order, a General Agreement on Tariffs and Trade (GATT) was quickly proposed (mainly due to the efforts of the British economist James Meade, who was later to receive a Nobel Prize for Economics).[8] GATT was to grow slowly in membership and in effectiveness as the years passed. It started with a modest programme of multilateral tariff reduction among the developed countries, leaving the decolonized countries pretty much to their own protectionist devices.

Thus the postwar economic order guaranteed exchange-rate stability and hoped for convertibility of the currencies – at least for trade purposes. Freer trade was to be promoted by this arrangement as well as by GATT (which came later, in 1948). The cost of this emphasis on trade and exchange-rate stability was control on capital movements. This was America's concession to the other developed countries, most of which were to have substantial problems of postwar recovery. Capital controls became an integral part of the system of national capitalisms over the next thirty years.

But while the Americans were generous to the Europeans in the postwar economic arrangements, they maintained a strong anti-imperial stance, welcoming the break-up of the British, French and Dutch empires in Asia. The British were antagonistic to the American stance in this respect. After VJ Day, the British sent part of the Indian Army to help the French recapture Indochina. They also tried to help the Dutch regain what soon became Indonesia. The Americans aided the independence movements. George Washington was a hero to Ho Chi Minh, who turned from fighting the Japanese to fighting the French. For East Asia, the dismantling of the Japanese and then the French Empire was to become entangled with the Cold War and last until 1975, by which time the Americans had abandoned their anti-imperialism in favour of an anti-Communist crusade.[9]

There were two crucial events soon after the war, but they were really a consequence of that war. The first event was Indian independence and partition in 1947. India's independence opened the floodgates of decolonization. Within twenty years of India leaving the Empire, Britain had given up almost all its overseas territories. The delay in handing over Hong Kong should not mislead in this respect. Asia, Africa and the Caribbean rid themselves of British colonial rule in rapid and – by and large – non-violent transfers of power. The French Empire was more violent in its dissolution, especially in Indochina and Algeria. But in terms of time frame, 1970 was about the outer limit of this process. Portugal, which stayed out of the war, did not join the decolonization process. In Goa, in Angola and in Mozambique, violent confrontation was necessary before Portugal ceded power. Only when Portugal became a democracy, after 1975, did it acquiesce in decolonization.

The other major event was the Communist Revolution in China. In a way the Chinese Revolution reinforced the earlier Russian one by taking place in a backward agrarian country. But in China's case – unlike that of Russia – the outgoing government was neither a monarchy nor a fledgling republic. China had been a republic since 1911, and its President, Chiang Kai-shek, was regarded by contemporaries as an outstanding Asian leader. He had inherited the mantle of Sun Yat-sen, a nationally and internationally revered hero. Japan's incursion into Manchuria and then into China had undermined the credibility of Guo Min Dang, Chiang's nationalist party. Regional warlordism became rife in the 1930s, as did corruption in the national government. Mao's campaign from his base in Yenan, against the Japanese as well as the Nationalists, was much more successful, and much sooner, than anyone had expected.

The establishment of a People's Republic of China (PRC) – not by Stalinist imposition but by a genuine Chinese Communist movement – enhanced the reputation of Marxism. Now Asia also had its own local Communist revolution. As an ally, China had been recognized as a Great Power during the war. Thus the Communists were now in power in two out of the five Permanent Members of the Security Council (though it took another twenty-two years before the Americans relented and recognized the PRC as China's legitimate government). But Chinese communism was different from Western communism inasmuch as it had grappled with the agrarian issue and recognized it as a central concern. The German SPD had taken on the agrarian question as a minority issue in Kautsky's *Die Agrarfrage.*[10] Lenin had been very impressed by Kautsky, and applied his concepts to the Russian peasantry. But Lenin's conception, influential though it was, could still be characterized as Western and urban-orientated. The Narodniks – and, later, the Social Revolutionaries – were much closer to Russian reality than the Marxists. A. V. Chayanov's outstanding work on the Russian peasantry gave a very different idea of the dynamics of agriculture from the works of Lenin.[11] Russian Marxism never managed to understand the peasantry. Marx himself had a low opinion of them until late in his life, when he studied Russia.

Mao was totally different in his understanding of the peasantry. In this respect he was much closer to Chayanov than to Lenin or Kautsky. He had grown up among the peasants. The urban-orientated Chinese Communist Party committed suicide in its adventurist uprising in 1927. Then Mao slowly and patiently established his control over the Party. The Long March to Yenan, and the establishment of autonomous Communist power there, confirmed his leadership. The Communists had to implement land reform and other policies catering to the well-being of the people. Thus when the Chinese Communists came to power, they, unlike the Bolsheviks, had already acquired the common sense of politics and policy implementation. They were much less theoretical and speculative.

They were also, however, a military power which had defied the Japanese and won battles, so the People's Army was part and parcel of the Chinese Communist Party's ruling machinery. Asian communism, wherever it was successful – in China, in Laos, in Vietnam or in Cambodia – had a military arm embedded in the Party. In the one country where that was not the case, Indonesia, there was a massive defeat of the Indonesian Communist Party (PKI). The Chinese People's Army soon showed its mettle in the first confrontation of the post-1945 Cold War world, in Korea. The ebb and flow of the campaign in Korea, and its settlement in 1954, should have warned the Americans about the tenacity of Asian Communist armies. The lesson was learned only at much greater cost in 1975, in Vietnam.

But again, I am running ahead of my story. The war created a contradictory situation for the liberal order. Capitalism was made safe, but it was a jigsaw puzzle of individual national capitalisms rather than a global system. There was a re-establishment of liberal democracy in Northwest Europe (Iberia remained authoritarian). But of course, Europe was divided into liberal-democratic and Communist camps, best illustrated by the partition of Germany as well as of Berlin. From the Elbe all the way to the China seas, there was a Communist government in Eurasia. Greece was caught in a civil war, which the Communists narrowly lost. It was there that the Americans chose to fight and halt the advance of communism.

The Cold War has seen multiple layers of revisionist history. American historians have given credit to the USA for starting the war in both a congratulatory and a critical tone. But the wartime alliance between the USA, the UK and the USSR was never going to be permanent. The removal of fascism clarified the battle. Now there was capitalism and anticapitalism, and the basic issue was a private-property-and-profitability-based system against its opposite. There was, of course, an element of 'planning' or mixed economy in postwar capitalism, but the bulk of industrial, financial and commercial capital was privately owned even at the height of the mixed economy.

The Cold War was fought on military and ideological grounds, and purely economic issues were not at the forefront. While the USA's ability to provide consumer goods on a massive scale became a weapon in the ideological struggle (as Nixon demonstrated when, as Vice-President, he visited the American Exhibition Pavilion in Moscow), the agenda of the liberals – free market, free trade, *laissez-faire* – was never adopted by the West. The battle was about growth rates, living standards, technology (in space and armaments). The capitalist world had diverse institutional arrangements when it came to liberal values, and the Cold War made the Americans tolerant of undemocratic regimes as long as they were in the camp of 'freedom'.

Thus the two systems became more alike than different as they confronted each other. Each caricatured the other in the propaganda it fed to the local population, and argued that the contest was 'value-free' (as economics was claiming to be). Even such a committed liberal as Joseph Schumpeter came to characterize the economy in a mechanistic way in terms of economic efficiency.[12] He was so impressed by the large corporation and its growing efficiency that he thought that its very efficiency would make capitalism converge to socialism. The individual entrepreneur would, he thought, become obsolete, and the corporation would rule. A capitalist corporation would then be no different from a socialist one.

Democracy, on the other hand, Schumpeter argued, would follow the logic of the market. Since the USA had only two large political parties, and they were ideology-free relative to Western Europe parties, Schumpeter could see them competing in the manner of sellers of ordinary products. Firms maximize profits, so politicians maximize votes. To do this they study what the voters want, and build a programme (a product) likely to appeal to the maximum number of voters (buyers). Schumpeter's insights were to be taken up in 1957 by an economist, Anthony Downs, who proposed *An Economic Theory of Democracy*.[13] So politics, no less than economics, could be seen through a positivist, instrumentalist framework. Politics thus became value-free. Systems delivered 'products' and were to be compared in terms of their efficiency. Communism's challenge to capitalism was now in terms of material production; human liberation no longer mattered for the self-styled inheritors of Marx's legacy, nor did the West argue back that it cared more for freedom and human rights than for GNP. Marx labelled the ruling ideology of capitalism – the displacement of human relations by commodity exchange – commodity fetishism. Now, of course, communism had also become commodity-fetishistic.

Two absolutely contrasting analyses of the mid-twentieth-century advanced capitalist societies were put forward at the end of the war. Both Polanyi and Hayek were from Vienna. They were both economists in the broad sense of the word. They both engaged with the role of the market in human societies, but one of them welcomed the restraints put on market relations by the Radical Whigs and Reformist Socialists, which had become the norm since the turn of the century. In *The Great Transformation*, Karl Polanyi saw the limits put on the labour market, which had been introduced as a result of political democratization, as proof that the liberal market order was an impossible utopia.[14] He characterized the liberal free market as the commodification of every aspect of life. Thus what Marx thought of as the distinguishing feature of capitalism – the buying and selling of labour-power – was, for Polanyi, a step too far. He interpreted the reform of the old Poor Law in the 1830s as introducing a free market in labour-power, but the reaction against this, and the introduction of legislation to restrict the commodification of labour, were for him significant pointers to the limits of the free market.

Polanyi's book was very influential. The notion of market failure had already been installed by Keynes at the heart of macroeconomic policy, and the Pigouvian version of microeconomic market failure complemented it. Thus markets were seen to be failure-prone, and in need of regulation from above. Polanyi takes the argument further by saying that even a well-functioning market is a failure in the sense that it is inconsistent with the democratic humanist polity. For Polanyi, the entire notion of an economy run on free-market principles is wildly dystopian (i.e. negatively utopian). Markets are worst when they are perfect, and have to be curtailed.

Polanyi's ideas have often been called Marxist, but Marx would not have sympathized with Polanyi. While capitalism lasts, markets are the defining institutions; exchange value is more important than use value in determining what to produce. Profits have to be realized by selling in the market; mere surplus-value is not enough. Markets can be transcended, Marx would say, only when private property is abolished. Markets in labour-power arise from the private property right every individual has in himself or herself. John Locke defined the origin of private property in the mixing of human labour with the soil. His theory has been much criticized by neo-Marxists, since it does not allow for accumulation through exploitation. But the origin of private property in human labour presumes private property in the human self. Marx would characterize market restriction on buying and selling of any commodity, including labour-power, as premature and Romantic. His stance on free trade and the Anti-Corn Law agitation was precisely that free trade was not ideal, but it was better than what went before. The alternative of protectionism was not better than free trade (as we saw in Chapter 7). The same impatience is clear in his 'Critique of the Gotha Programme'. He rejects Lassallean claims to the full product of labour, because he sees them as inconsistent with the needs of accumulation in a capitalist society. Later, under Bolshevik influence, Marxism became an anti-capitalist doctrine *in toto*, regarding the growth of capitalism as a backward movement. Markets came to be regarded as synonymous with inequality and exploitation under capitalism. Free markets and free trade became the *bêtes noires* of left-wing movements.

Polanyi's thesis, however, is very Eurocentric. Britain, which he took as the classic capitalist country, did indeed go through a bold liberalizing programme. In the fifteen years after the Great Reform Act of 1832, the old Poor Law was reformed, a Banking Act was passed to rationalize monetary policy, and free trade became the basis on which British agriculture was reorganized. Soon after this, a reversal of the policy commenced. One could even say that Britain's pioneering lead in the first Industrial Revolution made it a rich country, but it never became a fully capitalist one. To put it in Marxist terms: Britain never had a proper bourgeois revolution, because the aristocratic element in the British state did not lose its power in 1832. What happened was a class compromise in which a substantial liberalization of economic relations was traded for a sharing of political power with the middle class in a subordinate position, but full liberalization was soon checked by a cross-class alliance between the aristocracy and the growing workers' movement (Chartism, and then trade unions). This is reflected in Disraeli's novels – *Sybil* and *Coningsby* – as well as in his subsequent political career. The Tory Party after Peel was not a free-market liberal party. The Marquess of Salisbury, no less than Disraeli, built a career in British politics by representing the Tories as shielding the poor from the depredations of the market. The free-market champions (Gladstone, for example) were in the Liberal Party in the mid-nineteenth century. Later, the Radical Whigs chose to champion regulation of the market from the left. The British bourgeoisie split between manufacturers who wanted tariffs and the financial interests in the City of London, who stuck to their liberal credo.

The idea that Britain never had a bourgeois revolution became the focus of a vibrant debate between Perry Anderson and Edward Thompson in the *New Left Review* in the 1960s.[15] The occasion of the debate was a larger controversy about the British Disease: about the lagging British economy relative to the postwar dynamism of European capitalist economies. I do not wish to explore that debate here, merely to mention that – contrary to what Polanyi said – one could regard Britain as never having experimented with a free market for any length of time.

Of course, the obvious place to study capitalism in its full bloom is not Europe, but the USA. Since the USA did not have a hangover of feudal and aristocratic institutions, it could adopt free-market capitalism without the ideological opposition of precapitalist forces. Relative to European capitalism, American capitalism has always been much more free-market orientated. In the labour market, the USA is less regulated and has a much weaker system of entitlements. 'Welfare' has remained a politically contentious topic in American politics ever since the New Deal days. The long twenty years of Democratic Party rule in 1933–52, through Depression and war, created a climate for a welfare state. The fusion of the corporations, unions and government (a Big Government, as the Americans would call it) in the Keynesian quarter-century (see Chapter 14) led to a temporary political compromise and bipartisan support for an expanding welfare state epitomized by Lyndon Johnson's Great Society programme. But as we will see in Chapter 16, this compromise broke down with the return of the Republican Party to the presidency in 1981. If Britain had a brief experimentation with the free market lasting at most fifty years, the USA had a similar period of deviation from the free market.

The American society is not an ideal one – no society is – but its vigorous democratic tradition and socially egalitarian ethos were important in integrating millions of immigrants into the American economy. This would have been difficult without a free market in the buying and selling of labour-power. Had there been trade-union barriers to employment, or discrimination based on religion, as in Britain through much of the nineteenth century (Oxbridge prohibition of non-Anglicans; discrimination against Catholics and Jews in public employment, for instance), there would have been many more people in the Black underclass.

Thus the Polanyi thesis is spatially as well as temporally specific. Echoing

Lenin's debate with the Narodniks, one could say that it is the underdevelopment of capitalism that allows and supports substantial market intervention. As capitalism develops, it sheds rather than strengthens such restrictions. This is not uncontroversial, but as I shall return to this theme in the concluding chapters, it is worth pointing out that the Polanyi thesis is one of the axes on which the debate about the future of capitalism will turn.

It was Hayek's *The Road to Serfdom* which espoused the polar opposite of the Polanyi thesis about markets and the state. Hayek's ideas about economic rationality under socialism have already been discussed. But during the war, as bombs were falling over London, Hayek embarked on a deep and far-reaching critique of the collectivistic and corporatist departures from the liberal order which he saw to be at the root of totalitarianism. *The Road to Serfdom* was the first step in his long and lonely career searching for the philosophical foundations of (Adam Smith's) System of National Liberty. Hayek does not mark a dramatic break from earlier societies that capitalism represents as Marx does. But he takes over from Carl Menger, and from even earlier nineteenth-century German thinkers, the notion of society as a self-organizing organic process – a result of human action, but not of human design. The idea of society as a self-organizing entity is presented in his work as ageless, but historically it can be grounded only after the decline of religion and feudal authority (i.e. in the age of Enlightenment and after). Adam Smith's stadial theory is thus a backdrop for the emergence of a self-organizing society. How a society becomes self-organizing from its earlier stage – that is, the transition from earlier modes of production to capitalism or to the system of natural liberty – is a question Hayek does not address.

Hayek's concern was with a rival view of society – a constructivist view which he attributes to the French socialist philosopher Saint-Simon. This approach holds that societies can be changed by human design, by planning, by drawing up blueprints for a better society. But this project of constructivist rationalism is anti-libertarian, since it interferes with the organic processes of a self-organizing society. The Invisible Hand is maimed, and replaced by a mechanical signal that is prone to failure. The autonomous, self-equilibrating civil society (the market economy) is a guarantee of liberty.

Hayek's book was not the success that Polanyi's was. The latter was in tune with the spirit of the 1940s – interventionist, suspicious of the market, and confident that liberalism had finally been laid to rest. It is also an exciting book to read, with much blood and thunder. Hayek's book is serious, and his style is measured – almost antiseptic. Hayek was analysing the breakdown of European civilization, just as Polanyi was, but his vision was much more pessimistic. In the immediate aftermath of 1944, Hayek was shunted aside, but he had lit a slow fuse that was to blow up the Keynesian consensus thirty years later. But before I come to that, we must look at those thirty years.

14
The Golden Age of National Capitalism

The thirty years following the end of the Second World War were even more startling than the first forty-five years of the twentieth century, which had been already pretty eventful. These thirty years (some would say twenty-five: 1948–73) have been called 'the Golden Age of capitalism' or the Keynesian quarter-century, the 'Age of Keynes'.[1] But the period also saw the second stage of the dissolution of empires – the maritime empires of Britain, France, the Netherlands, Belgium and Portugal. It saw an explosion in state formation in many new independent territories (nations). The Golden Age of capitalism was very much a closed affair for the club of the advanced capitalist countries. The decolonization process brought a much larger part of the world's population into the global political system in its own right. The process of decolonization was neither smooth nor peaceful. There were new developments in the communist world. The revolution in China in 1949 immensely strengthened the followers of revolutionary socialism. There was a further involuntary addition to the communist camp as a result of the postwar developments in which the Soviet Union brought under its influence many of its European neighbours – Poland, Hungary, Czechoslovakia, Bulgaria, East Germany and Romania, as well as the Baltic States: Lithuania, Latvia and Estonia. The Golden Age of capitalism was perhaps not so golden for Eastern Europe either.

Paradoxically, this thirty-year period boosted the reputation of capitalism as well as that of socialism. The capitalism that became popular was the same capitalism which had failed in the interwar period, for now it was successful. It was national capitalism, or – as I have called it above – capitalism in one country. The diverse collection of national capitalisms in the advanced capitalist countries was able to achieve the widest and deepest improvement in human well-being those countries had ever seen. Full employment, sustained economic growth with only shallow cyclical interruption, high levels of mass consumption including public as well as private goods, improvements in health, housing and education – all these became common experience during those years. Not for the first time, people began to think that this was a new but permanent phase of capitalism in the advanced capitalist countries. It was the return of the Bernstein illusion.

But the socialist cause also gained ground. Many of the parliamentary reformist socialist parties came to power. One of the reasons for the popularity of capitalism was indeed that it was transformed by those whose agenda was Socialism within Capitalism (SwC). For the Second International (now the Socialist International), this was a golden age as well.[2] The other tendency, which I called Socialism outside Capitalism (SoC) – Leninist socialism – also became a formidable presence in this period. The works of Marx, Engels, Lenin and Stalin were translated and circulated. Others, such as Mao Tse-tung, Leon Trotsky and Che Guevera, were added as junior and often disputed members of the pantheon. Marxism flourished in universities, and in the print and other media, in the advanced capitalist countries as never before. The newly decolonized countries were enthusiastic about SoC, and practised their version of SwC – their own national socialisms. A few – such as Cuba, Vietnam, North Korea, Ethiopia and Cambodia (briefly and murderously) – even followed the SoC path.

There was a Cold War, of course, which went beyond this period. A confrontation between capitalism and communism, armed with nuclear weapons, persisted throughout. It reached a climax in 1962, with the Cuban missile crisis, but luckily, a nuclear confrontation did not lead to a real war. Arms expenditure became huge on both sides, and most aspects of public life in the principal protagonist countries became permeated with military culture. In the USA and France, a military hero of the Second World War came to power. There was nothing sinister about Eisenhower becoming President, with landslide victories in 1952 and 1956; nor was there reason to worry about De Gaulle's rise to power in 1945, but his return in 1960 was a Bonapartist coup. But it was not just that military leaders became political leaders. The Pentagon became a much larger presence in US politics than it had been in the previous 170 years of US history. The Soviet Union continued its pursuit of state capitalism/war socialism through its planning mechanism. Rosa Luxemburg's Department III was to loom large on both sides of the Cold War.

The Cold War produced a vulgarization of political language. We had the West versus the East, the North and the South, the First, Second and Third Worlds. For one camp, freedom became the sole possession of the West. The East said that their citizens had positive economic and social freedoms, while the West could only guarantee negative – political – freedoms. The West said it had democracy; the East called its system people's democracies. The decolonized countries denounced the West's democratic pretensions by pointing out the imperial depredations they had suffered.[3] The discord between the USSR and the USA, UK and France, as well as the changed political situation in China, the fifth Permanent Member of the UN Security Council, rendered the UN a talking shop incapable of fulfilling its function. The 'Concert of Great Powers' element of the UN was therefore dysfunctional. The democratic element – the General Assembly – became the floor for playing out the various postures. While its membership grew, and its agencies did useful work, the heart of the UN had sclerosis. Without Metternich's concept of power, Woodrow Wilson's democratic idealism was empty.

Through all this, the losers were the faithfuls of the nineteenth-century liberal order. Politically, the growth of adult franchise in democratic governments changed the nature of the democratic state. The non-interfering liberal state with a property-based franchise and protective of private property – the state idealized by A. V. Dicey[4] – disappeared from view. In the economic sphere, the liberals lost even more. Conservatives no less than socialists, capitalists and trade unionists were agreed on the merits of a 'mixed economy'. The degree of the mixture – the extent of the role of the state in the economy – differed as between the USA and Northwest Europe. Even within Europe, there were variations. But, in general, unregulated or free-market capitalism seemed to be a lost cause. The state's budget increased as a proportion of GDP to a high permanent level in peacetime, and went on increasing throughout the period. The idea of market failure, and the notion that taxes and/or subsidies were needed to correct the spillover effects caused by 'externalities' such as noise, pollution and congestion, became widely accepted. In macroeconomics, Keynesian solutions – in various combinations of monetary and fiscal policies – were adopted across the advanced capitalist countries, with only the rare exception of Germany. Keynes had pointed out the incidence of market failure at the macroeconomic level. Thus the notion that 'the market does not work' became a part of general conventional wisdom.

On the other hand, the planning practised by the Soviet Union seemed to many, especially in the decolonized countries, a superbly effective way of achieving economic growth. The Soviet Union appeared to have traversed the distance between an underdeveloped (or backward, to use a word then current) and a developed economy in record time. Despite having suffered extensive war damage, the Soviet Union impressed the world with its industrial achievements. It acquired nuclear and thermonuclear weapons soon after the USA. Then, in 1957, it launched Sputnik, the first unmanned spacecraft, and thus overtook the

USA in the space race. For the first time in the twentieth century, the Americans felt that they were behind another country. By the time of the 1960 US presidential election, it was said that the USA suffered from a 'growth gap' as well as a 'missile gap'. The new President made landing an American on the moon a major part of his programme. Kennedy did not live to see a man land on the moon, but it became a fact thanks to his determination.

The planned economy was, as we have seen above, a closed economy, seeking to achieve autarky. What the German war economy was forced to do – as was the Soviet Union in its isolation after 1927 – became a doctrine of best practice as far as the many decolonized countries embarking on their development were concerned. There was an export pessimism, as well as a new and powerful thesis advanced by the Latin American economist Raul Prebisch and a pioneer among British Keynesians, Hans Singer, which stated that the terms of trade were unfavourable to countries exporting primary products relative to manufacturing products.[5] Thus trade could not be an engine of growth for developing countries. They could not rely on the Ricardian doctrine of comparative advantage, since specializing in primary products would adversely affect their chances of obtaining manufactured imports. Developing countries had to industrialize, and in order to industrialize they had to go for import substitution.

This was one market failure on which the advanced capitalist countries (ACCs) begged to differ with the rest of the world. As I outlined in Chapter 13, there was a presumption in favour of freer trade, if not free trade, in the postwar settlement negotiated by the Allies (now without the USSR). Thus the failure to establish the ITO, due to the reluctance of the US Congress, was quickly corrected by the creation of GATT. As far as the ACCs were concerned, they would pursue the path of multilateral tariff reduction between themselves.

This push towards a steadily greater liberalization of international trade among the ACCs remained the sole surviving principle of the nineteenth-century liberal economic order. It was to prove to be a powerful thin end of the wedge to reverse the fortunes of the liberal economic order in the future. But for much of the Golden Age, it was protectionism and Friedrich List that defined the postwar economic ethos.[6] This was helped by the setting up of the European Economic Community among six West European countries. The EEC was a Listian organization, with high tariff walls against imports and progressively freer trade within. Japan also used a highly regulated trade regime to speed its path to becoming an advanced capitalist country. Thus even within the ACCs, the commitment to freer trade was more an Anglo-Saxon disease, since the largest capitalist country, the USA, was within the Anglo-Saxon camp. The extension of the GATT regime became a cornerstone of US economic foreign policy. It was to be a crucial long-term commitment.

Also – unlike in the aftermath of the First World War – this time the USA abandoned its isolation and became actively engaged in fashioning postwar Europe. Marshall Aid was a generous and powerful intervention which altered the balance in Northwest Europe in favour of capitalism, or even SwC, rather than a Leninist socialism or even a return of fascism. The size of the transfer – up to 5 per cent of US GDP – was enormous, and has never been repeated in any subsequent voluntary intergovernmental transfer. The transfer worked as much to US advantage as to those of the recipients, thus demonstrating the power of the Keynesian logic in yet another direction.

The Golden Age of capitalism coincided with an enormous growth in research and higher education in all the sciences. The social sciences grew much faster than the natural sciences. Economics, no longer the dismal science, benefited most from this growth. Its prestige as the most 'scientific' of the social sciences rested on its operational, mathematical/quantitative approach. Models of the economy came into greater and greater use, with economists playing a major and visible role as advisers. They underpinned the market-failure paradigm with a lot of research, and disseminated this research via textbooks and monographs. The dominant approach was positivist and instrumental. The economy was likened increasingly to a machine, a cybernetic system which could be studied and subjected to control and regulation.[7] Computers had been invented during the war, and they became better and faster – though also larger – as time went on. Economists took to computer modelling of the economy or its sectors. Leontieff had pioneered input–output analysis (see Chapter 5) just before the Second World War. This allowed detailed mapping of the intersectoral relations within a modern economy. It was, of course, also useful for military planning in many countries, and for planning for economic growth. Here was the practical implementation of the general equilibrium methodology of Walras, and an answer to the liberal economists who had questioned the feasibility of a socialist economy.[8]

During the war, the Allies had a shortage of shipping capacity and many destinations across the Atlantic to reach. It was in this context that a new mathematical technique to solve 'the transportation problem' was pioneered by the Dutch economist Tjalling Koopmans simultaneously with an American economist, George Dantzig. The generic name for the solution of the transportation problem came to be known as linear programming.[9] Some linear objective functions had to be maximized (tons of material delivered) or minimized (time spent idle by the ships). There were various constraints – capacity of the ships, distances to travel, maximum speed which they could attain, and so on. It turned out that this 'maximization subject to constraints' was also the classic problem economists dealt with. Consumers would maximize utility and minimize expenditure. The constraints would be the available income; the level of well-being to be achieved; rationing, if that was the case with some commodities. Or the firm had to maximize profits subject to constraints – production technology, et cetera. Linear programming simplified the problem at hand by using linear equations, but soon this was superseded by two Princeton mathematicians, Harold Kuhn and Abraham Tucker, who solved the non-linear programming problem.[10] What the economists had been talking about in general theoretical terms for nearly seventy years, ever since the marginalist revolution, was now exact and computable. The marriage of economics and mathematics was going to yield fruitful theoretical and practical results. This then led to the undermining of liberal economics in the immediate postwar period. It would be another thirty years before liberal economists could fight back.

The objection that quantitative calculations of physical relationships ignored market prices, and hence led to irrational allocations, was answered forcefully by Paul Samuelson, the most famous economist of his generation. He showed that corresponding to such physical allocations, a system of 'shadow' prices was automatically decided. This was a simple but imaginative use of the mathematics of linear systems, but its impact on the battle between the market-failure paradigm and the liberal paradigm was profound. Prices were no longer generated just in the marketplace, as Mises and Hayek had argued. Shadow prices could be calculated by using the mathematics of linear systems. They could be compared to the market prices, if these were available. Wherever there was a market failure, there would be a discrepancy between the two. But often markets did not exist – as, for example, for clean air or, within a firm or a government ministry, for intrafirm or interdepartmental allocation. In such cases, one had only shadow prices. Thus, the set of shadow prices was larger than the set of market prices. Far from being an example of socialist economic ignorance, the method of physical allocations led to a generalization of the market-failure argument, so that it became more powerful than market allocation.[11]

So economics led social sciences in a statist direction. The state became a major – if not the crucial – agency for securing the welfare of its citizens. As a philosophical category, as a social institution and as a political reality, the state became an object of fascination for the social sciences – economics, political science, sociology. The earlier idea of civil society as being autonomous, as formulated by Adam Smith, was now abandoned. Society was also no longer seen as an organic entity but as a mechanical one. Lenin had described the developments in Russia as an organic process. For Marx as well, capitalism was a self-organizing organic process, as it was for Smith, Hegel or Menger. Now, even for Marxists, economies were machines or buildings to be constructed or regulated from an a priori design. The state was to control the economy. It would be responsible for solving social problems – of marriage, divorce, teenage pregnancies, crime, and so on. Social sciences were to provide the tools for such reform, regulation and control. Like the natural sciences, the social sciences were happy to become part and parcel of the state's purpose. The notion that social sciences should be critical (in the sense of Hegel) lost favour. We were all positivists now.

The economic performance of Western capitalism during the Golden Age was spectacular. Output growth rate averaged 3.8 per cent, while the best performance in the period before 1914 was 1.4 per cent – miraculous relative to the interwar period. Labour productivity rose rapidly – 5.5 per cent per annum – and so did real wages. There was not only full employment but overfull employment, leading to net inward migration of foreign workers in Western European countries as well as the USA. But even within countries, there was a massive transfer of population from (low-productivity) agriculture to (high-productivity) manufacturing. This led to rural decay and urban overcrowding. The Black sharecroppers of the American South migrated to Chicago and Detroit and New York. At the end of the Civil War, the North had liberated the slaves but kept them confined to the South. Now, more than eighty years later, they were turning up in Northern cities. Agriculture became highly mechanized, transformed by new chemical inputs, and its productivity exploded. Food prices fell across the capitalist countries, and farmers had to lobby to get governments to buy off their surplus food at guaranteed prices.

But low prices for consumers meant better and more nutritious food. There was a baby boom in North America soon after the war. Infant mortality declined sharply, and longevity increased. Across advanced capitalist countries, women began to enjoy higher life expectancy than men – a sure sign of economic development. They had worked during the war, but were encouraged to get back to a wife-and-mother role after short, low-wage/secretarial work experience. Household drudgery was transformed by the new gadgets which were in increasing use – refrigerators, washing machines, dishwashers, vacuum cleaners.

Fashion, previously the preserve of the idle rich, now percolated much farther down the class structure. Women had magazines clamouring for their attention. If they felt caged during these years, it was at least a gilded cage.

But it was men, especially working-class men – or blue-collar workers, to use the American expression – men with only basic schooling, but a good physical working capacity, who had the best of times during the Golden Age. Trade unions grew, with massive memberships and recognized rights for workplace bargaining. A young man leaving school at fifteen or sixteen could look forward to the triple 48: 48 years of employment, 48 weeks per year, 48 hours per week. The weekly hours, of course, included overtime paid at a higher rate than the normal wage. The unions made sure their members' real wages went up each year. They could look forward to rising living standards with room enough to raise a family, acquire consumer durables – even a car; send their children to better schools, and even to college. By the late 1950s sociologists were starting to discover the bourgeoisified worker. Was this the end of the revolutionary proletariat? Was this the end of Marx?

Many social scientists, and even politicians, thought so. Anthony Crosland, a bright young British socialist, wrote *The Future of Socialism* at the height of the Golden Age.[12] Keynes had cleverly solved the problem of unemployment, and of course, steady economic growth was assured. Growth resolved the struggle between workers and capitalists over the share each got in income. The cake was growing, so that even if the share was the same, or declining, you got more cake to eat. Crosland, harking back to the aesthetic heritage of British socialism – William Morris, for instance – wanted a larger public share to improve the quality of consumption: subsidies for the arts, cafés in public parks run by municipalities, well-designed housing.

John Kenneth Galbraith became the most widely read celebrant of the Golden Age in the USA. Early in the 1950s, in *American Capitalism*, he saw that an equilibrium between big business and big unions was emerging in the USA.[13] This was his vision of countervailing power: the Marshallian notion of static equilibrium between demand and supply translated to modern times. There was stasis, but in stasis there was harmony, equilibrium. In the late 1950s, Galbraith wrote his most famous book, *The Affluent Society*, highlighting the problem that in the USA, unlike in Western Europe, there was little by way of public goods production. No municipal socialism, no subsidy for the arts, not even a decent infrastructure of roads and public transport. He was wrong about roads, perhaps, since Eisenhower had just implemented a very large programme of highway construction, but he was prescient about public-sector squalor in the midst of private affluence. What he perhaps did not see, however, was that the strength of American capitalism – its productivity, its profitability, its growth potential – was acutely dependent on the low level of public taxation that American capital enjoyed compared to Western European capital. No one else was to see this point, either, until much later, when profitability began to matter. For the time being, everyone thought we could have more of everything. Not only Marx had been killed off – even the calculus of scarcity was redundant.

For a generation of people – anyone born after 1920 and before 1945 in the West – the Golden Age became the normal form of capitalism, with growth and full employment, and an expanding welfare state. They grew up to think that active state intervention to ensure full employment was a regular feature of capitalism. Indeed, many thought – still do think – that providing full employment rather than making profits was the end purpose of capitalism. Trade cycles, mass unemployment, had been eliminated by Keynes for ever. But there was also a belief – mistaken, as it happens – that Keynes had said that budget deficits were not only harmless but beneficial, and that public debt was irrelevant, since that was what we owed to ourselves. Keynes himself advocated balancing the budget over the cycle – running a surplus in boom and a deficit in slump. He was not unmindful of the burden of debt; his passion throughout the Second World War was to get the British war debt financed at a low interest rate. He thought that was feasible, since he feared a glut of savings. In this he was not only wrong, but too much bound by interwar experience in the UK. It was to be some years before the fallacy was to be exposed. To be fair, though, British, Oxbridge Keynesians were much more aggressively fiscalist than their US counterparts.[14]

In 1945, American Keynesians forecast that the economy would face a postwar slump. New and confident econometric models were being deployed to sustain these predictions. As it happened, there was an immediate postwar boom, and no slump until 1949. There were many reasons for the boom. A pent-up demand existed, and grew as the baby boom started. People had saved in wartime, buying government bonds, and now they were ready to cash in. The American economy had been able to fight the war without undue strain, and it was ready to switch to peacetime production. New household gadgets flooded out from the factories. Families moved to new houses in the suburbs, bought their car for commuting and their new toy – TV – for entertainment.

The failure of the Keynesian forecasts did not destroy the model-building enterprise, but it did challenge it. Neoclassical critics of Keynes – especially his former teacher and King's College colleague, A. C. Pigou – had argued that

Keynes might have missed out on one mechanism of escape from a slump that was automatic to the market. A sustained fall in prices during a depression will increase the real value of savings – real balances. People will find themselves better off in terms of wealth – real balances being just one component of wealth – and will begin to spend. In Pigou's view, Keynes had underplayed the importance of real balances as a positive influence on consumption. So while he had shown that cuts in money wage or in interest rates would not restore full employment, here was a mechanism that could. As a liberal economist in the macroeconomic context, Pigou wanted to argue that state intervention was not necessary for full employment.[15]

As a theoretical argument in an academic debate, Pigou's was the first 'hit' against Keynes. It allowed a chink to appear through which much further criticism of Keynesian theory was to pass. But while the Full Employment Act was passed by Congress, American politicians remained suspicious of the fiscal profligacy that Keynesianism entailed. Once the Cold War started, there was also a left-wing taint on many young Keynesians. The Democratic Party stayed truer to Keynesianism than the rival Republican Party, but even among the Democrats it was the left-wing 'liberal' (in the US sense) Democrats who were more Keynesian than the rest. Throughout the 1950s, American Republicans and Conservative Democrats kept the wilder Keynesians at bay. It was only during Kennedy's presidency that the Council of Economic Advisers could be said to have been fully Keynesian. When he became President in 1968, Richard Nixon continued the Keynesian tradition, making him perhaps the first Keynesian Republican President.[16]

Keynesianism, in the sense of fine-tuning fiscal policy with a passive monetary policy, was much more a British practice. The balance-of-payments constraint was binding on British policymakers, and frequent changes in fiscal stance – stop–go – were necessary to reconcile full employment and fixed exchange rates. Britain's foreign debts accumulated in war also made severe capital controls necessary. Keynes had provided for all this in his Bretton Woods architecture. For British Keynesians, devaluation became a magic potion for their problems but, alas, a forbidden one. The two devaluations – 1949 and 1967 – were politically costly, but remained popular among economists.

The Americans did not have a balance-of-payments constraint – not in the 1950s, at least. They had capital to export, and vast reserves of gold, which was available for sale as foreign exchange reserves at $35 an ounce. The economy proved strong enough to bear the burden of rearmament, fight the Korean War, maintain an active engaged military posture throughout the 1950s, and still afford rising consumer expenditure. It was only in the 1960s that the balance-of-payments constraint began to bite. But in the 1950s, a prudent fiscal stance could be maintained. Arthur F. Burns, as Chairman of the Council of Economic Advisers, was no devotee of Keynes. It was in the early 1960s that Kennedy's Council Chairman, Walter Heller, advocated and obtained a pre-emptive tax cut to perpetuate the boom, which was beginning to flag in 1962. The boom lasted well into the 1960s, then the troubles began.

A premonition of the problem ahead was provided in the mild recession of 1957–58. This was the first time in post-1945 history that unemployment went up without inflation going down. It was not a Keynesian recession, but more akin to what Hayek had been warning about in the 1930s. But Hayek was otherwise engaged (finishing what became *The Constitution of Liberty*), and no one picked up the anomaly. Luckily for the Keynesians, an article by the LSE's A. W. Phillips, in 1958, traced out a relationship between unemployment and the change in money wage rates.[17] Phillips had looked at nineteenth-century data for the British economy. In the period 1861–1913, he traced six-and-a-half cycles of about eight years on average, but he also established a curve which traced the negative relationship between the two basic variables. Thus as unemployment rose, money wage rates fell till they reached a floor of about −10 per cent. But as unemployment fell to zero, money-wage-rate rise accelerated. Phillips then attempted to see how far interwar and postwar data matched the nineteenth-century curve. There was no close fit, but he thought there was a relationship.

Two prominent American economists, both subsequently Nobel Prize-winners, Paul Samuelson and Robert Solow, took Phillips's approach and extended it to price inflation.[18] They traced a smooth curve between inflation and unemployment in US data. While Phillips had doubts about the curve fitting all periods, Samuelson and Solow had none. Thus, in 1960, the Phillips Curve was baptized. Here was a recipe for Keynesian policymakers for fighting inflation: increase unemployment. The issue of how much unemployment was necessary for reducing inflation by one percentage point preoccupied many economists and econometricians. Preliminary results showed that an unemployment rate of 15 per cent might be required to get inflation to zero in the USA. Such results were disbelieved; many extensions and alternatives were explored. The recipe had to be perfected to make the dosage reasonable. But of the efficacy of the medicine, few had doubts. There was, after all, empirical econometric evidence.

Marxists who had been silenced in the West by the triumph of Keynesianism should have been thrilled by this discovery. Here was the reserve army of unemployed required to keep wage inflation, and thereby price inflation, down. The wage productivity ratio – the unit labour cost – was the crucial variable, and that – as I showed in Chapter 5 – is related to the rate of exploitation. But the first attack came not from the Marxists but from the hardy band of conservative and liberal economists concentrated in the University of Chicago. They had never signed up to Keynesianism, and asserted that money supply was a neglected but central variable explaining income fluctuations. It was not the Keynesian multiplier which explained the cycle, but money supply and the quantity theory. This group, headed by Milton Friedman, was the butt of many jokes in the early 1960s in American campuses, as I can personally testify.[19] But their persistence paid off. Inflation was a severe challenge to the Keynesians, and the Phillips Curve recipe was not only politically unpalatable – especially to left-wing Keynesians – but also proved ineffective. Direct controls on wage bargaining and price-setting – incomes policies – began to be advocated. Conservatives who had been happy with Keynesian policies broke rank.

The American economy faced particular problems in the 1960s. The Kennedy–Johnson tax cut of 1964 prolonged the boom, but then the Vietnam War began to add to the federal budget. There were labour shortages and inflation. America began to experience large trade deficits, and the dollar was beginning to look overvalued. The French, under De Gaulle, asked for their dollar reserves to be converted into gold, as was their right. American deficits were making the world awash with dollars. There were attempts to stem the outward flow by imposing a tax on capital movements. This led to evasion of this tax cut. American banks kept their dollars abroad; thus the Eurodollar market was born.

It was in this context that anti-Keynesian economists began to make inroads into the citadels of orthodoxy. Pigou's original objection about real balances had related to money deposits relative to prices. Money and monetary policy were said to be neglected by Keynesians, if not by Keynes himself. Money supply had to be controlled to control inflation. Keynesians argued that with the Phillips Curve, an optimal combination of unemployment and inflation could be chosen and maintained as an equilibrium. Friedman argued that workers would absorb inflation into their expectations, and bid up wages. Higher wages would mean either higher unemployment or – if the government tried to maintain unemployment at its target level – more expenditure and higher inflation.

The maintenance of low inflation and low unemployment entailed some regulation of the wage bargain. The reforming socialists and the Keynesians overlapped a lot. They had originally been friends and defenders of the trade unions. Here was a contentious issue which began to divide them. To have full employment without inflation was seen to be inconsistent with unregulated or free wage bargaining. In Sweden this had always been recognized, and the wage bargain was a national-level tripartite affair involving government, unions and employers. In Austria and Germany, similar 'social contracts' were prevalent. But in the Anglo-Saxon world, unions were relatively weak and fragmented. Employers were even more reluctant to combine for national wage negotiation. The 'political economy of inflation' became the buzz word for this messy mixture of politics, industrial relations and macroeconomics.

At this stage (the late 1960s) the monetarists were offering a simple answer – far too simple in the Keynesians' view: control the money supply. But that entailed eliminating budget deficits, and financing such deficits as there were by borrowing in the market rather than by 'printing money'. The monetarists were also free-market liberals in many cases. Thus Friedman attacked the fixed exchange rate system which was then causing America so many problems. Public debt became the bugbear of many right-wing political groups, and neoclassical economists (not necessarily monetarists or liberals) began to see debt as an intergenerational problem. We borrow; our children pay back. The simplicities of naive Keynesianism were being abandoned.

The full story of the demise of Keynesianism must await another chapter, but the nature of the problem could be – and was – seen with much greater clarity by Marxist economists in the late 1960s than by any other group. Inflation, especially wage-cost-led inflation, was really a problem of profitability. While there was surplus labour to recruit from agriculture, or from the baby boom, or from immigrants, and productivity kept growing, wages did not rise very fast, and the wage/productivity ratio remained low. Thus labour's share of income stayed constant, and afforded a reasonable share for profits. But productivity growth could be maintained only by larger investments to keep substituting expensive labour by new capital. Sustained full employment and powerful unions plus accommodating governments resulted in a rising share of labour. Real wages rose faster than productivity, and the share of profit began to erode. Profitability at the macroeconomic level was not a part of the Keynesian models by the 1960s. (In the late 1940s and early 1950s, there had been some attempt to model the wage/profit division as part of a Keynesian model in the work of Lawrence Klein, for instance. But the Cold War put a stop to all that.) Thus the inflation/profitability connection was seen by the Marxists rather than the Keynesians. Why Marxists, and what sort of Marxists?

Marxists in the West were never a single church. The Communist Party had prestige in the Soviet Union and a monopoly of Marxism in the immediate postwar period. In France, they had shared power for a while after 1945. Their reputation for anti-fascist struggle was high. There were dissident sects, though as yet very small, challenging the monopoly of the Communists – mainly the followers of Trotsky, who claimed to be the true heirs of Lenin and Marx. Their quarrel was with Stalin and Stalinism. It was about the nature of the Soviet Union and the importance of internationalism, but it was also about the possibility of a revolution in the West.

But in a paradoxical way, the Cold War helped the dissident Marxists. As Stalin moved into Eastern and Southeastern Europe, and as Germany was divided, Communists came under suspicion. But many Trotskyists were championed by the Cold Warriors. They had, after all, read all about Lenin, Stalin and the mysterious doings behind the Iron Curtain. Many Communists were in universities as scientists, historians, economists – especially in Europe. Now Trotskyists also entered academia and became accepted as public intellectuals. Isaac Deutscher, the biographer of Stalin and Trotsky, was one such. James Burnham, an American Trotskyist, became a guru when he wrote *The Managerial Revolution.*[20] The Trotskyists were less orthodox, less unquestioning, than the Stalinists. They were, of course, equally inclined to deify the words of Marx and Lenin, but their role was to free Marxism from the catechistic simplicities of Stalinist Marxism.

Then in 1956, from within the citadel itself, came the confessions of the enormities of Stalin. At the 20th Party Congress of the Communist Party of the Soviet Union, Nikita Khrushchev, Stalin's successor as General Secretary, gave a detailed and gory account of the concentration camps – the Gulags – of Russia. This caused a crisis for many Communists and many more bystanders in the socialist movement. A flood of literature was unleashed on Marx, Lenin, Stalin, and the revolutionary Communist movement. Marx's 1844 Manuscripts had become widely available in the 1950s, though the English translation was yet to come. A humanist Marx, long forgotten in the idiocies of Stalinism, was emerging into public view – a Marx in the Enlightenment tradition, concerned about alienation and the reintegration of man as a species being with his human essence.[21] (My use of the masculine is deliberate, since it reflects the original.) Marx's original works began to be read again. His views on democracy, different as they were from hegemonic liberal democracy, were in stark contrast to what the Bolsheviks had preached in his name, or what Lenin and Stalin – and, indeed, Trotsky – practised. A New Left was born in the advanced capitalist countries.

But in the 1950s, capitalism was still triumphant, and seemed free of problems. The doctrine of the Third International about capitalism being in a terminal crisis outlived the demise of the Comintern. Trotskyists no less than Stalinists were stuck with that vision. The New Left may have been anti-Stalinist, but Lenin was still infallible in its view, and Lenin's interpretation of Marx's theory was still swallowed whole. Yet in their daily lives, the Western leftist academics and activists could see that there was full employment, and that living standards were improving. The anticolonial struggle was one respect in which capitalism – especially European capitalism – was behaving as of old. France in Indochina and Algeria, the UK in Malaya and Africa, West or East, Belgium in the Congo and the Dutch in Indonesia had lived up to the imperialist image. But otherwise, Western capitalism was threatening to disprove Lenin's theories.

Conventional Cold War wisdom had reached a *modus vivendi* with the USSR. Happy with the anti-Stalinist propaganda which Khrushchev had given them, Western policymakers still respected Soviet military power and space technology. There was a tacit admission that industrialization, a pretty rough process historically anyway, had been accomplished by the Soviet Union. The newly decolonized countries' efforts to industrialize along similar lines were understandable. Economists had created a growth theory in the light of Keynesian macroeconomics: an operational, positivist and context-free theory. Growth of income occurred as a result of savings being invested. This investment was new capital and, with the technology available, became additional income. The higher the investment as a ratio of existing capital, the higher the income growth. Technology, represented by the ratio of output to capital, was – surprisingly for the time – taken to be constant. Growth thus became a matter of savings and the capital output ratio. It was a simple, single mathematical equation.[22]

But since growth was growth no matter where or how the savings were generated, the Soviet Union's growth performance was much admired by its Cold War rivals. Growth rates recently achieved could be mathematically projected to go on for a long time. The Soviet Union's growth rate was at least twice – if not more – that of the USA and the UK, despite the fact that the West was enjoying one of the highest income growths in the last hundred years. The roots of this growth were to become a subject of intense study, but the 'growth gap' in the 1950s between the USSR and the USA was to become a hot political potato in American politics.

There was thus admiration and envy of the enemy. Walt Rostow, an economic historian specializing in British economic history and Professor at MIT, gave the prestigious Marshall Lectures at the University of Cambridge in 1959. He called them *A Non-Communist Manifesto*,[23] but Rowstow's concept of 'the take-off into self-sustained growth' was actually very admiring of the Soviet system. Rostow identified five stages in the trajectory of any economy, of which the second was the 'take-off' once a savings income ratio of 10 per cent was achieved. But in the higher reaches was an economy of high mass consumption. The USSR was not there yet, but a convergence, Rostow argued, between the capitalist and the communist systems was very probable. It was the ruthless logic of exponential growth rate. Neither liberty nor property rights nor labour mobility mattered. Growth was an automatic mechanical process. There was to be no difference between the systems in economic terms.

Convergence was a strange doctrine for both sides. For the Leninists, it was a revisionist abandonment of the breakdown-and-terminal-crisis scenario. For the liberals, it meant admitting that freedom was irrelevant to economic well-being. But for the pragmatist shaping Cold War policy, convergence was a sound basis for calling off the hostilities – for a détente. It was the American 'liberals' – largely Democrats – who espoused convergence, since it got away from the virulent anti-communism of John Foster Dulles, American Secretary of State during much of the Eisenhower presidency. Communism might be evil, but it was 'their' system and it worked. Extreme economic determinists (denying Marx all the while) even hoped that prosperity might lead to democracy in the Soviet Union. It was another version of the old catechism: property → middle class → democracy. Once they have their own houses and refrigerators and cars, they are bound to want democracy next.

Rostow was soon to be engaged in a denial of his own thesis when he became a policy adviser to Presidents Kennedy and Johnson in the Vietnam War. It was this war more than anything else that made Marxism popular in the West. Sustained full employment had strengthened the demands for political equality everywhere. In the USA it was the coloured people, as they were then called (Negroes by their detractors, and subsequently Blacks, or Afro-Americans, or people of colour, as political fashions changed) who marched for civil rights in the South and in the North. The Cuban Revolution had brought a Marxist regime close to American shores, and made Latin Americans aware of alternatives to the many forms of dictatorship they were experiencing. Kennedy launched an Alliance for Democracy in Latin America and a peace corps to send American youth to the developing countries to show the peaceful anti-Communist face of America. But Kennedy's death in 1963 and the intensification of the war in Vietnam coincided with inflationary pressures and trade deficits in the USA. Students in the front line of compulsory military service discovered that the USA, which for many decades had been an anti-imperialist country, was merely perpetuating old-style French imperialism under the guise of anti-communism. The peasants of Vietnam became the scapegoats for an attack on American ideology as practised by the Pentagon, the State Department and the White House. It was the left-wing Democratic Party, friend of the unions and the Blacks and the poor, which was now under attack.

American radical movements never turned explicitly Marxist. They had their own traditions – Henry David Thoreau, for instance – to draw upon. But they began to question the military–industrial complex, the intricate but oligarchic power structure of multinational corporations cohabiting with the government machine. They took to violent as much as non-violent methods of protest. From Berkeley in 1964 to Columbia and Harvard and Stanford, and to the Democratic Party convention in Chicago in 1968, radical student protest raged.

It echoed with a loud thunder in May 1968 in Paris. France was shaken, and the students had explicit Marxist arguments. The French Communist Party disowned them, and the dissident Trotskyist and Maoist sects flourished. The anarchist tendencies in Marx were rediscovered; autonomy, self-organization, anti-bureaucracy became the new slogans of the Left. For a short time it even looked as if the French state was in peril. And soon, with the flowering of the Prague Spring in Czechoslovakia, it seemed to many that a non-Stalinist Marxism might capture Europe, both East and West.

But Rostow was right: the systems worked on both sides to crush rebellion. Student agitation and militant worker demonstrations in Paris or Prague were not to rock the respective systems. Inflation and the erosion of profitability were to be much more deeply threatening to the West. By this time, in the late 1960s, Marxist economics was flourishing. There were demands in universities everywhere that Marxist or radical political economy be taught. The smug satisfaction with the Golden Age of capitalism was being eroded. Strikes, trade-union militancy in defiance of leadership, shop stewards' movements, anti-discrimination struggles, began to increase. There was no meeting of minds between students and workers, but each group had its own complaints. The Marxist economists in the West, young and unencumbered by old orthodoxies, were able to return to a critique of capitalism as an ongoing system rather than merely awaiting its much-predicted demise.

Continuous full employment had begun to affect profitability. The first such results were analysed by the British Marxists Andrew Glyn and Robert Sutcliffe in an article in the *New Left Review*, itself a product of the post-1956 ferment in the Western socialist movement.[24] It was a careful exercise with macroeconomic data, but more on the income side than on output or expenditure accounts. Income data – wages and salaries, profits, rent – are more difficult to obtain and work with than expenditure data – consumption, investment, government spending. It is a problem to have to deal with taxation of incomes and profits. But to calculate the rate of profit, one must know the value of the capital stock. This is a statistical nightmare, since depreciation and obsolescence are slippery concepts. Accounting practices vary across companies and countries, and over time. What the accountant calls depreciation may depend on tax laws, and seldom corresponds to what economists mean by it. So in much of macroeconomic research, then and ever since, profit calculations are avoided.

But Glyn and Sutcliffe, as young Marxists, well educated in modern economics but also of a sharp critical mind, wanted to investigate the modern capitalist economy in Marxist terms. They did not go through the thicket of price–value transformation (and were much criticized by fellow Marxists for their less than pure approach), but they did construct capital measures to compute profitability. They were able to show that in the USA and the UK, profit rates were distinctly lower in 1970 than they were in 1960 – the USA had seen profit rates rise from 9.9 per cent in 1960 to 13.7 per cent in 1965, and fall to 8.7 per cent in 1970. For the UK, profit rates went down from 14.2 per cent (1960) to 11.8 per cent (1965) to 8.7 per cent (1970). But of course, the trend was not universal. In West Germany, profit rates were 23.4 per cent (1960), 16.5 per cent (1965) and 15.6 per cent (1970) – down, but not by much. In Japan, profitability was rising from 19.7 per cent (1960) to 22.7 per cent (1970). France saw a revival of profitability: 11.9 per cent (1960), 9.9 per cent (1965) and 11.1 per cent (1970).

Inflation was a much more serious problem in the Anglo-Saxon economies than in Japan or continental Europe. The difference was not only in the institutions of wage bargaining, with the much more decentralized and anarchic Anglo-Saxon system contrasted with the corporatist system elsewhere. The real issue was the erosion of profitability in the USA and the UK. The case of the UK was easy to explain. It had suffered great damage in the war, but failed to renew its capital stock because of a severe balance-of-payments constraint – stop–go, as I discussed above. But the USA was a dominant economic power. Its industry had been in the lead everywhere. Indeed, J. K. Galbraith, in *The New Industrial State*, had argued that the new technostructure allowed large corporations, such as the automobile giants Ford, GM and Chrysler, to shape consumer demand and control the market.[25] Now the American industry was facing competition from European and Japanese producers. In the automobile sector, VW from Germany, Fiat from Italy, Peugeot from France – small and fuel-efficient cars – were making inroads into the American market, as well as capturing a larger slice of their own domestic markets. Americans had to invest more to catch up with the competition, as well as cut costs in the face of rising real wages.

All this pressure was reflected in the decline in profitability. The remarkable thing about Glyn and Sutcliffe is that they saw it before anyone else did. If they had been Keynesians or monetarists, they would have been concerned with wages, and government deficits, and money supply. Important as these variables were, they were symptoms of the deeper underlying problem of profitability. Neoclassical and Keynesian economists ignored profitability. Only the Marxists – or rather, some Marxists, the younger, more critical ones – were concerned about profitability. This is because mainstream economists do not think of capitalism as a subject of study; they study the economy or the market. Profits and profitability play no role in their analysis. The Marxists care about capitalism, if only to hasten its demise.

The new crisis of capitalism was imminent. In 1971, when the *New Left Review* article came out, it attracted only mild attention. I remember a senior LSE economics professor asking me if I had a subscription to the *New Left Review*, and if I could show him this article he had heard about. But in 1971, even inflation had not taken off into double digits. In the UK, the recently elected Conservative government was alarmed about rising unemployment, which exceeded the 'unacceptable' figure of one million later that year, and panicked the government into a U-turn and massive reflation. Keynesianism was still official policy.

Across the Atlantic, the USA was also facing up to its problems. The Vietnam War was still raging, and was soon to spread to Cambodia. Nixon was ready to take advantage of the Sino–Soviet split, and make an overture to Mao. But most importantly, the USA had decided to shed its international responsibility as guardian of the dollar-exchange standard. On 15 August 1971, Nixon announced that the USA would not buy or sell gold at $35 per ounce. The Bretton Woods system of fixed exchange rates, so carefully constructed by Keynes, was dead. The anti-Keynesians had penetrated inside the castle walls. Flexible exchange rates – regarded as Milton Friedman's pet hobbyhorse, but dismissed as folly by the economics establishment throughout the 1950s and 1960s – had arrived.

15

The High Noon of Socialism

The twenty-five years after the Second World War saw the peak of the reputation of the Soviet Union and of Stalinism. But as in the case of Keynesianism, the seeds of its own destruction were also sown during that period, and though the final demise of the Leninist system occurred later, its reputation began to ebb by the end of this time. The problem, as in the case of Keynesianism, was the overweening ambition of later followers and political elites. The liberation of Europe by a Marxist revolution was an idealistic expectation in 1917, and although revolutions fizzled out everywhere except Russia, the idea of such an act of liberation remained alive for a while. The takeover of Eastern European governments, the abolition of all parties except the Communist Party and the imposition of a Stalinist regime was a tragic joke, an anti-liberation counter-revolution. It was an echo of Old European politics in which the Tsar shared the landmass of Eastern and Central Europe with the Habsburgs and the Hohenzollerns. The garb of communism was as false as the rhetoric of people's democracies. But since the Allies were keen not to break up so soon after the war, a Soviet zone of influence was allowed.

Yet despite this counter-revolution, the reputation of communism was high in the immediate postwar period. It was deemed to be a success, and a recipe for economic growth. Its adherents and fellow-travellers grew, despite the McCarthyite witch-hunts in the USA and in Western Europe. Its reputation in the developing countries was high, thanks to the Chinese Revolution, and – as we saw above – the unflinching support that Communist parties gave to anticolonial struggles.

Once the Cold War began, then, there were blocs. A French journalist, Tibor Mende, had the brilliant idea of labelling the decolonizing and still colonized countries the Third World. So the West was the First and the Soviet bloc the Second World. Labels, even imperfect ones, acquire a life of their own, and even become powerful forces. The Third World was one such. The question immediately arose as to whether the eventual destination of the countries of the Third World was going to be the First or the Second World. The First World, having been the imperial powers, had shaped (some would say misshaped) the consciousness of the anticolonial elite of these countries. There had been a liberal, constitutional wing in many countries clamouring for independence, but the repression these movements suffered had also spawned a left radical wing, reflecting the ways of the First World. A section of this wing was reformist in the tradition of the Second International, but the behaviour of socialist governments in Western Europe drove many in an anticapitalist direction. Thus at least three strands competed in the Third World for intellectual and political hegemony: liberal constitutional procapitalist; reformist and constitutional socialist; and anticapitalist, pro-communist.

As countries decolonized between 1945 and 1970, the manner of the transfer of power very much determined which strand came out on the top. India – crucially for the Third World – had a more or less peaceful transfer of power, without the necessity of an armed struggle. The liberal constitutional and reformist socialist strands coalesced in the Congress Party, led by Jawaharlal Nehru. It was in India also that much of the early thinking on economic development was done and tried out as policy. It was in India also that the notion of non-alignment as between the two blocs was first advanced; this gave cohesion to the Third World. It was also in India that a democratic polity and a mixed economy with planning were taken most seriously as a policy framework. The Third World was ambitious to create its own destination – neither the liberal capitalism of the First World nor the authoritarian communism of the Second.

But the economic policy bias of the Third World was anticapitalist rather than not. Nehru had imbibed British snobbery against trade and money. India's policy was protectionist, and in the mid-1950s it became formally wedded to an import-substitution strategy. Public ownership of new industrial sectors was taken for granted. The state was to take the lead in industrialization, and planning was to be its instrument. It was not that India had no native capitalist culture. Modern Indian industry had been started by a Gujarati Brahmin in Ahmedabad in the 1850s in the form of a cotton-spinning mill. After much agitation, India had acquired the powers to impose its own tariffs by the early twentieth century. At the time of independence, in 1947, India had the largest native capitalist class – merchants, industrialists, financiers – of all the Third World countries. Indeed, in terms of volume of industrial output (not *per capita*), it was the seventh largest industrial country in 1945.[1]

But the perception was that India had been deindustrialized and impoverished by British rule. In a perspective of, say, two hundred years, India was poorer in 1950 than it had been in 1750, though income calculations over such a long period are bound to be speculative. It was the Indian economist – later Liberal MP for Finsbury – Dadabhai Naoroji who, in *Poverty and Un-British Rule in India,* had pioneered the notion that India's wealth had suffered a steady 'drain' to British coffers.[2] India's trade surplus had been eaten into by 'home charges' – the cost of running the Empire imposed by Whitehall. Naoroji's critique had been backed up by Romesh Chandra Dutt, who had been a member of the Indian civil service. He blamed India's rural impoverishment on the land-tenure system. Bengal, which had zamindari with a single permanent settlement of revenue, had prospered during the nineteenth century because the surplus generated by cultivation stayed on the land. Elsewhere, however, land systems had been introduced which siphoned off the rising surplus as government revenue.

By 1950, rural poverty had engulfed Bengal as well. The years of the Depression had ruined many farmers and left them with unsustainable debts. The population of India rose by 60 per cent in the first half of the twentieth century, while its agricultural output had risen hardly at all. The availability of food grains had declined over the first fifty years of the twentieth century. So rural poverty had increased, while urban areas had acquired all the new industrial and commercial advantages. India had built up a textile industry in Ahmedabad and Bombay that could compete internationally, and a fledgling steel industry, but it lacked machinery and consumer durables.

So India was determined to industrialize, but it was not to build on the industries it had established. The path of growth through exploitation of comparative advantage – exports of agricultural and light industrial goods (especially textiles) – was rejected. The pessimism about terms of trade, as well as about the prospect of finding Western markets for its products, led India into a strategy of import substitution. Thus India was to build up its own machine-goods industries (Department I), restrict imports of 'non-essential' goods, and regulate its larger private firms, since they were liable to exercise monopolistic powers. Ricardo was rejected in favour not so much of Marx as of Stalin.

India was not alone in taking this path. Many Latin American countries – Mexico and Brazil, for example – also adopted this strategy. British colonies in Asia and Africa, as they became independent, also studied India's development policies. The recipe of import substitution, with the public sector playing a leading role in industrialization, became the standard one. The state had to mobilize savings in environments with fragile capital markets. There was little prospect of private foreign capital flowing to the periphery, as had happened in the years before 1914. There was soon a demand for foreign aid –

government-to-government transfer of capital – since domestic savings proved unequal to the task of ambitious industrialization. Thanks to the Cold War, aid flowed from both camps, each giving as much for political purposes as for economic assistance.

In this climate, markets were rejected as much as private capitalism. Prices, interest rates, exchange rates were regulated or fixed. The World Bank was happy with this approach, as were the Communist donors. Western universities took a leading role in helping India and other developing countries to build their planning models and devise their monetary, fiscal and trade policies. Western growth theory became a vital ingredient in the task of generating growth in the Third World.

There was, however, a solid onslaught from the Marxists on this mixed-economy strategy. In their view, rejection or regulation of markets was not enough. If they wanted to grow, developing countries would have to reject capitalism itself. An influential book at this time was Paul Baran's *The Political Economy of Growth.*[3] Baran, a Stanford Professor but a rare Marxist among American economists in the 1950s, argued that the 'bourgeois' regimes in developing countries would fail to mobilize the potential surplus that already existed in the form of wasteful consumption, luxury industries, bureaucracy, capital flight and tax evasion. This surplus, if mobilized, would remove the scarcity of savings. But he also argued that Western monopoly capitalism would not allow the growth of developing countries within its ambit, fearing competition from their cheaper products. This was because at home it was liable to secular stagnation, a slowing down of growth due to lack of investment opportunities. This idea of secular stagnation had come from Alvin Hansen, a Harvard economist who had been the Saint Paul of the Keynesian message. He foresaw excessive savings and insufficient investment in the advanced countries. Stagnation at home would make these countries defensive in trade. So the path of trade-led growth, or of private *laissez-faire* capitalism, was not open to the developing countries. They had to reject capitalism entirely in order to grow.

Baran's book was very influential in Third World countries. By the time he wrote it, in 1960, more countries were becoming independent. China had already shown that a 'backward' country could have a Communist revolution. It had implemented drastic land reform, and passed swiftly from co-operative farming to communes. It had stood up to American military might in the Korean War. Mao was promising to overtake America soon, and had launched the Great Leap Forward. If China and India were two rivals – one democratic and bourgeois, the other a Communist dictatorship – the contest between them was a peripheral version of the Cold War struggle (despite India's preferred non-alignment). China, it was said, showed the efficacy of communism for development.

Another strand of Baran's argument was taken much further in the Latin American context by Andre Gunder Frank.[4] The burden of Gunder Frank's thesis was that the developed capitalism of Europe and the USA caused backwardness and underdevelopment in South America. Western capital, engaged in extractive industries (copper in Chile) and underpricing raw material through hidden transfer pricing, transferred the surplus back north. This was a recapitulation of the Indian drain theory, but applied to industrial capitalism rather than imperialism. The profits of multinationals in these extractive industries were thus pure surplus – unearned rent.

So Baran and Frank reversed the nineteenth-century classical Marxian idea that capitalism, wherever it goes, destroys – but to the desirable end of developing productive forces. Lenin's dispute with the Narodniks was forgotten in favour of his *Imperialism.* In its new form of monopoly capitalism (neocolonialism), capitalism destroyed, but did not create. Thus – to quote the first few lines of Gunder Frank's preface – 'I believe, with Paul Baran, that it is Capitalism, both world and national, which produced underdevelopment in the past and which still generates underdevelopment in the present.'[5]

In the global context, the Marxists argued that capitalist accumulation helped the North no matter where it operated, and hurt the South, which became a victim of this process. The new discipline of the political economy of development became deeply suspicious of capitalism, of foreign trade, and of multinational capital.

There are several paradoxes here. Latin America had been politically independent throughout the twentieth century, having defeated Iberian imperialism in the nineteenth. Relative to Asia (excepting Japan) and Africa, it was prosperous – a middle-income rather than a low-income region. Argentina was classified as among the five richest countries by Colin Clark in his pioneering work *The Conditions of Economic Progress* published in 1940.[6] There was, of course, tremendous inequality in the distribution of land in much of South America – except in Mexico, which had, of course, undergone its own peasant revolution in the early twentieth century. Latin America had enjoyed a spurt of industrialization in the interwar period, and by the late 1950s it counted as moderately prosperous.

It would have been possible to analyse Latin America's backwardness in terms of internal, structural problems – land distribution, regionally unbalanced industrialization, non-democratic governments, racist discrimination by the Spanish (Portuguese)-speaking ruling classes against native groups, and so on. But shunning all this, the blame was fixed on an external agency: world capitalism. It was very neat, very convenient. Even the elite could agree, and Latin American universities became sold on the Baran–Frank thesis.

The Cuban Revolution reinforced this mood. Now the Americas had their own Marxist revolution. Small as it was, Cuba was near the USA, and had long been its playground (remember *Guys and Dolls*). Now it had a Marxist government, and took a sternly anticapitalist path to development. Alarmed by this event, the USA went out of its way to confirm the Baran–Frank thesis that Latin America was ruled informally by the Yankees. The economic blockade on Cuba has now lasted forty years. American alarm at the communist insurgency in the Americas led to gross interference in the affairs of Guatemala, Chile, Panama, Nicaragua, El Salvador, and other countries. But the USA was not singling Latin America out: at this time it was also bombing Vietnam, Cambodia and Laos.

The transformation of the USA from its anti-imperialist ways up to 1945 into the icon of imperialism for an entire generation of young men and women in the 1960s and 1970s was a result of the disastrous policies followed by successive American administrations. It was 'the best and the brightest' (to use David Halberstam's title for his book on US policies on Vietnam)[7] in the State Department, the Pentagon and the White House who crafted these policies. In constructing an ideology of anti-communism, the USA forgot much of its own history. In this enterprise, universities were seduced by the military–industrial complex to bend their research to the state's purposes. They accepted open as well as hidden grants, and manipulated their research agenda – as well as, sadly, some of their research students – to serve American foreign policy. While Galbraith was bemoaning the paucity of public funding in *The Affluent Society*, the CIA was acting as a great but secret patron of the arts and academe. It sponsored *Encounter*, a genuinely intellectual journal paying anti-communist authors of whatever hue large sums of money to join the cause. It supported abstract painting and opera, and even financed a research centre at MIT where some very good work on Indian economic planning was done. American corporate capitalism and the national security apparatus appropriated the best aspects of American culture. No wonder the students were revolting by the mid-1960s.[8]

The USA managed to win the title of an imperial power without adding an inch to its territory and, far from grabbing any surplus, spent a vast fortune of American taxpayers' money doing it. In the middle of the longest boom, and despite the spending on the war on poverty, American radical economists were able to mount an attack on the structural problems of their society. A lead was given by Paul Sweezy and Paul Baran, America's two senior Marxists, in *Monopoly Capital*.[9] In their view, American society had surplus enough to tackle poverty and combat racism, but it was the 'structure of social accumulation' – as a later book was to label it – which condemned America to be beset by these problems despite its wealth. The American critique was internal; at least American Marxists had no foreign power to blame for their ills.

The new generation of American radical political economists (they never called themselves Marxists) had one great advantage over their European counterparts: they did not have an emotional attachment, positive or hostile, to the Soviet Union. Their Marxism had come not from Bolshevism but from a contemporary critique of their own society. They were also much more concerned with (political) power structures, interlocking networks of power and influence. In a sense they were harking back to the anti-monopolist, anti-cartel heritage of American radicalism: their Louis Brandeis heritage. They saw the oligopolistic nature of American capitalism as the root cause of the cosy military–industrial complex which, in its turn, distorted taxation to take benefits from the poor and give them to the big corporations.[10]

Their indifference to the Soviet Union helped the American radicals to avoid many of the traumas of their West European comrades. It was in the 1950s and 1960s that the Soviet Union revealed its authoritarian nature abroad. The Hungarian Revolution of 1956 was crushed mercilessly, but the fact that the Suez adventure by Britain and France took place in the same week, obscured the impact of the Soviet outrage. In the UN debate, India, for example, voted with the Soviet Union rather than condemning the repression of the Hungarian Revolution. (Some brilliant film directors came out of Eastern Europe – Andrezj Wajda and Milos Forman, for instance, whose films conveyed the pain of living under the Soviet boot.) By the time the suppression of the Prague Spring in 1968 came around, the Soviet Union had lost much of its reputation among Western Marxists.

Western Marxism was a strange hothouse plant. It was critical – quite rightly so – of its own society. The Frankfurt School, uncomfortably naturalized in the USA during the 1930s but now back, led with a critique of capitalist culture.[11] Theodor Adorno, Max Horkheimer and Herbert Marcuse were worthy heirs of Georg Lukács in keeping up the critical tradition, but they eschewed economics. They did not, however, approve of the Marxist societies of the Soviet Union or China (or any East European country, of course), nor did they like where they lived. There was no actual example of a post-capitalist society to point to as ideal, but in the meantime, the 'repressive tolerance' (to use Marcuse's phrase) of the West was bitterly welcome. Thus the situation stayed as French, British and Italian New Left writers joined the broad church of Western Marxism. Much good scholarly work was done on the Marx manuscripts just being made available. Marx and Lenin were being studied in detail as they had not been since 1924, when Lenin died. Yet much of Western Marxism remained faithful to Leninism as enunciated by the Third and the Fourth (Trotskyist) International. Fideism was still the rule.

Soon after the war there was a split in the monolithic Communist bloc. The Yugoslavs, under Josep Broz Tito, were the first to split. But into the late 1950s, China quarrelled with the Soviet Union. Mao was angry with Khrushchev for denouncing Stalin. The Soviets became revisionist as far as the Chinese were concerned. Mao became a new icon in the Communist church; he was elevated to a high level. We had Marxism–Leninism–Maoism. China was more uncompromising, more revolutionary, than the Soviet Union. The split had a healthy effect in breaking the Soviet monopoly of Marxism. More publications of old Marx manuscripts followed. Maoism was anti-bureaucratic, more egalitarian, more agrarian than its Soviet alternative. China's support for Vietnam also raised its reputation among young Marxists. Mao's writings on the peasantry had great influence among Asian Marxists, rivalling Lenin's analysis. In India, a revolutionary Maoist movement – the Naxalites – arose which tried a violent attack on the Indian state. It lost immediately, but its echoes still reverberate in the tribal hinterlands of the provinces of Bihar and Andhra Pradesh.[12]

Mao plunged China into the Cultural Revolution, a messy, violent, upsetting event.[13] Its origins lay in Mao's critique of the Soviet Union as plagued by bureaucratism. He wanted to overhaul Chinese leadership (except himself of course), and sought the support of young students. For about eight years (1965–73), China had a constant revolutionary turmoil to deal with. The Party, the government (management) and the workers had to be in tripartite negotiations in every enterprise, every commune, every school and college. The issue of decentralized governance was thus raised for the first time in the annals of Marxism. Mao's analysis of the bureaucratic sclerosis of the USSR was correct, but his solution remained a Bonapartist rather than a democratic one.

But it was the Vietnam War which, from 1965 to 1975, constituted the central revolutionary struggle for the youth around the world. The battle of the Vietnamese peasantry against the American military juggernaut was as central to my generation as the Spanish Civil War had been to an earlier generation in the 1930s. It was not an intellectual but a deep emotional political battle in which Marxism gained reputation because Ho Chi Minh, as a Marxist, was fighting the American anti-Communist power. When the Americans lost and left Vietnam in 1975, it seemed to many that in Asia, at least, communism might win the day.

Vietnam, like China and much of Asia – and, indeed, Africa – was a peasant society. The issues of land reform, agrarian relations, agricultural productivity, were primary here. Asian Marxists, unlike Western Marxists, were rooted in the villages. Marx had said little about the peasantry except towards the end of his life, in as yet (in the early 1970s) unpublished notes. It was Lenin and Mao who were the basic sources for class analysis. The issue was one of mobilizing the small and middle peasants against the big ones. The capitalist class in China, small as it was, was denounced as collaborating with the imperialists (India never had that problem). Thus anticapitalism was ingrained in Asian communism but, being agrarian, it had a common sense about the market that the European Marxists lacked. Only in Cambodia did Asian Marxism take a virulent violent turn under the Khmer Rouge. Their idea – as articulated in a Sorbonne PhD by one of their leaders – was that to create a classless society it was necessary physically to eliminate all classes except the peasantry. Thus it was that Pol Pot and his friends killed one-seventh of the Cambodian population. It was almost a genocide, except that it was within the same country. Much worse than Stalin, the Khmer Rouge plumbed the anti-humanitarian depths. They were, of course, supported by the West, because in Cold War terms, they were the enemy of the enemy. And the enemy at the time was Vietnam.[14]

While East Asia remained locked in one war or another throughout the 1970s and 1980s, elsewhere economic development was changing societies. In Africa and Latin America, as well as South and Southeast Asia, GDP growth rates were in the respectable regions of 5 per cent or higher. *Per capita* incomes were improving. The first effects of a protectionist industrializing policy were not at all bad. The developing countries, now a majority in the UN General Assembly, asked for and got an anti-free-trade UN agency of their own: the UN Conference on Trade and Development (UNCTAD). There was also a UN Industrial Development Organization (UNIDO) whose goal was to improve the Third World share in world industrial output. It recommended an import-substitution-driven, state-led industrialization strategy around the Third World.

The Achilles heel in many of these programmes proved to be not industry but agriculture. Industrialization was taken to mean – though it is not necessarily – a neglect of agriculture at best, or its ruthless exploitation for surplus at worst.

Farmers proved very difficult to regiment, and most Communist regimes in Eastern Europe did not dare impose collectivization. The Chinese commune system seemed to work well in China, though the world was not to know about the 1962 famine, when thirty million died, until much later. In India, Nehru's policy of co-operative farming with land-pooling was defeated at the 1959 conference of the Congress Party. Charan Singh, who later briefly became Prime Minister, was the leader of the North Indian farmers who defended private ownership effectively, and saw off socialism in the countryside. Yet India faced a food shortage crisis in the late 1950s. It was a miraculous (unplanned) combination of high-yield seeds introduced by the Rockefeller Foundation, generous incentives by way of guaranteed output prices and subsidized input prices, and the enterprise of millions of Indian farmers which broke through the food barrier. The Green Revolution was denounced by the urban left intelligentsia and their Western social scientist friends. Its existence, efficacy and reach were doubted. Some even predicted (or hoped wishfully) that the Green Revolution would turn Red. Alas, they were to be disappointed.[15]

For the first time in at least a hundred years, if not longer, Indian agriculture became profitable. Capitalism entered the Indian countryside. India had been humiliated in the late 1960s by US President Lyndon Johnson, who used the weapons of food aid under American Public Law 480 to punish India for its stance on Vietnam. Within a few years, India did not need to rely on food aid. Industrial policy was statist in India for much longer, but at least in agriculture, sense had prevailed.

This Indian experience was not reflected in Africa. African governments flush with new independence went in for industrialization. The countries of West Africa which had a long history of agricultural exports – cocoa, coffee, palm – managed to wreck their agriculture in the pursuit of industrial growth. Agriculture and export marketing was a woman's job in West Africa; the men in urban areas had to have their new toys. But the effects of agricultural neglect were not to be felt in the 1960s – only later would the full extent of the policy distortion be tangible. For the time being, African intellectuals also subscribed to the idea that capitalism had underdeveloped Africa. Markets had to be rejected. There was even something called African Socialism for a while. And why not? Every national elite should have its own socialism, just as it has an airline. It is a 'must-have' middle-class luxury.[16]

But the leading country for both the Second World and the Third World was the Soviet Union. Its growth performance, as it recovered from the ravages of war, was stunning. Life began to get better for Soviet citizens in the 1950s.

There was a thaw, and consumer goods began to become available. The de-Stalinization campaign was pursued by Khrushchev and his partner in the government, Marshal Nikolai Bulganin. As they pursued détente, they travelled across the world, giving a genial face to the hoary myths of the totalitarian state. Khrushchev recognized that agriculture was the real limit on Soviet performance, and tried to bring more land under cultivation. The space triumph sealed Russia's reputation, and the rough treatment meted out to Boris Pasternak when he received the Nobel Prize for literature did little to detract from that. People around the world, especially in Asia, Africa and Latin America, saw the Soviet Union as bringing pride as well as a modicum of prosperity to its citizens. Education, public transport and health were well organized. If the USA had public squalor amid private affluence, the Soviet Union had good public provision alongside miserly private consumption.

Khrushchev's attempts to tackle the agricultural constraint did not bear fruit quickly. He was replaced by another team. Leonid Brezhnev became General Secretary of the Party, and Aleksei Kosygin became Prime Minister. There were signs of a re-examination of the Soviet economic doctrine. Soviet industry was not proving very efficient, though there was still adequate growth. It is easy to get growth: more inputs lead to more output. But efficiency requires getting more output (maximum output) from the same amount of input. Another way to look at this is to count the input cost relative to the output revenue. Minimum costs are a good objective to aim at; but this is true only if the input prices reflect the scarcity of materials relative to their productivity. Soviet planning was based on physical input–output ratios, ignoring prices or even shadow prices. The input coefficients were frozen at their old values, and no one was attempting to find cheaper methods.

There was a cautious search for market principles which could be appended to a centrally planned system. The capitalist system had markets; imperfect as they could be, there were prices as ready reckoners for comparing relative values. If production made a profit at existing prices, it was in the producer's interest at least. If the prices reflected 'true' scarcities, the whole society would gain. So could profits be used as a guide in a planned economy? After all, there was no danger of monopolists making excess profits. But were the prices right? What was right, by what criterion? These questions were debated in the Soviet bloc. Professor E. G. Liberman of the USSR became famous in 1962 for proposing that profits should be used as a criterion for choice of projects.[17] Throughout the mid-1960s there was some experimentation with market heresy in the Soviet bloc, especially in Hungary. Kosygin was identified with this experimentation. But soon after came the Czech Revolution and its suppression. Brezhnev took over as the sole leader, and orthodoxy was restored in the Soviet bloc.

But there had been experiments in Yugoslavia. There was much greater autonomy for individual enterprises within an overall planned system. Workers owned their enterprises. This gave them incentives to work hard, because their wages contained an element of profit. This was like capitalism without capitalists. Yugoslav socialism proved attractive to many in the West, since it was not distorted by Stalinism and hindered by autarkic quantitative planning. For the purist Marxist, this led to inequality among workers, since some might be working for profitable firms while others might not, and the profits might be due to extraneous factors. A good may go out of fashion, or another may become popular. In capitalism this happens all the time. Workers are expected to be hired and fired, or may move of their own accord. But a worker-owned company may not wish to hire anyone extra, lest the workers' share be diluted. Firing may also become a problem, because how is the worker to take away his equity when there are no shares to sell and no stock markets?

The Chinese had a different attitude towards work and reward. The rural communes were very large, with thousands of households spanning many villages. The payment to various types of skilled and unskilled labour was debated by the communes. There was a deliberate policy not to let interhousehold or intervillage inequalities increase. Those working on more fertile land or, say, with fruit trees had greater value productivity than their co-workers working on building or clearing. But the total product was a social product, joint fruit of all the various kinds of labour. Thus some sharing had to be done. The same rule was tried in urban industrial enterprises. When I visited China in 1973, during the days of the Gang of Four, there seemed to be a deliberate attempt to weaken the link between wages and the productivity of the enterprise where the worker was employed. There had to be a social dividend to be shared out with the less-well-placed workers. Lurking behind all these issues were the classical Marxian questions: where does surplus come from, and who appropriates it? Can a socialist society base its investment and wage policy on the criterion of productivity, which is only a hidden signal for profitability?

Such difficult issues are bound to arise in any economy which aspires to be socialist yet is not fully developed. Socialism outside Capitalism (SoC), as I labelled it above, flourished in this period. Issues of surplus creation and accumulation versus eliminating poverty and pursuing equality, of income differentials between the skilled and the unskilled, between consumer choice and the needs of future generations – all these had to be thrashed out. Marx had said very little about such questions, except for his remarks in the 'Critique of the Gotha Programme'. But these remarks are negative, since they advise against raising such questions while capitalism and scarcity still exist. Russians had debated those issues in the first ten years of their revolution, but settled on a hierarchical, managerial and productivity-based income-distribution system. While public goods – health, education, transport – could be shared by all, private income was still unequally distributed. The degree of inequality in any of the socialist countries was, of course, much lower than in any capitalist country, rich or poor.

And it seemed that within the SoC system, there was a growing diversity. The Soviet Union, Yugoslavia, China and Cuba represented a range of possibilities – and, indeed, a range of climates – across Europe, Asia and the Americas. There was the poor, agrarian, highly populated China; Cuba, a tropical island reliant on a single crop; a middle-income Southern European country, Yugoslavia; and, of course, the vast landmass of the USSR, taking in European and Asian ecologies. Superficially, it looked as if, while capitalism was confined to a corner of Western Europe and North America, socialism could be everywhere. It occupied the eastern half of Europe, and a large chunk of East Asia if you added North Korea, Vietnam and Cambodia. Was this what Marx would have predicted? Would he have applauded what was done in his name?

By now, of course, the Soviet Union had little to do with Marx or Marxism. His name was often taken, as in Marxism–Leninism, and his bearded face flew on banners alongside that of Engels. But the Soviet Union had given up any hope of a revolution in the West. Communist parties everywhere had been bewildered by the revelations of 1956. Some split when the USSR–China dispute flared up, but only in choosing a different master to be ideological slaves to. Thus in India, the Communists split into the Communist Party of India (CPI) and the Communist Party of India (Marxist) (CPM). The labelling was bizarre, since neither had renounced Marxism. It was merely that one continued to await dictates from Moscow, while the other obeyed Beijing. The CPI defended Soviet action in crushing Prague, in 1968, as the CPM did the Tian An Men Square massacre of 1989.

The Soviet Union abandoned the doctrine that capitalism was in terminal crisis, or ripe for revolution. There was to be peaceful coexistence between the two systems. Khrushchev predicted at the 22nd Party Congress in 1960 that the Soviet Union would bury the USA in an avalanche of commodities. It was to produce more steel and more cement, and other goods, than the USA in twenty-five years. This was a scenario not visualized by Marx or Lenin, before or after 1917. The two systems were to compete on grounds of economic size as measured by national income GNP. This was not an empty boast, and it was taken seriously by the rival military–industry complex.

The Chinese, of course, loathed such revisionism. Mao wanted the revolutionary proletariat to arise from the periphery, from the East. 'The East is Red' became a catch-phrase, as well as the title of a Beijing opera. The Chinese helped Vietnam and, indeed, any Communist Party that would reject Soviet passivity and foment revolution. Mao disowned his longtime comrade, Liu Shao-ch'i, a Soviet-style moderate Communist, and endorsed Lin Piao, who advanced the thesis that a world revolution would come from the East and defeat capitalism. He was soon discredited in the Byzantine politics of the Chinese Communist Party. Mao continued his egalitarian Cultural Revolution with the help of the 'Gang of Four' – younger Chinese Communists, including his wife.

At this time (late 1960s, early 1970s), Chinese universities had all their students read *The Communist Manifesto*, Engels's *Anti-Dühring* and Lenin's *Imperialism.* Marxism in China thus continued to be catechistic, as under the Third International. Even more amusing was the *Little Red Book* containing aphorisms described as 'Thoughts of Chairman Mao'. It had all the banality of a corporate CEO's homilies, but it became popular at radical-chic parties in New York. But for foreign consumption, the Chinese did produce rival and less bowdlerized editions of Marx's writings. The presence of a rival orthodoxy helped Western Marxists immensely, since now there were two versions of Leninism – or three, if you count Trotskyism. The anti-bureaucratic stance in Mao's thought chimed well with the growing dislike of bureaucracies – university, government, party – among the young in the West. While students were rising up in the West, and being fired at by governments, there was Mao fomenting a student rebellion. Cool cat!

In 1971, Henry Kissinger made a secret trip from Rawalpindi in Pakistan to China to open up a dialogue. Soon the ping-pong diplomacy grew, and Nixon's opening towards China became known. For the first time in two hundred years, the powerful white races (that is how the Chinese and many other Asians saw it) came to see a Chinese leader on a basis of equality. It was an acknowledgement not so much of the Soviet–Chinese schism as of America's difficulty in Vietnam. This time China had beaten the USA to a standstill. Asia had arrived.

But there was another power in Asia whose rise was underestimated by the Americans and, indeed, everyone else. The Japanese had defeated Tsarist Russia at the beginning of the century, fought in the two world wars, and ended up a defeated pile of rubble in 1945. General MacArthur had Americanized its constitution, its industries, and superficially even its culture. The Americans patronized the Japanese, and failed to notice Japan's economic growth. In August 1971, when the USA went off the dollar exchange standard by refusing to sell gold at $35 an ounce, they did not even bother to inform the Japanese government in advance, as they had done their Western friends. To this day the Japanese remember this shock. The Japanese, everyone said, had no originality. They were good at copying technology invented by others.

Japan was the first miracle capitalist country of the second half of the twentieth century, the first country to achieve double-digit growth rates, the first country to go from poverty to riches twice in a century. The Americans had intended Japan to be an agricultural country, as a punishment for its wartime conduct. But the Korean War and the Cold War soon changed all that. Japan was needed as a platform for American forces in the East. Japanese society responded to this opportunity. The government and the industrial elite collaborated to build up an industrial growth machine of awesome proportions. Japan imported raw materials, but kept out manufactured imports. It controlled the growth of consumption, and encouraged savings. This non-Keynesian policy was further bolstered by an aggressive drive to export manufactures. It was a Japanese version of National Socialism – economic planning with entrepreneurial capitalism. Private business was willing to be directed by the government (which, of course, it permeated and controlled) in order to pursue national objectives. There was no arm's-length nonsense here. Profits were made, but they were a secondary objective. The primary objective was to secure Japan's place in the Big League of advanced capitalist countries. This was managed capitalism. This was Asian capitalism.

Japan's arrival on the capitalist scene was to reshape the notion of a successful growth strategy. While everyone had been noticing the Soviet Union or China, or even the USA, it was Japan which was to show that a recipe for accelerated growth under capitalism was available. It was possible for a developing country to become an advanced capitalist one within a generation. Stalinist growth rates could be achieved without the Gulag. The future was capitalist.

And just then, in 1973, capitalism was plunged into another crisis.

16
Things Fall Apart

The summer of 1963 was a very pleasant one for me. I was in Philadelphia, finishing my Ph.D at the University of Pennsylvania. I had written my theses, got my supervisor's approval, and was waiting for the oral examination. We then had a debate at the nearby Swarthmore College. Paul Samuelson and George Stigler were to debate 'The Role of the State in the Economy'. Here indeed was a battle of giants – even at forty-seven Samuelson was the *enfant terrible,* the leading economist of his time. George Stigler, teaching at Chicago, was more senior, scholarly, and known for his sharp wit. This was MIT versus Chicago, salt water versus sweet water, progressive (liberal in American parlance) versus conservative. So it was not merely the hope of seeing some pretty young undergraduates that drove us down there.

The debate was a revelation for me. Samuelson was very funny. He told the audience a lot about himself, flattered us that he was in touch with the White House, but, in such a subtle manner that you would not call it vulgar, beat the Keynesian drum. He did not, however, address the question at hand. For him, there was nothing to debate. The state had a positive role to play, and was playing it. Kennedy was still alive; the tax cut bill would go through. Samuelson was no socialist; he was just a bit to the right of Galbraith.

Stigler was brilliant. He asked searching, shocking questions. Why did economists teach about markets, but accept the market-failure argument so uncritically? Could we privatize the post office or the fire service? If not, what was the economic rationale for state provision of many of these services? Naturally, he had arguments ready to demolish our firmly but uncritically held views. He was able to 'deconstruct' (in the original, not the postmodern sense) the market-failure argument. People bought insurance as well as fire-prevention services. So they did make a cost–benefit calculus about fire. Why not examine private provision of a firefighting service? Why should the post office have a monopoly of letter and parcel delivery? Was that efficient, since economic theory told us that monopolies were typically inefficient?

As I listened to Stigler, I realized that the pro-market economists at Chicago had not been defeated, and were not sitting idly by. They were willing to take on mainstream economists in an intellectual battle, and received wisdom would not be enough. They emerged not as conservatives, as defenders of the status quo, but as radicals – something which those of us on the Left thought we had a monopoly of. For ever afterwards, Stigler's speech stuck in my mind as a premonition of things to come.

Chicago became the unofficial new centre of the counterattack of middle-of-the-road, market-failure economics. In macroeconomics, Friedman led the charge against Keynesianism. After a decade of championing the quantity theory of money against Keynes, his payoff came in the mid-1960s when inflation began to be a problem which the Keynesians found hard to tackle (I recounted the early battle on this front in Chapter 14). But the battle was to get ugly as the oil-exporting countries quadrupled the price of crude oil in 1973, during the Arab–Israeli Yom Kippur War. In addition to the inflation due to higher wage share, and hence lower profits, we now had higher energy costs which fed through the input–output structure to the entire economy. The days of double-digit inflation had arrived. Keynesians were on the defensive.

But on the microeconomic side, as well, there were significant victories for Chicago. Regulation of airlines and of public utilities was questioned by the market radicals. Why should a cartel of airlines be sustained? Where was the consumer interest in control over flights, destinations and routes? Were the regulated public utilities making a wasteful use of capital because of a restriction on the rate of return they could make? Was it not more efficient to let them make the maximum rate of return? In a stunning piece of analysis in 1968, Ronald Coase – then at Chicago, later a Nobel laureate – showed that many cases of market failure arise from a failure to assign or clarify property rights.[1] If I had a private claim to a quiet neighbourhood because I had paid a premium price for my house, I could sue my noisy neighbours. People regularly litigate against extra property-building in their back yard. It is only when rights are diffuse that nuisances proliferate. Coase thus presented a very deep argument against market failure which economists had to address seriously. A large area of interdisciplinary studies of law and economics grew up around the Coase 'theorem'.

The comeback of free-market arguments in the 1970s surprised many people. They attributed it to the conservative revival or, later, even to the IMF and World Bank: the Washington consensus. I have recounted the story above to show that the free-market radicals were working hard in the 1950s and 1960s, thinking not the 'unthinkable' but the 'unthought of'. While Keynesian economists were smugly predicting that cycles were obsolete, and an optimal control of the economy awaited only a larger computer, market radicals concentrated on old-fashioned issues of human behaviour. They were ruthless in their self-criticism, as well as in examining their rivals' arguments. The battles were fought in learned journals, conference volumes, books. No blood was spilt, but a most profound change in economists' thinking – a veritable revolution – was brought about.

Thus when the oil shock plunged the advanced capitalist countries into an inflationary crisis, the alternative policies had been already articulated – albeit by an unfashionable minority which was growing larger by the day. The decade of the 1970s saw the battle moving from academia to the political arena. In every political party, not just those on the Right, there was a debate about how to reconcile full employment with inflation. Think tanks such as the Institute of Economic Affairs in London had been patiently publishing radical, market-orientated analyses of public policy issues. It took the breakdown of the Keynesian consensus in the mid-1970s – itself a result of the oil price rise and the ensuing inflation – for those think tanks to penetrate political parties and the print media. The editor of the London *Times*, William (now Lord) Rees-Mogg, became a passionate advocate of monetarism. Peter Jay, then editor of the business section of the *Times*, convinced his father-in-law, then Prime Minister Jim (now Lord) Callaghan, that the high inflation and high unemployment – stagflation – of the UK could not be cured by Keynesian remedies of deficits and devaluation.[2] It was a lesson bitterly learnt by the UK as the pound's value collapsed in the foreign exchange markets in the summer of 1976 and, just as Callaghan took over from Harold Wilson as Prime Minister, the IMF arrived (for the first time in the case of an advanced capitalist economy, not to say a key currency country) to lay down the law on how the UK should conduct its fiscal and monetary policies. Tony Crosland, who had inspired an entire generation of British democratic socialists with his book *The Future of Socialism*, said, in a much-quoted remark: 'The party is over'.

The Keynesian quarter-century had indeed been a party. Everything had stayed high – employment, hours worked, vacancies – or grown steadily – income, wealth. The public sector – central government, local government, public enterprises – had grown without causing any problems. Government ministers expected public spending to go up in real terms year after year. Indeed, the British Treasury settled the annual budget spending round in volume terms, translating it into money terms only after the growth had been agreed upon. Money did not matter; there was always plenty available.

While full employment and steady economic growth had lasted, Keynesian policies could be carried out without running budget deficits. That was the case throughout much of the 1950s and 1960s. But once inflation eroded profitability, unemployment rose in the private sector. There was an immediate move to create jobs in the public sector – local authorities, social services, teachers, health workers. They were paid from the public purse, but their services were typically not sold on the market. Thus the impact of these deficits was purely on the demand side via the spending of these workers. On the supply side, their impact was doubly negative. They kept wages high and demands for wage increases up by preserving full employment. But there was no increment to *saleable* output of goods and services. Once inflation had started, this double negative impact fuelled inflation. The negative effect dominated the positive one. With high wages and rising prices, costs went up in the private sector. Profits were squeezed first by market forces and then often as part of anti-inflation incomes polices. But profits were also squeezed because taxes went up. Tax bands and thresholds were fixed in money terms, and not revised upwards with inflation. As prices rose, money incomes rose, and so did profits. They had not risen in 'real' terms – that is, after allowing for price increases – anything like as they had done in money terms. But people previously outside the tax bands began to have to pay income tax. Small businesses and large ones were caught in the corporation tax net. During 1975, when the UK rate of inflation hit 25 per cent, the peculiar rules of evaluating inventories for tax purposes exaggerated the profits of many companies which had to pay crippling taxes.

Inflation brought taxes into the public consciousness, and tax resentment followed. Profit squeeze drove business into bankruptcy. Those who could, relocated abroad. Unemployment kept on going up, despite large budget deficits. Inflation alienated workers from everything the government did, even when they were recipients of state benefits – subsidized housing, free healthcare (in the UK), free education for their children. There were no votes in a Keynesian economic policy; there had to be retrenchment.

On the defensive, the Keynesians proposed incomes policies or forms of a 'social contract' between workers, employers and government. In countries where there were established institutions for national-level bargaining – Austria, Sweden – such social contracts were successful in keeping unemployment down. In Germany there had been an ethos of social partnership between employers and trade unions, and this corporatist model worked as a social compromise. But in the Anglo-Saxon economies – the USA, the UK – wage bargaining was decentralized. While there were trade unions, employers seldom had powerful organizations which could bargain with them. Incomes policies were *ad hoc*, depending on the party in power. There were duels between trade unions and governments, with employers staying out of the fray or playing rogues. Inflation was blamed on workers by Keynesians, and this led to a crisis in socialist parties which depended on union support for coming to and staying in power. If profits were taxed, this exacerbated rather than solved the problem.

The crucial relation between profitability and employment had never been articulated in Keynesian economics. Keynes took it for granted, but did not give it prominence. Michal Kalecki,[3] the Polish economist who had anticipated some of the macroeconomic insights of Keynes, theorized about profits as arising from monopolies and oligopolies. Implicitly, he took the Marshallian view that profits are low or zero where there is competition. But if there is monopoly power – due to entry barriers or concentration – then profits are high. This static model came to acquire a very high status among Keynesians, especially radical post-Keynesians. But Kalecki missed the dynamics of profits and innovation in a capitalist economy. Economics textbooks dealt with static economies in equilibrium. Capitalism is a dynamic disequilibrium system. Profits are an evil in the former, but essential lifeblood in the latter. But once profits are seen as coming from monopoly power, lower profits become a desirable thing. Thus, a profit squeeze was welcomed by left Keynesians. They saw radical – not to say revolutionary – possibilities in the stagflationist scenario. The state could nationalize much more of private business, give workers what they wanted, and control prices by fiat.

The Marxists should have clearly seen the connection between the profit squeeze and stagflation. Since it was evident early on that profitability was declining, and inflation was rising, the answer – one that Marx or a young Lenin would have given – was to raise profitability if you wanted more employment. But this insight was lost due to two major confusions. Since inflation was being blamed on workers' wage rises, the Marxists began to defend workers' wage rises as defensive and correct. That left them with the puzzle of explaining the causes of inflation. Ernest Mandel, the leading Marxist economist during the 1970s, took the monetarist view that it was excessive money supply which caused inflation; thus it was caused by the government.[4] This union of monetarists and Marxists was a surprising one, but it kept the Marxists in the trade unions' good books. But the question remained: why was the state issuing excess money supply? The answer to this question led to the second confusion.

Government expenditure had gone up to finance public-sector jobs. These jobs replaced the lost jobs in the private sector. But public-sector jobs – unlike private-sector ones – generated no surplus-value and no profits. Marx had labelled such jobs unproductive. Productive jobs were those where the workers were employed by capitalists in order to make a profit. Unproductive workers were hired for consumption services, not for profit. They were paid out of income, not capital, as productive workers were. Productive workers aided accumulation by generating profits for the capitalists. Unproductive workers were an expenditure, a diversion of savings.

The distinction did not lie in whether the final product was goods or services. Adam Smith, who made a similar distinction, came close to adopting physical concreteness of the product as a criterion. Marx saw the generation of profits as the deciding factor. Through much of classical political economics, the central purpose of an economy was deemed to be wealth creation – expansion of productive forces and accumulation of capital, as Marx would say. Consumer satisfaction or well-being, which is the central objective in neoclassical economics, did not play any significant role, save for the odd exceptional author who excites scholars of the history of economic thought. But the major theme – from Smith to Marx and John Stuart Mill – was wealth creation. The distribution of income was interesting to Ricardo as an aid to understanding the wellsprings of accumulation. Thus the more that went to merchants and industrialists who were prone to invest in productive activities, and the less to landlords who would fritter it all away employing servants and hangers-on, the better for accumulation. This is why rent was a burden on accumulation.

Now the growth of state activities over the twentieth century, but especially since 1945, meant employment of workers not for profit but for consumption of the services they rendered. Teachers, social workers, prison officers, police, civil servants and, in the UK, all those employed in the National Health Service – all these workers were unproductive in Marx's sense. They were not useless in terms of people's well-being, but they were paid out of taxation which diverted savings away from accumulation. For Keynesians this distinction is irrelevant, since what concerns them is the contribution of employment in keeping up effective demand.

Many of the New Left were classic unproductive workers – university and high-school teachers, government employees at various levels, trade-union officials. Thus their normal instinct had been to defend the role of the state, and agitate for its extension. They believed strongly in the value of the welfare state, and state provision of education, health and housing. But Marx, in his perverse way, seemed to be arguing for privatization of all this into profit-making hands. Were Marxist writers, revolutionary though they saw themselves to be, unproductive labour? Or did Marx need yet another revision?

By a fateful coincidence, a new generation of radical economists, well trained in mainstream economics and mathematically proficient, began re-examining the foundations of Marx's theory. An exact parallel process occurred with the foundations of Keynes's theory, though here the attack came from a new generation of Chicago economists. One common thread in their attacks was a revival of Walras's theory of general equilibrium.[5] This theory – first put forward in the 1870s, and later in the four editions of Walras's *Elements of Pure Economics* – had been popular on the Continent, while the Anglo-Saxon tradition, nurtured by Alfred Marshall at Cambridge, had been one of partial equilibrium. But beginning in the 1930s, English-speaking economists began to take Walras's mathematically rigorous arguments seriously. The challenge for the theorist was to demonstrate that all the various markets for individual commodities and services could clear at the same time, their demand curves intersecting with their supply curves at positive prices without any interference from any outside forces such as governments.

This was not a project of descriptive realism about how an actual economy worked on a daily basis. It was a logical, analytical project to show that on the basis of minimal assumptions about consumer behaviour, producer behaviour and technology, an equilibrium of all goods and services could be shown to exist simultaneously. Walras had not been able to prove this. He could not tackle the problem that, where supply exceeded demand at every positive price, one could not think of an equilibrium. Then Abraham Wald, a mathematician who later made pioneering contributions to statistics, was able to show, using some recently developed mathematical techniques, that one could encompass that problem and require that prices be only non-negative. Thirty years of further work by other economists such as John Hicks and Kenneth Arrow (joint winners of the Noble Prize) climaxed in a book in 1959 by a French mathematical economist who had migrated to the USA. Gérard Debreu's slim book *Theory of Value*[6] was more mathematics than economics for most economists of that time, but he established new standards of mathematical analytical rigour in proving the existence of a Walrasian equilibrium. While most economists choked at the use of calculus and linear algebra, Debreu used methods of topology which had only been recently developed to extend the scope of economic theory.

Debreu was also awarded the Nobel Prize, but when interviewers asked him on the day of the announcement what he thought could be done about American inflation, he replied without hesitation that his kind of economics did not help with answering such practical questions. But his theory changed the prospects of Keynesian economics profoundly, and also dented the prestige of Marxian economics. He accomplished this, however, by making his theory about as an unrealistic as you can get. The Arrow–Debreu economy has agents – consumers and producers. Consumers have preferences; they can rank all commodities pairwise – as either one being preferred to another, or the consumer being indifferent. More income is preferred to less. Each commodity or service has a date and location pair to identify it – apples in London today being a different commodity from apples in Birmingham today or in London tomorrow. But even more than date and place, people may also demand commodities in various contingent circumstances. Thus I may wish to demand an umbrella on 10 July 2010 if it is raining, but not if it is not. There are markets for contingent commodities which are promises to deliver in case the hypothesized circumstances become real.

If one multiplies commodities in this ingenious way, there are obviously a large number of demand-and-supply responses to specify, which in turn lead to equilibrium prices. In a dazzling thought experiment, you imagine millions of consumers making known their demands for the millions of commodities from today until any time in the future for real dates as well as for hypothetical circumstances – in different 'states of nature'. And then, as in the Big Bang theory of the origin of the universe, all the millions of prices could be shown to be solved out as equilibrium prices by the market in an instant. This is general equilibrium, 1960-mathematical-economist style. The book occupies less than a hundred pages. It is a work of mathematical elegance and breathtaking simplicity.

But if the generation of 1960 found the book abstruse, within ten years young graduate students in their twenties were able to deploy the arguments of Debreu's theory with great skill. This was microeconomics of considerable subtlety. Yet if it was correct – and there was a proof to say that it was – how could one reconcile Keynes's macroeconomics with Walrasian general equilibrium? If all markets clear, why is the labour market peculiar in the sense that there is involuntary unemployment? If supply of labour exceeds demand for it, why does not the price of labour – real wage – move down to clear the market? Where are the microfoundations of Keynesian macroeconomics?

If the battle between Keynesians and monetarists was polemical, and concerned with practical policy matters, the search for the microfoundations was academic and theoretical. The argument centred around unemployment – was it voluntary, that is, due to preferences of the presently unemployed for a higher real wage than existed, or was it involuntary in the sense that workers were willing to work at the going real wage, but there was a demand failure? Keynes had emphasized uncertainty, especially about the long-term future over which an investor had to recoup his investment, and said that in a monetary economy, bargains and contracts were in money terms rather than real terms. Workers may not be able to cut their real wages even if they want to, only their money wages. Even cutting money wages might not be enough to cut real wages if prices fell as wages fell. In any case, if investors were pessimistic they would fail to invest and generate the demand for labour.

The dismantling of this edifice was the accomplishment of a young Chicago economist, Robert Lucas, who won the Nobel Prize for his work in 1995.[7] He began by questioning the logic of the Phillips Curve, which purported to show that a variety of combinations of inflation and unemployment were available for the policy-maker to choose from. This would imply a multiplicity of equilibria in the labour market. But Debreu had shown that Walrasian equilibrium was unique in most circumstances. So the labour market, along with all other markets, should be in a single – unique – equilibrium. The level of unemployment in that equilibrium situation was the natural rate of unemployment. The word natural did not mean inevitable or God-given. The Swedish economist Knut Wicksell had used the words 'natural rate of interest' in his pre-1914 book *Interest and Prices.* Natural was a surrogate word for equilibrium. Lucas set out to show that, despite uncertainty and the use of money, the economy would have a unique equilibrium – that is, natural rate of unemployment – whatever the level of inflation. No government policy choice could lower, or even raise, that equilibrium rate. The government could, however, determine the rate of inflation by the money supply it created in pursuit of its policy to alter the natural rate of unemployment.

This was as much against Keynesian theory as it could be. Keynes had argued that the market economy, left to itself, could produce a situation of less than full employment, and then get stuck there – underemployment as an equilibrium situation. He was also sceptical of the usual cures for this situation – flexibility of prices, wages and interest rates. Hence the need for action from an authority not subject to market pressure. This was the state, echoing Hegel's disquiet about how the market (civil society), left on its own, could go wrong. Lucas denied the possibility of an underemployment equilibrium. Since economists, in teaching microeconomic theory, had agreed upon competition as a market-clearing process, macroeconomics could not deny these foundations in an *ad hoc* manner. The Keynesians put up with all sorts of objections – sticky prices, rigid wages, liquidity traps making interest rates inflexible and inefficacious. But these were empirical objections. In theory, no one had shown that an equilibrium could exist with sticky prices, et cetera. The behavioural foundations of this institutional realism were lacking. If you had no rigorous complete proof of your theory of underemployment, then you had to surrender.

Keynesians from the East Coast universities – saltwater economists – fought back. Many empirical tests were tried, and battles raged on about whose theory fitted the data better. The Keynesians had dominated econometrics throughout much of the 1950s and 1960s. The monetarists, led by Friedman, were at that time deriding the technical superstructures built by the Keynesian econometricians, and boasted about the superior efficacy of their simpler approach. This was hardly likely to appeal to the new breed of young economists who loved technique. But in the 1970s, Lucas and other Chicago and Minnesota economists associated with him – Thomas Sargent, Edward Prescott, Neil Wallace, Lars Hansen – were also on top of their econometrics. Lucas undermined most of the fashionable econometric models of the 1970s by showing that their estimates of economic relationships – demand for money, Phillips Curve, and so on – were highly unstable and fragile. This was not for any statistical or empirical reason. Their very basis of theorizing had missed out on the ways in which private agents – consumers, workers, producers – could nullify government intervention by taking evasive action. The models were assuming that government policies would have the intended effect. But governments can only propose; the individuals in the economy – the market – will dispose.

Despite the large number of equations and the huge computers they used, the Keynesian econometricians frequently had to revise their predictions. This was routine, since new data were thrown up as time went by. The relationships thus established were not 'constant', as in the natural sciences. They were not 'invariant' to changes in the policy regime, or even the odd random shock such as quadrupling of the oil prices. Lucas argued that this lack of structural invariance rendered most of these models useless. The right way to go about this was to base the equations on what economic theory told us about behaviour. Consumers would maximize satisfaction within the limits of their budgets; workers would seek to maximize income, short of being unemployed; and producers would maximize profits. All would face uncertainty about the future, and would need to form expectations about future government policies, or movements in prices, and so on. In forming these expectations, they would behave rationally and use all the information at their disposal. Since economic theory could show that prices and wages were linked, and that real wages affected employment, as an economic model-builder one had to take these insights on board. You had to assume that people would use the same model as economists taught.

John Maynard Keynes, more than anyone else this century, made liberal-democratic capitalism a popular proposition. He could be said to have made capitalism safe for democracy. But he was an elitist. If he trusted government to run the economy, he meant by that himself and the few Eton or Winchester and Oxbridge men who were in the Treasury. Economists took their cue from him. One may assume, for the sake of argument, that people were rational, but only the Americans took it literally. Reality was different, as we all knew. Civil servants – British, French or Dutch – normally assumed that the natives in India or Indochina or Indonesia were not rational. They were bound by custom and practice, slow to respond or change. Salt of the earth, but not rational – no, never. What became known as Development Studies inherited this bias. For them it was anti-neoclassical economics. The peasant was not rational. Indeed, the notion of rational calculation by the masses smacked of Eurocentricity.

It was the economists of the Right – Peter (Lord) Bauer, who taught at the LSE for many years, or Theodore Schultz, Professor at Chicago – who did patient fieldwork among the peasants and traders, and attributed rationality to them, just as they did to themselves. The Left was patronizing and elitist; the Right perversely democratic. By the 1970s, elitism was under attack from both sides – from students, Blacks, women, Third World movements, and so forth. The assumption that people are rational is so basic to economic thinking that the only thing people could accuse Lucas of was taking it seriously. Thus, while technical details were contested and empirical results thrown about by each side against their opponents, the simple point had to be conceded that if you took economic theory seriously, then Keynesians had a problem. They had not bothered to construct an anti-Walrasian microeceonomics to suit their Keynesian macroeconomics. Some maverick post-Keynesians argued that the world was not competitive, but full of oligopolies. But that said, they had no general equilibrium story to offer. It was all *ad hoc* – who-said-what-to-whom sort of stuff. Lucas was offering a well-known alternative, with an up-to-date technical language to question Keynes.

Within four years spanning 1972 to 1975, and in the course of no more than five articles in learned journals, Robert Lucas reversed the hegemony of the Keynesian Revolution in economics: involuntary unemployment could not be an equilibrium phenomenon. Government policy, if pre-announced, could be frustrated by the agents if it did not dovetail with their well-being. Ricardo's dismal science was restored to the top after a few decades of Bloomsbury indulgence. This restoration of pre-Keynesian economics was reinforced when Milton Friedman received the Nobel Prize in 1972, followed in 1974 by a joint award for Friedrich von Hayek and Gunnar Myrdal. Myrdal was a Swedish Social Democrat and a pioneering social theorist in a variety of fields, including an analysis of racism in America. Hayek was his distinct opposite as a libertarian. But Myrdal's sun was setting, and Hayek's reputation had come around like a comet after a lapse of nearly thirty years. This was the birth of new classical economics.

The helplessness of Keynesian policymakers did not improve matters. Incomes policies were leading to bitter strikes and splits within political parties. Government budgets were out of control, and deficits were mounting. The oil price rise of 1973 was followed by another in 1979. Within that decade, the USA finally gave up the ghost and fled from Vietnam, defeated. Richard Nixon narrowly escaped impeachment, and an unelected President, Gerald Ford, came to office. A strike by coalminers undermined the government of Edward Heath in Britain. In the two elections that followed, during 1974, Harold Wilson established a fragile majority for his Labour government. But the battles over wages and prices between the trade unions and the Labour government raged. Incomes policies were tried, and eventually failed. The IMF came and imposed a monetarist discipline on the UK Treasury.

Capitalism was in crisis. The old compromise between unions, corporations and governments was breaking down. It seemed that left-wing forces would gain strength. Worker militancy had been aroused by the inflationary spiral and the rising burden of taxation. There was a tax revolt as well as a wage revolt. Here was an opportunity for a Left takeover by waging a battle to bring capitalism to a halt. There were violent Marxist anarchist groups such as Bader–Meinhoff in Germany, the Weathermen in the USA, the Angry Brigade in the UK and others in France, Italy, the Netherlands. The PLO guerrillas disrupted the Munich Olympics.

Marxists also found that their theories, too, had no microfoundations. Marxism had become popular in university economics courses. Students wanted to learn about Marx's critique of capitalism, but here again they were used to a new level of theoretical rigour. As in the Keynesian–monetarist debate, the first wave of attack came from the elders of the profession. Paul Samuelson pointed out in a widely read academic journal that Marx's 'proof' of exploitation was defective, and his 'transformation problem' was not so much wrong as otiose.[8] Prices could be determined by the technical coefficients of any input–output table. There was no need to calculate 'values' or 'surplus-values'. The maximum profit rate a system could make was also given by the technology. Labour was required as an input, but you could calculate 'energy values' as well as 'labour values'.

An oblique attack came from an Italian economist, long settled in Trinity College Cambridge. Piero Sraffa had exploded on to the economic scene in 1926 with an article which pointed out that Marshall's theory of competition, the basis of all English economics, was logically flawed. This had spanned a large literature on imperfect competition, monopolistic competition, et cetera. Sraffa was the opposite of the prolific economists of his generation: he hated teaching, and disliked writing even more. But he was a scholar, and he put together the collected writings of David Ricardo, working through the 1930s and 1940s. He stayed on the sidelines of the Keynesian Revolution. But in a short preface to the first volume of his Ricardo collection, he let slip the simple idea that for Ricardo, the rate of profit was determined by the productivity of agriculture. Discounting rent, in a corn economy the inputs could be calculated in the same commodity as the output. Seeds were required as inputs. If workers were paid subsistence wages, you could think of that as corn as well. So profit, as pure surplus between corn output and corn input, can be calculated independently of prices or the market. Since profit rates were equal across the economy, the profit rate in agriculture was the crucial one. And it was determined not by exploitation but by nature and technology.

The year after Debreu published his *Theory of Value,* Sraffa published a book somewhat idiosyncratically entitled *The Production of Commodities by Means of Commodities: Prelude to a Critique of Economic Theory.*[9] In this book he generalized the argument he had made in his Ricardo preface. One could calculate a rate of profit for an economy (described by an input–output table) independently of prices, purely as a consequence of the technology of the system. Labour, labour-power or surplus-value were not required.

Sraffa was sympathetic to Marxism, and was a friend of the Italian Communist Antonio Gramsci, supplying him with an account to buy books while Gramsci was in prison. Ludwig Wittgenstein considered Sraffa so bright that he said he felt naked in his presence. The book was only about Sraffa's third publication and his first and only book, a slim volume of about a hundred pages. But it was profoundly undermining of Marx's theory. If Marx thought he had improved upon Ricardo and the other classical economists in providing a theory of profits, a century later, his claim was being questioned – from the Left of the political spectrum, not the Right.

Sraffa first derived a 'wage–profit frontier'. This indicated a rate of profit associated with each wage rate. The maximum rate of profit was determined by technical conditions when wages were zero. The actual rate of profit that would prevail depended, however, upon the social and political conditions – 'class struggle' – since it affected wages. Sraffa himself did not mention this sociopolitical context, but his followers, the neo-Ricardians, did.

Sraffa had meant to undermine neoclassical economics, especially the marginal productivity theory of distribution. This theory said that rewards to factors of production – labour and capital – were determined by their marginal productivity – that is, their respective contribution to output when an extra unit of the factor was put to use. The marginal productivity theory thus denied the existence of exploitation. Sraffa wanted to show that since actual rates of profits and wages depended on the outcome of distribution, one could not justify wages or profits in terms of productivity. Actual profitability came not from technical conditions so much as from the political economy of distribution. Only the maximum rate and the wage–profit frontier were technically determined.

Throughout the 1960s, this resulted in a series of articles for and against neoclassical economics. The contestants were economists from MIT in Cambridge, Massachusetts – Paul Samuelson, Robert Solow – and from Cambridge, England – Joan Robinson, Luigi Pasinetti. It came to be known as the capital controversy, because the issue became the possibility of measuring the value of capital independently of the profit rate. That controversy had died down by the beginning of the 1970s. The real sting in the Sraffa theory was for the Marxists.

Sraffa's theoretical structures had a great similarity to a paper by the Hungarian–American mathematician John von Neumann. In a paper given at Princeton in 1932, entitled 'A Model of General Economic Equilibrium', von Neumann, as befits a genius mathematician, wrote one of the most influential papers in economics. He showed that the maximum rate of profit was determined by the input–output technology where the inputs were machines and raw materials as well as labour. But while raw materials were consumed during the production process, and the labour input was renewed each period, the machines were durable. How could one take account of the durability of machines? The valuing of old machines was one of the great puzzles of economic theory. There were few markets for a five-year-old steel-rolling mill to give an accurate value. Accountants use various formulas for depreciation and amortization, but the economic value of an old piece of capital is an elusive notion. Much of the capital controversy had tried to tackle that issue, but got nowhere.

John von Neumann was innocent of the troubles of economists. He made the simple assumption that among the outputs of the process were machines one period older, as well as final output. Thus the value of output included the value of older machines as well as final goods, with inputs being fewer old machines, less labour and fewer raw materials. The problem of old capital was solved by considering it not just as input but also as output which could again become input. This was called joint production. A classic example is winemaking. When grapes are harvested and crushed, labour is used. But then the grape juice is left to ferment for some time before we have wine. The value of the wine exceeds that of the grape juice by a large factor, yet labour contributes nothing to the extra value. Thus, value and surplus-value could arise from factors other than labour.

Now Marx had discounted the contribution of capital inputs by putting it all in constant capital – translating the value of the wear and tear of capital in production in terms of its labour value. He struggled with the problem of durable capital in the middle third of *Capital Volume 2*, but did not think it modified his basic thesis. But now one had to face up to the possibility that the surplus-value came not from labour alone, but from other sources. Ian Steedman, a student of Sraffa, argued that the new techniques introduced by Von Neumann and Sraffa could be used to show up anomalies in Marx's argument. One could have negative surplus-value, yet positive profits.[10]

At one level, Steedman was pointing to logical possibilities, not a real-world outcome in real-life capitalism. There was, however, a fierce debate around his ideas that spanned political as well as mathematical issues. The Marxist Left was divided, and fell to quarrelling. To many outside academia, it sounded like debating how many angels could dance on a pin. After all, the dynamic disequilibrium nature of capitalism was nowhere at issue. The problem was that the Marxists had always been proud of the 'scientific' basis of Marx's notion of exploitation. At the macroeconomic level, as we saw in Chapter 5, exploitation is very similar to the notion of competitiveness. But just as Keynesian macroeconomics was found to be without sound microfoundations, so was it to be the case with Marx.

While the Marxists were in disarray, the communist economies were not doing much better. The Soviet economy had begun to slow down in the 1970s, no longer able to generate the additional inputs required for growth, nor to raise the productivity of existing inputs. In Marx's terms, the system was failing to produce relative surplus-value. Committed to full employment of all who could work (there being no unemployment benefits), the Soviet Union often employed workers who were producing negative surplus-value – that is, worth less than the wages they were getting. This was not mathematics, this was the political economy of Soviet planning. Outside the armaments and space industries, there were few innovations and no incentive to improve efficiency. Every worker was guaranteed a job, as was the manager, the banker and the planner. Productivity was low, and the products of the Soviet bloc were not competitive on world markets.

The oil price rise helped the Soviet Union. As an exporter of oil, it began to earn good foreign exchange. There was, however, a revolt in Poland by workers who, in 1971, wanted a better standard of living. Edward Gierek, the Polish Communist leader, boldly borrowed abroad. The Soviet Union did not obstruct this. Soon the many economies of Eastern Europe were able to borrow petrodollars. Since the Soviet Union had good reserves, it looked on benignly at this engagement with Western banks. In its foreign trade relations with the Eastern European countries, the Soviet Union reversed its former conduct and began to subsidize the rest of the Comecon countries whom it had exploited. Life became somewhat easier for the citizens of the Soviet bloc. The oil price bonanza hid the structural fault of stagnation.

The first few dollops of happiness after twenty-five years of Communist austerity encouraged dissident activity in the Soviet bloc. In Poland, Hungary and Czechoslovakia, individual dissidents outside the political system, and without a programme of violent overthrow of the Communist regime, began to form groups. This was not Hungary 1956 or Czechoslovakia 1968. This was a non-violent, individual dissidence, mocking the authorities. It led to the big strike in the Lenin shipyards in Gdansk in Poland, and the birth of Solidarity. The dissidents were afforded some cover by the agreement in Helsinki in 1975, as part of the Cold War détente, that human rights would be respected in the Soviet bloc.

There was also a new form of non-party-political dissidence developing in the West. The struggle for civil rights for Black Americans in the 1960s had been the pioneer on this. But in the 1970s the women's movement erupted. It baffled the established political parties of both Right and Left, parliamentary as well as revolutionary. Women questioned the nature of democracy, the definition of equality and the emphasis on paid work to the detriment of household work. Marxists who had worked on the notion of class and class struggle found themselves attacked for ignoring gender and the power relations within society across all classes. All authority was doubted, as it was often male authority. Neither capitalism nor socialism had faced up to the gender question. Power as much as profits had to be understood, fought for and won.

Women everywhere in developed capitalist economies were emerging as a new force. The same was happening in the developing countries. As profitability declined in the North, capital began to move to developing countries, where wages were lower. In many industries, women proved more adept at working with technology than men. They were dextrous, likely to be docile, and willing to work flexible hours. Women's employment began to increase in many of the developing countries which were receiving foreign capital. But employment and income are empowering, and the women began to assert themselves in both their homes and their societies. They also linked up with their sisters in the North.[11]

The oil price rise was a boon for many Third World countries. Some, of course, were oil exporters. With their sudden large fortunes, they began to import skilled and unskilled labour from their neighbours. Thus the oil-rich countries of the Gulf invited Muslim workers from South and Southeast Asia as immigrants. This meant literally billions of dollars of capital inflow for India, Pakistan, Bangladesh and Sri Lanka, as well as Malaysia, as these workers' remittances home piled up.

The biggest benefit was more indirect. The oil-exporting countries could not absorb the large inflows of their export revenue. Much of the wealth ended up in Western banks as deposits. This meant a fall in interest rates, despite high rates of inflation. In 1975, the UK had an inflation rate of 25 per cent, and the nominal interest rate was 5 per cent. Banks became eager to lend, and for the first time since 1914, private capital began to flow into the developing countries. Of course, these were bank loans, and the larger the better as far as the banks were concerned. There was finance for oil exploration, for finding oil substitutes, even for outlandish projects such as clearing the Amazon jungles of Brazil. Some equity capital was also moving from the West, but most of it was bank debt.

It was in this period – the second half of the 1970s – that four Asian economies – South Korea, Taiwan, Singapore and Hong Kong – astonished the world by their export growth performance. What Japan had done in the 1960s, and kept on doing, was now emulated by the Asian Tigers.[12] They were open export-orientated economies which penetrated markets all over the world by their competitive pricing. South Korea modelled itself on Japan, building up close-knit partnerships between banks, manufacturing conglomerates and government. But there was also a solid foundation of universal literacy and land reform. People in the countryside were prosperous enough to save, and their savings were mobilized by the banking system to fund investment by the *chaibol* – the small number of large conglomerates. Taiwan had few such large corporations, but its strategy was similar – universal literacy, land reform, high savings and high export-orientated investment. The other two – Singapore and Hong Kong – were island economies with a long history of being entrepôts. Foreign trade had been growing throughout the previous three decades, thanks to GATT and a successive round of tariff-cutting by its members. The island economies benefited from being at the crossroads of a growing business, but also by having low wages and flexible markets. They had avoided the statist pattern of many other Asian economies. The state played a large role, but it went with the grain of the market rather than impeding it. They subjected their industrialists to the objective test of export competition.

The oil price rise amounted to a transfer of nearly 5 per cent of GDP from the advanced capitalist countries to the oil-exporting economies. This was as much as the USA had transferred to Western Europe as Marshall Aid, but this time it was not voluntary. The transfer was paid in unemployment, slower growth in real wages, cuts in public expenditure, erosion of public services. But through much of the 1970s, official policy stayed Keynesian. Governments went on printing money to finance higher expenditure, but much of that was eaten up by inflation. There was also a bit of coin-clipping as far as the oil exporters were concerned. The dollar price was higher for oil, but the dollar was worth less. If gold was $35 an ounce in early 1971, by the end of the decade it was about $300. The dollar had depreciated, and that meant the oil exporters were able to buy less back from the advanced oil-importing countries.

Thus inflation was a solvent. At the very least, it postponed the problems caused by lower profitability and competitiveness. There were strikes and disruptions, which at times looked very threatening. There was a rise of racism in many countries, especially the UK. As industry moved out of old established areas and relocated to Asia or Latin America, blue-collar jobs were threatened. De-industrialization and rust belt became words that the North had to come to terms with. But people were redeployed elsewhere – not all of them, of course, because unemployment rose across most Western countries.

The glue of inflation did not stick for long, nor could it have done so. If inflation was not to accelerate and get out of government control, it had to be tackled. Despite rising wages, labour was dissatisfied as inflation ate into purchasing power. Strikes and walkouts mounted across capitalist countries. This was worse than student rebellions or civil rights agitation. Continuous accommodation to labour's demands was neither possible nor effective. Profitability of the capitalist order had to be restored. If not, the alternative might well have not been socialism, as many hoped, but could easily have been fascism.

The second oil price rise in 1979 forced a drastic solution. By one of those accidents of history, the Cunning of Reason, new political leaders came to office in the USA, the UK and Germany around the late 1970s/early 1980s. They were able to transcend the old rules, and restructure capitalism. The social cost was enormous, and the risk was always that the gamble might fail and democracy itself might go under. But Ronald Reagan, Margaret Thatcher and Helmut Kohl were radical leaders from the Right of the political spectrum. Radicalism was no longer the monopoly of the Left. In challenging the Left's hegemony of radicalism, the New Right proceeded to change the language and culture of liberal democracy. It also changed the chances of the survival of capitalism.

17

Up from the Abyss

The 1970s saw the common crisis of the capitalist and the communist worlds. For the Third World, it was a case of easy money from petrodollars: either earning them or borrowing them. Primary commodity prices rose throughout the decade until around 1977. The one UN institution that the Third World thought of as its own – UNCTAD – proposed a New International Economic Order. This New Order was to redress centuries of injustice caused by the imperial connection, and the alleged exploitation of the Third World by the First. There was to be a new arrangement for stabilizing, if not increasing, primary commodity prices – on the analogy of the quadrupling of oil prices – and new and fair arrangements for trade. For a while the USA, beleaguered in Vietnam and elsewhere, jollied the Third World along. But then the second oil price rise came, and the tables were turned. The crises of the 1980s were different for the capitalist and the communist worlds, and the Third World came to its knees.[1]

The reactions in the leading countries of the First World – the USA, the UK, France and Germany – to the second oil shock were as unexpected as they were radical. But while the 1960s and 1970s had brought the radicalism of the Left on to the streets, it was the Right which won the battle of ideas and, indeed, even of the ballot box. The crucial year was 1979, when the second oil price rise took place. Paul Volcker, as the new Chairman of the Federal Reserve, shifted the monetary policy of the USA to a monetarist one, and Margaret Thatcher won the election for the Conservative Party in the UK. Volcker installed control of the money supply as the central tenet of monetary policy and this, in turn, implied allowing the interest rate on government debt to find its own level. Within months of coming to power the Conservative government deregulated capital movements, thus following the USA's example of 1972. These two events rocketed the interest rate to double-digit figures, practically trebling it. This was because the rich countries – which, throughout the 1970s, had 'printed money' to finance their deficits – began to borrow instead. As inflation was receding at the end of the 1970s to low single figures – 5 per cent in the UK during 1978–79

– interest rates were climbing to 15 per cent. After a bonanza of negative real interest rates since 1974, during which billions had been borrowed, now the real costs were coming home at last.

The crisis that ensued in the US and UK economies upon the adoption of monetarist policies was one of the most severe since the Great Depression. With real rates going positive for the first time since 1973, output dropped sharply, and a steep rise in unemployment was the consequence. Levels of unemployment not seen since 1945 were reached, and would not be reduced for a decade. Full employment as conceived by the Keynesians – a permanent tight labour market – was now abandoned openly and explicitly by democratically elected leaders. Inflation was the new enemy. Bringing inflation down became the sole objective of macroeconomic policy. A rise in unemployment, a deep recession, a precipitous fall in industrial output, were all 'a price worth paying'.

In the UK, GDP at factor cost reached a peak of 79.6 (1990 = 100) in the second quarter of 1979. This level was not to be reached again until four years later, in 1983. Industrial production suffered even more. The peak of 89.1 (1990 = 100) in 1979 was not reached again until 1985. At its lowest level, in the last quarter of 1980, it was 77.8, a decline of 12 per cent in eighteen months. Unemployment was 1.38 million in 1978, doubled to 2.92 million in 1982, and went on climbing for the next four years, despite much massaging of the unemployment statistics which hid the actual rise.

The slowdown in the USA was milder. Output stagnated between 1979 and 1980, the last year of the Carter presidency, rose slightly in 1981 and fell about 3 per cent in 1982, but recovered in 1983. In the advanced capitalist countries as a group, growth rate of GDP slowed down from 3.8 per cent during 1950–73 to 2.1 per cent during 1973–89. In this slowdown, the USA and the UK suffered the least. They had been relatively slow growers between 1950 and 1973 – 2.2 per cent and 2.5 per cent respectively – and fell to 1.6 per cent and 1.8 per cent. But Japan fell from 8.0 per cent to 3.1 per cent, Germany from 4.9 per cent to 2.1 per cent, France from 4.0 per cent to 1.8 per cent.

The real change, however, was not in the nature of the recession but in governments' reaction to it. The textbook Keynesian response would have been to increase government expenditure, even at the cost of a higher budget deficit, and reflate the economy to bring the level of unemployment down. This had been the reaction of the previous Conservative government under Edward Heath in 1971, when the level of unemployment reached one million. The Thatcher government not only refused to reflate the economy, but made a virtue of the need to eliminate the budget deficit and, more especially, to finance any deficit by market borrowing rather than by 'printing money'. This was a dramatic rejection of the Keynesian orthodoxy, and following the 1981 Budget, 364 economists from British universities wrote a letter to *The Times* denouncing the Chancellor of the Exchequer, Geoffrey Howe. He ignored them.

This was a historic moment. Just as the British government was rejecting Keynesian reflationary policies, French Socialists – who had just come to power in 1981, with François Mitterrand as President – decided to pursue an aggressive Keynesian policy. Here was an unusual situation in the realm of economics – an experiment to test the rival theories. Of course, the experiment was not conducted under ideal laboratory conditions, but the UK and France were similar enough to be suitable guinea pigs. There was also a clear ideological demarcation between a Conservative government in the UK and a Socialist one in France. Each government had sufficient legislative strength to implement its programme.

The immediate outcome was startling, and has been the subject of much subsequent debate. The British economy began to turn around soon after the deflationary budget of 1981. The bottom of the recession was in the second quarter of that year. Helped by a war in the South Atlantic in 1982, the Thatcher government went on to win the 1983 election with an enhanced majority, while unemployment was still above three million – despite the fact that the government did not even promise to reduce unemployment. All it said was that it would combat inflation. This abandonment of the old Keynesian commitment to full employment did not prove an electoral liability. More trade-union members voted for the Conservative Party than for their traditional ally, the Labour Party. It took another three elections and fourteen years before the Labour Party could defeat the Conservatives.

The French experiment had to be abandoned and reversed in 1983. The prospect of a Keynesian reflation alarmed the financial and foreign exchange markets. Unfortunately for the French Socialists, these markets had recently learnt to operate on a global scale. There had been a decade of floating exchange rates following the collapse of the Bretton Woods system. The French, along with their German ally, attempted to rebuild a fixed exchange rate system – the European Monetary System, with its Exchange Rate Mechanism (ERM) – in 1979. This system confined the range of fluctuations in the exchange rate for the French franc against all other currencies to 2½ per cent. The adoption of Keynesian policy, with its concomitant rise in deficit, led to a capital flight from France, and a collapse in the market for French government debt. A large trade deficit, as well as capital flight, compelled France to depreciate the franc. The ERM, launched only four years previously, had to deal with a crisis in one of its major currencies. The franc had to be 'realigned'. The reflationary policy had to be abandoned. Indeed, following this blow to its national prestige, the French government moved over completely to a policy of exchange rate stability – the *franc fort* – and let unemployment go up to whatever level was necessary to defend this exchange rate.

This double blow to Keynesian policies was reinforced by the experiences of the West German economy. Keynesian policies had never been part of German economic orthodoxy. After the launching of liberal free-market policies by Ludwig Erhard in the 1950s, Germany had followed orthodox fiscal policies. The Bundesbank had an autonomous status, enshrined in the Federal Constitution, and it had long followed a monetarist policy. It watched its money supply like a hawk, and gave priority to fighting inflation. Germany relied on high savings and high investment rather than consumption demand as the driving force of the economy. As the 1970s passed, and the crisis of stagflation hit European economies, the reputation of the Bundesbank – and, by implication, of West Germany – rose. Germany had always emphasized low inflation, low government debt and high investment. It was a major exporter of manufactured products, and enjoyed a trade surplus. The citizens of West Germany had lower consumption levels, but higher employment and lower inflation levels. There was a social partnership between trade unions, employers and the state which became the envy of other countries. But none of these virtues had come from the adoption of Keynesian policies. It was classical policies that Germany advertised. The Deutschmark became one of the key currencies alongside the dollar, the yen being the other.

Germany and Japan emerged as major economic powers in the 1970s. Thirty years after they had been totally physically devastated, these two former enemy countries became exemplary capitalist economies. But their national capitalisms did not follow the Anglo-Saxon logic of equity-financed firms and an adversarial logic in labour–capital relations. In Japan as in Germany, there was labour–capital partnership in the large corporations. Equity ownership played a smaller part than debt finance, and to the extent that there was equity finance, it was very tightly held. There was a large degree of intercorporate ownership, and banks played an active role in financing as well as managing business. In Japan, the government presided over an industrial strategy in which corporations and banks were inducted as willing partners. The large business houses with conglomerate holdings across industries and services – Mitsui, Mitsubishi, and so on – were pivotal to the success of Japan's strategy. This was the same philosophy as was used by the German National Socialists (with no pejorative association with the evil consequences of Nazism).

It was also a protectionist strategy in which Japan exported but did not import manufactures; imported raw materials but not raw foods, especially rice; kept foreign capital from ownership in Japanese industries. Germany was part of the European Economic Community, which was also a Customs union, discouraging imports. Both Germany and Japan played their part in tariff-cutting in many of the GATT rounds, yet their strategy was more a Friedrich List than an Adam Smith one.

As the Anglo-Saxon economies faltered through the 1970s, the Axis economies prospered. When the Anglo-Saxon economies went through a painful process of restructuring in the 1980s, the contrast between the two approaches became even more pronounced. In the UK and the USA, unemployment increased, as did interest rates. Manufacturing imports were liberalized; this caused the closure of domestic industries. The UK government foresaw the depreciation of sterling as a weapon, as did the USA, but the dollar stayed overvalued through the first half of the 1980s. The pound sterling rose at first in the wake of the second oil price rise since, thanks to North Sea oil, the UK had become a net oil exporter. As oil prices fell from their 1979 height, sterling began to fall against the dollar and the Deutschmark. Either way, the open-economy approach of the Anglo-Saxon countries, with a hands-off attitude towards foreign exchange, seemed to lead to high unemployment and the destruction of old-established industries. While this strategy was bold, it was an embattled one. To many in the advanced countries, it seemed that the German/Japanese model of caring, socially responsible capitalism was preferable to the Anglo-Saxon model.

The abandonment of Keynesian policies was deliberate in the UK, but only rhetorical in the USA. Reaganomics rejected the welfare state and espoused supply-side economics. Control over money supply was implemented by the Federal Reserve System under Paul Volcker's chairmanship. But unlike Thatcher, Reagan did not control public spending. Spending on defence rocketed, and the budget became unbalanced. Despite stern speeches on controlling the state, or slimming it down, all that happened was a reduction in the growth of welfare budgets, overcompensated by defence spending and generous tax cuts. Reaganomics in practice was Keynes without Beveridge, using Keynes's own injunction in 1938 (albeit without formally acknowledging it) that arms spending is a good way of pump-priming the economy out of a recession.

Real output grew every year from 1982 onwards, and by 1989 it was a third higher. Yet the anti-Keynesian rhetoric was winning.

In microeconomic policies, deregulation and privatization became the norm. In the USA, public regulation of airlines, of communications, of electricity companies (public utilities) had been subjected to a wide-ranging and telling critique by many economists, among whom Ronald Coase was prominent. Airlines were deregulated as to their fare structures and flight schedules. Radio frequencies were auctioned on the market rather than rationed by a bureaucracy. Large electricity and telephone utilities were broken up and allowed to maximize profits without any ceiling. In the UK, the publicly owned industries were not just restructured – they were privatized. Airlines, steel, telephones, gas, electricity – one after another – the 'commanding heights' were sold off to private buyers. The process of privatization was designed to give the ordinary citizen a stake in the gains to be made by selling off public property. Citizens were exhorted to take a gamble on the shares being underpriced at the outset, and hence likely to go up in price as soon as they started being traded. Big hoardings yelled out the message: 'Tell Sid'. Sid was your ordinary Britisher, by instinct and habit a gambler, now being invited to play the stag and make a killing out of privatization. This was privatization with a populist appeal.

It was not all plain sailing by any means. Riots in inner-city areas – Brixton in London and Toxteth in Liverpool; Watts in Los Angeles; long and bitter industrial strikes – coalminers and newspaper printers and journalists in the UK; the rise and growth of racist and fascist parties in the UK, Germany, the USA, France – these were boils on the surface of polity as it was subjected to a drastic cure. The women's movement became widespread, vocal and much more effective. It had no favourites among political parties, since from a feminist point of view, all parties were part of the problem, not necessarily a solution. Claims for entitlements and for positive discrimination proliferated in the USA – Blacks, Native Americans, women, the disabled, the elderly. While the forms of democracy stayed the same, their context was changing. Citizens were no longer satisfied to be ordinary autonomous voters in an electoral graveyard. As the state abandoned welfarism, citizens formed voluntary associations and political action committees to pursue their entitlements through law courts and by lobbying for special treatment.

The most surprising aspect of this restructuring was that while trade unions, intellectuals and 'progressives' opposed it bitterly, voters approved of it. The Left had always thought that it represented the majority of the people, and that only devious devices kept it from perpetual power. Here was a situation in which governments adopted an anti-worker rhetoric, chose to dismantle well-entrenched industrial structures, defied orthodoxies about progressive taxation and public spending. And yet they got elected again and again. Margaret Thatcher's victory in 1983 is dismissed as due to the Falklands conflict, but the opinion polls had begun to turn up from rock bottom for her before Falklands. The divisions in the Labour Party did help. But even discounting 1983, she won in 1987 and her successor, John Major, won in 1992. People did not seem to mind the pain, if there was clear gain at the end of the hard road. Reagan proved this by winning in 1984, and Bush in 1988. Mitterrand was re-elected in 1988 despite high unemployment through the 1983–88 period.

What had happened was that the social contract struck in 1945 was rewritten. Full employment was no longer central to it. Low inflation and stable growth became pivotal. A richer electorate wanted quality public services, and did not mind who provided them or how they were paid for. Luckily for the West, political leaders emerged who could see the need to rewrite the social contract. They were in fact restructuring the economy to restore profitability. They were only half-conscious of the emerging global context in which capital flows were to reshape the economies of individual countries. The migration of capital to cheaper production locations impelled a search for new economic activities – services rather than goods, sophisticated innovative goods rather than the stable manufactures on which postwar economies had been built. New technologies were also being introduced in a parallel process unguided by the visible hand of government planning. Computers became faster, more efficient and then smaller, defying all the predictions of gigantism. The introduction of the microchip in pocket calculators, and then in personal computers, led to the biggest industrial revolution since the 1890s.

The new technology was a result of a Schumpetarian process. Entrepreneurs relying on venture capital and a talent for risk-taking came together in Silicon Valley. In an unorganized, unplanned way, their competitive activity helped to create the IT revolution. For the first time in many decades, there was a cluster of products in which quality improved as prices dropped. Information-gathering and telecommunications became cheaper by the day, and soon began to transform production as well as consumption. It was a process in which the well-established giants of the 1970s – IBM, Bell – were practically destroyed by intrepid new companies; a process that defied the logic by which many critiques of capitalism had thought the world worked. For an economist such as Galbraith, corporate giants were powerful and permanent. Technostructures were invincible. Radical critiques from the Left emphasized the degree of concentration of industries, the share of the largest three or four firms in an industry's total sales. But here were new firms toppling the giants from their perches. New industries were being created. Capitalism was not a static, or even a steady-state, growing process. It sought profits where it could, and innovation was the one 'sure' process by which profitability could be revived. This was 'creative destruction' in our lifetime.

The Communist world, meanwhile, failed to restructure. Where democracies could rewrite the social contract with their citizens, dictatorships proved to be too timid. When Brezhnev died in 1982, his successors were the worst examples of Soviet gerontocracy. Yuri Andropov and Konstantin Chernenko are not even footnotes in history. As successors to Lenin as upholders of the Bolshevik torch, they are invidious figures. As the West retrenched and rebuilt, the Soviet Union dithered. Mikhail Gorbachev came to power in 1985, promised much and almost succeeded. His glasnost was welcome, and led eventually to the dismantling of the Soviet Empire in Eastern Europe. But his perestroika was a dismal failure. The Soviet economy badly needed deep structural reform. It was failing in its basic task of producing surplus and restoring growth, which had collapsed. The goods being produced no longer enjoyed a competitive, or even technical, edge over those in the West. Despite its success in military and space hardware, the Soviet economy lagged behind on computers, telecommunications, fibre optics – the new horizons. In its ability to produce consumer durables, or services, the Soviet economy had always been backward. It was a high-cost, low-quality economy in which citizens had little alternative but to consume what was there. The Soviet Union appeared to be a middle-income country, but estimates of GDP were misleading. If the goods had been revalued at the much lower international prices, it would have been clear that apart from its military–space complex, the USSR was a Third World country. It failed the stern test of the law of value, as an old-fashioned Marxist would have said.

This was made starkly obvious not so much in the USSR as in its dependencies. The loans taken from Western banks by the Eastern European economies had to be repaid in hard currencies. By 1985, oil prices had collapsed, and the Soviet Union could not cushion its dependants. Poland or Czechoslovakia could not export their manufacturing products to the West because – not to put too fine a point on it – they were junk, and high-priced junk at that. They had to export agricultural products, putting up the price of food for their citizens. There was a sudden realization – though not in these terms – that the industrial structures built up over years of relentless accumulation were worthless. Capital, as Marx said, is not a thing; it is a social relationship – a relationship for producing surplus-value. Poland, Czechoslovakia, the GDR (East Germany) had ceased to have productive economies, though here again, measurements of GDP and its growth were misleading. (This is not an ideological matter but a predictable consequence of autarky. West European agriculture is similarly overpriced and overvalued. If free trade in agriculture were to become the norm, it would collapse, and the sooner the better.)

Across Eastern Europe and the USSR, the 1980s proved both exhilarating and troublesome. Many illusions were shattered. Some people thought that market socialism could provide a way out. But they failed to recall that in the original debate about market socialism (see Chapter 12), it was a mature capitalist economy being transformed into a market socialist one. The task of producing surplus-value was taken as having been accomplished. Markets were assumed to be active and deeply permeating in labour and goods. The Eastern European economy could not be market socialist, since it was not capitalist enough, and innocent of market discipline. This paradox was beyond the grasp of many who thought that as Soviet-style 'Socialism outside Capitalism' collapsed, capitalism could be avoided.

The lasting achievement of these economies was not in the production of goods and services (except, of course, armaments and space technology). It was in education and health. In areas where critical thought was not essential – engineering, mathematics, natural sciences – they excelled. In humanities and social sciences, they stagnated. Individuals – poets such as Václav Havel or thinkers such as George Konrad, journalists such as Adam Michnik – provided the innovative ideas which eventually transformed these regimes. They were the entrepreneurs – ideological entrepreneurs who took the risks and led the creative destruction of the *ancien régime*. But behind them was an articulate, literate mass readership that could march behind these ideas. The ideas were anarchist, libertarian. They invoked not Marx but Locke, Hayek and Popper. Marx, for them, had become the monster that Stalin had made him – a monster of repression. They rejected all forms of socialism, but endorsed self-management, decentralization, individual dissent. These ideas undermined the *ancien régime*. The images that East Germans could see on their black-and-white TVs told them that they had been left behind by West Germany. Stalinism had promised plenty for the price of unfreedom, but all it had delivered was poverty and unfreedom. Yes, the degree of inequality was low, but this merely confirmed Adam Smith's tenet that equal societies were poor societies.[2]

This was not how it was meant to be. Socialism had arisen to challenge the inegalitarian tendencies of capitalism. Its promise was to abolish scarcity along with inequality. It was also a programme of human liberation. But the twentieth-century priests of orthodox Marxism had done things in Marx's name that forever compromised his message. Leninism became a doctrine of oppression, scarcity, unfreedom. Socialism outside Capitalism had been born prematurely in 1917, and withered away – thankfully without bloodshed – in 1991, when the USSR ceased to be. No one who had championed it as the beacon of hope, or lamented the distortion of the Revolution, had expected its demise. Its worst enemies overestimated its strength, and were surprised by the sudden collapse. The Wizard of Oz was just a little, frightened old man. All those who had travelled the yellow brick road to his temple were to be disillusioned.

The death of Leninism as a ruling ideology impacted badly on its socialist rival, but even before then, there was trouble. Reformist socialism of the Second International met its biggest challenge in the 1980s, and flunked it. In France, Spain, Portugal, Italy and Greece, Socialist governments held power. Socialists were hegemonic in Austria, Sweden, Denmark. But since the good fortunes of Socialism within Capitalism (SwC) were crucially dependent on capitalist prosperity, SwC was caught in the task of restructuring and retrenching. Capitalism in one country, with its Keynesian protective belt, was on the way out. Deregulated capital flows and flexible exchange rates put severe limits on the autonomy of national economic policy, as France discovered. Markets – now armed with fast telephone and computer links, getting faster and cheaper daily – started speculating on interest rates and exchange rates. Money began to flow in and out of countries in massive amounts.

This was a new world. While the Bretton Woods era lasted, exchange rates were fixed within narrow bands, capital was not mobile, phones were slow and computers beyond the nexus of stockbrokers. In March 1973, during a currency crisis, $3 billion were traded in one day. By the late 1970s, daily turnover was $100 billion, and in the late 1980s, $650 billion. In 1960, a transatlantic cable could carry 138 conversations simultaneously. By 1995, thanks to fibre optics, this had gone up to 1.5 million.

The speed and size of these transactions unnerved many, but especially all those who had relied on using state power to control the economy. To many it seemed immoral that such large transactions could be carried out in paper assets. There has always been a fascination for the concrete in the economic imagination. Solid things have value, should have value, and should engage people. To attribute value to manipulation of abstract numbers seems obscene, especially to anyone immersed in a crude labour theory of value. Manufactures are good things. Services, especially financial services, are bad. For socialist parties built on unionized labour from manufacturing industries, this seems axiomatic. But the moralists have the wrong economics. They also have severe myopia. In any society beyond a simple self-sufficient village economy (a hoary myth), the number of buying and selling transactions is always a multiple of the number of people. The value of these transactions is also a multiple of the value of the final output. It takes many transactions of buying inputs and selling semi-finished goods for refashioning further down the line to produce a consumable good. The value added at each stage is a fraction of the value of total input purchased or value of output sold. A pair of shoes may be a result of fifteen or twenty previous stages of production – getting the hide, tanning, cutting and shaping, combining with sole and heel – themselves results of a separate process: stitching, polishing, transporting to the wholesalers, then to retailers, until you buy them. Some of these processes may involve international trade, with the leather coming from India, the material in the sole/heel from another country. These inputs have to be transported, too – within India to the ports, through a chain of traders, and then upon arrival. If we 'double-counted' the gross value of other transactions at each stage, it would be a multiple of the final sale value.

The moralist rejects such arguments. In his world, goods are somehow directly purchased from the primary producer, and all intermediaries are superfluous. But if you want to eat fresh organic food, sitting in your urban dwelling, the stuff has to be transported along country lanes and highways and urban roads to your local supermarket in order that you may be able to satisfy your craving. The fresher you want it, the faster the lorries will have to travel. You want your food hygienic and healthy, so it will need plastic or Cellophane packaging, multiplying the transactions.

As we become more prosperous, we become more demanding. This is no problem, since the division of labour on which modern economies are based is designed to cater for such sophisticated demands. But the chain from the original product to the final consumer gets longer, and acquires extra layers. It summons resources from farther away. The advantage is that despite this elongated chain and multiple layers, what we get is delivered at a reasonable price. Things which kings could rarely afford are now ours, thanks to the division of labour. But it involves middlemen, multiple transactions and multi-sectoral co-ordination. All this is, of course, done by the market. That, after all, was what Adam Smith liked about his system of natural liberty.

The case of financial transactions is no different, except that it caters not to ordinary consumers but to firms – banks, non-financial corporations, pension funds, stockbrokers. The output is abstract; it is a service which is non-durable, much like the music of a street busker, or the lesson a teacher gives to students, or the diagnosis of a doctor. When these are delivered, there is nothing concrete to show, but a service has been rendered. When there was a Gold Standard, there were no foreign exchange markets. With fixed exchange rates across the world, the same would be the case. (There would be other adverse consequences of an unalterable exchange rate, but I leave those aside for the moment.) If a pair of currencies becomes flexible, then there is one exchange rate to determine for the immediate – spot – transaction. But there may be anticipatable needs of trade in the future. So there will be forward transactions. These can be many, depending on dates of delivery. But there may be probable future events – 'states of nature' – in which the currencies may change in value. People may wish to guard against such contingencies, causing them loss. They hedge. So even for a single pair of currencies, there could be many ways of transacting around their exchange rate. As long as the future is uncertain, people will want to hedge against a future loss or bet on a possible gain.

As you multiply the number of currencies, the number of exchange rates goes up fast: only one exchange rate for two currencies; three rates for three currencies; forty-five rates for ten currencies; four thousand nine hundred and fifty for a hundred currencies. Thus as exchange rates became flexible, and more and more countries deregulated their capital markets (all EU countries by 1988, all OECD countries by 1990), the possible number of tradeable currencies exploded. Corporations trading in several countries needed to hedge against exchange rate fluctuations in the many currencies they made or received payments in. And there were not only spot transactions but forward transactions, as well as those allowing for contingent circumstances. The costs of not anticipating currency fluctuations and hedging against them became severe for corporate treasurers.

Exchange rate movements were triggered by expected shifts in budget deficits and money supplies. A government seen as soft on inflation, as likely to run budget deficits, experienced a depreciation in its currency. To stave this off, it needed to increase interest rates on its short-term debt. Thus, anticipated movements in interest rates also became an object of speculation by the market, often forcing governments to take action sooner than they intended. Rules of orthodox finance – balanced budgets, control over money supply – became *de rigueur* for governments.

This went against the grain of socialist parties. They were committed to Keynesian policies – full employment, growth, and in some cases redistribution of income in favour of the poor. The instruments for such policies were budget deficits, low interest rates, progressive taxation. But it took skill to navigate the fiscal ship of state in the new turbulent international markets. The conservative parties championed tax cuts and reverse redistribution. Reagan cut income taxes on the advice of the California economist Arthur Laffer, and Thatcher followed suit. Socialist parties could not reconcile balanced budgets and low taxation with an active expenditure policy to create jobs. European socialist governments had also imposed the straitjacket of the Exchange Rate Mechanism on themselves. This limited their freedom to devalue, and forced a quick reversal of any move that might depreciate their exchange rates. One such policy was public spending to boost employment. In the new context of open economies, public spending had limited domestic multipliers with large import leakages. Thus the old-fashioned self-liquidating budget deficit that Keynes had advocated was no longer operative. Public spending led to small multipliers and trade deficits.

It was not immediately obvious to socialist parties that a change had taken place, requiring fresh thinking. To begin with, there was resistance to abandoning old policies. Many of these parties had to come to power for the first time after decades, and wanted to try out the nostrums they had championed. Their supporters expected nationalization, rapid growth, higher wages and full employment. They were faced with compulsions from outside which they had not anticipated. One after another, European socialist parties in office had to learn the lesson that France learnt in 1983.

There was scope for progressive policies within the fiscal bounds. Governments could meet the challenge posed by the women's movement, by ethnic minorities, by an ageing population. They tried to build a 'rainbow coalition', but many of these people were poor. It became necessary to think of ways to direct public spending specifically to the poor. There was also revulsion on the Left against bureaucratic and elitist administration of welfare benefits. Decentralization, devolution, self-organization, were imperative demands. These were fiscally neutral, and socialist parties experimented with new and cost-effective ways of meeting these new demands.

The shift in the electoral base of socialist parties was the reason behind these new demands. Large-scale manufacturing industry was declining in importance as the biggest provider of jobs. Products which were now well known, with their technology standardized – mature manufactures – were being relocated abroad to Asian and Latin American countries where labour was cheap and skilled. Blue-collar jobs were under pressure in the OECD countries by the 1980s, albeit to varying degrees. The Anglo-Saxon economies – the UK, the USA – were in the forefront of manufacturing decline. But France and Germany were not able to resist the tide. Everywhere in advanced capitalism, manufacturing had to specialize in new knowledge-intensive products – pharmaceuticals, aerospace, telecommunications, information technology – while shipbuilding, automobiles, textiles and electrical goods were moving away. New service industries took their place. Financial services were the fastest-growing, but also information-processing, communications, advertising, design, fashion. These were the new 'abstract' goods. But these industries employed graduates, and were typically small enterprises with flexible working hours and non-hierarchical structures. The traditional working class was shrinking. A new heterogeneous collection of white-collar employees was supplanting the proletariat. The Left had to come to terms with the middle-class electorate.

In Marxist theory as well, the old certainties were being challenged. Marx's theory of history, with the daisy chain of modes of production and the base–superstructure articulation within any mode – was re-examined: once from the perspective of French philosophical tradition by Louis Althusser, and then from an English philosophical angle by Gerry Cohen.[3] There was no Cartesian mathematical certainty, as a French philosopher would have liked, nor the logical tightness that English philosophy demanded. Marx's historical materialism was a late product of his Hegelian youth. Like Adam Smith's theory of modes of substance, it is, in my view, a useful story for explaining how Western Europe arrived at the threshold of capitalism in the eighteenth century, but it is not – and should not be made into – a universal logical scheme. It is a millennial epochal scheme abounding in broad generalities. When he came to discuss specific historical episodes – as in France in 1848, 1851, 1871 – Marx used a much more detailed framework of political economy. A two-class scheme was replaced by multiple classes and factions. The dynamic of chance and accident was given prominence. There were few inevitabilities. And as his correspondence with the Russian Marxists showed (see Chapters 5 and 6 above), Marx was aware of the specificities of his theory. He would have been the last to elevate his youthful speculations into a general universal theory. That was the result of Stalinism elevating Marxism to a religion.

The notion of a proletariat ever eager to challenge the capitalist system was itself under scrutiny. Trade-union membership was shifting largely to white-collar workers in the public sector, or in the knowledge-based private industries. The traditional worker with a lifetime job – 48 years, 48 weeks per year, 48 hours per week (including overtime) – was disappearing. But his image as a revolutionary was also being questioned. Women's movements highlighted the exploitation in household work, and the sturdy proletarian became part of patriarchy. The emergence of Third World countries in the international arena brought out questions of colonialism, and the ways in which the 'labour aristocracy' of the advanced capitalist nations had benefited from imperialist exploitation. Was there a proletariat? How were classes defined?

The growth of Marxist sociology and political economy continued in the 1980s, but this was a Marxism steeped in the methods of Western social sciences. Marx's notions were re-examined and tested. Was class the same as occupation, for which a lot of statistical information was available? Was there mobility between classes? A rigorous examination of the notion of class and exploitation by the American economist John Roemer concluded that it was the initial endowment of assets that determined a person's class position – the proletariat had no endowments; the petty bourgeois had some, but insufficient to live off the profits of production; the bourgeois had enough to hire others, but not to work himself.[4] Once it was placed in this position, Roemer's schema allowed for no mobility. But it was a static, one-period model; thus questions of accumulation over the life cycle, or mobility due to acquisition of skills, or even chance, could not be posed in it. Marx's notion of exploitation had already been modified, as we saw in Chapter 16. The importance of capital and time in the production of surplus-value had to be acknowledged. These were technical considerations not unknown to the original Austrian critic of Marx, Eugen von Böhm-Bawerk. But even this objection undermined Marxism's scientific aura. From the demanding standpoint of Walrasian economics, Marx's theories were found to be insufficiently general. Of course, Walrasian economics – even in its latest avatar as the Arrow–Debreu economy (Chapter 16) – was static. It did not deal with cycles, innovations, crises. It had no role for profits or accumulation. Yet for the young social scientist in the 1980s, it was Marx's failure to pass the Walras test that undermined his appeal.

If there was no definable proletariat with impeccable revolutionary credentials, the only opposition to capitalism could come from reformist socialism. Yet the 1980s showed the weakness of reformist socialism – or, rather, reconfirmed what German debates about social democracy in the decades before 1914 had already established. Reformist socialism thrives when capitalism prospers, but unfortunately, it was usually called to office only when capitalism was in trouble. As soon as problems were solved, the bourgeois parties reaped the benefits of prosperity. In the 1980s, bourgeois parties had shown much tougher attitudes to solving the structural problems of capitalism. The reformist socialists had to follow suit lest, in good times as well as bad, they were supplanted by their enemies.

Socialist parties ended the 1980s with the future of socialism very bleak. They never had a revolutionary programme, but they had now lost their coherent class support. Their preferred economic philosophy – Keynesianism – was in retreat. Welfare spending was under pressure as their following became more middle-class. Then came the fall of the Berlin Wall, and the demise of Leninist parties in Eastern Europe. The path chosen by these countries was not that of reformist socialism but that of unbridled capitalism. They saw socialism of any variety as a dead end. Rightly or wrongly, it was capitalism that was the liberating path for the Eastern Europeans.

The situation was even worse – not to say catastrophic – for many countries of the Third World during the 1980s. But it was also during this decade that differences among its members emerged. The Third World, or its organized lobbying counterpart the G-77, began to lose homogeneity. Just as some countries were abysmal failures, others emerged as successes. A new paradigm of development was about to be unleashed.

The root of the catastrophe was excessive borrowing of petrodollars. After years of being starved of financial resources by miserly governments of the OECD, the developing countries could borrow as much as they liked, and the larger the loan demanded, the quicker the response of the commercial banks. By the 1970s, the idea that such borrowing could be ill-advised was dismissed. This was the early fruit of the swing towards a faith in the markets. The IMF, which should have behaved like a world central bank, or at least monitored the effects of such large injections of bank credit, stood by silently. It had just lost any *raison d'être* with the demise of the Bretton Woods exchange rate system. It was too confused during the 1970s to reinvent itself; the 1980s gave it the platform for its rejuvenation.

The petrodollars had been borrowed at nominal interest rates of about 5 per cent (real rate being negative, around minus 10 per cent). The commodity price boom of the 1970s proved short-lived, and a long downward trend persisted throughout the 1980s. The money had been borrowed when Keynesianism, though coming under attack, still ruled the policymakers' circles. The favourite model of economic development in the 1970s was still state-led, import-substituting industrialization. The money had been borrowed to implement many schemes, some in oil exploration, with long gestation periods, low payoff and little export potential.

By the time the interest rate rise made debt repayment a problem, the intellectual climate in the policymaking circles of the IMF and some developed countries had changed. Budget deficits were thought to be bad, trade deficits were a sign of macroeconomic imbalance, and fixed exchange rates were ill-advised. The turnaround in the climate was very sudden; the counter-revolution was quick to capture policymaking circles in the IMF and the US Treasury. The confident nostrums of the 1960s and early 1970s were now targeted as the source of the problem.

The academic battle between Keynesians and monetarists was at its hottest in the US and the UK during the ten years following the oil price rise of 1973. By 1981, the Keynesians were fighting a rearguard battle. Older Keynesians refused to concede the monetarist argument. But for the younger generation of Keynesians, educated on the East and West coasts of the USA, the technical elegance of Robert Lucas was attractive. They conceded the basic truth of his theory that the economy had an equilibrium at the natural rate of unemployment. The quarrel was about whether this was a permanent situation with no short-run deviation – no gain, that is, from following old-fashioned or even newly refurbished Keynesian policies – or whether there was some slack. The argument took a technical form, with mathematical and econometric subtleties deployed by both sides. But the hegemony of Keynesian economics ended. We now had the new classical economics of Lucas confronting a new Keynesian economics which had all but signed up to the Walrasian equilibrium message. The Lucas notion of the natural rate was relabelled NAIRU (Non-Accelerating Inflation Rate of Unemployment) to save the honour of the New Keynesians.

There had, of course, been disagreement among Keynesians before this battle commenced. Many left Keynesians in Cambridge (UK) and elsewhere denounced the Americans' 1960s theories as bastard Keynesianism. The post-Keynesians had textual and hermeneutic disagreements with all other schools of Keynesianism. They had always labelled the official Keynesian policies as more or less neoclassical. When they were outflanked on their right, the Keynesians – neo-, left and post – were stranded.

In the developing countries, there had been a long-held argument that Keynesian theories were not applicable. All varieties of neoclassical economics were suspect as slavishly following market principles. Third World economists saw market failures everywhere, and the need for comprehensive state intervention. Where the neoclassical and even neo-Keynesian economists talked of competitive markets, the Third World economists found oligopolies and cartels.

They concocted a mixture of Soviet planning, Listian protectionism and structural theories of macroeconomic rigidities.

But their countries suddenly faced large trade deficits, big debt repayment bills, and an acute shortage of foreign exchange. Mexico, a leading example of the policy of state-led import-substitution industrialization, was the first to announce its inability to pay its debt in 1982. Many other indebted countries had the same problem. Could countries go bankrupt, and could they undermine the solvency of their lenders? There was much talk of the crisis of capitalism that summer. Keynes was quoted by some as saying that when you owe your bank a thousand pounds, you spend sleepless nights, but if you owe a million, your banker does.

This gallows humour was misplaced. The IMF took charge of the debt-ridden countries, which had to seek IMF assistance in meeting their shortage of foreign exchange. This was why Keynes had given the IMF powers of short-term lending. Granting loans, he had argued, would obviate any need to deflate. But that was in 1944; now it was 1982, and Keynes was deader than ever before. The IMF insisted on severe deflation, on the prompt cutting of budget deficits, on devaluation of fixed exchange rates and control of the money supply. Instead of allowing controls on imports, or even temporary tariffs, borrowing countries had to remove protection and liberalize imports. They had to abandon import substitution and adopt export-expanding policies.

The IMF's pretensions to omniscience would have been farcical if their consequences had not been so tragic. Every economy, regardless of its history, geography or culture, was reduced to an Identikit model of two or three equations. There was the demand-for-money equation, an equation for inflation and output (the Phillips Curve), and maybe – just maybe – an exchange rate equation. Every country was supposed to have an equilibrium (Lucas had said so) at some level of output where its inflation would be eliminated and its trade deficit would disappear. Such an equilibrium might be at a level of national income half of what prevailed, but no matter. There had to be some zero-inflation equilibrium. The IMF advised the debtor countries how to achieve this.

A curious but unhappy development aided the IMF. In one way it was progress of a kind, but its effects were damaging. The explosion in the number of new territorial states which had emerged after decolonization was a phenomenon of the 1960s. New countries had to have their paraphernalia of statehood – their own currency, their own central bank, their own airline. They also now had their national income measured by dedicated economic statisticians trained by the UN or in Western universities. These income numbers were seemingly scientific, but often left out large swathes of the traditional economies. At best, they tried to grapple with valuing activities in the countryside and among pastoralists, as well as in urban informal sectors. At worst, these were ignored, and only formal urban activities were captured. Money supply was measured often with IMF help, and again bore little relation to many economic activities.

Yet there were numbers to fit new econometric models. The IMF had to have 'estimates' of demand for money equations, and it got them. Thus there was some distorted map of the economy which was now to serve as a device for its control. An automobile dashboard of controls was fitted to a bullock cart, and everyone pretended they knew how to steer this new vehicle. The results were disastrous.

Throughout the 1980s, country after country had signed a 'letter of intent', in fact promising the IMF that it would reform its economy so that it would not need the IMF's loans. These letters had, of course, been dictated by IMF advisers. These countries had to cut their budget deficits, to liberate their foreign exchange rate to boost their exports, to cut their tariffs. The incidence of cuts in budget deficits fell on the poor, naturally, because the ruling elites who had borrowed the petrodollars (and in many cases salted them away as private fortunes in Switzerland) were not about to suffer hardship. Their armies continued to be favoured, but food subsidies were abolished as inefficient. The meagre amount spent on public education and health was cut. The IMF, of course, had to respect the sovereignty of these countries. All it cared about was that the deficit should be cut; it could not possibly suggest that such cuts should be progressive, or protective of the poor.

The exhortation to increase exports performed worse. Many of the debtor countries, especially in Sub-Saharan Africa, were single-commodity exporters. Taken in isolation, each could be advised that 'given' a 'world demand curve' for its exports, the income and price elasticities could be estimated. These in turn could be used to work out the price reduction via devaluation plus cost-cutting, which would be sufficient to boost exports. But of course, taken together, these exporting countries could not all increase their exports by cutting their prices. They were competing against each other. The world demand curve was not 'given' in any sense. The IMF, looking at the problem in its totality, should have been able to see that. But it didn't. Its economics was naive, and in any case, the 'country desks' were separately run.

These Structural Adjustment Programmes (SAPs) became hate objects throughout the indebted countries. Most indebted countries had negative income growth and, despite that, rampant inflation due to devaluation. There was real suffering among the population of these largely poor countries. Getting away from national income statistics, the misery was reflected in infant mortality and life-expectancy calculations. These, though imperfectly measured, related to real events, not virtual entities. With progress in public health, infant mortality had been declining and life expectancy rising during the previous two decades. Now this progress was halted, if not reversed. These numbers were not part of the IMF's measure of the effectiveness of its policy. They were not macroeconomic numbers, which was all that the IMF cared about.[5]

Thus, for many developing countries, their first experience of integration into the world of international bank lending and finance after independence turned tragic very suddenly. The bulk of the debt was, however, owed by Latin American countries which were neither newly independent nor among the poorest in terms of *per capita* income. Their predicament was largely self-inflicted, since they used the borrowed money in public-sector projects with low yields and little export potential. As they passed the costs of SAPs on to their poor people, it became clear that the problem was as much in their unequal structures of wealth and political power as their economic policies. While their elites could blame the IMF, they had to counter the criticism that the governments they ran were not democratically accountable, nor pursuing policies which tackled poverty.

By contrast, there were some real success stories among the developing countries. It was in Asia that this new paradigm of development was discovered. The Asian Tigers – South Korea, Taiwan, Singapore and Hong Kong – emerged in the 1980s as economies with fast income growth and healthy exports of manufactures. They also had high levels of education and health, with a good balance between rural and urban sectors. Their income and wealth distributions displayed low inequality. How had they done this? Could their experience be emulated?

The four Asian Tigers were soon joined by the other Asian countries – Malaysia, Indonesia, Thailand and, to a lesser extent, the Philippines. They had rejected the import-substitution autarkic model. They were export-orientated. Their manufacturing sectors were not state-owned, but private. Yet the state played a major role in promoting export efficiency. The ideal model for the East Asians was not the USSR but Japan. In postwar Japan, there had been a single-minded pursuit of national economic prosperity by a coalition of interests: government, corporations and banks. The banks mobilized the savings of a frugal population at low interest rates. These funds were channelled to those corporations which the government assigned to pursue export growth in specific sectors – steel, cars, radio/TV, computers. This was an ideal corporatist state, with a single-minded purpose of economic growth.

The Asian Tigers copied this model. South Korea and Taiwan had also undertaken radical land reforms in the 1950s, and this had reduced wealth inequalities in the countryside. They had provided free education, achieving total literacy. Their healthcare systems were also better than those in many developing countries. They built their manufacturing industries by carefully chosen subsidies which directed products to exports. This automatically ensured that the quality of their products had to be such that they could compete in world markets. Corporatist collusion was the key to the success of the Asian Tigers.

The paradox of the Asian Tigers was that they had successful economies in the dual sense of good market performance and a high level of well-being, despite authoritarian political structures. While Brazil had achieved high growth rates under authoritarian governments in the 1960s and 1970s, it had neglected equity and popular well-being. Mexico had a one-party democracy which had experimented with public-sector corporatism, but failed to benefit the ordinary people. In India, there was democracy with a weak corporatist mix of public and private sector, orientated to the domestic sector but failing in growth or equity stakes. South Korea and Taiwan, with Singapore and Hong Kong, had found the one justification for authoritarian rule – an ability to be responsive to the poor.

The success of the Asian Tigers was claimed as a vindication of their philosophy by all sides in the ideological battle. Those who favoured open economy and private ownership hailed the miracle (as Milton Friedman did) for its avoidance of state ownership and hostility to foreign trade. Those who favoured state control of the economy over the market celebrated the Tigers' ability 'to govern the market'.[6] The many voices which had been complaining since the beginning of the 1960s that economic growth did not lead to poverty reduction were happy about the equity and well-being achieved. Many of the leaders of those countries, particularly Lee Kuan Yew of Singapore, found in their success a riposte to Western democratic decadence. Here were Asian values of thrift, hard work and discipline, with a firm authoritarian guiding force, as the key to success.

Corporatism of the sort practised by Japan and the Asian Tigers, with collusion between politics, industry and finance, had been tried in the interwar period as an alternative to the liberal economic and political order. Its association with

Nazism discredited it but, as I have emphasized, the innovation of planning in a capitalist economy with a mixture of public and private enterprise was undoubtedly the achievement of National Socialism. It should be dissociated from the destructive anti-Semitism that the Nazis practised. Its problems lay elsewhere – its lack of democracy, its selective protectionism from international competition (compare Japan, with its import restrictions), and its fostering of cartels in domestic production. There was a consequent sacrifice of consumption standards. In the Asian countries there is an accepted tradition of high savings which helps to sustain the underconsumptionist strategy of export promotion. Yet it is a moot point as to how far these savings propensities are truly voluntary, and how far they are due to the control mechanisms.

The test of the national corporatist model was to come in the 1990s, but that was still in the future. By the end of the 1980s, there was a convergence of views that the new development paradigm was embedded in Asian experience. On the one hand, it showed that sustained and rapid growth was possible within a capitalist context – that is, without taking the path that Paul Baran had thought was the only escape from backwardness: the path of Socialist Revolution that Cuba had taken. This path could be combined with equity, and high levels of education and health. The United Nations Development Programme (UNDP) labelled this mix the Human Development Paradigm. It was market-friendly but pro-poor; it welcomed the open economy orientation but celebrated the positive role of the state. It valued economic growth as much as health and education.

The new classical economists concurred. Robert Lucas and Paul Roemer formulated the New Endogenous Growth Theory.[7] The neoclassical growth model formulated in the mid-1950s by Nobel Prize-winner Robert Solow had shown how accumulation of capital led to higher output, yet as capital per worker rose, the extra input would be smaller. If this was so, rich countries with a high capital output ratio should grow more slowly than poor countries. This was an equalizing result. The experience of forty years of postwar economic growth was that no such equalizing was taking place – or certainly not at any noticeable speed. What was the explanation?

The Lucas–Roemer model emphasized the increasing returns to education and knowledge, which led to innovation and improvements in technology. As each new innovation lifted the production function, returns to higher capital per worker did not diminish, but were enhanced. This insight shifted attention from fixed capital to human capital, from hardware to software, from steel factories to schools. In a rare example of prescience, it anticipated the knowledge economy of the subsequent decade.

But the next decade was going to see more than just the knowledge economy. It was to see a rejuvenation of global capitalism not seen since 1914. It was to see the death of Bolshevism and the return to the world of *The Communist Manifesto.*

18
A Bonfire of Illusions

What happened in the decade following 1989, the bicentenary of the French Revolution and the centenary of the Socialist International, was most unexpected. The massive structures of Socialism outside Capitalism (SoC), the entire edifice of the Leninist state and its extension across Eurasia from the Elbe to the Pacific – the USSR, along with its Eastern European satellites – collapsed.[1] There had certainly been trouble brewing. There were dissident movements in East Germany, Poland, Hungary and Czechoslovakia. But there had been such dissidence before, and the Soviet Union had crushed it all in 1953, in 1956 and in 1968. There had even been occasional opposition inside the Soviet Union, which had led to the exile of leading troublemakers such as Nathan Sharansky.

No one, but no one, forecast the collapse of the Soviet system. There are multiple explanations, *ex post facto,* why it was inevitable. But all the social scientists, and all the Kremlinologists, and all those who thought it was the Evil Empire, failed to see that, as in the case of Dorothy, the fear of the mighty Wizard of Oz was much exaggerated. It was a ramshackle outfit kept alive more by the respect of its enemies than by any real material power.

The boast of socialism is that it is superior to capitalism. As far as Socialism within Capitalism is concerned, it had steadily lost the argument in the area of relative efficiency of production, and the boast had narrowed down to the claim that it was in distribution of the fruits of production that socialism could improve upon capitalism. The superiority of nationalized industries, of public ownership of the commanding heights, was harder to claim. But the Leninist alternative, SoC, claimed much more. Socialism was to be superior to capitalism in production and in distribution. The only ground left for dispute was about negative freedoms of political and civil liberties as against positive freedoms of economic and social rights.

Throughout the 1960s and 1970s, it was capitalism that had faced massive changes in its own back yard. The struggle for equality had shifted its focus away from economic (income and wealth) equality to social equality, equality of status for women, for Blacks, for native people, for the disabled. To this had been added an awareness in the West of the continuing struggle of colonial and ex-colonial peoples against repression from their local elites, often in cahoots with Western governments. Thus, Vietnam, South Africa, Nicaragua, Chile became rallying cries for protest movements in the West. Many of these struggles, especially the women's movement,[2] took place outside the classic Right/Left political party framework. The SwC parties were sometimes in support, but as often as not they were in office, and therefore ambivalent (e.g. the Labour government in the UK about the Vietnam War).

At the same time – with the economic crisis in the West, with rising unemployment and high inflation – the economic superiority of capitalism was being questioned. The SwC parties had to struggle with these problems, and often ended up adopting a conservative economic agenda (France under Mitterrand, for example). It seemed to many that oppressive as they were politically, the socialist countries were free of these economic problems. The deep economic crisis that SoC economies were going through, in the 1980s especially, was hidden from public view. The high price of oil had allowed the Soviet Union, as a major oil producer, some breathing space. It was able to relax political repression at home, and even allowed a reverse surplus flow in its trading relations with its satellite economies. This is why the outlook for the Solidarity movement in Poland was better than for similar protests in the 1950s and 1960s. Even as General Jaruzelski maintained a political grip on power, the economic bargain with the workers was not driven very hard. The Soviet system had come some distance from the worst excesses of Stalinism.

Just over a decade later, this may seem an exaggeration. In the West, socialists had long turned away from Stalinism. They had read about the Gulag. Membership of the orthodox Stalinist Communist parties had dwindled. There was Eurocommunism, a fashionable reworking of the Old Communist themes. The Italian Communist Party, the largest in Western Europe, had come to terms with power-sharing with 'bourgeois' parties. In the developing countries, however, communism still retained its appeal. China, despite its market deviations, remained a one-party Leninist state. But in South Asia, Africa and Latin America, the Soviet experiment had its champions. Rejection of the market and of private property in the means of production was attractive to many Third World leaders who wanted accelerated growth. The appeal of Cuba, Vietnam – even Ethiopia – was potent.

There was a revival of the debate on the feasibility of market socialism which consciously went back to the earlier debate in the 1930s (see Chapter 12).[3] But this time there was a more sophisticated appreciation of this Walrasian system.

The new debate could also draw on the experience of the socialist experiment in the USSR and Eastern Europe. There had been some relaxation in the direction of market calculation in Hungary after 1968, and in Poland during the 1980s. Around that time, in 1989–91, there was even some hope that the centrally planned economies could make a smooth transition to a market socialist arrangement rather than a fully fledged capitalist one.

In this phase of the debate, the starting point was the Lange solution. Thus the idea of replacing the market by having 'calculation in kind' – Otto Neurath's idea – was abandoned. There would be prices, there would be consumer choice as well as freedom in the labour market. The one way in which market socialism was to be different from capitalism was that investment decisions would not be left to private profit calculation. Thus capital was to be owned by the public via vouchers, but these vouchers were not meant to be tradeable. The central defect of capitalism in this view is that private investment is driven by the expectations of future profitability in an irrational manner. This is much as Keynes had argued in the *General Theory*. The answer, then, was to socialize investment decisions, but to avoid state ownership by vesting the ownership of capital among all the citizens. Given such widespread ownership, profits can be distributed equally.

This new model of market socialism thus concentrates on avoiding cyclical instability, and minimizing income and wealth inequality. The Hayek problem of motivating managers to be efficient remains, of course. But there is also the Schumpeterian problem of innovation. Those who take risks and innovate expect large rewards. As Adam Smith had argued two hundred years previously, inequality is the spur to the growth of productivity. There is also the possibility of acquiring a large amount of wealth by buying and selling claims on already existing capital, that is, equity. While the stock market has a tendency to be volatile, it also acts as a discipline, however imperfect, on managers who cannot maximize the net worth of their firms.

The new market socialists were ready to design ingenious schemes for monitoring managerial performance, but they all involved supervision of one type or another rather than the carrot of enrichment, or the stick of bankruptcy or takeover. Given that their model capital economy was Walrasian, risk or uncertainty, and dynamic disequilibrium of growth and cycles, had no place in their schemes. Yet capitalism does not work to a Walrasian scheme. It works via instability and cycles, inequality of wealth and income. It is not possible, outside mathematical models, to reconcile productivity growth with restrictions on wealth accumulation. The new models remain more in the realm of mathematical socialism than anything else.

Yet there was a general desire to avoid both the worst aspects of Soviet-type central planning, and the boom and bust of capitalism. Somehow, capital had to be tamed and labour empowered. This was the utopia whose blueprints were prepared in the course of this new debate.

There was even a living example of this utopia: Yugoslavia was the model economy. It had workers' ownership rather than state ownership. It had planning, but with a large degree of provincial autonomy in a federal system. Market calculation was not ruled out. Yugoslavia seemed to be a human version of the Soviet Union, and a workers' paradise compared to Western capitalism. It was a middle-income country, not a poor one like Cuba.

The idea of a labour-managed economy proved very attractive to some economists. Workers could own their firms, and hire and fire managers.[4] Thus, there is an ironic symmetry to the capitalist hiring and firing workers. Instead of all citizens owning vouchers or coupons, as in the new schemes of market socialism, it is the workers who own, but they own only the firm in which they work, and draw its profits as part of their income. Besides Yugoslav firms, there are also co-operatives in Spain (Mondragon) and in France or Belgium, where similar arrangements prevail.

In theory, labour-managed firms can work as well as shareholder-owned firms. In either case, the managers are hired and can be asked to maximize net worth. This leaves out the problem of innovation, which is a major flaw. But even ignoring that, there are problems if the firms' equity is tradeable. When a worker quits a firm, he is obliged to sell his shares in it, but he cannot sell to an outsider. If the market is confined to his erstwhile fellow-workers, they have every incentive to give him a low price. Similarly, a newly hired worker immediately gets all the equity built up by workers who have been in the firm for many years. And, of course, the last thing such a labour-managed firm would be able to do is to restructure by reducing the labour force if that proved necessary for survival.

No doubt there are many inequities within capitalism. Alternatives can be devised which, in theory, avoid its disadvantages. But the advantages of capitalism – its wealth-producing ability, its dynamism and innovativeness – are dialectically connected to its disadvantages. Outside mathematical models, it is difficult to separate the two. But even in the capitalist mode, there is a wide diversity of outcomes ranging from egalitarian Scandinavian economies to grossly unequal Latin American ones. Thus inequalities of income and wealth can be mitigated or exacerbated, and often the causal variables may not be central to the dynamics of capitalism. An inequality of wealth which is a result of innovative, risk-taking activity is much less of a problem than one that is due to entrenched semi-feudal inequalities of landownership, or elite control of political power and rent-seeking. This is probably why Eastern Europe chose the unstable prospect of capitalism to the experience of Stalinism or the utopia of market socialism.

On the Leninist Left, there was always a hope that the distorted Revolution in Russia would be subverted from within by the working class. Since Stalinism had betrayed the Leninist legacy, and duped the heroic working class of Russia (so the analysis went), the next step would be a regaining of power by the workers. They would smash the state capitalist system, and establish a genuine revolutionary socialism. By now, despite all the distortions, enough capital accumulation would have taken place. So the workers would be taking over a somewhat mature (state) capitalist machine.

The Berlin Wall did not collapse. It was destroyed piece by piece by East and West Germans. Gorbachev's decision not to enforce Soviet hegemony in Eastern Europe was as radical as decolonization. He had seen that the Soviet Union needed fundamental reform. In the political sphere this meant greater openness, though not yet multiparty democracy. It meant a tolerance of dissent: glasnost. But it also required a restructuring of the economy: perestroika. He had no clear answer in that respect. He knew he had to give enterprises greater autonomy, but he did not grasp the importance of clarifying property rights. The enterprises, though state-owned, stopped paying back their profits. There was no corporate tax. The fiscal system collapsed.

Between 1989 and 1991, much more was lost than just the Soviet hegemony over Eastern Europe and Eurasia. The complete death of the Soviet Union was as remarkable as the end of the *ancien régime* in France.[5] It left no scope for recovery for Russia as a market socialist economy, or rejuvenation as a revolutionary socialist one. There was no future left for Bolshevism. It turned out to have a finite life after all, like many organisms, except that it was a short one in the life-scale of political ideologies. In one sense it was not so much the 'End of History' as the End of Hope. Socialism has always been based on a hope that the future will be better than the present. It is a doctrine of optimism. Its eclipse is the End of Hope.

In its wake, the Soviet Union also damaged the prospects of its other – SwC, the reformist socialist alternative. Although their relations were antagonistic, both alternatives shared a socialist dream that life could be better than what capitalism had to offer; that it was by regulation, control – and, indeed, abolition of private property – that the next stage of human history would be defined. In rejecting Leninist authoritarianism and collectivization, SwC had made its provisional peace with capitalism. But it meant eventually to tame capitalism into a better system: by a steady expansion of the sphere of public consumption; by demonstrating the superiority of public over private ownership; by running the economy for use, not for profit; by catering better to the needs of the many rather than the greed of the few.

The death of the Soviet Union made the claims of reformist socialism untenable. It is not fair, of course. No controlled experiment had been conducted to prove that reformist socialism could not work. Even the record of nationalized industries in the UK was being defended late into the 1980s. Yet suddenly, the idea that the state could run the economy better by planning and/or public ownership began to lose its appeal. Even the Scandinavian countries discovered that their achievement of a high-tax-financed welfare capitalism had to be rethought, because their capitalists could invest abroad rather than pay tax or buy government debt. An ideological tidal wave hit and swept away the sandcastles of socialism in its existing variants. For the generation born in the 1970s and after, it seemed inexplicable that anyone thought socialism could work. I should know – my teenage children told me so in the early 1990s.

The ideological tidal wave was, of course, a revival of liberal ideology. It is – wrongly, in my view – called neoliberal. What is called neoliberalism is often attributed to the international financial institutions – the IMF, the World Bank. Multinational corporations are also tarred with the same brush. But there is a need to distinguish between mere conservatism and liberalism. The former retains a large role for the state in helping capitalists via tax holidays and subsidies, union-busting and even protectionism. Incidentally, it is also militarily aggressive, though that may be an accident of the Cold War. Fiscal conservatism and an anti-inflationary monetary policy ruled the roost in a neoliberal programme, but they still put the state at the helm of the economy. Monetarism, the first avatar of neoliberalism, celebrates government control (via the central bank) of the money supply. Ronald Reagan was a fiscal conservative in words, but a wild spender of public money in fact. Margaret Thatcher did more to centralize economic power than any of her predecessors. Even she chose to sell public assets to private monopolies rather than to unleash the forces of competition.

But such neoliberalism was midwife to the much more deep-seated change which came in its wake: the revival of nineteenth-century liberal beliefs. They are now labelled libertarian, but they are basically the set of ideas that all nineteenth-century thinking – Left and Right – espoused. The basic notion is civil society (the market, as well as larger society) as an organic process which is a result of human action, but not of human design. Thus, no one single agency, or even a handful of conspiring institutions, is responsible for the course of events which unfolds every day. Marx does not blame monopoly capitalists; he talks of class monopoly of ownership. Even capitalists only seek to make profit and accumulate. They do not control the market, nor can they overcome competition. Indeed, competition is not understood, as in neoclassical economics, as a game of numbers of firms producing an identical product and earning zero profits. The firms can be few or many, large or small. They may try to control the market by patents, cartel agreements, price-fixing. But eventually there will be substitutes and innovations and rival products. A giant corporation like IBM can be undermined by an innovating minnow such as Microsoft which, in its turn, can become a giant corporation. In its own turn, Microsoft, or any of the other giants, will be undermined by the constant search for profits, by innovation, by the gale of creative destruction. By the same token, the state is not seen as being able to control the economy, or even to be an agent that should interfere with the economy. If neoliberalism is a conservative version of the twentieth century's love of the state, libertarianism is its nineteenth-century radical cousin.[6]

The revival of this liberal ideology – of libertarianism – has, of course, a material base. The crucial role played by the neoliberal ideology was in deregulating capital movements. As I have already shown, this was an endogenous response to the decline of profitability. But as in many other things, there were larger, unforeseen as much as unintended consequences of this policy move. As the UK followed the US lead in deregulating capital movements as well as plumping for a floating rather than a fixed exchange rate, a basic building block for the state's control over the economy was removed. It is not that the state is not still very powerful. It retains control over its currency (no Gold Standard, as there was in the nineteenth century), over public taxation and expenditure and, of course, over entry/immigration into its territory (no freedom of movement for labour, as there was in the nineteenth century).

Yet the state does not control the economy, as it used to in the halcyon quarter-century of the Golden Age of capitalism. It controls the public purse, but is constrained in its ability to run large deficits. Much more significantly, there is no longer any belief that such deficits can achieve full employment. The state holds the monopoly over its currency, but again, it is conscious that the consequences of monetary mismanagement are severe. A deregulated global capital market limits the extent to which the interest rate within a country can diverge from the interest rate at which other countries borrow. If the exchange rate is flexible, there are immediate movements to offset any possible gains from monetary indulgence. If it is fixed, the country will lose reserves defending its parity.

This downsizing of the powers of the state in controlling the economy had profound consequences for a certain model of national capitalism. Japan had built itself up by state guidance of the elite corporations, with the help of banks mobilizing savings to finance the industrial expansion. Once it became possible to invest abroad as well as at home, Japanese banks took to exporting their capital. Even Japanese corporations like Sony diversified out of manufacturing, and got into media and entertainment companies in the USA. The cohesion of the old policy was soon lost. Japan discovered that neither its banks nor its companies could operate abroad efficiently and compete outside the narrow lines laid down by the old strategy. A long recession gripped Japan in the 1990s which shows no signs of ending because the powers that be are unable and unwilling to restructure the economy drastically, as Margaret Thatcher or Ronald Reagan dared to do.

A similar crisis hit South Korea, a miracle economy of the 1970s and 1980s. The challenge of liberalizing its capital markets and opening its economy to foreign competition exposed the fragility of the structures painstakingly built up with the tripartite collaboration of banks, corporations and the state. Unlike Japan, South Korea has embraced political change as well as economic change, and it has embarked on a painful restructuring under the regime of a President who has come from outside the old political elites. But the state, which was so powerful in shaping the economy in the national capitalist or Leninist versions, had now been assigned the difficult task of undoing its achievements and adapting to the market.[7]

Globalization, as this phase has come to be known, is a combination of deregulated capital movements, advances in information/communication/ transport technologies, and a shift in the ideology away from social democracy and statism towards neoliberalism and libertarianism.[8] All three aspects appeared in the 1970s after the breakdown of Bretton Woods and the OPEC oil crisis, and they gathered pace in parallel, eventually reinforcing each other throughout the 1980s and 1990s. Keynesianism was the first to lose the battle as a dominant economic ideology.[9] State intervention in the economy was on the retreat in the 1980s, as deregulation and privatization began to be tried as innovative alternatives. Although these trends originated in the USA and the UK in the 1980s, other developed economies began to come on board in the early 1990s. The transition economies of Eastern Europe joined in this abandonment of state ownership at the same time. By the late 1990s, even developing countries had embraced the doctrine of deregulation and privatization.

This change is still going on. Even now, the pace is different in different countries. France is a reluctant liberalizer compared to the UK, but Germany and Italy are accelerating their pace. India held out against liberal economic reforms for a long time, but by the end of the 1990s it had seen the wisdom of the policy change.[10] Everywhere policymakers began to repeat that governments do not create jobs, do not bring about economic expansion, merely provide the conditions for the private sector to accomplish job creation and income growth.

There was also a change in attitudes to foreign capital. The presence of foreign companies was not welcome even in developed countries, especially if they were not 'cousins' from across the Atlantic. As recently as the early 1990s, the incursion of Japanese cars and television sets invited resentful comments from some British trade-union leaders. British jobs, it was thought, could be generated only by British-owned capital. Americans were shocked by the Japanese invasion of Hollywood and buying up of the Rockefeller Center. But soon these attitudes changed. Governments, even governments of rich countries, realized that one of their tasks was to attract foreign capital to equip labour to perform productive, high-value-added tasks. One corollary of this was that the new technology needed skilled, educated workers. Education became a much-publicized responsibility of governments. Capital and labour were not antagonistic in this new paradigm. Even SwC governments (or their American counterparts, Clinton Democrats) saw that an active government policy had to perform these new tasks – attracting capital and educating workers by training and reskilling.

One consequence of this new phase is that the state no longer controls the economy, but is one player (a major one, of course) among many. The state has to adapt and adjust to forces which it cannot control but must respond to. While the dominant analogy in economics in the 1950s and 1960s was of a car driving down a turnpike (maximal growth being achieved), or of a jet taking off (development), the present world is more analogous to sailing a ship on high seas. The ship has some machinery for control, but in navigating it, the captain does not control the waves or the wind. These forces can be studied, but they cannot be controlled. The captain who ignores or defies these forces may well run the ship aground, and sink altogether.

Economies did crash in just such a manner. France in the early 1980s ran aground, and had to change course. Peru under Alan García crashed because of reckless overspending. Many developing countries are still left holding the unproductive assets built up in the days when such considerations as competition or markets were neglected. India had to change its state-orientated economic policy in the early 1990s.

Even so, old attitudes and outmoded habits of thought persist. This is most clearly seen in the financial markets. There has been a tremendous expansion in the volume of transactions on these markets, and this has raised concern about the volatility of prices – interest rates, share prices, exchange rates. Even George Soros, best known for his bold speculation about the pound sterling's exit from the ERM in September 1992, is now on record deploring excess volatility.

Cycles, with their manias, crashes and panics, are endemic to capitalism.[11] This is especially the case now, where there is unregulated capital movement, as in the nineteenth century. In the heyday of Keynesianism, with restrictions on capital movements, cycles remained shallow and infrequent. Indeed, by the late 1960s economists were asking whether the business cycle was obsolete. But from the early 1970s onwards, some severe recessions began to occur. Even then, the full-scale cycle with a financial crisis came in 1997 with the Asian currency upheaval. This was a global crisis, since it spread from Asia to Russia to the USA, and on to Brazil. Yet like all cycles in the previous phase of globalization, there was a recovery, but more rapid than in the nineteenth century: within two years. The Mexican peso crisis of December 1994 was localized, but even that proved short and sharp, with recovery within eighteen months.

There will be more such cycles, more financial crises, crashes of stock-market prices. But they are unlikely to be like the Great Depression of 1931. That was a rare and unique experience in which an agricultural oversupply (thanks to Soviet collectivization and dumping by Russian farmers) played a significant part. The inexperience of the US central bankers in running the international Gold Standard caused a liquidity crunch. Today, this is unlikely. Indeed, it was the US decision to lower interest rates in quick succession in September–October 1998 that brought the world economy out of the Asian crisis.

There are three competing visions of the global financial market.[12] The first is a classical liberal/Marxian view: cycles are endemic to capitalism, but they are also self-correcting and self-sustaining. In such a world, there is no need for overarching governance of the market. Marx subscribes to this theory, though he also emphasizes the self-destructive capacity of the system. Modern liberals, such as Hayek and the neo-Austrians, highlight the spontaneity of the underlying order.[13]

A diametrically opposite view is that the market is subject to frequent failure, and may crash if it is not governed properly. Memories of the Great Depression colour this view. The answer is a New Deal such as Roosevelt conducted. If the market is now global, one needs a global governing order, a World Financial Authority. Of course, since the interstate system is hierarchical, any such governing order will be democratic only if things go incredibly better than they have for the last hundred years. But the vision of a dysfunctional market is central here. Polanyi is the spirit behind this vision.

In the middle is a vision which asserts that the system is normally, and usually, self-regulating but has an occasional tendency to go haywire. This requires a light touch on the rudder, a correction flowing with rather than against the tide. The action of the US Federal Bank in the autumn of 1998 was an example of such effective intervention. Central banking was, after all, invented during the liberal heyday of the nineteenth century in England for just such purposes. The person most associated with such a vision would be Keynes. Unlike many Keynesians, he was a liberal who believed that the market should be allowed to work as far as possible, with an occasional corrective. Hegel, with his critique of the civil society, would be another.

These three visions – Marx/Hayek, Polanyi and Keynes/Hegel – span all the possible views one can have of the workings of the capitalist system. There is no reason to believe that any one is the correct one. Indeed, capitalism may mostly be in the Marx/Hayek mould, but may occasionally slip into the Keynes/Hegel deviation. Rarely has it reached the depths that Polanyi feared for it. After all, the boast of Talleyrand after the French Revolution could be echoed by capitalism: 'I survived'.

19

The Future of Capitalism II: Endgame or the Only Game?

Capitalism survived the twentieth century. Indeed, it did not just survive; it triumphed over the major challenges posed to it: fascism and Leninism. It has eliminated Socialism outside Capitalism as a serious prospect. Socialism within Capitalism is still around, but it is a pale shadow of its former self. It may be argued that SwC is dormant because it has achieved most of its aims. This could have been argued in the 1960s (the Crosland idea), or even in the 1970s, when SwC came once again to manage the latest crisis of capitalism. But not only did it botch the job, but in conceding the democratic victory to neoliberal governments (Thatcher, Reagan, Kohl), or even apeing their methods (Mitterrand after 1983; the British Labour Party after 1994), it has conceded intellectual supremacy to its enemies. What is more, its gains which seemed so solid in the 1970s – full employment, the welfare state, state control of industries and public utilities – have been eroded.

Capitalism has not just survived; it has been rejuvenated, and shows no prospect of imminent collapse, or even ageing. This is the totally unpredictable outcome of the twentieth century. It is still unbelieved in many circles. Many point to the injustices, inequities and costs of the new dispensation. Others wish for a return to the heyday of Keynesianism. Indeed, Keynesian policies have become the sole aim of those who still champion the older version of SwC. Commentators extol German or Japanese corporatism in contrast to the Anglo-Saxon system, where corporate ownership is both contestable and frequently contested. Labour markets with strong union entrenchment in bargaining and recruitment are praised, as against the flexible options of the USA and the UK. The size of the fiscal take, the solidity of the safety net, the degree of insularity against foreign trade and foreign capital, have all become indicators of the alternatives to capitalism.

Yet they are all only different versions of capitalism. There is no rival mode of production on the horizon as a viable alternative. Capitalism is the only game in town. The contest is between rival versions: Anglo-Saxon versus Continental-Japanese.[1] The forces of free movement of capital liberalization of financial markets, the new technology of transport, information transmission and communication appear, at least for the present, to favour the Anglo-Saxon model. This is because in terms of profitability – the sure and only test of capitalism's success – the Anglo-Saxon economies fared better in the first full decade of globalization – the 1990s – than the corporatist economies. Profits have been increasing; what is more, despite earlier gloomy predictions about 'The End of Work', high levels of employment prevailed in the Anglo-Saxon economies, in contrast to the Continental European ones. In terms of GDP growth and growth of earnings, things have been looking up.

As I have argued in previous chapters, much of the intellectual thinking about the economy and society during the twentieth century was predicated upon the prospect of capitalism being enfeebled, if not dead. All social science became 'statist', with the state being in control of the economy and the principal actor in alleviation of social problems. The idea that instead of that kind of world, we are faced with a capitalism that is unlikely to go away and, indeed, dictates the pace of change to which individual states have to adapt, has unhinged and confused many. There is denial, of course. Globalization has not happened, is nothing new, or is a mislabelling of internationalization – all these assertions have been forcefully made.[2] The state, it is passionately argued, is not powerless in the face of globalization. The market shall not triumph; it shall be a servant, not a master, is how the French Socialist Prime Minister Lionel Jospin described his position. Polanyi's powerful critique of the market as an impossible, destructive, dysfunctional dystopia has been revived partly in the (fearful) hope that globalization may (will?) self-destruct.

There are also triumphalist accounts of globalization. A world without borders, the End of History, untold prosperity for everyone, with democracy in every country and a VCR in every home, have been forecast.

What is missing in these analyses is the notion of dialectical contradictions of the mode of production that is capitalism. Capitalism is a profit-driven system of accumulation and incessant search for new technologies to increase productivity. As such it is prone to cycles, crashes and panics. It is the best arrangement for the alleviation of poverty and misery, even as it destroys jobs and restructures economies. The global financial markets act as a powerful discipline on individual states, yet are themselves volatile and highly fragile. As in previous revolutionary phases – the first Industrial Revolution of the late eighteenth century, or the second one of the late nineteenth century – inequalities increase markedly as old industries and employment wither, and new technologies and skills come into prominence.[3]

Yet the previous Industrial Revolutions largely affected Northwest Europe and the USA. They impacted on the rest of the world via imperialism, and hence largely in a negative way – destruction of old modes without construction of a new one. This phase, however, is truly global. The influence of capital – either as portfolio finance or as direct investment – the hegemony of financial markets, the increasing penetration of trade, have been experienced by all the worlds: First, Second and Third. Indeed, this numerical categorization is now otiose. The benefits and costs of capitalism fall symmetrically – though not equally – on all parts of the world. For the first time in two hundred years, the cradle of capitalism – the metropolis, the core – has as much to fear from the rapidity of change as does the periphery.

This is why, in the crowds demonstrating outside the WTO conference in Seattle in November 1999, there were more unionized workers belonging to the AFL–CLO demanding protectionism for their high-earning jobs than there were people concerned with environmental or redistributional issues.[4] By depicting free trade as the common enemy, the prosperous citizens of the advanced capitalist countries can have their cake and eat it too. After all, the cake would be whisked away to other countries with lower-paid workers by free trade.

But there is also a genuine coalition of interests – of poor and rich countries, as well as people who have shown their anger against globalization in varied locations: Seattle, Washington DC, Davos, Prague, or wherever the IMF/World Bank/WTO/G-7 meet. To understand the logic as well as the illogicalities of these concerns, it is necessary to see the present phase of capitalism as an outcome of recent historical processes. This is because globalization has hardly begun. It is in some sense only as old as the new century, which began at the end of the 'short twentieth century' in 1989. The logic of the post-1945 global order, symbolized by the IMF/World Bank, is in contradiction with the market-led logic of this new phase of capitalism. It is for this reason that we have to retrace our steps once more, but for the last time, and go back to Marx as well as recent history.

Capitalism in a Long Perspective

The advent of the twenty-first century is thus a beginning as well as a resumption. The world has come back to where it left off in 1914. Yet it is not a circle, but a spiral. This is because of the many ways in which the present is different from the nineteenth century.

This is not only a new century, but also a new millennium. The calendar is, of course, European and Christian, yet the date is more than a cliché. At the advent of the previous millennium, Europe was in the 'Dark Ages'. The dynamic force at that time was the world-conquering power of Islam. China was technologically the most advanced and, perhaps, the most prosperous country. The universities of Cairo and Baghdad were preserving, transmitting and adding to the knowledge that came from Ancient Greece and contemporary India.

It was in the second half of the previous millennium that the balance between Europe and the Rest of the World (itself a peculiarly Eurocentric expression) changed. Light and speedy sailing ships, mounted with guns, were the crucial innovation enabling Iberian adventurers to establish contacts with the Americas, Africa and Asia. Columbus in 1492 and Vasco da Gama in 1498 mark the start of capitalism as a world system. This inaugurated the period of modern imperialism. Empires had been around for ever, but they were mainly land-based expansions. Now, for the first time, we had maritime empires.

It was the innovations in warfare and navigation which enabled this expansion.[5] But it effected a transfer of surplus from the colonies to the metropolis, executed with much violence. It also marked the beginning of racial arrogance fuelled by religious fanaticism. God and guns were used to get gold. It is ironic that Iberia, which had been colonized by Muslims in the earlier centuries of the millennium, was now in the arrogant vanguard of European racism.

What changed the prospect for European imperialism was the technological leap in the late eighteenth century. Now Western Europe could *generate* surplus faster and in larger amounts than all the rapacity of pioneering imperialists. Capitalism had a new lease of life after the Industrial Revolution. It was loom and lathe, rather than God and guns, which marked this new phase. Imperialism continued, and even extended in the nineteenth century further into Asia and Africa. But its basis had changed. It sought markets and natural resources. There was not only a transfer of surplus, but also the export of surplus-enhancing technology.

The end of the twentieth century marked not just the end of the challenges to capitalism as a mode of production but, along the way, imperialism, both continental and maritime, lost out as well. Europe, with its deep and long-standing identification with imperialism over hundreds of years, lost its empires in two distinct stages. The land-based empires – Ottoman, Habsburg, Romanoff – went after 1918. The Romanoff Empire was rejuvenated, of course. But then, after 1945, the maritime empires of Britain, France and Holland went with those of Portugal and Belgium, the last and most reluctant to go. Thus, the triumph of liberal-democratic capitalism saw the end of all empires of the half-millennium. This did not happen without struggle by the colonized. Indeed, in its final stages, the USA, long a champion of anti-imperialism, got entangled in Vietnam in a long war of decolonization which lasted from 1945 to 1975.

It is the existence of a large number of new territorial (nation-) states which makes the twenty-first century different from the nineteenth-century phase of globalization. In the second half of the twentieth century (1945–89), decolonization interacted with the Cold War to produce many distortions in the economy and polity of the new nation-states. Dictators were sponsored by both sides in a cynical play of power politics. Yet as the century of war ended in a peaceful collapse of the Leninist state in Europe, the liberal-democratic phase began in the scores of decolonized states of Asia, Africa, Latin America and, indeed, Eastern Europe.

Classical liberalism championed freedom, but was wary of democracy. This is why Marx's unfinished critique of Hegel was so radical for its time.[6] To admit the propertyless (proletariat) into the elective Estates was beyond the imagination of Locke or Mill. For classical liberalism, freedom was freedom to hold and enjoy the fruits of property. This included, of course, property in your own labour-power. Yet once you extended the economic freedom of property to the political freedom of franchise, the contradictions implicit in liberal democracy became clear.

The young Marx, in his critique of Hegel, thought that extending the franchise to the propertyless would destroy a polity in which the right to representation in an Estate required property. Thus, removing a property qualification for voting was to be the act of removing property altogether. But this was because he had not yet understood political economy: how the system produced and reproduced the proletariat – how, that is, the worker voluntarily entered into a contract which led to his exploitation. This took time. This is what he understands by the time he publishes *Capital Volume I*, in which the sixth chapter is devoted to the Buying and Selling of Labour-Power.

The creation of the proletariat had profound, unintended consequences. Once the freedom to contract, to sell labour-power, had been granted, the parity of status in the sphere of contracts could not but lead to a demand for status equality everywhere else. All previous societies had been based not only on inequalities of wealth and power, but on a hierarchy of status, a narrow pyramid. But once people became subjects of exchange and sellers of labour-power, status inequalities became unsustainable. Workers' franchise was the first step, though it took long enough in the Old World. (The USA and the Antipodes did much better in the early introduction of adult male franchise.)

The next step was women's suffrage. The gender issue is still not resolved. This is because while male workers' economic freedom to contract was established before their political rights, women's economic empowerment lagged half a century behind their political rights. But the movement for women's and workers' political enfranchisement led to the impetus for decolonization. This in turn fed back into movements against racial discrimination and the civil rights movement in the USA. The removal of status inequalities is a logical consequence of the economic right to contract. The Greeks did not have status equality in their democracy; neither women nor slaves could vote. Paradoxical though it may sound, it is contractual freedom which leads to status equality.

But neither enfranchisement nor the removal of status inequalities contributes decisively to the solution of economic inequality.

Marx saw clearly that once labour-power became a community, it had freedom and mobility. It had the juridical right to enter into contracts. Yet this equality coexisted with an economic inequality of wealth. The employer (Mr Moneybags) could match hundreds, if not thousands, of his employees in terms of income/wealth. Exchange conducted on the basis of juridical equality was carried out in the context of economic inequality.

But in 1867, or even later, Marx did not reconnect with his own critique of Hegel's *Philosophy of Right.* Wealth gave disproportionate power to the employer, but the workers' strength was in numbers. In the market for labour-power, numbers matter in determining bargaining strength, but here again, Marx's own theory of the cycles shows how capital can displace labour when profits are threatened. Political combination in a world of widespread – if not universal – franchise is more robust than economic combination (though they are related). This is because the fluctuations in political power do not form a cycle like the economic one. Democracy thus becomes a challenge to the market.

However, it also proved to be a challenge to Socialism outside Capitalism. The failure of the German Revolution led by Karl Liebknecht and Rosa Luxemburg was due to the German workers' deliberate decision to stick with the moderate reform which made Germany a republic. They did not want the revolutionary alternative of abolishing property rights that was on offer from the USPD. This is because with the republic, a blow was dealt to the status inequalities so prevalent under the Reich. The SPD had been instrumental in the removal of the Hohenzollern dynasty which made the German polity more inclusive.

And thus the enfranchised worker, by being brought into democracy, buys into capitalism. Democratic power can push the bargaining strength of the worker up to a certain point. If it threatens profitability too much, then capital withdraws or migrates. Standing Marx on his head, I argued above that there is a need for a longer-term complementarity between capital and labour, despite – or perhaps because of – the short-term cyclical conflict. This also makes sense if we interpret Marx's overall vision in *Capital* as one which highlights the cyclical nature of capitalism, with no guarantee of a fall in the rate of profit sufficient to undermine the system. And the rate of profit has not fallen catastrophically. This complementarity is reinforced even in the short run if the outcome of the workers winning the battle with capital is not the abolition of capitalism but the shortage of capital, with consequent unemployment.

This was the conclusion, I would argue, to which the workers of the advanced capitalist countries came, albeit at the end of the 1980s. Social-democratic parties everywhere saw that restoration of profitability mattered once capital became mobile. But once it had become mobile, it demanded co-operation from the workers, not conflict. And it got that co-operation. This was most dramatically described by Ambalavaner Sivanandan, in a critique of the direction the British Left was taking in the late 1980s: 'Capital had been freed from labour – [this] had escaped the Left altogether'.[7]

Conflict is endemic to capitalism, but if it is seen that capitalism is not about to die, then the beliefs, as well as behaviour, of the workers undergo a modification. Not all at once, of course. Not evenly in every country. But the general retreat of SwC parties in the 1990s was due to the realization of this complementarity between capital and labour on the part of labour and its political agents.

The proliferation of nation-states in the late twentieth century introduces another conflicting logic to the logic of capitalism: the nature of the interstate (often called international) political system. Starting with the Treaty of Westphalia in 1648, the European state system evolved in a Eurocentric way over three centuries, but its outward extension and universalization belong to the late twentieth century. Woodrow Wilson failed, but Franklin D. Roosevelt succeeded in undermining the Eurocentricity of the interstate political system. The United Nations adopts the Westphalian logic of sovereign states, and it is by treaties that the system orders itself. When, during the twentieth century, global capitalism broke up into a set of national capitalisms after 1919, the treaty-based logic was extended to the international economic sphere. In constructing the post-1945 global order, institutions such as the UN and the Bretton Woods financial bodies – the IMF and World Bank – were created. These institutions superimposed on the Westphalian idea of nominally equal sovereign states the idea of a superpower condominium – a Concert of Europe extended to the world. Thus the UN has a General Assembly (Westphalia) and a Security Council with five Permanent Members (Concert). The voting rights in the IMF and the World Bank are allocated not on a one-country, one-vote basis, but on the basis of the quotas subscribed by countries to the capital of the IMF and the World Bank. Here again, the G-7 dominate.

Economic or *de facto* inequality thus lives in an uneasy accommodation with political or *de jure* equality. This is no different from Marx's depiction of the labourer's freedom under capitalism. Beneath the phenomenal level of equality lurk the structural inequalities of wealth and power. This logic of an interstate system prevailed throughout the latter half of the twentieth century. It was helped by the Cold War, as well as its material basis in the system of capitalisms in one country. This made the world order fragmentary. On the one hand there were the Cold War divisions of West and East. The newly independent ex-colonies constituted the Third World, whose members had a varying allegiance to the rival camps, while also convening the Non-Aligned Movement. The economic division between rich and poor countries took on the label North and South.

The effect of this contradiction between political equality and economic inequality was to render the global institutions less than effective. Thus, within the UN, the General Assembly was seen to be identified with the Third World, while the Security Council was paralysed by the East–West division among the Permanent Members. The IMF and World Bank were seen to be First World institutions run by the G-7 (as it came to be known) in the interests of the First World. The Third World demanded and got UNCTAD, which was thought to be its own institution, more friendly to its concerns about tariffs and development than was the IMF or even the World Bank. Under this arrangement there was some scope for the acting out of conflicts between the rich and poor nations.

The analogy between the contradictions of the proletariat and of the newly independent nation-state should not be carried too far. There were, however, attempts to do so. Thus for a while, there was the Chinese Communist idea that the countries of the Third World might rise like the proletariat to undermine the global order/world capitalism. This was an extreme version of Trotsky's weak-link hypothesis. Thus, in complete opposition to Marx's theory, the weakest link was to be the farthest advanced towards socialism, and was to lead world revolution. Less revolutionary versions of the solidarity of the South versus the North were also popular for a while, especially during the 1970s, when the oil price crisis weakened the OECD countries.

Much of this proved to be a delusion. There was little that could be achieved by the South alone, solidaristic as it could be. Very much as the SwC parties realized that their cause gained when the economy prospered, the South had to admit that the route to its own prosperity lay in exchange with the North. This was the analogue at the interstate level of the 'standing Marx on his head' idea that an exchange is more a complementary than a conflictual process, even when parties to that exchange have unequal endowments.

An opportunity to implement this logic arose from the negotiations which took place in the one institution of the 1945 arrangement which was not set up on a hierarchical basis: the General Agreement on Tariffs and Trade (GATT). The divergence in the development experience of the South (see Chapter 17) had made some countries 'newly industrialized' and eager to gain access to the markets of the North. They took the initiative to start the Uruguay Round of GATT. This finally led to the negotiation and the signing of the Treaty which set up the World Trade Organization. Trade is a reciprocal relationship, and the WTO requires all its members to agree to extend the Most Favoured Nation clause to all countries they trade with. Reciprocity and symmetry are thus at the heart of the WTO process. Its structure is the most egalitarian of any of the international institutions – one country, one vote. Yet its operations resist any populist demagogy – unlike the UN General Assembly. Its procedures have led to the chastisement of powerful Northern members – the USA and the European Union – which neither the UN nor the IMF has ever managed.

The WTO is the first institution of the new phase of globalization. Membership is voluntary, but not automatic. Countries have to satisfy certain criteria on freer trade and avoidance of discriminatory trade barriers. Thus China had to negotiate at length before it could join, while it is a Permanent Member of the UN Security Council. By showing an eagerness to join the WTO, developing countries have demonstrated that the fragmentation of the 1945–89 period is past.

This is the ultimate paradox of present times. One world is being created, slowly but surely, by the forces of market-led globalization. The WTO is the premier institution for global governance in this phase. The UN/IMF/World Bank belong to an older interstate system. Inequality of power is codified in their operations. Unlike trade, political (power) relations between the states are neither symmetrical nor, even, always reciprocal. The presumption of sovereign equality is not the same as the fact of the reciprocity of an exchange relationship.

This is best illustrated, perhaps, in the divergent ways in which the debt problem of developing countries was settled in the 1980s as against the recent agitation by Jubilee 2000 for the cancellation of debt. The debts incurred in the 1980s arose from commercial lending of petrodollars by Western commercial banks to sovereign states in Latin America, mainly in the 1970s. Mexico signalled the debt crisis in 1982, when it could not service the debt. The outcome, after lengthy negotiations, was to write off a lot of that debt as unpayable. Much financial ingenuity – Brady Bonds, and so on[8] – was deployed in devising this solution, but in the end, only a negligible proportion of the debt was paid. This is because when that debt is equitized, the financial markets put a low realistic value on it – a fraction of its nominal value.

The outstanding public debt owed to governments and multilateral public lending agencies is proving much more difficult to cancel. Its incidence is even more severe than in the case of the earlier debt, because in the present case the debtor countries are largely from Sub-Saharan Africa. A large part of the debt is the result of non-payment of earlier servicing instalments being added to the original debt, and compounded. There is no serious prospect that the debt can ever be repaid. Yet the interstate system cannot accept what the market did in the 1980s, and either cancel the debt or equitize it. So we get the strange outcome that the market, much maligned as the evil genius of globalization, proves much more forgiving and much less harmful than the interstate system, many of whose members (France, Germany) preach socialism or, at least, some form of progressive social philosophy.

Another problem which is genuinely global is that of the ecosystem. The hole in the ozone layer and the excessive emission of greenhouse gases leading to global warming are two issues which obviously transcend the interstate system, to say nothing of the individual sovereign state. The awareness of the adverse impact on the environment of industrial processes and consumption patterns began in the early 1960s with Rachel Carson's *Silent Spring*. Much of the perspective then was national, with environmental groups battling with government and industry in the many developed and a few developing countries. From the Stockholm Conference in 1972 to the Bruntland Report on Sustainable Development (1989) to the UN Conference on Environment in Rio (1992), the environmental movement has gained prominence in public policy discussions.

One perspective on the environmental issue is that it is a market failure on a drastic scale. In search of profits, business neglects to consider the true environmental costs of its operations. Consumers are also encouraged by the market to pursue unsustainable consumption patterns. There is some truth in this. Yet the market may also prove to be an efficacious solution to the same problem, in the sense that it is by modifying the incentives for consumers and business via taxes and subsidies that a modification will occur which is more reliable than fiat. The biggest improvement in energy efficiency was triggered by the quadrupling of crude oil prices in 1973, followed by another increase in 1979.

There have also been very stringent regulations imposed on products and processes which guarantee lower environmental damage. It is naive to think that markets operate without rules or regulations of any kind. Financial markets everywhere are heavily regulated, and also subject to laws about fraud, bankruptcy, embezzlement, and so forth. It was in the Soviet Union and Eastern Europe that perhaps the most eco-damaging industrial policies were followed. The market was absent, and the allocating authority chose to ignore environmental problems.

But the more serious problems are those that are truly global in scope. Here, despite its conferences, the UN system has been ineffective. What has worked, as in the case of GATT/WTO, is the coming together of governments with business negotiating a global arrangement. The Montreal convention on chlorofluorocarbons was the first successful tackling of the ozone-layer problem; it imposed restrictions on the technology of production of refrigerators, and so on, which use chlorofluorocarbons. Here the industry – including among its members powerful global corporations – co-operated by accepting these restrictions.

The global-warming problem is proving more elusive. Here again, the Kyoto Conference in 1998 was another global conference, outside UN auspices, which set a timetable. But in this case, some of the larger producers are sovereign states rather than just companies. The solution which is on the table, and which will work, is the introduction of tradeable permits. This is an example of the Coase solution to market failure – introduce property rights in a clean environment, and allocate these rights in the form of tradeable permits. Its adoption will not be easy, since the logic of the market clashes with that of the interstate system. Sovereign states are insulated from the competitive pressures banks have to face. In this case, as in the case of debt cancellation, the market logic is kinder and more effective than the logic of power.

Capitalism is not a kind or a benevolent system. It is the most effective mode of production discovered so far in wealth creation. It has no overarching objective, since it works through the profit-seeking efforts of millions of capitalists. It generates economic growth, prosperity, employment as side-effects. It also causes much misery and destruction in its tendency towards incessant change. But over the last two hundred years, it has achieved the largest gain in well-being in all previous millennia. For one thing, many more people are alive now than in 1800 (around six times as many), and they live longer on average – between ten to twenty years longer – than they did then. In this sense Malthus was wrong, though this has not prevented Malthusians continuing to follow him. If length of life can be taken as a crude measure of potential well-being, a billion people living, say, forty years on average in 1800 compared to six billion people living sixty years today speaks volumes for the success of capitalism. In 1800, perhaps two thirds of that billion were poor; today, at most a quarter of the six billion are poor. Yet the reduction of poverty is neither automatic, nor to be taken for granted.[9]

Adam Smith was not wrong, however, in saying that the new system of natural liberty imposed the cost of inequality while delivering a universal betterment of living standards. More people have been brought out of poverty in the last two hundred years, especially since 1945, than ever before in history. The very idea that poverty could be eliminated could not have occurred in any precapitalist stage. Capitalism provides the means for eliminating poverty, but these means were not directed immediately, or evenly, in the course of its development. Absolute poverty began to be addressed in the heartland of capitalism – Great Britain – only in the late nineteenth century, a hundred years after the Industrial Revolution. Poverty disappeared as a public concern even as it intensified as private experience in the dysfunctional interwar phase.[10]

It was in the climactic years of the Keynesian Golden Age – the 1960s – that poverty reappeared as an issue in rich countries. By this time the focus was not on absolute poverty but on relative poverty. In the decolonized countries, economic growth was given priority for national advancement, but poverty reduction was only an unintended consequence. Again, it was only in the 1980s and 1990s when countries, especially in Asia, began to adopt open-economy market-orientated policies that the more phenomenal growth took place. There was the wisdom in many of these Asian countries to provide literacy and good healthcare. Then Asia, the most populous and poorest continent for centuries, began its climb out of poverty in a most remarkable and unforeseen way.

China, perhaps, best illustrates the Adam Smith proposition. From the Revolution establishing the People's Republic of China in 1949 until 1978, it followed policies which kept it poor but equal. Much industrial progress happened under a Soviet-type economy, but the arbitrariness of Mao's policies led to a large famine and much destruction during the Cultural Revolution. Foundations were laid, however, with literacy and good healthcare in the communes. It was after 1978 and the restructuring of the communes with the more individualistic responsibility system in agriculture, the opening up of the economy to foreign capital and the encouragement of local enterprises that China started experiencing double-digit growth rates. Its GDP has increased eightfold in the last twenty-two years. Regional inequalities have grown, income inequality has also grown, yet poverty has come down. China remains a one-party state with a sad human rights record. But it has gone from a poor but equal society to one that is not so poor yet more unequal.

Marx's challenge to Adam Smith therefore remains yet to be met. Knowing full well the potential capitalism had to eliminate scarcity, Marx did not see that inequality as well as poverty could be eliminated in a capitalist society. Yet between his juvenilia in the 1840s, and his mature writing in *Capital*, he became less sure that the system would disappear imminently. Sadly, his youthful rhetoric rather than his mature analysis became his legacy. Untold crimes were committed in his name, evoking the prophecy that capitalism would die soon, defeated by the new order created in the Soviet Union. The idea that capitalism, while it lasted, was a progressive mode of production whose unfettered development was preferable to reactionary alternatives was forgotten. Now it has come back with a vengeance. Capitalism has become truly global, and it has not yet reached its limits. So what happens to Marx?

Recall Marx's reluctance to prophesy what would follow capitalism in any detail. It was to be socialism, followed after some time by communism. Yet how it would come about and what it would look like, how it would work, are all issues he left untouched. After twenty years devoted to a critique of political economy – an analysis of how capitalism worked – he never came back to the questions he posed in his youthful manuscripts. Is it possible to have a society that is not merely self-organizing, but consciously so? A society fully self-conscious of its own workings, and able to direct them, where individuals are not alienated from their work, or from themselves, but fully participate in their self-emancipation, and realize the full potential of the species-beings that they are – in other words, Socialism beyond Capitalism?

Marx diverted himself from the task of answering these questions to studying capitalism, and excoriating contemporary socialists for their delusions about the prospect of achieving socialism. Yet these delusions reappeared after his death, and had murderous consequences after 1917. That sad, violent and barbaric episode in the world's history is over. Marx has had his revenge. But will he ever get his reward? Will there be Socialism beyond Capitalism?

Notes

Chapter 1

1. François Furet (1988/1992), *The French Revolution 1770–1814*); English translation by Antonia Nevill from *Révolution* (1988), Hachette, Blackwell, Oxford; Simon Schama (1989), *Citizens: A Chronicle of the French Revolution*, Viking, London.

2. Francis Fukuyama (1992), *The End of History and the Last Man*, Hamish Hamilton, London; Karl Popper (1945), *The Open Society and Its Enemies*, 2 vols, Routledge & Kegan Paul, London. I am referring here to vol. 2, *The High Tide of Prophecy: Hegel, Marx and the Aftermath.*

3. Harold Laski (ed.) (1948), *The Communist Manifesto: The Centenary Edition*, published for the Labour Party by Allen & Unwin, London, pp. 123–5.

4. Friedrich Engels (1845/1892), *The Condition of the Working Class in England in 1844*, first published in German in 1845, translated into English by Florence Kelly-Wischnewetzky in 1885 and published in New York in 1886 by John W. Lovell, and in London in 1892 by George Allen & Unwin. Engels wrote a preface to the English edition.

5. Sidney and Beatrice Webb (1923), *The Decay of Capitalist Civilisation*, Harcourt Brace, New York.

6. Lenin (1916) *Imperialism: The Highest Stage of Capitalism* (various translations), also in *Collected Works*, 45 vols, Lawrence & Wishart, London, vol. 22; Ernest Mandel (1972/1975), *Late Capitalism*; translation by Joeis de Bres of *Der Spätkapitalismus* (1972), Suhrkamp Verlag, Berlin, New Left Books, London.

Chapter 2

1. In this chapter I have been much influenced by two books: Istvan Hont and Michael Ignatieff (eds) (1993), *Wealth and Virtue: The Shaping of Political Economy in the Scottish Enlightenment*, Cambridge University Press, Cambridge. The two essays that are useful background to this chapter are: Hont and Ignatieff, 'Needs and Justice in *The Wealth of Nations*', an introductory essay, and Donald Winch, 'Adam Smith's "Enduring Particular Result": A Political and Cosmopolitan Perspective'; and Donald Winch (1978), *Adam Smith's Politics: An Essay in Historiographic Revision*, Cambridge University Press, Cambridge.

For a recent biography of Adam Smith, see Ian Simpson Ross (1995), *The Life of Adam Smith,* Clarendon Press, Oxford. All references to Adam Smith's works are from the marvellous six-volume Glasgow edition of *The Works and Correspondence of Adam Smith,* edited for the Smith bicentenary by a group of Smith Scholars: J. C. Bryce, R. H. Campbell, A. L. Macfie, E. C. Mossner, D. D. Raphael, I. S. Ross, A. S. Skinner, P. D. Stein, W. B. Todd and W. P. D. Wightman. This is a most civilized act by the University of Glasgow, published by Oxford University Press. In particular, I use *Lectures on Jurisprudence,* ed. R. L. Meek, D. D. Raphael and P. D. Stein (1978); and of course, *An Inquiry into the Nature and Causes of the Wealth of Nations,* 2 vols, ed. R. H. Campbell and A. S. Skinner, textual editor W. B. Todd.

2. The quote from John Millar is in the editors' Introduction to *Lectures on Jurisprudence,* p. 3.

3. LJ (A) 14 refers to the *Lectures on Jurisprudence* – the lecture notes taken from 1762–63 and published as A in the Glasgow edition, p. 14.

4. The Early Draft of Part of the *Wealth of Nations* is included as an Appendix to the *Lectures on Jurisprudence.*

5. Cited by Donald Winch in *Adam Smith's Politics,* p. 71.

6. The reference is to Part V, p. 50 of vol. 2 of the two-volume Glasgow edition of the *Wealth of Nations,* cited above.

7. The quotation from *The Theory of Moral Sentiments* is on pp. 340–41 of D. D. Raphael and A. L. Macfie (eds), *The Theory of Moral Sentiments,* Part VII, Section 4, para. 36.

Chapter 3

1. The two books which form the background to this chapter are Laurence Dickey (1987), *Hegel: Religion, Economics and the Politics of Spirit 1770–1807,* Cambridge University Press, Cambridge; Charles Taylor (1975) *Hegel,* Cambridge University Press, Cambridge.

2. The reference is to Winch, *Adam Smith's Politics.*

3. On Dugald Stewart's revamp of Smith, see Emma Rothschild (2001), *Economic Sentiments: Adam Smith, Condorcet and the Enlightenment,* Harvard University Press, Cambridge, MA.

4. The reference is to K. J. Arrow (1951), *Social Choice and Individual Values,* John Wiley, New York; Marie Jean Antoine Nicolas de Condorcet (1785), *Essai sur l'application à la probabilité des decisions rendue à la pluralité des voix* (Paris).

5. James Madison, Alexander Hamilton and John Jay (1789), *The Federalist Papers,* ed. Isaac Kramnick (1987), Penguin, London.

Chapter 4

1. See Leopold Schwarzschild (1948), *The Red Prussian: The Life and Legends of Karl Marx,* Pickwick Books, London.

2. For the background to Bruno Bauer and the Young Hegelians, see David McLellan (1969), *The Young Hegelians and Karl Marx,* Macmillan, London; Harold Mah (1987), *The End of Philosophy and the Origins of Ideology,* University of California Press, Berkeley; Daniel Brudney (1998), *Marx's Attempt to Leave Philosophy,* Harvard University Press, Cambridge, MA.

Karl Marx (1844/1970), *A Contribution to the Critique of Hegel's Philosophy of Right,* ed. and introduced by Joseph O'Malley (1970), Cambridge University Press, Cambridge; introduction, first published in Deutsche–französiche Jahrbücher (Paris), trans. included in O'Malley (1970), pp. 131–42, also reprinted in Karl Marx (1975), *Early Writings,* Pelican Marx Library, introduced by Lucio Colletti, trans. Rodney Livingstone and Gregor Benton, Penguin, Harmondsworth, pp. 243–57.

Karl Marx and Friedrich Engels (1845/1956), *The Holy Family, or Critique of Critical Criticism Against Bruno Bauer and Company,* first published in German in 1845 by Literarische Anstalt, J. Rutten, Frankfurt; trans. Richard Dixon and Clemens Dutt, Progress Publishers, Moscow, 1956.

Karl Marx and Friedrich Engels (1846/1964), *The German Ideology: Critique of Modern German Philosophy According to Its Representatives,* Feuerbach, Bauer and Stirner (vol. I); and of *German Socialism According to its Various Prophets* (vol. 2). First published in German in 1932 by the Institute of Marxism–Leninism (Moscow), and in trans. (translators not given) by Progress Publishers, Moscow, 1964.

3. On Marx's abandonment of philosophy, see Brudney, *Marx's Attempt to Leave Philosophy.*

Karl Marx and Friedrich Engels (1848/1888), *The Communist Manifesto.* Published in German by The Communist League, first translated in English by Helen Macfarlane, who serialized it in *The Red Republican,* November 1850. The widely available translation was by Sam Moore with Engels (1888).

For recent accounts of the history of the publication and reception of the Manifesto, see Mark Cowling (ed.) (1998), *The Communist Manifesto: New Interpretations,* Edinburgh University Press, Edinburgh, especially articles by Terell Carver: 'Re-Translating the Manifesto: New Histories, New Ideas', pp. 51–62; and Ian Thatcher: 'Past Receptions of the Communist Manifesto', pp. 63–74.

Leo Panitch and Colin Leys (1998), *The Communist Manifesto Now: Socialist Register 1998*; see especially Sheila Rowbotham, 'Dear Mr Marx: A Letter from a Socialist Feminist', pp. 1–17.

Karl Marx (1859/1904), *A Contribution to the Critique of Political Economy,* Meisner, Hamburg. English translation (1904) by N. Stone, Charles Kerr, Chicago.

Karl Marx (1867/1887), *Capital Volume 1: Capitalist Production*, German Publication Otto Meisner (Hamburg), trans. from the third German edition by Samuel Moore and Edward Aveling in 1887, Swan Sonnenschein, Lowry & Co., London. Since then several editions, including Pelican Library.

4. Karl Marx (1871/1951), *The Civil War in France*, originally published by International Workingman's Association (London). English translation in *Selected Works of Karl Marx and Frederick Engels*, Progress Publishers, Moscow, 1951. This is the earliest reference to an English translation I can find.

5. Karl Marx (1885/1919), *Capital Volume 2: The Process of Circulation of Capital*, ed. Friedrich Engels, first published in Germany by Otto Meisner, Hamburg, first English translation published 1919 by Charles Kerr, Chicago. Various editions since by Progress Publishers, Moscow, Lawrence & Wishart, London. Also in Pelican Marx Library.

6. Eugen von Böhm-Bawerk (1896/1949) 'Zum Abschluss des Marxschen Systems', in O. V. Boenigk (ed.), *Staatswissenschaftlische Arbeiten: Festgaben für Karl Kneis*, Berlin. English translation in Paul M. Sweezy (ed.) (1949), *Karl Marx and the Close of His System*, Augustus M. Kelley, New York.

7. For Edouard Bernstein, see Peter Gay (1952), *The Dilemma of Democratic Socialism: Edouard Bernstein's Challenge to Marx*, Columbia University Press, New York; Edouard Bernstein (1899), *Die Voranssetzungen des Sozialismus und die Aufgaben der Sozialdemokratie*, J. H. Dietz, Stuttgart; trans. (1909) *Evolutionary Socialism*, Huebsch, New York.

8. Rosa Luxemburg (1913/1951), *The Accumulation of Capital*, first published in German in 1913, trans. Agnes Schwarzschild (1951), Routledge & Kegan Paul, London.

9. Karl Marx (1859/1971), *A Contribution to the Critique of Political Economy*, trans. S. W. Ryazanskaya, ed. Maurice Dobb, Lawrence & Wishart, London, p. 21.

10. For Marx as a stylist, see Stanley Edgar Hyman (1961), *The Tangled Bank: Marx, Darwin, Frazer and Freud*, Athaneum, New York; S. Prawer (1976) *Karl Marx and World Literature*, Clarendon Press, Oxford.

11. Marx, *Early Writings*, p. 248.

12. Ibid., p. 256.

13. On the Asiatic mode of production, there is a large literature: Stephen Dunn (1982), *The Fall and Rise of the Asiatic Mode of Production*, Routledge & Kegan Paul, London; Brendan O'Leary (1989), *The Asiatic Mode of Production*, Blackwell, Oxford; Lawrence Krader (1975), *The Asiatic Mode of Production*, Assen, New York; Karl Wittfogel (1957), *Oriental Despotism: A Comparative Study of Total Power*, Yale University Press, New Haven, CT.

14. Some of these issues about external versus internal causes for the transition from feudalism to capitalism are explored in the articles by Sweezy and others in

Paul Sweezy (ed.) with an introduction by Rodney Hilton (1978), *The Transition from Feudalism to Capitalism*, Verso, London. For an orthodox Marxist history of capitalism's origins, see Maurice Dobb (1946), *Studies in the Development of Capitalism*, Routledge & Kegan Paul, London.

15. Marx, *Critique*, p. 20.

16. Ibid.

17. John Millar (1806), *The Origin and Distinction of Ranks*, Edinburgh, 4th edn, also published in William C. Lehmann (1960), *John Millar of Glasgow 1735–1801: His Life and Thought and his Contribution to Sociological Analysis*, Cambridge University Press, Cambridge. See also Michael Ignatieff (1983), 'John Millar and Individualism' in Hont and Ignatieff (eds) (1983), pp. 317–44.

18. Marx, *Critique*, p. 21.

Chapter 5

1. Engels, *The Condition of the Working Class in England in 1844.*

2. David Ricardo's collected works were edited by Piero Sraffa with the help of Maurice Dobb. In his introduction to Ricardo's *Principles of Political Economy and Taxation*, Sraffa argued that in Ricardo's theory, the profit rate on the marginal land can be seen to be a pure ratio independent of market prices. Wages were paid in corn, and output was in corn. If fixed capital was not important, then profit and capital (wage fund) are both measured in corn. The rate of profit on agriculture can then be the pivot around which all other profit rates equalize. Other Ricardo scholars – Professor Samuel Hollander, for example – have disagreed with this. But Sraffa's extension of this argument later in his 1960 *Production of Commodities by Means of Commodities* (Cambridge University Press, Cambridge) was to become a source of much controversy among Marxists in the 1970s. I discuss it in Chapter 17.

3. Marx's method of measuring the labour content of the commodities is one direct measure. Modern-day statisticians measure the labour *commanded* by wages by asking, for example, how many hours of work of an average worker it takes to buy bread or a bicycle. Such measures are now widely available.

4. Engels's objections and Marx's replies are in letters which have been conveniently collected in: Marx and Engels (1954/1983) *Letters on Capital*, first published in German as *Briefe über Das Kapital*, Dietz Verlag, Berlin, trans. Andrew Drummond (1983), published by New Park Publications, London. I have discussed the 'prehistory' of the price–value transformation problem in 'The Transformation Problem', in G. Caravale (ed.) 1991, *Marx and Modern Economic Analysis* (Edward Elgar), Cheltenham).

5. For those not familiar with mathematical notation, Σ represents summation.

6. Ladislaus von Bortkiewicz (1907/1949) *On the Correction of Marx's Fundamental*

Theoretical Construction in the Third Volume of Capital; originally published in Jahrbücher für National Ökonomie und Statistik, July 1907, trans. in Sweezy (ed.), *Karl Marx and the Close of His System*, pp. 199–221. I have discussed Bortkiewicz's solution in Meghnad Desai (1979), *Marxian Economics*, Blackwell, Oxford.

Solving the Price–Value Puzzle

In the preface to *Capital Volume 2*, Engels teased the many critics of Marx who had said that his theory of profits could not be coherent. If surplus-value came from variable capital alone, how come constant capital earned the same average rate of profit as variable capital? Marx had either to contradict his theory of value or to challenge the law of equal profits on all activities. (Empirically, of course, all firms do not make the same rate of profit, even after many adjustments. But in economics, battles are fought and won on grounds of theory, never by citing empirical data.) Engels asked people to hurry up and solve the problem before he published the last volume of *Capital*. Many took up the challenge, but none was thought to have resolved it. When Marx's own solution came out, it satisfied nobody. The Viennese economist Eugen von Böhm-Bawerk denounced Marx's system as incoherent in 1896 in his article 'Karl Marx and the Close of His System'.

Eleven years later, a German Professor of Statistics, Ladislaus von Bortkiewicz published an elegant solution. While Böhm-Bawerk's critique occupies a hundred pages of somewhat turgid prose, Bortkiewicz's solution takes up 25 pages of some simple algebra and numerical tables. Being a mathematician, he was able to pose the problem in its generality, take up an example that could be tackled, and provide numerical results to make his solution accessible.

He started by assuming three Departments (sectors) producing machines, wage goods and luxuries. He used Marx's scheme for Simple Reproduction as a basis, but extended it to three Departments. He set out the accounts for each sector in value terms – the $C \rightarrow C'$ circuit (inside the box on p. 62 above) and set up a parallel account in money terms – $M \rightarrow M'$ circuit. The only connecting link was that total surplus-value had to be equal to total profits. He had thus to solve for three prices and one average profit rate. This is as follows;

Value Accounts

$$C_1 + V_1\ (1 + r) = C_1 + C_2 + C_3$$
$$C_2 + V_2\ (1 + r) = V_1 + V_2 + V_3$$
$$C_3 + V_3\ (1 + r) = S_1 + S_2 + S_3$$

The first equation says that constant capital plus variable capital and surplus-value (r being the rate of exploitation) produces machine goods output that has to be brought for use by each of the three sectors. The second Department produces wage goods bought from the wage bills of workers, while the third Department produces luxuries bought by the capitalist from their surplus-value.

Money Accounts

$[P_1C_1 + P_2V_1]\ (1 + \varrho) = P_1\ (C_1 + C_2 + C_3)$
$[P_1C_2 + P_2V_2]\ (1 + \varrho) = P_2\ (V_1 + V_2 + V_3)$
$[P_1C_3 + P_2V_3]\ (1 + \varrho) = P_3\ (S_1 + S_2 + S_3)$

Here the first equation sets up the cost of inputs by multiplying machine input by price P_1 and labour input by price P_2, and then adds a rate of profit ϱ which has to be met by the revenue from selling the output at price P_1. Similarly for the wage goods. Luxuries are not used as inputs in production, but their costs of production have to be recovered. The last equation is:

The 'Bridge'

$(S_1 + S_2 + S_3) = \varrho\ [(P_1C_1 + P_2V_1) + (P_1C_2 + P_2V_2) + (P_1C_3 + P_2V_3)]$
i.e. total surplus-value equals total profits.

Thus P_1, P_2, P_3, and ϱ are the unknowns, and we have the Cs, Vs and r as givens. To reduce the complexity of his task, Bortkiewicz assumed $P_3 = 1$ – or, as we say today, normalized all prices in terms of price of the luxury good. (Many people thought that luxury was gold, and hence money. But that is not necessary, nor is the normalization. It is just a convenient starting point.) It can then be shown that profit rate can be solved from a quadratic equation. I will spare you the details.

The numerical example was as follows:

Dept	Constant capital	Variable capital	Surplus-value	Total value	Machine costs	Wage bill	Profits	Total revenue
I	225	90	60	375	288	96	96	480
II	100	120	80	300	128	128	64	320
III	50	90	60	200	64	96	40	200
	375	399	200	875	480	320	200	1,000

Numbers are arbitrary, of course, and nothing hinges on them. We see above that total surplus-value (200) equals total profits (200). But the distribution of surplus-value as profits among the three Departments as determined by prices is different. Dept I makes profits above its surplus-value, and the other two departments lose out. The price of constant capital is $1\frac{7}{25}$, of variable capital $1\frac{1}{15}$, and the profit rate is 25%. Of course, in real life we know the prices and profit rate, and need to get back to the rate of exploitation. Bortkiewicz's solution was too neat, too clinical, to satisfy anyone. Many other solutions were offered. The reason, as I say in the text, is that Marxists want from this exercise more than a solution to a technical problem. They want the key to the destruction of capitalism. So they will keep looking.

7. For the capital controversy, see Geoffrey C. Harcourt (1972), *Some Cambridge Controversies in the Theory of Capital*, Cambridge University Press, Cambridge; Christopher Bliss (1975) *Capital Theory and the Distribution of Income*, North Holland, Amsterdam.

8. For the empirical results see Anwar Shaikh (1984), 'The Transformation from Marx to Sraffa', in Ernest Mandel and Alan Freeman (eds), *Ricardo, Marx, Sraffa: The Langston Memorial Volume*, Verso, London; P. Petrovic (1987), 'The Deviation of Production Prices from Labour Values: Some Methodology and Empirical Evidence', *Cambridge Journal of Economics*, 11, 197–210. I have discussed these papers in: 'Methodological Problems in Quantitative Marxism', in Paul Dunne (ed.) (1990), *Quantitative Marxism*, Polity Press, Oxford.

9. The formula is as follows. If W is the real wage rate, L total employment, Q total output (value added), then $WL/Q = \alpha$ is the share of wages in total output, but Q/L is output per worker, so we can rewrite as:

$\alpha = W/[Q/L]$. Now W is variable capital per worker and Q/L is value added (surplus-value plus variable capital) per worker, hence:
$\alpha = v/(s + v) = 1/(1 + s/v) = 1/1 + e$

10. Clément Juglar (1862), *Des Crises commerciales et de leur retour périodique en France, en Angleterre et aux États-Unis* (Paris).

11. A. W. H. Phillips (1958), 'The Relationship of the Rate of Change of the Money Wage Rate and Unemployment', *Economica*, new series, 1–18.

12. Richard M. Goodwin (1967), 'A Growth Cycle', in C. H. Feinstein (ed.), *Capitalism, Socialism and Economic Development: Essays in Honour of Maurice Dobb*, Cambridge University Press, Cambridge. See also Meghnad Desai (1973), 'Growth Cycles and Inflation in a Model of the Class Struggle', *Journal of Economic Theory*, December, reproduced in Desai (1995d) *Macroeconomics and Monetary Theory: Selected Essays of Meghnad Desai, Volume 1*, Edward Elgar, Cheltenham.

Goodwin's article led to a number of extensions, some of which are in R. Goodwin, M. Kruegar and A. Vercelli (1984), *Non-Linear Models of Fluctuating Growth*, Springer Verlag, Berlin.

13. I discuss these schemes in Meghnad Desai (1979), *Marxian Economics*, Blackwell, Oxford.

14 Michio Morishima (1973), *Marx's Economics,* Cambridge, Cambridge University Press, discusses the balanced growth result. He was the first to point out how powerful Marx's result was in terms of modern economics.

15. Friedrich von Hayek (1938), *Profits, Interest and Investment,* Routledge & Kegan Paul, London, p. 4.

16. The copy in my possession has no publication date, but it is described as *Karl Marx, Selected Works in Two Volumes: Prepared by Marx–Engels–Lenin Institute, Moscow,* ed. V. Adoratsky, Martin Lawrence, London.

17. Karl Marx, *Capital Volume 1,* Lawrence & Wishart edn, London 1974, ch. 32, pp. 714–15.

Chapter 6

1. Germany began to base its mark on gold in 1871, France in 1878; the USA began to redeem its currency fully in gold in 1879.

2. The full quotation from William Jennings Bryan, Democratic Presidential Candidate in 1896 is: 'You shall not press down upon the brow of labour this Crown of thorns, you shall not crucify mankind upon a cross of gold.' Still, Bryan lost the election to the Republican candidate, William McKinley.

3. Most of the income and price data quoted in this book are from Angus Maddison (1991), *Dynamic Forces in Capitalist Development: A Long Run Comparative View,* Oxford University Press, Oxford. The book contains much more than the most reliable and comprehensive set of comparative statistics on income, population, productivity, capital formation and prices. It is also an analysis of the development of capitalism which, in many ways, has informed my work.

4. The number of years it takes any quantity to double depends on the annual compound rate of growth. The simple calculation is number of years n to double x, n = 72/annual growth rate of x. Thus 6% growth doubles a quantity in 12 years, etc.

5. N. D. Kondratieff was a Russian economist who did pioneering work on long waves as Director of the Business Cycle Research Institute in Moscow. His first publication on this subject was: 'Die Langen Wellen der Konjunktur', in *Archiv für Sozialwissenschaft und Sozialpolitik,* December 1926. His work is extensively discussed by J. A. Schumpeter (1939), *Business Cycles,* McGraw-Hill, New York.

6. Income inequality data are notoriously difficult to calculate over a sustained period of time. For a good summary of the British and American income and wealth inequality data, see David Hackett Fisher (1996), *The Great Wave: Price Revolutions and the Rhythm of History,* Oxford University Press, Oxford. In a tabulation entitled 'The

Victorian Equilibrium', Fisher displays a Gini ratio (a measure of inequality) for wealth in Northern and Southern USA, and for income inequality in England, for 1801–1913. While inequality does not change, it is very high compared to what we have today. The income inequality in England has a Gini ratio of 0.50, while today the value would be around 0.35. (A value of zero is perfect equality, and a value of one is complete inequality where one person gets all the income and the rest get nothing.)

7. Robert Owen's *A New View of Society or Essays on the Principle of the Formation of the Human Character and the Application of the Principle to Practice* was written during 1813–16. He was the first to use the word 'exclusion', now so much in vogue to describe the debilitating effects of poverty. Thus in his First Essay he writes:

> [I]t is now obvious that the system must be destructive of the happiness of the excluded by their seeing others enjoy what they are not permitted to possess; and also that it tends by creating opposition from the justly in injured feelings of the excluded, in proportion to the extent of the exclusion, to diminish happiness even of the privileged . . .

Robert Owen [1991] *A New View of Society and Other Writings*, ed. Gregory Claeys, Penguin Harmondsworth, p. 15.

John Ruskin (1958), *Unto This Last and Other Writings*, ed. Clive Wilmer; Penguin, Harmondsworth.

Charles Booth mapped poverty in London in great detail over the years 1887–97. For a succinct account of his discovery of the 'poverty line', see Alan Gillie (1996) 'The Origin of the Poverty Line', *Economic History Review*, vol. XLIX, no. 4, 715–30. Gillie gives an extensive bibliography of Booth's writings, including his nine volume *Labour and the Life of People*; see also B. Seebohm Rowntree (1922), but first published in 1901, *Poverty: A Study in Town Life*, Longmans Green, London.

8. There is extensive literature on the German SPD. The classic work is Carl Schorske (1955), *German Social Democracy 1905–1917: The Development of the Great Schism*, Harvard University Press, Cambridge, MA.

9. Karl Marx's 'Critique of the Gotha Programme', written in May 1875 but published in 1891 in the SPD journal, *Vorwärts*. For an English translation, see Karl Marx and Friedrich Engels (1968), *Selected Works*, Lawrence & Wishart, London, pp. 315–35 (p. 317).

10. Ibid.

11. Ibid., p. 319.

12. Ibid.

13. Karl Marx and Friedrich Engels (1974), *The First International and After*, ed. David Fernbach, Penguin, Harmondsworth, pp. 344–5.

14. For an analytical and sympathetic study of Karl Kautsky, see Massimo Salvadori (1979), *Karl Kautsky and the Socialist Revolution 1880–1938,* Verso, London.

15. Donald Sassoon (1996), *One Hundred Years of Socialism: The West European Left in the Twentieth Century,* I. B. Tauris, London, p. xx.

16. Ibid., p. xxii.

17. Karl Kautsky (1891/1910), *The Class Struggle (Erfurt Programme),* trans. William e. Bohm, Charles Kerr, Chicago, p. 8.

18. Peter Gay (1952), *The Dilemma of Democratic Socialism: Edouard Bernstein's Challenge to Marx,* Columbia University Press, New York, p. 63.

19. Ibid., pp. 67–8.

20. A major critic was Bukharin. See, for his criticism and Rosa Luxemburg's reply to her critics, Rosa Luxemburg and Nikolai Bukharin (1972), *Imperialism and the Accumulation of Capital,* trans. Rudolf Wickman, ed. Kenneth Tarbuck, Allen Lane, London.

The wide-ranging debate is also discussed in M. C. Howard and J. E. King (1989), *A History of Marxian Economics, Volume I 1883–1929*; and (1992) *Volume II 1929–1990,* Macmillan, London.

21. Rudolf Hilferding (1927/1981), *Finance Capital,* first published in German by Wein, trans. T. Bottomore, Routledge & Kegan Paul, London.

22. The debates among the Fabians were influenced by economists such as Wicksteed and Edgeworth. I have described these in Meghnad Desai (1974), *Marxian Economic Theory,* Gray-Mills, London. See also Eric Hobsbawm 'Dr Marx and the Victorians', in E. Hobsbawm (1964), *Labouring Men: Studies in the History of Labour,* Weidenfeld & Nicolson, London.

23. Alfred Marshall (1890), *Principles of Economics,* Macmillan, London; A. C. Pigou (1920), *The Economics of Welfare,* Macmillan, London.

24. M. C. Howard and J. E. King, *A History of Marxian Economics,* vol. 1, has a good discussion of Russian Marxism.

25. For Vera Zasulich's letter and Marx's reply, along with four drafts, see Teodor Shanin (ed.) (1984), *Late Marx and the Russian Road: Marx and the Peripheries of Capitalism,* Routledge & Kegan Paul, London.

26. Karl Marx, letter to the editorial board of *Otechestvenniye Zapiski,* in Karl Marx and Friedrich Engels (1955), *Selected Correspondence,* Progress Publishers, Moscow, p. 293.

27. Laski (ed.), *The Commnist Manifesto,* p. 104.

28. For a complete list of all of Lenin's economic writings, see Meghnad Desai (ed.) (1989), *Lenin's Economic Writings,* Lawrence & Wishart, London; Lenin (1893/1937), 'On the So-Called Question of the Home Market', written in 1893, first published in 1937, reprinted in *Lenin: Collected Works Volume I,* also in Desai (1989); Lenin (1897), *A Characterization of Economic Romanticism: Sismondi and Our Native*

Sismondists, first published in four issues of *Novoye Slovo*, April–July 1897, signed K T . . . n. English translation in *Collected Works Volume 2*. I am quoting from a Progress Publishers 1971 pamphlet.

29. W. A. Lewis (1954), 'Economic Development with Unlimited Supplies of Labour', *Manchester School*, vol. 22, pp. 139–91.

30. Lenin in Desai, *Lenin's Economic Writings*, pp. 81–2.

31. Ibid., pp. 134–5; original emphasis.

32. Ibid., p. 135.

Chapter 7

1. Bernard Shaw's biographer, Stanley Weintraub, has brought this out in his study of Shaw's *Heartbreak House*: Stanley Weintraub (1973), *Bernard Shaw 1914–1918: Journey to Heartbreak*, Routledge, London.

2. The resolution is quoted from Schorske, p. 83.

3. Massimo Salvadori makes this judgement in his book on Kautsky:

> What integrated Social Democracy into German society . . . was not erroneous ideology; it was the product of real historical conditions. Between the end of the nineteenth century and 1914, the SPD experienced a situation completely unforeseen by the heritage of Marxism, which was nonetheless its official ideology. Its integration into the Second Reich was fundamentally determined by objective processes, which met with the active accord of some sectors of the party and the opposition of others: above all by the peculiar combination of a powerful and conservative state apparatus, based on an alliance of aristocratic militarism and elite bureaucracy, and an unprecedented industrial development dominated by a brutal finance capital. In these conditions, the real 'motor force' of integration was actually the trade-union movement. German social democracy was the first great workers' party that was compelled to deal, squarely and bluntly, with a capitalist system whose rapid end of its theory had led it to expect, which instead exploded outwards in an imperialism that rallied wide mass support. (Salvadori [1979] p. 19)

4. Schorske, p. 106.

5. Ibid., pp. 290–91.

6. German war socialism is discussed in Paul Auerbach, Meghnad Desai and Ali Shamsavari (1988), 'The Dialectic of Plan and the Market: On the Transition from Actually Existing Capitalism', *New Left Review*, 170, September–October. The debate among economists about planning is discussed in Chapter 12 below.

7. For a Left sympathetic history of the events of the revolt in Germany see Chris Harman (1982), *The Lost Revolution: Germany 1918–23*, Bookmarks, London.

8. There is such a large literature on the Russian Revolution that it is difficult to cite all the relevant material. There is, of course, E. H. Carr (1950), *The Bolshevik*

Revolution, 3 vols, Macmillan, London, which is by now a classic. See also Alexander Rabinowitch (1968), *Prelude to Revolution: The Petrograd Bolsheviks and the July 1917 Uprising*, Indiana University Press, Bloomington.

More recent works include Orlando Figes (1996), *A People's Tragedy: The Russian Revolution 1891–1924*, Jonathan Cape, London.

The arguments about the betrayal of the Revolution have been made by Trotsky and his followers, but also by Mensheviks. See Tony Cliff, *Lenin* 4 vols (1975–79) [vol. 1, *Building the Party*; vol. 2, *All Power to the Soviets*; vol. 3, *Revolution Besieged*; vol. 4, *The Bosheviks and World Communism*, Pluto Press, London; Tony Cliff (1989), *Trotsky: Towards October, 1879–1917*, Bookmarks, London.

9. Cliff, *Lenin*, vol. 2, p. 156.

10. On the Kronstadt revolt, see Paul Avrich (1970), *Kronstadt 1921*, Princeton University Press, Princeton, NJ. This was a revolt in March 1921 by the sailors of the naval fortress Kronstadt, in the Gulf of Finland. Kronstadt was the 'pride and glory' of the 1917 Revolution, and its rising against the Bolshevik government under the slogan 'free soviets' was a very serious event for the Bolsheviks. After sixteen days it was ruthlessly put down. Lenin announced his New Economic Policy soon after.

11. Raphael Samuel (1994), *Theatres of Memory*, vol. 1, *Past and Present in Contemporary Culture*; vol. 2, *Island Stories: Unravelling Britain*, Verso, London and New York.

12. Isaac Deutscher (1954–1963), *The Prophet Armed: Trotsky, 1879–1921*; *The Prophet Unarmed: Trotsky, 1921–29*; *The Prophet Outcast: Trotsky, 1929–1940*, Oxford University Press, Oxford.

Tony Cliff in *Lenin*, vol. 4, chs 8–9, argues along lines similar to Deutscher's.

13. Karl Kautsky (1919), *The Dictatorship of the Proletariat*, reprinted with a new introduction (1964); trans. H. J. Stenning, University of Michigan Press, Ann Arbor.

Karl Kautsky (1946), *Social Democracy versus Communism*, ed. and trans. D. Shub and J. Shaplen, Rand School Press, New York.

Rosa Luxemburg (1935), *Leninism or Marxism*, Anti-Parliamentary Communist Federation, Glasgow; also (1961), *The Russian Revolution and Leninism or Marxism*, University of Michigan Press, Ann Arbor.

14. Cliff, *Lenin*, vol. 4, p. 127.

15. E. Preobrazhensky (1966), *The New Economics*, Clarendon Press, Oxford. Michael Ellman (1975), 'Did the Agricultural Surplus Provide Resources for the Increase in Investment in the USSR during the First Five Year Plan?', *Economic Journal*, December.

Chapter 8

1. The story of Europe's encounter with Asia, Africa and America is long, complex and controversial, but a recent book may suffice for many readers: Mark Cocker (1998), *Rivers of Blood, Rivers of Gold: Europe's Conflict with Tribal Peoples*, Jonathan Cape, London.

2. J. A. Hobson, *Imperialism: A Study*, 1st edition 1905, Archibald Constable, London; 3rd edition 1988, Unwin Hyman, London.

3. J. A. Schumpeter (1919/1951), *Imperialism and Social Class*, trans. Heinz Norden, Augustus Kelley, New York.

4. I have taken the quotation from Kenneth E. Boulding and Tapan Mukerjee (eds) (1972), *Economic Imperialism: A Book of Readings*, University of Michigan Press, Ann Arbor, p. 39.

5. Ibid.

6. Desai, *Lenin's Economic Writings*, pp. 29–30.

7. Ibid., p. 306.

8. Ibid., p. 317.

9. W. W. Rostow (1960), *The Stages of Economic Growth: A Non-Communist Manifesto*, Cambridge University Press, Cambridge.

10. John Wells (1997), *The House of Lords: From Saxon Wargods to a Modern Senate*, Hodder & Stoughton, London, p. 155.

11. Marx, *Capital Volume 1*, Lawrence & Wishart edn, p. 720.

Chapter 9

1. Chris Harman (1997), *The Lost Revolution: Germany 1918–1923*, Bookmarks, London.

2. Alfred Döblin (1983), *Karl and Rosa: November 1918, A German Revolution, A novel*, trans. John Woods, International Publishing Corporation, New York.

3. George Dangerfield (1980), *Strange Death of Liberal England*, G. P. Putnam's Sons, New York.

4. Arno Mayer (1981), *The Persistence of the Old Regime: Europe to the Great War*, Croom Helm, London.

5. The split in the Second International and the formation of the Third International are well described, albeit from a Leninist viewpoint, in Cliff, *Lenin*; and Sassoon, *One Hundred Years of Socialism*.

6. The course of post-1918 inflation in Europe is charted in J. M. Keynes (1923), *A Tract on Monetary Reform*, London, Macmillan.

On the return to Gold Standard, see J. M. Keynes (1925), 'The Economics

Consequences of Mr Churchill', published as a pamphlet but included in (1972) *Essays in Persuasion: The Collected Works of John Maynard Keynes, Volume IX*, Macmillan, London.

7. On German hyperinflation see Gerald Feldman (1993), *The Great Disorder: Politics, Economics and Society in the German Hyperinflation 1914–1924*, Oxford University Press, Oxford.

On the Weimar Republic, see Anthony Kaes, Martin Jay and Edward Dimendberg (1994), *The Weimar Republic Sourcebook*, University of California Press, Berkeley.

8. For interwar financial history, see C. P. Kindleberger (1973), *The World in Depression 1929–1939*, Macmillan, London; A. J. Brown (1938), *International Gold Standard Reinterpreted*, 2 vols, Princeton University Press, Princeton, NJ.

9. On Lenin's policy, see his pamphlet 'The Tax in Kind', reprinted in Meghnad Desai (ed.) (1989), *Lenin's Economic Writings*, Lawrence & Wishart, London.

On the history of Bolshevik Russia, see Carr, *The Bolshevik Revolution*. On the suppression of workers' opposition, see Robert V. Daniels (1960), *The Conscience of the Revolution*, Harvard University Press, Cambridge, MA.

10. The label 'social state' was applied by Nigel Harris (1995), *The New Untouchables: Immigration and the New World Worker*, I. B. Tauris, London.

11. On the Marxian roots of Russia's First Five Year Plan, see Meghnad Desai (1979), *Marxian Economics*, Blackwell, Oxford.

12. For a heterodox view of Marx on imperialism, see Bill Warren (1980), *Imperialism, the Pioneer of Development*, New Left Books, London.

13. On fascism in Italy and Germany, see Stanley G. Payne (1995), *A History of Fascism 1914–45*, UCL Press, London.

14. On cinema, see David Putnam and Neil Watson (1998), *Movies and Money*, Alfred Knopff, New York.

Chapter 10

1. On chaotic dynamics, see Richard Goodwin and Lionello Punzo (1987), *The Dynamics of Capitalist Economy: A Multi-Sectoral Approach*, Polity Press, Oxford, especially Appendix A3.

2. For the Depression in the USA, see Arthur Schlesinger (1957), *The Crisis of the Old Order 1919–1933* vol. 1 of *The Age of Roosevelt*, Houghton Mifflin, Boston, MA; Charles Kindleberger (1973), *The World in Depression, 1929–1939*, Macmillan, London.

3. On the crash of 1929, see J. K. Galbraith (1980), Fiftieth Anniversary Edition (first published 1955), *The Great Crash, 1929*, André Deutsch, London.

4. The Federal Bank was blamed for the Depression in Milton Friedman and

Anna Schwarz (1963), *A Monetary History of the United States 1867–1960,* Princeton University Press, Princeton, NJ.

5. For hegemon, see Kindleberger, *The World in Depression.*

6. On Hitler's economic policy, see Richard Overy (1994), *War and Economy in the Third Reich,* Clarendon Press, Oxford.

7. On the New Deal, see Arthur Schlesinger (1959), *The Coming of the New Deal,* vol. 2 of *The Age of Roosevelt,* Houghton Mifflin, Boston, MA.

8. On the Labour Party's fortunes in 1929–31, see Robert Skidelsky (1967), *Politicians and the Slump: The Labour Government of 1929–1931,* Macmillan, London.

9. David Marquand (1977), *Ramsay MacDonald,* Jonathan Cape, London.

10. On Sweden's socialist success, see Sassoon, *One Hundred Years of Socialism.*

11. On Trotsky in the 1930s, see Deutscher, *The Prophet Outcast.* On the history of Russian politics and economics, see E. H. Carr (1958), *Socialism in One Country,* 3 vols, Macmillan, London.

12 Moshe Lewin (1975), *Russian Peasants and Soviet Power: A Study of Collectivization,* Norton, New York.

13. Sidney and Beatrice Webb (1935), *Soviet Communism: A New Civilization?* Longman, London. After its first edition in 1935, it was republished with revisions in 1937 and 1941 – that is to say, after the show trials had been exposed.

14. On the Frankfurt School, see Martin Jay (1984), *Marxism and Totality: The Adventure of a Concept from Lukács to Habermas,* University of California Press, Berkeley.

15. On Marxian Economics, see M. C. Howard and J. E. King (1989, 1992), *A History of Marxian Economics,* vol. 1, 1883–1929; vol. 2, 1929–90, Macmillan, London.

Chapter 11

1. Technopol is a word we owe – as far as I am aware – to the international economist John Williamson.

2. Ludwig von Mises (1922), *Socialism.* For a complete reference, see the notes to Chapter 12.

3. Ibid., p. 51.

4. For Wicksell, see Erik Lundberg (1996), *The Development of Swedish and Keynesian Macroeconomic Theory and its Impact on Economic Policy,* Cambridge University Press, Cambridge.

5. On Hayek's statement about the profit rate being renamed as natural rates, see Hayek, *Profits, Interest and Investment.*

6. Joseph A. Schumpeter (1913/1934), *The Theory of Economic Development,* Harvard University Press, Cambridge, MA.

7. Schumpeter made an attempt to substantiate his theory empirically, but by the time he published his two-volume study on business cycles in 1939, Keynes's *General Theory* had come out, and economists lost interest in older themes: Joseph A Schumpeter (1939), *Business Cycles*, 2 vols, McGraw-Hill, New York.

8. Friedrich von Hayek (1931), *Prices and Production*, 1st edition 1935, revised and enlarged edition, Routledge, London.

9. Paul Sweezy made his remark at the memorial meeting for Professor David Glass, held at the LSE. I was present.

10. J. M. Keynes (1936), *The General Theory of Employment, Interest and Money*, Macmillan, London.

11. Samuel Brittan, 'Voices in the Air', *Financial Times*, 2 September 1999.

12. For details of Keynes's activities during the years of writing the General Theory, see Robert Skidelsky (1992), *John Maynard Keynes*, vol. 2, Macmillan, London.

13. The expression 'territorial social state' is from Harris, *The New Untouchables.*

14. On Marxists' attitude to Keynes, see Paul Mattick (1969), *Marx and Keynes: The Limits of Mixed Economy*, Merlin Press, London.

15. J. M. Keynes (1940), *How to Pay for the War* Macmillan, London, reproduced in J. M. Keynes (1972), *The Collected Writings of John Maynard Keynes. Volume 9, Essays in Persuasion*, Macmillan, London.

The original edition of *Essays in Persuasion* was published in 1931. This is a revised and enlarged edition published in the collected works edition.

16. Seymour E. Harris (ed.) (1952), *The New Economics: Keynes' Influence on Theory and Public Policy*, Alfred Knopff, New York.

17. Lawrence R. Klein (1947), *The Keynesian Revolution*, Macmillan, New York.

Chapter 12

1. On Otto Neurath, see Nancy Cartwright, Jordi Cat, Lola Fleck and Thomas Hebel (1996), *Otto Neurath: Philosophy Between Science and Politics*, Cambridge University Press, Cambridge. All my discussions of Neurath rely on this excellent book. For the growth of marginal theory, the most accessible source is Mark Blaug (1987), *Economic Theory in Retrospect*, 4th edition, Cambridge University Press, Cambridge.

2. Neurath in Cartwright *et al.*, p. 29.

3. Ibid., p. 37.

4. The Mises reference is Ludwig von Mises (1923/1936/1981), *Socialism: An Economic and Sociological Analysis*, first published in German as *Die Gemeinwirtschaft*, Gustav Fischer, Jena, 2nd edition 1932, trans. J. Kahane 1936, published by Jonathan Cape, London. I quote from the 1981 Liberty Classics edition (Liberty Fund Inc. Indianapolis, IN).

5. Ibid., p. 95.

6. Ibid., p. 101.

7. Friedrich von Hayek (ed.) (1935), *Collective Economic Planning: Critical Studies on the Possibilities of Socialism,* Routledge, London. This contains two essays by Hayek on the subject of socialist calculations:

(1) 'The Nature and History of the Problem' (pp. 1–40);

(2) 'The Present State of the Debate' (pp. 201–43).

A third essay is, 'The Competitive Solution'; a review article on Lange–Taylor and Dickinson, *Economica,* vol. VII no. 26, May 1940. All three essays were brought together in Friedrich von Hayek (1948), *Individualism and the Economic Order,* University of Chicago Press, Chicago, pp. 119–208.

8. Enrico Barone's article 'The Ministry of Production in the Collective State' was first published in Italian in 1908; trans. in Hayek, pp. 245–90.

9. The Lange–Taylor references are F. M. Taylor (1929), 'The Guidance of Production in a Socialist State', *American Economic Review,* March. This was reproduced along with Lange's essay in B. E. Lippincott (ed.) (1938), *On the Economic Theory of Socialism,* University of Minnesota Press, Minneapolis.

10. Hayek, *Collective Economic Planning,* pp. 207–8.

11. H. D. Dickinson (1939), *Economics of Socialism,* Oxford University Press, Oxford.

12. Lippincott, 1938.

13. Friedrich von Hayek (1937), 'Economics and Knowledge', *Economica,* IV, pp. 33–54. This essay is also reprinted in Hayek, *Individualism and the Economic Order.*

14. Hayek, 'Economics and Knowledge', pp. 45–6.

Chapter 13

1. Friedrich von Hayek (1944), *The Road to Serfdom,* Routledge, London.

2. On Keynes's importance in deflecting the anti-cartel attack, see Arthur Schlesinger (1959), *The Age of Roosevelt, Volume 3: The Politics of Upheaval,* Houghton Mifflin, Boston, MA.

3. Joseph Schumpeter (1942), *Capitalism, Socialism and Democracy,* 5th edn 1996, Routledge, London; Joan Robinson, (1942), *An Essay on Marxian Economics,* Macmillan, London; Paul Sweezy (1948), *The Theory of Capitalist Development,* Monthly Review Press, New York; Böhm-Bawerk (1949), *Karl Marx and the Close of His System.*

4. Laski (ed.) (1948), *The Communist Manifesto: The Centenary Edition.*

5. On the wartime negotiations which led to the IMF and the World Bank, see Robert Skidelsky (2000), *John Maynard Keynes: Battling for Britain, Volume 3,* Macmillan, London.

6. Skidelsky (ibid.) argues that Harry White was in secret collusion with the Soviet Union. Even without that, anti-British sentiment was strong in the USA.

7. Paul Rosenstein-Rodan (1943), 'Problems of Industrialisation in Eastern and South-Eastern Europe', *Economic Journal* 53, pp. 202–11.

8. James Meade told me personally that he thought up the arrangement for GATT in a note he wrote while he was in the UK Cabinet Office. This note is in Susan Howson (ed.) (1990), *The Collected Papers of James Meade: Volume 4: The Cabinet Office Diary, 1944–46*, Unwin Hyman, London.

9. On US attitudes to the British Empire, see Christopher Thorne (1979), *Allies of a Kind: The United States, Britain and the War against Japan 1941–1945*, Oxford University Press, Oxford.

10. Karl Kautsky (1902), *Die Agrarfrage: eine Übersicht über die Tendenzen der modernen Landwirtschaft und die Agrarpolitik der Sozialdemokratie*, J. H. W. Dietz Nachf, Stuttgart, trans. Peter Burgess, Swan, London.

11. A. V. Chayanov (1966), *The Theory of the Peasant Economy*, trans. Basile Kerblay, ed. Daniel Thorner, Basile Kerblay and R. E. F. Smith, Richard D. Irwin, Homewood, IL.

12. Schumpeter, *Capitalism, Socialism and Democracy.*

13. Anthony Downs (1957), *An Economic Theory of Democracy*, Harper & Row, New York.

14. Karl Polanyi (1944), *The Great Transformation*, Farrar & Reinhart, New York.

15. These arguments and all the references are in Perry Anderson (1992), *English Questions*, Verso, London.

Chapter 14

1. The literature on the Keynesian Golden Age is extensive. On the 30th anniversary of the *General Theory* Robert Lekachman (1966) published *The Age of Keynes*, Random House, New York. Andrew Schoenfield's *Modern Capitalism* (1965) appeared at the peak of the Golden Age, and embodies mixed-economy Keynsianism in the best, most astute way: Oxford University Press, Oxford.

2. For the history of the Socialist International, see Sassoon, *One Hundred Years of Socialism.*

3. For decolonization, see V. G. Kiernam (1982), *European Empires: From Conquest to Collapse, 1815–1960*, Fontana, London.

4. A. V. Dicey (1914), *Introduction to the Study of the Law of the Constitution* (8th edition), Macmillan, London, was a classic liberal text first published in 1885. It was republished as a Liberty Classic by Liberty Classics of Indianapolis, IN (1982).

5. The Prebisch–Singer hypothesis, as it is called, is best described in John Eatwell *et al.* (eds) (1990), *The New Palgrave Dictionary of Economics*, Macmillan, London.

6. Friedrich List (1837/1856), *The National System of Political Economy*, trans. Sampson Lloyd, Longmans Green, London.

7. Econometric model-building for national economies as well as on a global scale is associated with the name of Lawrence Klein, who was awarded a Nobel Prize in 1984 for his work. For a simple introduction, see Meghnad Desai (1976), *Applied Econometrics,* Philip Allan, London.

8. Input–output models were used in the immediate postwar period by the US government. After Eisenhower came to power, this was discontinued for any policy-making in the civilian economy, but continued to be in use for defence planning. I recall that a fellow research student at the University of Pennsylvania was asked to work on input–output for the PARM programme in Washington during the 1960s. He was not told that PARM stood for Post-Attack Resource Management. Outside the USA, input–output models continued to be successful. Leontieff was awarded the Nobel Prize in Economics.

9. George Dantzig (1963), *Linear Programming and Extensions,* Princeton University Press, Princeton, NJ. Koopmans shared the Nobel Prize for Economics with the Soviet economist Leonid Kantorovich. See also C. Tjalling Koopmans (ed.) (1951), *Activity Analysis for Production and Allocation,* John Wiley, New York.

10. Harold Kuhn and Abraham Tucker (1951), 'Nonlinear Programming', in Jerzy Neyman (ed.) (1951), *Proceedings of the Second Berkeley Symposium on Mathematical Statistics and Probability,* University of California Press, Berkeley.

11. The connection between shadow prices and market prices was first shown by the Nobel laureate Paul Samuelson in a memorandum for the Rand Corporation in 1949. It has been published as 'Market Mechanism and Maximization', in *The Collected Scientific Papers of Paul Samuelson, Volume 1,* MIT Press, Cambridge, MA, pp. 425–92.

12. Anthony Crosland (1956), *The Future of Socialism,* Jonathan Cape, London.

13. John Kenneth Galbraith (1952), *American Capitalism; The Concept of Countervailing Power,* Harcourt Brace Jovanovich, Boston, MA; (1958), *The Affluent Society,* Hamish Hamilton, London.

14. Keynes's views on policy after publication of the *General Theory* are fully described in the third and final volume of Robert Skidelsky's biography: R. Skidelsky (2000), *John Maynard Keynes: Battling for Britain 1937–1946,* Macmillan, London. But even in the early years, the advocates of Keynesian ideas were cautious: Harris (ed.) *The New Economics.*

15. Pigou's real-balances argument was fully developed by Donald Patinkin (1949/1965), *Money, Interest and Prices: An Integration of Monetary and Value Theories,* Harper & Row, New York.

16. The American adoption of Keynesian policies is fully described in Herbert C. Stein (1969), *The Fiscal Revolution in America,* University of Chicago Press, Chicago.

17. Phillips 'The Relationship . . .'.

18. Paul A. Samuelson and Robert M. Solow (1960), 'The Analytics of the Anti-Inflation Policy', *American Economic Review* 50, pp. 177–94.

19. Milton Friedman (ed.) (1956), *Studies in the Quantity Theory of Money,* University of Chicago Press, Chicago, was the first salvo in this battle. The climax was in R. J. Gordon (ed.) (1974), *Milton Friedman's Monetary Framework: A Debate with the Critics,* University of Chicago Press, Chicago. By 1974, Friedman had won. He also got the Nobel Prize in economics.

20. James Burnham (1942), *The Managerial Revolution, or, What is Happening in the World Now,* Putnam, London.

21. For an early account of the humanist Marx, see Eric Fromm (1967), *Marx's Concept of Man,* Ungar, New York. See also Robert Tucker (1972), *Philosophy and Myth in Karl Marx,* Cambridge University Press, Cambridge.

22. In growth theory, the seminal contribution was that of Robert Solow, See Robert M. Solow (1970), *Growth Theory,* Oxford University Press, Oxford, for an explanation.

23. W. W. Rostow, *The Stages of Economic Growth.*

24. Andrew Glyn and Robert Sutcliffe (1971), 'The Collapse of UK Profits', *New Left Review,* 66 (March–April) was the first article to notice the decline in profitability. The argument was later expanded in Andrew Glyn and Robert Sutcliffe (1972) *British Capitalism, Workers and Profit Squeeze,* Penguin, Harmondsworth; and Andrew Glyn and John Harrison (1980), *The British Economic Disaster,* Pluto Press, London.

25. J. K. Galbraith (1971), *The New Industrial State,* Houghton Mifflin, London. See also a critique in Auerbach, Desai and Shamsavri (1988), 'The Dialectic of Plan and the Market'.

Chapter 15

1. For an economic history of India's industrialization, see D. R. Gadgil (1971), *Industrial Evolution of India in Recent Times, 1860–1939,* 5th edition, Oxford University Press, Bombay.

2. Dadabhai Naoroji (1901), *Poverty and Un-British Rule in India,* Swan Sonnenschein, London. The original was republished in 1962.

Romesh Chandra Dutt (1908), *Economic History of India,* 2 vols, Kegan Paul, Trübner Trench, London.

Many of the facts about India's economic history are disputed. See Dharma Kumar (ed.) (1983), *The Cambridge Economic History of India 1757–1970* (vol. 2), Cambridge University Press, Cambridge, for revisionist views. See especially the chapter by Morris David Morris, 'The Growth of Large-Scale Industry to 1947', for industrial growth in pre-independence days.

India had the world's largest jute industry, fourth- or fifth-largest textile industry, and third-largest railroad network by 1914.

3. Paul Baran (1960), *The Political Economy of Growth,* Monthly Review Press, New York.

4. Andre Gunder Frank (1967), *Capitalism and Underdevelopment in Latin America: Historical Studies of Chile and Brazil,* Monthly Review Press, New York.

5. Ibid., p. xi.

6. Colin Clark (1940), *The Conditions of Economic Progress,* Macmillan, London. This was a pioneering book in national income measurement. Clark was a student and associate of Keynes at Cambridge.

7. David Halberstam (1972), *The Best and the Brightest,* Random House, New York.

8. On the CIA's support of culture, see Francis Stonor Saunders (1999), *Who Paid the Piper? The CIA and the Cultural Cold War,* Granta, London.

A Centre for International Studies was set up at MIT where bright young economists from India collaborated with their US counterparts. Much good work was done on mathematical model of planning. There was great embarrassment when it was discovered that the centre was CIA-financed. After all, many of the Indian economists regarded themselves as socialists, if not communists!

9. Paul Baran and Paul Sweezy (1968), *Monopoly Capital,* Monthly Review Press, New York.

10. For a general critique of the American economy, see Samuel Bowles, David Gordon and Thomas Weiskopf (1991), *After the Wasteland: A Democratic Economics for the Year 2000,* M.E. Shape, Armonk, NY.

Bowles and his American Marxist colleagues have devised a theory of 'the structure of social accumulation' as 'a critique of the inequities and wastefulness of American capitalism'.

The Union of Radical Political Economists (URPE) publishes a *Review of Radical Political Economy* in which many articles analysing American capitalism from a Left perspective are published.

11. The best source on the Frankfurt School, is Jay, *Marxism and Totality.* See also Perry Anderson (1979), *Considerations of Western Marxism,* Verso, London.

12. On the Naxalite movement, see Sumanta Banerjee (1982), *India's Simmering Revolution: The Naxalite Uprising,* Zed Books, London. This book was first published in 1980 under the title *In the Wake of Naxalbari: A History of Naxalite Movement in India,* Subarnarekha, Calcutta.

13. On the Cultural Revolution, Roderick MacFarquhar's multi-volume history is the best source: Roderick MacFarquhar (1974/1983/1997), *The Origins of the Cultural Revolution,* 3 vols, Oxford University Press, Oxford.

14. On Cambodia, Ben Kiernan (1985), *How Pol Pot Came to Power,* Verso, London, is the best account.

15. On the Green Revolution and other matters see Meghnad Desai (1975) 'India: Contradictions of Slow Capitalistic Development', in R. Blackburn (ed.),

Explosions in a Subcontinent, Penguin, Harmondsworth. This was an expanded and revised version of Meghnad Desai (1970), 'The Vortex in India', *New Left Review* 170, September–October.

16. The pioneering African Socialists – Léopold Senghor, Kwame Nkrumah and Julius Nyerere – were all sincere and dedicated politicians. Still, the fact remains that African socialism remained an intellectual pastime. Efforts to implement a socialist policy prematurely in a barely capitalist context were uniformly disastrous, as the examples of Ghana and Tanzania show. See Léopold Senghor (1959), *African Socialism,* American Society for African Culture, New York.

17. E. G. Liberman (1971), *Economic Methods and the Effectiveness of Production,* International Arts and Sciences Press, New York.

Chapter 16

1. Ronald Coase's articles have been collected and issued with an introduction by Ronald Coase (1988), *The Firm, the Market and the Law,* University of Chicago Press, Chicago.

For Stigler's more popular pieces, see George Stigler (1982), *The Economist as a Preacher and Other Essays,* Blackwell, Oxford.

2. For a multicountry study of stagflation, see Michael Bruno and Jeffrey Sachs (1985), *The Economics of Stagflation,* Blackwell, Oxford.

3. I confess to a blind spot about the merits of Kalecki. For much more favourable views, see the writings of post-Keynesians such as Malcolm Sawyer: Malcolm Sawyer (1985), *The Economics of Michal Kalecki,* Macmillan, Basingstoke.

Kalecki's original papers are in Michal Kalecki (1968), *Theory of Economic Dynamism,* Monthly Review Press, New York; also (1971), *Selected Essays on Dynamism of the Capitalistic Economy,* Cambridge University Press, Cambridge.

4. Ernest Mandel, (1978), *The Second Slump,* New Left Books, London.

5. For the history of ideas about Walras's general equilibrium and proofs of its existence, see E. Roy Weintraub (1993), *General Equilibrium Analysis: Studies in Appraisal,* University of Michigan Press, Ann Arbour.

6. Gérard Debreu (1959), *Theory of Value,* John Wiley, New York.

7. For a reader-friendly account of Robert Lucas's work, see Thomas J. Sargent (1996), 'Expectations and the Non-neutrality of Lucas', *Journal of Monetary Economics* 37, pp 535–48.

The paper commemorated the twenty-fifth anniversary of Lucas's paper 'Expectations and the Neutrality of Money', *Journal of Economic Theory* 4, pp. 103–24, which made the anti-Keynesian argument. Other articles by Lucas are also listed in Sargent's references.

8. Paul Samuelson (1971), 'Understanding the Marxian Notion of Exploitation:

A Summary of the So-called Transformation Problem between Marxian Values and Competitive Prices', *Journal of Economic Literature* 9 (2), pp. 399–431. Most recently Samuelson has written an amusing *divertissement* on this: Paul Samuelson (1999), 'Sherlock Holmes and the Swarthy German: The Case of Inanely "Transforming" *Mehrwert* to Prices' in Martin Faase *et al.* (eds), *Economics, Welfare Policy and History of Economic Thought: Essays in Honour of Alfred Heertje*, Edward Elgar, Cheltenham.

9. Piero Sraffa (1960), *The Production of Commodities by Means of Commodities: Prelude to a Critique of Economic Theory*, Cambridge University Press, Cambridge.

10. Ian Steedman (1977), *Marx After Sraffa*, New Left Books, London.

11. For a recent account of these forces in the context of Bangladeshi women in the UK and Bangladesh, see Naila Kabeer (2000), *The Power to Choose: Bangladeshi Women and Labour Market, Discussions in London and Dhaka*, Verso, London and New York.

12. The Asian Tigers have been well described in: Alice Amsden (1989), *Asia's Next Giant*, Oxford University Press, Oxford.

See also Robert Wade (1990), *Governing the Market: Economic Theory and the Role of the Government in East Asian Industrialization*, Princeton University Press, Princeton.

Chapter 17

1. For some background to the 1970s and 1980s, see Meghnad Desai (1981), *Testing Monetarism*, Pinter, London.

2. See Mary Kaldor (ed.) *The Ideas of 1989*, LSE, Centre for the Study of Global Governance Publication, forthcoming.

3. Louis Althusser (1969), *For Marx*, Verso, London; G. A. Cohen (1978), *Karl Marx's Theory of History: A Defence*, Princeton University Press, Princeton, NJ.

4. John Roemer (1982), *A General Theory of Exploitation and Class*, Harvard University Press, Cambridge, MA. For a critique, see Roberto Veneziani (2000), *Exploitation and Time*, unpublished, LSE.

5. See especially Giovanni Cornia, Richard Jolly and Frances Stewert (eds) (1987), *Adjustment with a Human Face*, Clarendon Press, Oxford.

6. Wade, *Governing the Market*.

7. Robert Lucas (1988), 'The Mechanism of Economic Development', *Journal of Monetary Economics* 22, pp. 3–42; Paul Romer (1986) 'Increasing Returns and Long-Run Growth', *Journal of Political Economy* 94, pp. 1002–37.

Chapter 18

1. For a discussion of the collapse of the USSR, see Michael Cox (ed.) (1999), *Rethinking the Soviet Collapse: Sovietology, the Death of Communism and the New Russia*,

Pinter, London; Robert Skidelsky (1995) *The World After Communism*, Macmillan, London; János Kornai (1992), *The Socialist System: The Political Economy of Communism*, Princeton University Press, Princeton, NJ.

2. On the women's movement, there is an extensive literature. See Sheila Rowbotham (1972), *Women, Resistance and Revolution: A History of Women and Revolution in the Modern World*, Allen Lane, London; Nancy Folbre (1994), *Who Pays for the Kids? Gender and the Structure of Constraints*, Routledge, London.

3. There are many books and articles on market socialism. See especially Alec Nove (1983), *The Economics of Feasible Socialism*, Allen & Unwin, London.

There has been a revival of the socialist debate by some modern economists, who recommend the socialization/public control of investment. See John Roemer and Pranab Bardhan (1993), *Market Socialism: The Current Debate*, Oxford University Press, Oxford; Joseph Stiglitz (1994), *Whither Socialism?* MIT Press, Cambridge, MA.

4. Worker ownership was first discussed extensively by Jaroslav Vanek. James Meade also wrote on it: J. Vanek (1977), *The Labour Managed Economy*, Cornell University Press, Ithaca, NY; James Meade (1972), 'The Theory of Labour Managed Firms and Profit Sharing', *Economic Journal* 82, pp. 402–28.

5. On the demise of socialism, see Meghnad Desai (1992) 'Is Socialism Dead?', *Contention*, Indiana University Press, Indianapolis.

6. On the contrast between neoliberal and libertarian theories, see Meghnad Desai (2000d), 'Neither Ideology nor Utopia', *Cambridge Review of International Affairs*, November.

7. On the debate about the powerless state, see Linda Weiss (1998), *The Myth of the Powerless State: Governing the Economy in a Global Era*, Polity Press, Cambridge; Kenichi Ohmae (1990), *The Borderless World: Power and Strategy in the Interlinked Economy*, Collins, London.

8. There are many books on globalization. See Paul Hirst and Graeme Thompson (1996/2000), *Globalization in Question: The International Economy and the Possibilities of Governance*, Polity Press, Cambridge; David Held (1999), *Global Transformations*, Polity Press, Cambridge; Meghnad Desai (1995b), 'Global Governance', in Meghnad Desai and Paul Redfern (eds), *Global Governance: Ethics and Economics of the World Order*, Pinter, London; Meghnad Desai (1998), 'Profitability and the Persistence of Capitalism', in R. Bellofiore (ed.), *Marxian Economics: A Reappraisal, Volume 2, Essays on Volume III of Capital Profit, Prices and Dynamics*, St Martin's Press, New York, pp. 291–305; Meghnad Desai (2000b), 'Rejuvenated Capitalism and No Longer Existing Socialism', in Jan Toporowski (ed.), *Political Economy and New Capitalism: Essays in Honour of Sam Aaronovitch*, Routledge, London.

9. On the demise of Keynesianism, see Meghnad Desai (1996), 'Hayek, Marx and the Demise of Official Keynesianism', in Mauro Baranzini and Alvaro Cencini (eds), *Inflation and Unemployment*, Routledge, London.

10. On Indian reforms, see Meghnad Desai (1993), *Capitalism, Socialism and Democracy in India,* EXIM Bank, India; Meghnad Desai (1995a), 'Economic Reform: Stalled by Politics?', in Philip Oldenburg (ed.), *India Briefing: Staying the Course,* M. E. Sharpe, New York/London; Will Hutton (1995), *The State We're In,* Jonathan Cape, London.

For a review, see Meghnad Desai (1997), 'It's Profitability, Stupid', in Gavin Kelly, Dominic Kelly and Andrew Gamble (eds), *Stakeholder Capitalism,* Macmillan, London, pp. 203–18.

11. On cycles, see Charles Kindleberger (1978), *Manias, Panics and Crashes: A History of Financial Crises,* Macmillan, London; George Soros (1998), *The Crisis of Global Capitalism: Open Society Endangered,* BBS/Public Affairs, New York.

12. I have dealt with the three versions of capitalism in Meghnad Desai (2000a), *Financial Crises and Global Governance,* unpublished, LSE.

13. For the Marx/Hayek debate, see Chris M. Seccavaccia (1995), *Marx, Hayek and Utopia,* State University Press of New York, Albany, NY.

Chapter 19

1. For alternative capitalisms, see Hutton, *The State We're In,* Chapter 10: 'The Political Economy of World Capitalism' pp. 257–84.

2. On globalization; besides the references cited in the notes to Chapter 18, see also: Peter Burbach, Orlando Núñez and Boris Kagarlitsky (1997), *Globalization and Its Discontents: The Rise of Post-Modern Socialisms,* Pluto Press, London (a largely negative view of globalization from a Left perspective, but rather optimistic about the imminence of change. The authors plead diverse socialism.)

Samir Amin (1997), *Capitalism in the Age of Globalisation: The Management of Contemporary Society,* Zed Books, London (a critique from a senior Marxist–Leninist, somewhat hopeful that the European Union will challenge American hegemony).

Saskia Sassen (1998), *Globalisation and its Discontents: Essays on Mobility of People and Money,* New Press, New York (an account of migration and informal economy as they shape globalization from a feminist perspective).

3. The dialectical 'classical Marxist' view has been developed in Desai, 'Profitability and the Persistence of Capitalism'; and Desai, 'Rejuvenated Capitalism and No Longer Existing Socialism'.

4. On Seattle and the WTO, see Meghnad Desai (2000c), 'Seattle: A Tragi-Comedy', in Barbara Gunnell and David Timms (eds), *After Seattle: Globalisation and Its Discontents,* Catalyst Pamphlet, London.

5. For innovations in warfare and navigation which were crucial to the Iberian expansion, see Carlo Cipolla (1966), *Guns, Sails and Empires,* Pantheon, New York. The classic study is Emmanuel Wallerstein (1980), *The Modern World System II:*

Mercantilism and the Consolidation of the European World Economy, Academic Press, New York.

6. Karl Marx (1844/1970), *A Contribution to the Critique of Hegel's Philosophy of Right*, ed. with an intro. by Joseph O'Malley, Cambridge University Press, Cambridge.

7. Ambalavaner Sivanandan (1990), *Communities of Resistance: Writing on the Black Struggle for Socialism*, Verso, London.

The quotation comes from Chapter 2, 'All that Melts into Air is Solid; The Hokum of New Times', p. 23. The full quotation is:

> [I]n throwing out the tool of economic analysis along with the ideological baggage of economism, the new Marxists were unable to bring to New Times [a new programme of the Communist Party of Great Britain published in *Marxism Today*, October 1988], the understanding that all the seismic changes in society and culture that they so adroitly and bravely described stemmed from (and in turn contributed to) the revolutionary changes at the economic level, at the level of productive forces, brought about by the new technology. Here was an ongoing revolution, the size, scope, comprehensiveness of which had never been known in the history of humankind and it was passing the Left by – till Thatcherism inadvertently brought it to their notice. And even then, what the Left understood was the scientific and technical magnitude of its achievements, summed up in Sir Iewan Maddock's phrase, that electronics had replaced the brain as once steam had replaced muscle. But its sociological size – that Capital had been freed from Labour – had escaped the Left altogether. The Labour Party was too sunk in its own stupor of trade unionism to see that the working class was decomposing under the impact of the new forces of production and the old forms of labour organization were becoming frangible. (pp. 23–4).

While I doubt that Sivanandan will agree with my analysis, there is much in his book that has enriched my understanding of globalization.

8. Nicholas Brady was US Treasury Secretary in the Reagan–George Bush days. To solve the debt problem, he introduced bonds with a US government guarantee which would induce indebted countries to buy up debts from banks.

9. For population and poverty estimates, see World Bank (2000), *World Development Report*, Oxford University Press, Oxford.

10. For poverty in the UK, see Peter Townsend (1979), *Poverty in the UK*, Penguin, Harmondsworth.

There were similar 'discoveries' of poverty in the USA. See Meghnad Desai (1995e), *Poverty, Famine and Economic Development: The Selected Essays of Meghnad Desai, Volume II*, Edward Elgar, Aldershot, especially Chapter 13 on 'Poverty and Capability: Towards an Empirically Implementable Measure' (pp. 185–204).

Bibliography

Althusser, Louis (1969) *For Marx*, Verso, London.

Amin, Samir (1997) *Capitalism in the Age of Globalisation: The Management of Contemporary Society*, Zed Books, London.

Amsden, Alice (1989) *Asia's Next Giant*, Oxford University Press, Oxford.

Anderson, Perry (1979) *Considerations of Western Marxism* Verso, London.

Anderson, Perry (1992) *English Questions*, Verso, London.

Arrow, Kenneth J. (1951) *Social Choice and Individual Values*, John Wiley, New York.

Auerbach, Paul, M. Desai and A. Shamsavari (1988) 'The Dialectic of Plan and the Market: On the Transition from Actually Existing Capitalism', *New Left Review* 170, September–October.

Avrich, Paul (1970) *Kronstadt 1921*, Princeton University Press, Princeton, NJ.

Banerjee, Sumanta (1982) *India's Simmering Revolution: The Naxalite Uprising*, Zed Books, London.

Baran, Paul (1960) *The Political Economy of Growth*, Monthly Review Press, New York.

Baran, Paul and Paul Sweezy (1968) *Monopoly Capital*, Monthly Review Press, New York.

Baranzini, Maurizio and Alvaro Cencini (eds) (1996) *Inflation and Unemployment*, Routledge, London.

Bellofiore, R. (ed.) (1998) *Marxian Economics: A Reappraisal, Volume 2, Essays on Volume III of Capital – Profits, Prices and Dynamics*, St Martin's Press, New York.

Bernstein, Edouard (1899/1909) *Evolutionary Socialism*, English translation of *Die Voranssetzungen des Socialismus und die Aufgaben der Sozialdemokratie*, J. H. Dietz, (Stuttgart) Huebsch (New York).

Blackburn, Robin (ed.) (1975) *Explosion in a Subcontinent*, Penguin, Harmondsworth.

Blaug, Mark (1987) *Economic Theory in Retrospect*, fourth edition, Cambridge University Press, Cambridge.

Bliss, Christopher (1975) *Capital Theory and the Distribution of Income*, North Holland, Amsterdam.

Böhm-Bawerk, Eugen von (1896/1949) *Karl Marx and the Close of His System,* originally published in German in O. Boenigk (ed.) *Staatwissenschaftlische Arbeiten: Festgaben für Karl Kneis* (Berlin), ed. and trans. Paul Sweezy and published in Sweezy (ed.) (1949).

Bortkiewicz, Ladislaus von (1907/1949) *On the Correction of Marx's Fundamental Theoretical Construction in the Third Volume of Capital,* originally published in *Jahrbücher für National Ökonomie und Statistik,* July 1907, trans. in Sweezy, (ed.) (1949).

Boulding, Kenneth E and Tapan Mukerjee (eds) (1972) *Economic Imperialism: A Book of Readings,* University of Michigan Press, Ann Arbor.

Bowles, Samuel, David Gordon and Thomas Weiskopf (1991) *After the Wasteland: A Democratic Economics for the Year 2000,* M. E. Sharpe, Armonk, NY.

Brown, A. J. (1938) *International Gold Standard Reinterpreted,* 2 vols, Princeton University Press, Princeton, NJ.

Brudney, Daniel (1998) *Marx's Attempt to Leave Philosophy,* Harvard University Press, Cambridge, MA.

Bruno, Michael and Jeffrey Sachs (1985) *The Economics of Stagflation,* Blackwell, Oxford.

Burbach, Peter, Orlando Núñez and Boris Kagarlitsky (1997) *Globalization and Its Discontents: The Rise of Post-Modern Socialisms,* Pluto Press, London.

Burnham, James (1942) *The Managerial Revolution, or, What is Happening in the World Now,* Putnam, London.

Caravale, G. (ed.) (1991) *Marx and Modern Economic Analysis,* Edward Elgar, Cheltenham.

Carr, E. H. (1950) *The Bolshevik Revolution,* 3 vols, Macmillan, London.

Carr, E. H. (1958) *Socialism in One Country,* 3 vols, Macmillan, London.

Cartwright, Nancy *et al.* (1996) *Otto Neurath: Philosophy Between Science and Politics,* Cambridge University Press, Cambridge.

Chayanov, A. V. (1960) *The Theory of the Peasant Economy,* trans. Basile Kerblay, ed. Daniel Thoner, Basile Kerblay and R. E. F. Smith, Richard D. Irwin, Homewood, IL.

Cipolla, Carlo (1966) *Guns, Sails and Empires,* Pantheon, New York.

Clark, Colin (1940) *The Conditions of Economic Progress,* Macmillan, London.

Cliff, Tony (1975–79) *Lenin,* 4 vols, Pluto Press, London.

Cliff, Tony (1989) *Trotsky: Towards October,* Bookmarks, London.

Coase, Ronald (1988) *The Firm, the Market and the Law,* University of Chicago Press, Chicago.

Cocker, Mark (1998) *Rivers of Blood, Rivers of Gold: Europe's Conflict with Tribal Peoples,* Jonathan Cape, London.

Cohen, G. A. (1978) *Karl Marx's Theory of History: A Defence,* Princeton University Press, Princeton, NJ.

Condorcet, M. de (1785) *Essai sur l'application à la probabilité des décisions rendue à la pluralité des voix,* Paris.

Cornia, Giovanni, Richard Jolly and Frances Stewart (eds) (1987) *Adjustment with a Human Face,* Clarendon Press, Oxford.

Cowling, Mark (ed.) (1988) *The Communist Manifesto: New Interpretations,* Edinburgh University Press, Edinburgh.

Cox, Michael (ed.) (1999) *Rethinking the Soviet Collapse: Sovietology, the Death of Communism and the New Russia,* Pinter, London.

Crosland, Anthony (1956) *The Future of Socialism,* Jonathan Cape, London.

Dangerfield, George (1980) *Strange Death of Liberal England,* G. P. Putnam's Sons, New York.

Daniels, Robert V. (1960) *The Conscience of the Revolution,* Havard University Press, Cambridge, MA.

Dantzig, George (1963) *Linear Programming and Extensions,* Princeton University Press, Princeton, NJ.

Debreu, Gérard (1959) *Theory of Value,* John Wiley, New York.

Desai, Meghnad (1970) 'The Vortex in India', *New Left Review,* 170, September–October.

Desai, Meghnad (1973) 'Growth Cycles and Inflation in a Model of the Class Struggle', *Journal of Economic Theory,* December, reproduced in Desai (1995d).

Desai, Meghnad (1974) *Marxian Economic Theory,* Gray-Mills, London.

Desai, Meghnad (1975) 'India: Contradictions of Slow Capitalist Development', in Blackburn (ed.) (1975).

Desai, Meghnad (1976) *Applied Econometrics,* Philip Allan, London.

Desai, Meghnad (1979) *Marxian Economics,* Blackwell, Oxford.

Desai, Meghnad (1981) *Testing Monetarism,* Pinter, London.

Desai, Meghnad (ed.) (1989) *Lenin's Economic Writings,* Lawrence & Wishart, London.

Desai, Meghnad (1990) 'Methodological Problems in Quantitative Marxism', in Dunne, P. (ed.) (1990).

Desai, Meghnad (1991) 'The Transformation Problem', in Caravale (ed.) (1991).

Desai, Meghnad (1992) 'Is Socialism Dead?', V. S. Desai Memorial Lecture, 15 December 1990, *Contention,* Indiana University Press, Indianapolis.

Desai, Meghnad (1993) *Capitalism, Socialism and Democracy in India*, EXIM Bank, Bombay, India.

Desai, Meghnad (1995a) 'Economic Reform: Stalled by Politics?', in Oldenburg (ed.) (1995).

Desai, Meghnad (1995b) 'Global Governance', in Desai and Redfern (eds) (1995).

Desai, Meghnad (1995c) *Poverty and Capability: Towards an Empirically Implementable Measure*, in Desai (1995e).

Desai, Meghnad (1995d) *Macroeconomics and Monetary Theory: Selected Essays of Meghnad Desai, Volume 1*, Edward Elgar, Cheltenham.

Desai, Meghnad (1995e) *Poverty, Famine and Economic Development: The Selected Essays of Meghnad Desai, Volume II*, Edward Elgar, Aldershot.

Desai, Meghnad (1996) 'Hayek, Marx and the Demise of Official Keynesianism', in Baranzini and Cencini (eds) (1996).

Desai, Meghnad (1997) 'It's Profitability, Stupid', in Kelly, *et al.* (1997).

Desai, Meghnad (1998) 'Profitability and the Persistence of Capitalism', in Bellofiore (ed.) (1998).

Desai, Meghnad (2000a) *Financial Crises and Global Governance*, LSE, unpublished.

Desai, Meghnad (2000b) 'Rejuvenated Capitalism and No Longer Existing Socialism', in Toporowski (ed.) (2000).

Desai, Meghnad (2000c) 'Seattle: A Tragi-Comedy', in Gunnell and Timms (eds) (2000).

Desai, Meghnad (2000d) 'Neither Ideology nor Utopia', *Cambridge Review of International Affairs*, Autumn/Winter.

Desai, Meghnad and Paul Redfern (eds) (1995) *Global Governance: Ethics and Economics of the World Order*, Pinter, London.

Deutscher, Isaac (1954–63) *The Prophet Armed: Trotsky, 1879–1921; The Prophet Unarmed: Trotsky, 1921–1929; The Prophet Outcast: Trotsky, 1929–1940*, Oxford University Press, Oxford.

Dicey, A. V. (1885/1914/1982) *Introduction to the Study of the Law of the Constitution*, first edition 1885, eighth edition 1914, reprinted as a Liberty Classic in 1982, Liberty Fund Inc., Indianapolis, IN.

Dickey, Laurence (1987) *Hegel: Religion, Economics and the Politics of Spirit 1770–1807*, Cambridge University Press, Cambridge.

Dickinson, H. D. (1939) *Economics of Socialism*, Oxford University Press, Oxford.

Döblin, Alfred (1983) *Karl and Rosa: November 1918, A German Revolution, A Novel*, trans. by John Woods, International Publishing Corporation, New York.

Downs, Anthony (1957) *An Economic Theory of Democracy*, Harper & Row, New York.

Dunn, Stephen (1982) *The Fall and Rise of the Asiatic Mode of Production*, Routledge & Kegan Paul, London.

Dunne, Paul (ed.) (1990) *Quantitative Marxism*, Polity Press, Oxford.

Dutt, Romesh Chandra (1908) *Economic History of India*, 2 vols, Kegan Paul, Trübner Trench, London.

Eatwell, John, Peter Newman and Murray Milgate (1990) *The New Palgrave Dictionary of Economics*, Macmillan, London.

Ellman, Michael (1975) 'Did the Agricultural Surplus Provide Resources for the Increase in Investment in the USSR during the First Five Year Plan'?, *Economic Journal*, December.

Engels, Friedrich (1845/1892) *The Condition of the Working Class in England in 1844*, first published in German, trans. Kelly-Wischnewetzky (1885), published in New York (1886) (John W. Lovell); and in London (1892) (George Allen & Unwin) with a preface by Engels.

Faase, M. *et al.* (eds) (1999) *Economics, Welfare Policy and History of Economic Thought: Essays in Honour of Alfred Heertje*, Edward Elgar, Cheltenham.

Feldman, Gerald (1993) *The Great Disorder: Politics, Economics and Society in the German Hyperinflation 1914–1924*, Oxford University Press, Oxford.

Feinstein, C. H. (1967) *Capitalism, Socialism and Economic Development: Essays in Honour of Maurice Dobb*, Cambridge University Press, Cambridge.

Figes, Orlando (1996) *A People's Tragedy: The Russian Revolution 1891–1924*, Jonathan Cape, London.

Fisher, D. H. (1996) *The Great Wave: Price Revolutions and the Rhythm of History*, Oxford University Press, Oxford.

Folbre, Nancy (1994) *Who Pays for the Kids? Gender and the Structure of Constraints*, Routledge, London.

Frank, Andre Gunder (1967) *Capitalism and Underdevelopment in Latin America: Historical Studies of Chile and Brazil*, Monthly Review Press, New York.

Friedman, Milton (ed.) (1956) *Studies in the Quantity Theory of Money*, University of Chicago Press, Chicago.

Friedman, Milton and Anna Schwarz (1963) *A Monetary History of the United States 1867–1960*, Princeton University Press, Princeton, NJ.

Fromm, Eric (1967) *Marx's Concept of Man*, Ungar, New York.

Fukuyama, Francis (1992) *The End of History and the Last Man*, Hamish Hamilton, London.

Furet, François (1988/1992) *The French Revolution 1770–1814*, trans. Antonia Nevill from *Révolution* (1988) (Hachette), Blackwell, Oxford.

Gadgil, D. R. (1971) *Industrial Evolution of India in Recent Times, 1860–1939*, fifth edition, Oxford University Press, Bombay.

Galbraith, J. Kenneth (1952) *American Capitalism: The Concept of Countervailing Power*, Harcourt Brace Jovanovich, Boston, MA.

Galbraith, J. Kenneth (1955/1980) *The Great Crash, 1929*, Fiftieth Anniversary Edition, André Deutsch, London.

Galbraith, J. Kenneth (1958) *The Affluent Society*, Hamish Hamilton, London.

Galbraith, J. Kenneth (1971) *The New Industrial State*, Houghton Mifflin, London.

Gay, Peter (1952) *The Dilemma of Democratic Socialism: Edouard Bernstein's Challenge to Marx*, Columbia University Press, New York.

Gillie, Alan (1996) 'The Origin of the Poverty Line', *Economic History Review*, vol. XLIX, no. 4.

Glyn, Andrew and John Harrison (1980) *The British Economic Disaster*, Pluto Press, London.

Glyn, Andrew and Robert Sutcliffe (1971) 'The Collapse of UK Profits', *New Left Review* 66, March–April.

Glyn, Andrew and Robert Sutcliffe (1972) *British Capitalism, Workers and Profit Squeeze*, Penguin Books, Harmondsworth.

Goodwin, R. M. (1967) 'A Growth Cycle', in Feinstein (ed.) (1967).

Goodwin, R. M., M. Krueger and A. Vercelli (1984) *Non-Linear Models of Fluctuating Growth*, Springer Verlag, Berlin.

Goodwin, Richard and Lionello Punzo (1987) *The Dynamics of Capitalist Economy: A Multi-sectoral Approach*, Polity, Oxford.

Gordon, R. J. (ed.) (1974) *Milton Friedman's Monetary Framework: A Debate with the Critics*, University of Chicago Press, Chicago.

Gunnell, Barbara and David Timms (eds) (2000) *After Seattle: Globalisation and Its Discontents*, Catalyst Pamphlet, London.

Halberstam, David (1972) *The Best and the Brightest*, Random House, New York.

Harcourt, Geoffrey C. (1972) *Some Cambridge Controversies in the Theory of Capital*, Cambridge University Press, Cambridge.

Harman, Chris (1982) *The Lost Revolution: Germany 1918–1923*, Bookmarks, London.

Harris, Nigel (1995) *The New Untouchables: Immigration and the New World Worker*, I. B. Tauris, London.

Harris, Seymour E. (ed.) (1952) *The New Economics: Keynes's Influence on Theory and Public Policy*, Alfred Knopf, New York.

Hayek, Friedrich von (1931) *Prices and Production*, Routledge, London.

Hayek, Friedrich von (ed.) (1935) *Collective Economic Planning: Critical Studies in the Possibilities of Socialism*, Routledge, London.

Hayek, Friedrich von (1938) *Profits, Interest and Investment*, Routledge & Kegan Paul, London.

Hayek, Friedrich von (1944) *The Road to Serfdom*, Routledge, London.

Hayek, Friedrich von (1948) *Individualism and the Economic Order*, University of Chicago Press, Chicago.

Held, David (1999) *Global Transformations*, Polity Press, Cambridge.

Hilferding, Rudolf (1927/1981) *Finance Capital*, published in German by Wein, trans. Tom Bottomore, Routledge & Kegan Paul, London.

Hirst, Paul and Graeme Thompson (1996/2000) *Globalization in Question: The International Economy and the Possibilities of Governance*, Polity Press, Cambridge.

Hobsbawm, Eric (1964) 'Dr Marx and the Victorians', in *Labouring Men: Studies in the History of Labour*, Weidenfeld & Nicolson, London.

Hobson, J. A. (1905/1988) *Imperialism: A Study*, Archibald Constable, London, first edition; Unwin Hyman, London, third edition.

Hont, Istvan and Michael Ignatieff (eds) (1993) *Wealth and Virtue: The Shaping of Political Economy in the Scottish Enlightenment*, Cambridge University Press, Cambridge.

Howard, M. C. and J. E. King (1992) *A History of Marxian Economics, Volume 1 1883–1929; Volume 2 1929–90*, Macmillan, London.

Hutton, Will (1995) *The State We're In*, Jonathan Cape, London.

Hyman, Stanley Edgar (1961) *The Tangled Bank: Marx, Darwin, Frazer and Freud*, Athaneum, New York.

Jay, Martin (1984) *Marxism and Totality: The Adventure of a Concept from Lukács to Habermas*, University of California Press, Berkeley, CA.

Juglar, Clément (1862) *Des Crises commerciales et de leur retour périodique en France, en Angleterre et aux États-Unis*, Paris.

Kabeer, Naila (2000) *The Power to Choose: Bangladeshi Women and Labour Market, Discussions in London and Dhaka*, Verso, London and New York.

Kaes, Anthony, Martin Jay and Edward Dimendberg (1994) *The Weimar Republic Sourcebook*, University of California Press, Berkeley, CA.

Kaldor, Mary (ed.) (forthcoming) *The Ideas of 1989*, LSE, London, Centre for the Study of Global Governance.

Kalecki, Michal (1968) *Theory of Economic Dynamism*, Monthly Review Press, New York.

Kalecki, Michal (1971) *Selected Essays on Dynamism of the Capitalist Economy*, Cambridge University Press, Cambridge.

Kautsky, Karl (1891/1910) *The Class Struggle (Erfurt Programme)*, trans. William E. Bohm, Charles Kerr, Chicago.

Kautsky, Karl (1902) *Die Agrarfrage: eine Übersicht über die Tendenzen der modernen Landwirtschaft und die Agrarpolitik der Sozialdemokratie*, J. H. W. Dietz Nachf, Stuttgart, trans. Peter Burgess, Swan, England.

Kautsky, Karl (1919/1964) *The Dictatorship of the Proletariat*, reprinted with a new introduction, trans. H. J. Stenning, University of Michigan Press, Ann Arbor.

Kautsky, Karl (1946) *Social Democracy versus Communism*, ed. and trans. D. Shub and J. Shaplen, Rand School Press, New York.

Kelly, Gavin, Dominic Kelly and Andrew Gamble (eds) (1997) *Stakeholder Capitalism*, Macmillan, London.

Koopmans, Tjalling C. (ed.) (1951) *Activity Analysis for Production and Allocation*, John Wiley, New York.

Keynes, J. M. (1923) *A Tract on Monetary Reform*, Macmillan, London.

Keynes, J. M. (1925) 'The Economic Consequences of Mr Churchill', published as a pamphlet by Hogarth Press, reprinted in Keynes (1972).

Keynes, J. M. (1936) *The General Theory of Employment, Interest and Money*, Macmillan, London.

Keynes, J. M. (1940) *How to Pay for the War*, Macmillan, London, reprinted in Keynes (1972).

Keynes, J. M. (1972) *Essays in Persuasion: The Collected Works of John Maynard Keynes*, vol. 9, an expanded version of the original 1931 book, Macmillan, London.

Kiernan, Ben (1985) *How Pol Pot Came to Power*, Verso, London.

Kiernan, V. G. (1982) *European Empires: From Conquest to Collapse, 1815–1960*, Fontana, London.

Kindleberger, Charles (1973) *The World in Depression, 1929–1939*, Macmillan, London.

Kindleberger, Charles (1978) *Manias, Panics and Crashes: A History of Financial Crises*, Macmillan, London.

Klein, Lawrence R. (1947) *The Keynesian Revolution*, Macmillan, New York.

Kondratieff, N. D. (1926) 'Die Langen Wellen der Konjuktur', *Archiv für Sozialwissenschaft und Sozialpolitik*, December.

Koopmans, C. Tjalling (ed.) (1951) *Activity Analysis for Production and Allocation*, John Wiley, New York.

Kornai, János (1992) *The Socialist System: The Political Economy of Communism*, Princeton University Press, Princeton, NJ.

Krader, Lawrence (1975) *The Asiatic Mode of Production*, Assen, New York.

Kuhn, Harold and Abraham Tucker (1951) 'Nonlinear Programming', in Neyman (ed.) (1951).

Kumar, Dharma (ed.) (1983) *The Cambridge Economic History of India Volume 2: 1757–1970*, Cambridge University Press, Cambridge.

Laski, Harold (ed.) (1948) *The Communist Manifesto: The Centenary Edition*, published for the Labour Party, Allen & Unwin, London.

Lehmann, William C. (1960) *John Millar of Glasgow 1735–1801: His Life and Thought and His Contribution to Sociological Analysis*, Cambridge University Press, Cambridge.

Lekachman, Robert (1966) *The Age of Keynes*, Random House, New York.

Lenin, V. I. (1893/1937) 'On the So-Called Question of the Home Market', written in 1893, first published in *Collected Works*, vol. 1, also reprinted in Desai (ed.) (1989).

Lenin, V. I. (1897) *A Characterization of Economic Romanticism: Sismondi and Our Native Sismondists*, first published in four issues of *Novoye Slovo*, April–July 1897; also *in Collected Works*, vol. 2.

Lenin, V. I. (1916) *Imperialism: The Highest Stage of Capitalism*, in *Collected Works*, vol. 22.

Lenin, V. I. (1921) 'The Tax in Kind', reprinted in Desai (ed.) (1989).

Lenin, V. I. (1955) *Collected Works*, 45 vols, Lawrence & Wishart, London.

Lewin, Moshe (1975) *Russian Peasants and the Soviet Power: A Study of Collectivization*, Norton, New York.

Lewis, W. Arthur (1954) 'Economic Development with Unlimited Supplies of Labour', Manchester School, vol. 22.

Liberman, E. G. (9171) *Economic Methods and the Effectiveness of Production*, International Arts and Sciences Press, New York.

Lippincott, B. E. (ed.) (1938) *On the Economic Theory of Socialism*, University of Minnesota Press, Minneapolis.

List, Friedrich (1837/1856) *The National System of Political Economy*, trans. Sampson Lloyd, Longmans Green, London.

Lucas, Robert (1971) 'Expectations and the Neutrality of Money', *Journal of Economic Theory* 4.

Lucas, Robert (1988) 'The Mechanism of Economic Development', *Journal of Monetary Economics*, 22.

Lundberg, Erik (1996) *The Development of Swedish and Keynesian Macroeconomic Theory and Its Impact on Economic Policy*, Cambridge University Press, Cambridge.

Luxemburg, Rosa (1913/1951) *The Accumulation of Capital*, trans. Agnes Schwarzschild, Routledge & Kegan Paul, London.

Luxemburg, Rosa (1935) *Leninism or Marxism*, Anti-Parliamentary Communist Federation, Glasgow.

Luxemburg, Rosa (1961) *The Russian Revolution and Leninism or Marxism*, University of Michigan Press, Ann Arbor.

Luxemburg, Rosa and Nikolai Bukharin (1972) *Imperialism and the Accumulation of Capital*, trans. Rudolf Wickman, ed. Kenneth Tarbuck, Allen Lane, London.

MacFarquhar, Roderick (1974/1983/1997) *The Origins of the Cultural Revolution*, 3 vols, Oxford University Press, Oxford.

McLellan, David (1969) *The Young Hegelians and Karl Marx*, Macmillan, London.

Maddison, Angus (1991) *Dynamic Forces in Capitalist Development: A Long Run Comparative View*, Oxford University Press, Oxford.

Madison, James, Alexander Hamilton and John Jay (1789/1987) *The Federalist Papers*, ed. Isaac Kramnik, Penguin, London.

Mah, Harold (1987) *The End of Philosophy and the Origins of Ideology*, University of California Press, Berkeley, CA.

Mandel, Ernest (1972/1975) *Late Capitalism*, trans. Joeis de Bres of *Der Spätkapitalismus* (1972) Suhrkamp Verlag, Berlin New Left Books, London.

Mandel, Ernest (1978) *The Second Slump*, New Left Books, London.

Mandel, Ernest and Alan Freeman (eds) (1984) *Ricardo, Marx, Sraffa: The Langston Memorial Volume*, Verso, London.

Marquand, David (1977) *Ramsay MacDonald*, Jonathan Cape, London.

Marshall, Alfred (1890) *Principles of Economics*, Macmillan, London.

Marx, Karl (1844/1970) *A Contribution to the Critique of Hegel's Philosophy of Right*, ed. with an intro. by Joseph O'Malley, Cambridge University Press, Cambridge.

Marx, Karl (1859/1904) *A Contribution to the Critique of Political Economy*, originally published in German by Otto Meisner (Hamburg), trans. N. Stone, Charles Kerr, Chicago; Lawrence & Wishart edn trans. S. W. Ryazanskaya, ed. Maurice Dobb, London 1971.

Marx, Karl (1867/1887) *Capital Volume 1: Capitalist Production*, German publication Otto Meisner (Hamburg), trans. from the third German edition by Samuel Moore and Edward Aveling in 1887, Swan Sonnenschein, Lowry & Co, London; Lawrence & Wishart, London 1974.

Marx, Karl (1871/1951) *The Civil War in France*, originally published by International Workingman's Association (London), in English in *Selected Works of Karl Marx and Friedrich Engels*, Progress Publishers, Moscow.

Marx, Karl (1885/1919) *Capital Volume 2: The Process of Circulation of Capital*, ed. F. Engels, published in German by Otto Meisner (Hamburg); trans. N. Stone, Charles Kerr, Chicago.

Marx, Karl (1894/1909) *Capital Volume 3: The Process of Capitalist Production as a Whole,* ed. F. Engels, published in German by Otto Meisner (Hamburg); trans. N. Stone, Charles Kerr, Chicago; Lawrence & Wishart, London 1974.

Marx, Karl (1974) *The First International and After,* ed. David Fernbach, Penguin, Harmondsworth.

Marx, Karl (1975) *Early Writings,* Pelican Marx Library, trans. Rodney Livingstone and Gregor Benton, intro. Luccio Colletti, Penguin, Harmondsworth.

Marx, Karl (no date) *Selected Works in Two Volumes: Prepared by the Marx–Engels–Lenin Institute, Moscow,* ed. V. Adoratsky, Martin Lawrence, London.

Marx, Karl and Friedrich Engels (1845/1956) *The Holy Family, or Critique of Critical Criticism Against Bruno Bauer and Company,* first published in German 1845 (Literarische Anstalt, J. Rutter, Frankfurt); trans. Richard Dixon and Clemens Dutt, Progress Publishers, Moscow.

Marx, Karl and Friedrich Engels (1846/1964) *The German Ideology: Critique of Modern German Philosophy According to Its Representatives, Feuerbach, Bauer and Stirner* vol. I and of *German Socialism According to Its Various Prophets* vol. 2, first published in German in 1932 and in English translations (translators not given) Progress Publishers, Moscow.

Marx, Karl and Friedrich Engels (1848/1888) *The Communist Manifesto,* first trans. by Helen Macfarlane, serialized in *The Red Republican,* November 1850.

Marx, Karl and Friedrich Engels (1954/1983) *Letters on Capital,* originally published in German as *Briefe über Das Kapital,* trans. Andrew Drummond, New Park Publications, London.

Marx, Karl and Friedrich Engels (1955) *Selected Correspondence,* Progress Publishers, Moscow.

Marx, Karl and Friedrich Engels (1968) *Selected Works,* Lawrence & Wishart, London.

Mattick, Paul (1969) *Marx and Keynes: The Limits of Mixed Economy,* Merlin Press, London.

Mayer, Arno (1981) *The Persistence of the Old Regime: Europe to the Great War,* Croom Helm, London.

Meade, James (1972) 'The Theory of Labour Managed Firms and Profit Sharing', *Economic Journal,* 82.

Meade, James (1990) *The Collected Papers of James Meade Volume 4: The Cabinet Office Diary,* ed. Susan Howson, Unwin Hyman, London.

Millar, John (1806) *The Origin and Distinction of Ranks,* Edinburgh.

Mises, Ludwig von (1923/1936/1981) *Socialism: An Economic and Sociological Analysis,* first published in German as *Die Gemeinwirtschaft* (Gustav Fischer, Jena), second edition 1932, trans. J. Kahane (1936), Jonathan Cape, London, republished as a Liberty Classic by Liberty Fund Inc., Indianapolis, IN.

Morishima, Michio (1973) *Marx's Economics*, Cambridge University Press, Cambridge.

Morris, David (1983) 'The Growth of Large-Scale Industry to 1947', in Kumar (ed.) (1983).

Naoroji, Dadabhai (1901) *Poverty and Un-British Rule in India*, Swan Sonnenschein, London. Republished 1962.

Neyman, Jerzy (ed.) (1951) *Proceedings of the Second Berkeley Symposium on Mathematical Statistics and Probability*, University of California Press, Berkeley, CA.

Nove, Alec (1983) *The Economics of Feasible Socialism*, Allen & Unwin, London.

Ohmae, Kenichi (1990) *The Borderless World: Power and Strategy in the Interlinked Economy*, Collins, London.

Oldenburg, Philip (ed.) (1995) *India Briefing: Staying the Course*, M. E. Sharpe, New York/London.

O'Leary, Brendan (1989) *The Asiatic Mode of Production*, Blackwell, (Oxford).

Overy, Richard J. (1994) *War and Economy in the Third Reich*, Clarendon Press, Oxford.

Owen, Robert (1991) *A New View of Society and Other Writings*, ed. Gregory Claeys, Penguin Books, Harmondsworth.

Panitch, Leo and Colin Leys (1998) *The Communist Manifesto Now: Socialist Register 1998*, Merlin Press, London.

Patinkin, Donald (1949/1965) *Money, Interest and Prices: An Integration of Monetary and Value Theories*, first edition 1949, second edition 1965, Harper & Row, New York.

Payne, Stanley G. (1995) *A History of Fascism 1914–45*, UCL Press, London.

Petrovic, P. (1987) 'The Deviation of Production Prices from Labour Values: Some Methodology and Empirical Evidence', *Cambridge Journal of Economics* 11.

Phillips, A. W. H. (1958) 'The Relationship of the Rate of Change of the Money Wage Rate and Unemployment', *Economica*, new series, February.

Pigou, A. C. (1920) *The Economics of Welfare*, Macmillan, London.

Polanyi, Karl (1944) *The Great Transformation*, Farrar & Reinhart, New York.

Popper, Karl (1945) *The Open Society and Its Enemies*, 2 vols, Routledge & Kegan Paul, London.

Prawer, S. (1976) *Karl Marx and World Literature*, Clarendon Press, Oxford.

Preobrazhensky, E. (1966) *The New Economics*, Clarendon Press, Oxford.

Putnam, David and Neil Watson (1998) *Movies and Money*, Alfred Knopf, New York.

Rabinowitch, Alexander (1968) *Prelude to Revolution: The Petrograd Bolsheviks and the July 1917 Uprising*, Indiana University Press, Bloomington.

Ricardo, David (1821/1951) *Principles of Political Economy and Taxation Volume 1 of Collected Works*, ed. Piero Sraffa with Maurice Dobb, Cambridge University Press, Cambridge.

Robinson, Joan (1942) *An Essay on Marxian Economics*, Macmillan, London.

Roemer, John (1982) *A General Theory of Exploitation and Class*, Harvard University Press, Cambridge, MA.

Roemer, John and Pranab Bardhan (1993) *Market Socialism: The Current Debate*, Oxford University Press, Oxford.

Romer, Paul (1986) 'Increasing Returns and Long-Term Growth', *Journal of Political Economy* 94.

Rosenstein-Rodan, Paul (1943) 'Problems of Industrialisation in Eastern and South-Eastern Europe', *Economic Journal* 53.

Ross, Ian Simpson (1995) *The Life of Adam Smith*, Clarendon Press, Oxford.

Rostow, W. W. (1960) *The Stages of Economic Growth: A Non-Communist Manifesto*, Cambridge University Press, Cambridge.

Rothschild, Emma (2001) *Economic Sentiments: Adam Smith, Condorcet and the Englightenment*, Harvard University Press, Cambridge, MA.

Rowbotham, Sheila (1972) *Women, Resistance and Revolution: A History of Women and Revolution in the Modern World*, Allen Lane, London.

Rowntree, B. Seebohm (1901) *Poverty: A Study of Town Life*, Longmans Green, London.

Ruskin, John (1958) *Unto This Last and Other Writings*, ed. Clive Wilmer, Penguin, Harmondsworth.

Salvadori, Massimo (1979) *Karl Kautsky and the Socialist Revolution 1880–1938*, Verso, London.

Samuel, Raphael (1994) *Theatres of Memory*, 2 vols, Verso, London and New York.

Samuelson, Paul (1949) *Market Mechanism and Maximization*, Rand Corporation, reprinted in Samuelson (1966) *The Collected Scientific Papers of Paul Samuelson*, vol. 1, ed. Joseph Stiglitz, MIT Press, Cambridge, MA.

Samuelson, Paul (1971) 'Understanding the Marxian Notion of Exploitation: A Summary of the So-called Transformation Problem between Marxian Values and Competitive Prices', *Journal of Economic Literature* 9 (2).

Samuelson, Paul (1999) 'Sherlock Holmes and the Swarthy German: The Case of "transforming" *Mehrwert* to prices' in Faase *et al.* (eds) (1999).

Samuelson, Paul and Robert Solow (1960) 'The Analytics of the Anti-Inflation Policy', *American Economic Review* 50.

Sargent, Thomas J. (1996) 'Expectations and the Non-Neutrality of Lucas', *Journal of Monetary Economics* 37.

Sassen, Saskia (1998) *Globalisation and its Discontents: Essays on Mobility of People and Money*, New Press, New York.

Sassoon, Donald (1996) *One Hundred Years of Socialism: The West European Left in the Twentieth Century*, I. B. Tauris, London.

Saunders, Frances Stonor (1999) *Who Paid the Piper? The CIA and the Cultural Cold War*, Granta, London.

Sawyer, Malcolm (1985) *The Economics of Michal Kalecki*, Macmillan, London.

Schama, Simon (1989) *Citizens: A Chronicle of the French Revolution*, Viking, London.

Schlesinger, Arthur (1957/1959/1981) *The Age of Roosevelt: The Crisis of the Old Order 1919–1983* (vol. 1), Houghton Mifflin, Boston, MA; *The Age of Roosevelt: The Coming of the New Deal* (vol. 2); *The Politics of Upheaval* (vol. 3) (vols 2 & 3 Heinemann, London).

Schoenfield, Andrew (1965) *Modern Capitalism*, Oxford University Press, Oxford.

Schorske, Carl (1955) *German Social Democracy 1905–1917: The Development of the Great Schism*, Harvard University Press, Cambridge, MA.

Schumpeter, Joseph (1913/1934) *The Theory of Economic Development*, original in German (1913), trans. 1934, Harvard University Press, Cambridge, MA.

Schumpeter, Joseph (1919/1951) *Imperialism and Social Class*, trans. Heinz Norden, Augustus Kelley, New York.

Schumpeter, Joseph (1939) *Business Cycles*, 2 vols, McGraw-Hill, New York.

Schumpeter, Joseph (1942) *Capitalism, Socialism and Democracy*, George Allen & Unwin, London, fifth edition, reprinted with an intro. by Richard Swedberg (1996), Routledge, London.

Schwarzschild, Leopold (1948) *The Red Prussian: The Life and Legends of Karl Marx*, Pickwick Books, London.

Seccaraccia, Chris M. (1995) *Marx, Hayek and Utopia*, State University Press of New York, Albany, NY.

Senghor, Léopold (1959) *African Socialism*, American Society for African Culture, New York.

Shaikh, Anwar (1984) 'The Transformation from Marx to Sraffa', in Mandel and Freeman (eds) (1984).

Shanin, Teodor (ed.) (1984) *Late Marx and the Russian Road: Marx and the Peripheries of Capitalism*, Routledge & Kegan Paul, London.

Sivanandan, Ambalavaner (1990) *Communities of Resistance: Writing on the Black Struggle for Socialism*, Verso, London.

Skidelsky, Robert (1967) *Politicians and the Slump: The Labour Government of 1929–1931*, Macmillan, London.

Skidelsky, Robert (1983/1992/2000) *John Maynard Keynes*, 3 vols: *Hopes Betrayed 1883–1920; The Economist as Saviour 1920–1937; Battling for Britain 1937–1946*, Macmillan, London.

Skidelsky, Robert (1995) *The World After Communism*, Macmillan, London.

Smith, Adam (1757/1976) *The Theory of Moral Sentiments*, ed. D. D. Raphael and A. L. Macfie, Oxford University Press, Oxford.

Smith, Adam (1776/1976) *An Inquiry into the Nature and Causes of the Wealth of Nations*, ed. R. H. Campbell and A. S. Skinner, 2 vols, Oxford University Press, Oxford.

Smith, Adam (1978) *Lectures on Jurisprudence*, ed. R. L. Meek, D. D. Raphael and P. D. Stein, Oxford University Press, Oxford.

Solow, Robert M. (1970) *Growth Theory*, Oxford University Press, Oxford.

Soros, George (1998) *The Crisis of Global Capitalism: Open Society Endangered*, BBS/Public Affairs, New York.

Sraffa, Piero (1960) *The Production of Commodities by Means of Commodities: Prelude to a Critique of Economic Theory*, Cambridge University Press, Cambridge.

Steedman, Ian (1977) *Marx After Sraffa*, New Left Books, London.

Stein, Herbert C. (1969) *The Fiscal Revolution in America*, University of Chicago Press, Chicago.

Stigler, George (1982) *The Economist as a Preacher and Other Essays*, Blackwell, Oxford.

Stiglitz, Joseph (1994) *Whither Socialism*, MIT Press, Cambridge, MA.

Sweezy, Paul M. (1948) *The Theory of Capitalist Development*, Monthly Review Press, New York.

Sweezy, Paul, M. (ed.) (1949) *Karl Marx and the Close of His System*, Augustus Kelley, New York.

Sweezy, Paul M. (ed.) (1978) *The Transition from Feudalism to Capitalism*, Verso, London.

Taylor, Charles (1975) *Hegel*, Cambridge University Press, Cambridge.

Thorne, Christopher (1979) *Allies of a Kind: The United States, Britain and the War against Japan 1941–45*, Oxford University Press, Oxford.

Toporowski, Jan (ed.) (2000) *Political Economy and New Capitalism: Essays in Honour of Sam Aaronovitch*, Routledge, London.

Townsend, Peter (1979) *Poverty in the UK*, Penguin, Harmondsworth.

Tucker, Robert (1972) *Philosophy and Myth in Karl Marx*, Cambridge University Press, Cambridge.

Vanek, Jaroslav (1977) *The Labour Managed Economy,* Cornell University Press, Ithaca, NY.

Veneziani, Roberto (2000) *Exploitation and Time,* LSE, unpublished.

Wade, Robert (1990) *Governing the Market? Economic Theory and the Role of the Government in East Asian Industrialization,* Princeton University Press, Princeton, NJ.

Wallerstein, Immanuel (1980) *The Modern World System II: Mercantilism and the Consolidation of the European World Economy,* Academic Press, New York.

Warren, Bill (1980) *Imperialism, the Pioneer of Development,* New Left Books, London.

Webb, Sidney and Beatrice (1923) *The Decay of Capitalist Civilization,* Harcourt Brace, New York.

Webb, Sidney and Beatrice (1935) *Soviet Communism: A New Civilization?* Longman, London.

Weintraub, E. Roy (1993) *General Equilibrium Analysis: Studies in Appraisal,* University of Michigan Press, Ann Arbor.

Weintraub, Stanley (1973) *Bernard Shaw 1914–1918: Journey to Heartbreak,* Routledge, London.

Weiss, Linda (1998) *The Myth of the Powerless State: Governing the Economy in a Global Era,* Polity Press, Cambridge.

Wells, John (1997) *The House of Lords: From Saxon Wargods to a Modern Senate,* Hodder & Stoughton, London.

Williamson, John (1999) 'Economic Reform: Content, Progress, Prospect', *www.icrier.re.in.*

Winch, Donald (1978) *Adam Smith's Politics: An Essay in Historiographic Revision,* Cambridge University Press, Cambridge.

Wittfogel, Karl (1957) *Oriental Despotism: A Comparative Study of Total Power,* Yale University Press, New Haven, CT.

World Bank (2000) *World Development Report,* Oxford University Press, Oxford.

Index